SUPERV...
STUDIES
A Managerial Perspective

P. W. Betts
MTech, PhD, FInstAM(Dip), FBIM, FIIM, MIM

FIFTH EDITION

PITMAN PUBLISHING
128 Long Acre, London WC2E 9AN

A Division of Longman Group UK Limited

© P. W. Betts 1989

Fifth edition published in Great Britain 1989

British Library Cataloguing in Publication Data
Betts, P. W. (Peter Wilfred, *1924*–)
 Supervisory studies.−− 5th ed
 1. Management. Supervision
 I. Title
 658.3′02

ISBN 0 273 03071 X

Printed and bound in Singapore

Contents

transmission; Non–verbal communication; Managerial receptiveness; Process models; Communication flow; Causes of misunderstanding; Questions; Case study

networks, simulation; Statistical method; Establishing standards; Questions; Case study

Preface

This book has been written both for those who are actively engaged in supervision at work and for those who wish to train and qualify in this subject. It covers in detail the guidelines issued by the National Examinations Board for Supervisory Studies (NEBSS) and the Institute of Supervisory Management, and the syllabus for the paper in Supervisory Studies at BTEC National Diploma level.

Until recently, the importance of supervision to the success of an organisation has not been fully realised. Supervision permeates all levels of business activity, from the top executive who supervises senior management through close contact, to the shopfloor supervisor or office supervisor who controls the output of the workforce. To achieve a real competitive advantage in modern business and industry, there must be effective and continuing collaboration between all departments and employees and here the role of the supervisor is crucial to the performance of the company as a whole. The book sets out to equip people in this key position with the knowledge, awareness and practical techniques essential to the development of sound supervisory skills.

The new edition looks at the role of the supervisor across a range of organisational structures, from manufacturing and commerce to service industries. The text incorporates all recent developments in business and industrial technology, modern job design, industrial relations and employment legislation. End-of-chapter test questions and case studies help the reader relate all that has been learnt to his or her own workplace and suggestions for investigative project work give scope for exploring topics of particular interest further.

The book is divided into three parts. Part One, Building and Maintaining an Efficient Organisational Structure, introduces the various aspects of supervision: organisation of work; group activity; supervision in industry and business; and the principles, practice and role of management.

Part Two, Creating an Effective Working Force, concentrates on human relations, motivation, behaviourism, leadership and power, many aspects of communication, and various other personnel aspects of supervision.

Part Three, Controlling the Work, examines the nature of control along with work study, production control, quality assurance, financial and cost control, and improving productivity.

Thanks are due to many friends who have offered advice and their experiences. I gratefully acknowledge the assistance given me by the British Standards Institution, the Department of Employment, the Training Commission, the Department of Trade and Industry, the National Institute of Industrial Psychology, and IBM (UK) Limited. Finally, my personal thanks go to my wife, Rosalinde, who has patiently listened to discussions and advised.

PWB 1988

Part One Building and Maintaining an Efficient Organisational Structure

1 The supervisor

Introduction

During this century more has been written on supervision in its various guises than on any other topic in industry or business. Most managers and employees now recognise its importance, yet supervision remains a thankless task. Supervisors are often poorly trained and neglected; when things go wrong they are usually blamed by management; employees appear to resent their interference, while trade union representatives seldom help.

Increasingly, claims are made that UK managers also are below average when compared with standards set in other developed countries; a common charge is that few managers understand fully the supervisor's role. Essential support is, therefore, lacking in many organisations and this tends to upset relations between supervisors and employees and trade unions.

Effective supervision has, however, always been seen as a vital feature in improving productivity. Achieving high rates of competence is becoming more of a challenge as the implementation of information technology and other technologies in the workplace means that supervisors begin to work more closely with senior management and are further removed from the workforce. Modern organisation development programmes are already highlighting the urgent need for well-trained supervisors − a skills-gap that is of growing concern for managers and in Government. Statistics clearly show that, to date, national and local schemes to train supervisors to cope with changing work patterns have been only sparsely supported by industry and business. However, as UK industrial performance continues to lag behind productivity levels set by competing nations, organisations face mounting pressure to take the training of supervisors seriously. The rapid developments in new technologies, too, will force managers and employees to adapt more quickly.

A more enlightened industrial society envisaged for the UK in future years gives today's supervisors a unique opportunity − with appropriate education and training they will be able to influence as well as oversee the inevitable structural changes within the work environment.

What is a supervisor?

A supervisor is any person who is given authority and responsibility for planning and controlling the work of a group by close contact.

In the broad sense this definition means that supervisors may be delegated the authority to deal with the following matters:

- engagement, transfer, reprimand, and dismissal of staff under their control
- staff grievances
- staff discipline
- quantity and quality of output
- recommendations to management

In the narrow sense it can include anyone who directs the work of others by:

- giving instructions on production
- co-ordinating specialist departments
- recommending courses of action to management

This classical approach to supervision is commonplace and fits conveniently into traditional formal organisation. It conforms to many organisation principles described in the next chapter and to the theory of teams involving managers, supervisors and employees explained in Chapter 7.

Range of supervisory jobs

No two supervisory jobs are exactly alike. Two apparently similar supervisory jobs may in fact be very different, depending on such factors as status, company size, the product, the type of company and its structure, relationships between management, supervision, trade unions and operators, production tempo, growth problems, staffing and the use of specialists.

This variation in supervisory jobs depends mainly upon the range of duties, the complexity of each duty and the particular level of supervision. An understanding of the latter aspect is most important.

The many levels of supervision can be grouped in a number of ways according to factors such as titles, salary, number of employees controlled, or degree of authority and responsibility.

A typical example of grouping supervisors into levels, based on the last two factors, is given below.

- Primary group supervision
- Section supervision
- Department supervision
- Works supervision

Primary group supervision

Included in this level are operators, leading hands and charge-hands who are given additional responsibility for supervising small groups. Such a cluster of six to twelve operators forms a primary working group, and the person in control is known as the *primary group leader*. This position is important because the leader represents the vital link between operators and management. Weakness at this point is obviously dangerous, and often not fully appreciated by management, although this extremity of control can easily nullify the efforts of higher management levels.

Section supervision

This level includes all supervisors who are responsible for sections consisting of about six primary groups. Various titles are used, such as *section supervisors*, junior foremen, and assistant foremen. They rarely do any manual work; instead their authority and responsibility is generally restricted to allocating duties, ensuring smooth work flow by co-ordinating the activities of the primary group leaders, and dealing with the day-to-day running of the section.

Department supervision

A control group, consisting of about six sections, is headed by a foreman. The group is also termed a department, and the foreman may be called department superintendent, or *department supervisor*. General responsibility for the department includes planning and controlling the work. This is the level most often thought of when considering what is meant by supervision. Procedures and policy normally originate from higher levels.

Works supervision

All senior supervisors come under this category. There are many titles used to describe this level, including general foreman, senior foreman, production foreman, *shop supervisor*, and shop superintendent. They have substantial authority and responsibility in order to control effectively the six to eight departments which generally make up the shop or works.

In most cases a supervisor will fit into one of these groups. Generally, all four levels are seen in the medium and large size companies whereas in the small firm only the second and last would be apparent.

Supervision and employees

In general terms the difference between employees and their supervisors is that employees perform their own work using their technical knowledge manually, whereas supervisors control the work of others using their technical knowledge theoretically combined with supervisory techniques.

In modern terms the supervisor should concentrate more on developing the co-operation and direct involvement of employees who, it is hoped, will behave more responsibly and feel committed. Emphasis is placed on team-work, participation, autonomy and flexibility – key factors that allow employees to work within much wider control limits. Indeed, the supervisor must adopt new roles associated strongly with co-ordination, advice, adap-tability and associated specialisms, to be successful.

Often logical changes are not acceptable to employees through fear of the consequences, such as less autonomy or redundancy. This apprehension may be reduced by discussion in advance, divulging plans, noting responses and suggestions, and endeavouring to gain support. Without ample discussion the supervisor risks ridicule. The usual accusations are discourtesy, igno-rance, lack of understanding and having no idea of employees' capabilities and experience.

The old sayings still hold good: treat an adult like a child and he will behave like one; treat him like a dog and he may bite; treat him like an idiot and he·will behave like one.

Basic elements of supervision

The three basic elements were outlined in the Preface. Each one contains many aspects which demand appropriate techniques some of which are used instinctively by applying sound common sense. Others demand training and practice. Applying the right principles at the right time needs something more than knowledge alone since the basic elements must interact closely although they are outlined independently.

A representative sample of ten supervisory activities is given for each basic element in Fig. 1.1. These activities or duties are interdependent in practice. For instance no decision should be made on facts and theory alone; the human factor must be given due consideration along with control features in a given situation. Finding and maintaining the right balance is difficult, time-consuming and often frustrating.

Responsibilities of a supervisor

A supervisor is responsible for subordinates, the activities and the workplace which he or she is given formal authority to control. Within this over-all definition, the finer points of responsibility should now emerge which make possible the performance of the job.

One way of thinking about these responsibilities is to examine again the list of duties given under each basic element and to summarise them in a list of responsibilities, as follows.

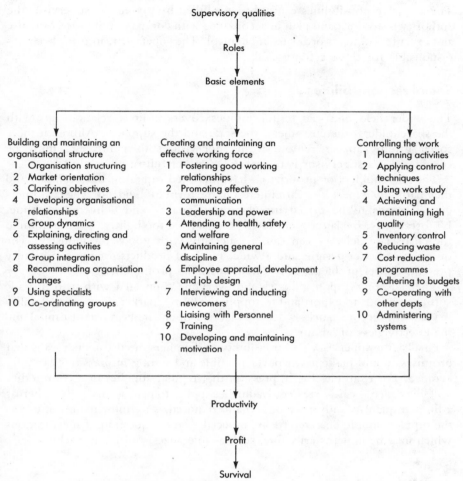

Fig. 1.1 *Basic elements of supervision*

The three elements interact although portrayed independently. A representative sample is shown of ten major activities for each basic element

1 *Staff:* morale, consultation, discipline, welfare, safety, employment, induction, training.
2 *Work:* quantity, quality, and timeliness.
3 *Cost:* maximum economy.
4 *Machines and equipment:* maintenance, loading, operation.
5 *Materials:* supplies, waste, suitability.
6 *Workplace:* layout, tidiness, good housekeeping.
7 Co-ordinating with other sections.

The above responsibilities can only be fulfilled by giving the supervisor the authority to forecast and plan in accordance with company policy, to organise and execute and to co-ordinate and control. The supervisor, in turn, becomes responsible for these activities.

Social responsibilities

The wider field of social responsibilities covers indirect relationships with the shareholders, the customers, the state and the suppliers. Although these social groups appear remote from supervision, their interests must be considered if a supervisor is to realise his or her full responsibility.

The shareholders or proprietors have invested capital in the business, and they naturally expect it to earn interest in the form of dividend. The customers expect goods to be priced in relation to quality and delivered on time. Unfortunately, the latter point often is considered too lightly, bearing in mind the chaos late delivery can cause, especially with goods for industry. The question of better designs and a wider range of products for the community presents deeper problems of research, cost, and profitability.

The state relies upon industry and everyone connected with it to provide sufficient goods to export and to supply the home market. Economic stability is vital to everyone; success depends largely upon the best use of capital and the effectiveness of labour.

Finally, the supervisor's responsibility to suppliers or customers means that promises should be kept whenever possible and wrong impressions carefully avoided. For example, the impression that regular supplies of a commodity will be needed is easily created, leading a supplier to plan accordingly, whereas a limited quantity only may be actually required. Any information of use to the supplier should be given freely, especially on the question of specifications which may be unnecessarily fine, such as tolerances, finish and packing.

Qualities of a good supervisor

The main problem when discussing personal qualities is the measurement of degree. For example, when people refer to intelligence as a quality, they use such terms as average, reasonable, high level, low level, and general level. Unfortunately there is no standardised method of dealing with these matters and each individual will naturally interpret these terms in a slightly different way.

It should be appreciated that a general foreman may possess no more qualities than a primary group leader, but he or she will possess them in greater degree. Moreover, a comprehensive list of an outstanding general foreman's qualities would correspond with specifications for general management. Nevertheless, the same qualities appear at the lower levels of supervision, but in a less intensive form.

The main differences in supervisory job specifications occur in the technical and administrative aspects, which vary considerably depending upon the industry, company size, or different circumstances within the same factory, e.g. special qualities may be desirable in supervising particular groups that contain an unusual feature.

The five essential qualities are:

- Drive
- Leadership
- Intelligence
- Skills and knowledge
- Character

They are discussed below, but not in order of importance; each job demands a different proportion of all these requirements.

Drive

The basic need for vitality, energy and enthusiasm is good health. Physical and mental fatigue impair judgment and are demoralising for subordinates who need to be 'caught up' by the supervisor's example and vigour. Making the best use of time and energy requires careful planning. Whenever possible, over-excitement and bursts of stop-gap measures should be avoided to conserve nervous energy. An even spread of effort sustained over long periods is desirable for good performance, which can then be expected from others. This sustained effort or drive demands self-discipline and conscientiousness in the face of outside distractions and the general pace of living.

Leadership

A good leader must be an outstanding member of the group who gets along easily with people and has above-average competence. Leadership is difficult to define accurately; its intangible qualities cannot be learned, yet they are easily recognisable.

Naturally, ability is not enough. Previous environment, which moulds personality and character, should provide a balanced background for an individual to feel at ease, mix easily with many types of people, and sense the ability to supervise well. Some people, of course, manage to overcome an unhappy past, while others who were more fortunate fail to make the grade.

Good leaders set high standards of performance for themselves, keep to them, and expect similar performance from others. They mix easily with people by understanding them and using clear and constructive methods of handling everyday problems. They are not always more skilful or more intelligent than their subordinates, but they appreciate their own technical and human limitations. They recognise their responsibilities and use their authority in a fair and impartial manner. This implies that they are temperamentally suited for the task of solving problems, are sufficiently far sighted to see potential ones before they arise, and can take appropriate early action.

An important management task is to create conditions under which leaders can become effective but, at the same time, avoiding the development of a situation where leaders struggle for power among each other. If the well known 'rat-race' is allowed, subordinates suffer, and organisation is badly affected. Given the opportunity and the right conditions, the leader can push people beyond their normal capabilities towards a higher level of effectiveness, with greater work satisfaction.

Intelligence

Most supervisory posts require average intelligence, similar to the general level of intelligence found among skilled operators. Some people expect supervisors to be more intelligent than their subordinates, which is naturally desirable.

A high level of intelligence is essential in some supervisory jobs, where technical and administrative problems are intricate and demanding. On the other hand, many supervisory jobs contain a large proportion of routine work which would soon frustrate the highly intelligent person.

In reality, supervisors need shrewdness, judgment, and an acute mind with plenty of common sense. They must be quick-witted, able to distinguish between major and minor problems, apportioning sufficient time to deal with each problem. They must decide whether permanent or temporary arrangements are needed. They must understand clearly the many and varied written and spoken instructions and be able to pass on information clearly to a number of different types of subordinates.

Skills and knowledge

Three main skills are distinguishable: technical, interpersonal, and conceptual. They apply to all managerial and supervisory jobs but the ratios between them differ, depending on the organisational level.

As top levels are approached technical skills tend to reduce, interpersonal skills should remain the same, while conceptual skills increase. Understandably collaborative philosophies demand more emphasis on interpersonal and conceptual skills for supervisors since a crucial appreciation of the total organisation and the involvement of employees are needed to achieve high performance levels.

These two skills are major supervisory assets, rated above many other qualities such as IQ, knowledge, and job skills.

Technical skills

An inherent part of any supervisory job is technical competence. Supervisors need a good knowledge of every operation or process under their control to be able to eliminate common faults, wastage and any dangerous practices. Practical and theoretical knowledge plus varied experience help to command respect and help others. To train successfully, supervisors should illustrate *why*, as well as *how*, a job should be done, and at the same time appreciate the trainee's problems. Supervisors do not necessarily have to be the best operator in the group, but certainly they should not be the worst.

A reasonable elementary education and further education are essential. Technical skills are learned relatively quickly by repetition and are specific in behavioural activity. They are classified by referring to an established management principle or methodology, and are measurable. Implementation and appraisal are learned through practice. A general definition is the capability to apply knowledge, experience, techniques and methods, to perform specific tasks with the aid of appropriate machines and equipment.

Interpersonal skills

Often called human skills or interactive skills, they use motivational and behaviourist techniques to extract higher performance. They stimulate ideas, concentrate on needs and goals, and encourage participation.

A general definition is the capability and judgment to work with employees and to utilise fully their talents through leadership and various behavioural theories. Generally they take a long time to develop since learning and experience are needed, along with patience, perseverance, and tolerance.

Conceptual skills

Abstract in nature, these multiple skills are drawn from knowledge and experience over a long period. Considerable training and the opportunity to gain insight into corporate activities and problems is needed.

They concentrate on broader issues, corporate and organisational planning and policy, and systems. Collectively a definition is the capability to act in accordance with the objectives of the company as a whole. Conflict often exists between the objectives visualised by the group or section and the objectives of the corporate whole. Being able to reconcile the two and convince all those concerned is one difficulty.

Character

Nobody possesses all the qualities of character of the ideal supervisor. A compromise is inevitable and the choice will be governed by the particular circumstances.

Some of the important qualities are honesty and trustworthiness, with a strict sense of fairness and justice. A stable personality is essential for an even temper, steadiness and reliability. A direct, open and positive approach is desirable, giving due consideration to all parties when dealing with problems and grievances. Cheerfulness and enthusiasm, coupled with a sense of humour, are essential to provide the right type of industrial atmosphere.

In brief, good supervisors must possess something besides technical competence, clearly placing them above their particular group. Someone without higher intellect can still shine by having more drive, or inherent qualities of leadership. A person displaying strength of character who 'bubbles over' with activity can make up for other faults.

Each particular combination of qualities would suit a certain group in a particular work situation. Thus, one person stands out in a group and, provided his or her outlook is reasonably aligned with management policy and not objectionable, he or she is a likely choice.

Selection of supervisors

The importance of careful and fair selection of supervisors is often overlooked by management. Promotions from the shop floor and appointments in the lower levels of supervision are viewed very critically by operatives who are often directly affected.

Poor selection may destroy the efforts of previous supervisors who have managed to improve the industrial climate. Overlooked employees may feel frustrated and suspicious of management if the appointed individual is obviously unsuitable. The working harmony of the group or groups may be upset and resentment tends to spread like a disease – in all directions. The disgruntled individuals, who may have a legitimate complaint, mention the 'injustice' to everyone and a sense of frustration may develop throughout the concern.

Some observations on selection

Before considering the methods of selection, some circumstances which can affect selection must be mentioned. A common fault among supervisors is to baulk the promotion of individuals because they are considered to be indispensable in their present positions, although they are eminently suitable for promotion. Sometimes the supervisor cannot be bothered to train a replacement and the easiest remedy is deliberately to penalise a person's chances of promotion, often forcing the person to seek employment elsewhere.

It is not uncommon for superiors who are able to influence promotion, or who actually select the individual, to allow unimportant incidents (such as a heated political discussion at the company's Christmas dinner, or failing to acknowledge the general manager in the High Street) to dominate their impressions or opinions of subordinates, sometimes holding a trivial misdemeanour against a person for years. In some cases, even the suspicion of wrongdoing is sufficient reason to by-pass an individual. A true understanding of reality makes due allowance for human errors, and it is wiser and fairer to give other people the benefit of the doubt.

Type to suit management

Managers' opinions on the type of supervisor required are diverse and also vary with company size. The manager in a small concern may demand a 'Yes-man' who carries out orders to the letter, while in a large establishment the opposite type may be required, those who show initiative, make their own decisions and with a powerful personality. Some prefer the outsider with new ideas, others favour internal promotion. No two managers agree entirely on the qualities they seek for a particular position and usually compromise is necessary.

Methods of selection

The methods of selection are divided into two groups to highlight the importance of using scientific methods.

Unsubstantiated methods

All methods that do not allow for systematic selection and result in the detrimental effects of poor selection upon employees and the company come under this heading. These methods do not necessarily imply spontaneous selection — some are planned well in advance — but selection is based not on true grounds but on such grounds as:

1 favouritism, promoting friends and relatives
2 length of service or age seniority
3 high standard of skill alone
4 haphazard recommendations by a supervisor
5 chance, through stop-gap arrangements, i.e. someone being at the right place at the right time.

Scientific methods

Any method that attempts to reduce the possibility of error comes under this heading. The aim is to find the best person available for each vacancy. All employees, therefore, initially have equal opportunity and those with ability have good prospects of promotion which will not depend upon influence and favouritism. The essential requirements for any scheme with these aims are as follows:

1   planning ahead by estimating the vacancies which are likely to occur
2   preparation of a job specification listing all the main requirements of the vacancy
3   advertising internally and externally with the understanding that promotion from within will always take precedence where suitable internal applicants are available
4   careful investigation of *all* employees as promotion prospects
5   interviews of all candidates who are likely to be suitable. These must be conducted by skilled, objective interviewers and supplemented by appropriate tests
6   final choice or approval by top management or a selected panel.

Scientific choice, although not perfect, has obvious advantages. Many factors which may have been omitted are now included in the job specification, there is less chance of potential supervisors being overlooked, better assessment of individuals is now assured, and unbiased selection is more likely.

Frankness and open dealings are needed to make the scheme acceptable. Any queries should be discussed openly. Every applicant should be fully informed of proceedings and the unsuccessful candidates must be told (in confidence) why they failed.

A fair scheme must be seen to be fair by everyone. This is essential to smooth the way for the new supervisor, who may have to face special problems if he or she comes from the group to be supervised. This type of change can be a big wrench and it will help the person to adjust quickly if everyone accepts the selection as fair.

Training of supervisors

Informal training

Most supervisors learn their jobs by actually doing them, making mistakes, and correcting them as they gain experience. Although this system of trial and error is considered to be an essential part of training, practical experience must be supplemented by formal training to form a sound working basis.

Working with an effective supervisor is an invaluable experience but, to gain full benefit, a knowledge of the basic elements of supervision helps considerably. Techniques, built up through the experiences of many supervisors and specialists who have spent years studying supervision, need ideally to be learned and integrated with informal training.

Formal training

Many of the half a million supervisors in this country have not received any formal training although a variety of courses have been on offer for a number of years. Any successful training scheme must have suitable training facilities, the right syllabus, appropriate lecturers and back-up staff, and strong support from management who should ensure adequate follow-up and assessment after the course.

Although managers often agree that some form of supervisory training is essential, and show enthusiasm when the matter is discussed, few seem prepared to take any practical steps. Some managers say either that supervisors cannot be spared or that they are too busy to make the arrangements. Others ignore the facilities offered possibly because they think the subject is unimportant — or perhaps they fear that the supervisor, after training, may know more than the superior.

Questions

1 Give a detailed definition of a supervisor.
2 Outline the range of supervisory jobs under the headings of supervisory levels, range of duties and complexity of each duty.
3 List the typical duties of a supervisor.
4 What are the likely qualities to be seen in a successful supervisor?
5 What is meant by interpersonal and conceptual skills?
6 Outline a typical training programme for supervision.
7 How would you judge the effectiveness of a supervisory training course?
8 Outline some of the problems of selecting supervisors.
9 Would you expect the supervisor to be the best worker in the department? Explain your answer fully.
10 Outline the qualities of a supervisor for whom you would like to work.
11 Describe a suitable code of conduct for a new supervisor.

Case method of training

Case studies are provided at the end of each chapter. A complex situation typical of a real–life problem is outlined in a case study. This enables a supervisor to relate theory and his or her practical experience, and apply problem-solving and decision-making techniques. Such analysis and evaluation develop insight into how organisations succeed or fail and show what a supervisor can do to avoid disastrous situations.

The case method provides a theme for discussion in a group who may concentrate on a variety of topics including: what to do? how could the problem have been avoided? and what are the main policy issues involved? Thus, the benefits of discussion, practice in problem-solving and decision-making, and stimulation of enquiry into the principles of human relations are achieved.

The general approach

A case situation is intentionally incomplete since a full account of personalities, organisation climate and background data would partially defeat the objectives. Imagining the overall situation by using inferences, intuition and value judgments enables group members to assess each other's reactions and ideas as there is no single or correct answer. Thus the case and its implications should be related to each member's own working environment, noting the differences and possible reasons.

General guidelines

Certain fundamental guidelines apply regardless of the technique to be chosen for solving the case study. These are:

1 Read the case completely and make immediate notes that come to mind.
2 Develop a feel of the situation and elaborate on the questions if considered necessary to ensure a full understanding of requirements.
3 Read the case again but this time try to relate each person mentioned to others and the situation. Make appropriate notes and the sequence of events.
4 Draw up a rough profile of each person involved, trying to be completely objective in your analysis. Note (a) any obvious personal bias that you feel you are applying, and (b) any issues that were not immediately obvious before.
5 List any information not available that is important. Verify the facts that have emerged with evidence given, avoiding any assumptions.
6 Attempt to determine real issues and their significance. Refer these to theory and practical experience.
7 Relate the issues to the questions and identify the courses of action and possible answers.
8 Plan the answers bearing in mind various viewpoints and using appropriate diagrams.

Techniques

The main problem-solving techniques are intuition; analytical thinking; and creative thinking through discussion, brain storming, lateral thinking, synectics and morphological analysis. These are described in Chapter 8 along with guides to planning, characteristics of a sound plan and decision-making; all of which are useful in solving case studies.

Case study 1

Having attended a course on supervision it was very clear to Jane, a supervisor for twenty years, that it was impossible to implement many of the practices that had been explained. She was convinced that management would not agree to the changes she had in mind and that her superior would certainly not co-operate.

Gradually she became more frustrated over this assumption until one day an incident occurred which caused her to lose her temper — a further complaint from her staff that the employees in the sales department nearby were allowed to come and go as they pleased. She stormed into the sales manager's office and complained in very strong terms. Fortunately the sales manager was an understanding man and after explaining adequately why some of his staff had to work odd hours he suggested there should be more liaison between the two departments. Jane readily agreed, having calmed down, and maintained that she had always thought that a liaison committee was essential for good communication and alignment of objectives but she was sure her boss would not hear of it. To her amazement her boss responded positively to the idea. Indeed, she reproached Jane for not being more forthcoming before.

How much blame could be attributed to the training course, management, the superior, and Jane in these circumstances?

Case study 2

John Cummings, aged 36 years, had worked for Newland Techniques Ltd for six years. His supervisor was transferred and John as senior became the new supervisor.

He muddled his way through the week feeling thoroughly incompetent. After a month, to his surprise, his superior mentioned that she thought John had settled down well in his new job.

Whenever there were queries John simply contacted the specialist departments concerned and waited for answers which he then implemented. He used the same technique with the shop steward when decisions were needed, passing the problems over to his superior.

After six months two changes occurred; his superior retired and the company lost one of its major contracts. His new superior, about the same age as John, soon made it clear that there would be no buck-passing and that John would be taking full responsibility in future for a number of duties that he listed.

After a fortnight John was severely disciplined for not properly controlling his section. John was confused; he had no idea what else to do but give in his notice.

1 What factors contributed to John's downfall?
2 What advice could John possibly receive from an experienced supervisor?

2 Background: the development of supervision

The changing role of the supervisor

The climax of supervisory power was reached in the eighteenth century. The supervisor could dictate practically every aspect of production. He could engage and dismiss employees as he wished with little interference from the owners, so long as profits were acceptable.

The accuracy of this view of high status is unimportant for it holds no place in the modern supervisor's outlook. New supervisory roles have appeared and disappeared as a result of changing economic situations, the gradual organising of employees, the introduction of various concepts by management pioneers, a growing emphasis on behavioural science research, improved education, the efforts of industrialists to improve productivity, and the impact of new technologies.

As would be expected, the changing roles of a supervisor coincide with the phases of management thinking.

Autocratic management

During the Middle Ages, supervision through force was commonplace, both for free and slave labour. Output was probably very low and life was cheap. This barbaric use of labour died slowly – slaves were still being used in the British Empire even as late as 1833.

Semi-autocratic management

The early modern period, from about 1500 to 1940, saw the introduction of a more subtle form of supervision through fear of dismissal, although driving and bullying continued. In an era of unemployment dismissal could mean near-starvation for the worker and his family. The supervisor also faced similar treatment from management, with many employees standing by to take his place at a moment's notice. The supply of labour continued to outpace industrial growth owing to a huge increase in the population from three million in 1500, to forty-five million in 1935. Those who were employed submitted, at various times, to truck, cheating, and low wages. Underemployment also occurred through trade cycles.

The inevitable conflict between labour and capitalists first took on an organised form early in the nineteenth century. Local trade clubs were set up, followed by trade unions on a national level towards the end of the century. By 1940 waves of amalgamations had strengthened the bargaining power of the trade unions.

By 1900, F. W. Taylor, who is often known as the 'Father of Scientific Management', developed new techniques in the USA which included ideas of fostering close co-operation between management and men, and functionalising many of the foreman's duties. His methods eventually 'caught on' and were extensively used in the USA to speed up production.

In Britain, Taylor's teaching was ignored. Some articles on Taylorism appeared in the press about 1913–14 but, with the exception of a few large, progressive firms, little interest was shown until 1940.

Constitutional management

The critical war situation in 1940 demanded about four times the existing output in industry. Soon it became obvious that working overtime was not the complete answer to this problem. Attempts were made, therefore, to increase production in other ways.

Ernest Bevin transformed working conditions; welfare officers were introduced, and the unions and employers agreed to set up joint production committees. Although the effectiveness of these committees varied, it began to be recognised that the first steps towards maximum efficiency were only possible when human relations and machine operations were considered to be of equal importance.

Close consultation between the government and trade unions led to many trade union leaders and officials entering government departments. Wages were guaranteed and claims were settled at a national level between the unions and employers' associations.

A new era had commenced, with the unions gathering strength and consolidating, with government co-operation and consultation, and with employers gradually changing their attitude towards employees.

The concept of a fundamental common interest existing between all groups within a society slowly began to be recognised. Management, however, was viewed as the best-qualified to pursue these common interests. Opposition from employees was considered to be irrational and misguided, organised by 'trouble-makers' or politically motivated fanatics. The supervisor's role gradually absorbed the ideas of consultation, more emphasis was placed on human relations and loyalty, and the 'one big happy family' approach appeared.

The concept is often referred to as the *unitary framework* and at national level it includes the idea of acting within the national interest. Thus, anyone or any organisation who is construed to be acting against it is considered to be holding the country to ransom, or acting in a subversive manner. An example is to question the legitimacy of a trade union's activities.

Democratic management

In the 1960s it became increasingly obvious that employees were not responding to the previous approach. Management was forced to recognise that a variety of different and conflicting interests existed and it was assumed that these could, to some extent, be balanced out through compromises. The employee, therefore, has to surrender autonomy and recognise some rights of management, while management recognises employees' rights to organise, loyally oppose and bargain over procedures and financial rewards.

This *pluralist* approach, benign in character, became the basis for dealing with industrial relations issues. For the supervisor it meant a change in persuasive techniques, the use of logical argument, even more emphasis on good personal relationships, and the encouragement of a free exchange of information.

Contingency management

In the 1970s several fundamental working assumptions became more acceptable. The pluralist framework became suspect, arising from research the *systems* approach gained support, and *contingency* theory developed as a result.

The radical framework

Pluralism failed to account adequately for the marked inequalities and unfair opportunities in society. It could not overcome various fundamental social issues such as an unequal distribution of wealth and a lack of principled basis for income. Among many other criticisms, pluralism wrongly assumed a stable balance of power between employers and employees and as a result the *radical framework* became more acceptable on the basis of its analytical power, *not* its political emphasis.

Briefly the approach goes to the roots of issues and analyses contradictions in social, economic and political structures. Moreover, it locates internal tensions or strains within 'systems' which tend to lead to collapse or adaptation by those who wish to retain basic features. For example, in a culture where freedom, independence, choice, and autonomy are important values, conflict is inevitable when most employees are in a work situation which does not agree with these cultural expectations.

From this analysis conflict is fundamental, has to be expected, and taken into account. Co-operation however is also fundamental in society and industry. Herein lies the basic problem of supervision and management, and of organisation design, to avoid narrow tasks and the dehumanising of jobs.

The systems approach

In addition to the social aspects, research revealed the importance of technical and economic factors in achieving organisational effectiveness. Consequently new theories viewed organisations as complex systems of individuals, tasks and technology which interacted with, and were part of, a larger environment. Collectively these concepts become known as an *open-system*.

Briefly, the systems approach analyses activities to see how they communicate with, and relate to, each other; and how they are controlled. Basically systems are groups of parts that are dynamically combined and interrelated into a purposeful whole. In other words, to be effective any collection of activities that has a common objective should ensure that each activity is recognised as having an effect on all other activities, especially when any changes occur.

This simple explanation becomes complex when an organisation is examined. For example, obviously it is pointless for marketing to accept orders that production cannot manufacture. Therefore marketing activities affect production and finance, and their effectiveness depends on relating them to other activities to ensure that co-ordination is achieved. Activities that ignore this approach establish boundaries that isolate, cause communication and control problems, and defeat co-ordination.

Expanded further, interrelationships operate through complex communication networks that self-regulate (control mechanisms) and adapt to internal and external environmental changes. Networks are examined in Chapter 14, self-regulation in Chapter 22 (and homeostasis in Chapter 9), and environmental aspects in Chapters 3 and 6.

The contingency approach

From 'systems' emerged contingency theory which determines organisation design and management style for a particular situation. It relies upon finding the best combination or compromise considering the existing or forecasted conditions associated with human skills, technological aspects and the external environment.

This situational approach to management uses all the previous approaches but in the right consistency depending upon circumstances. The supervisor must be knowledgeable, adaptable, and able to cope with boundaries problems. Key supervisory roles emerge: achieving co-ordination; encouraging participation; developing group autonomy; and recognising situational changes and rapidly adapting to them.

Collaborative management

A clearer forecast of the 1990s is already emerging as companies – especially in the USA – take account of their difficulties experienced over the past twenty years. These difficulties have included increased strong competition from certain countries; unfavourable economic circumstances; degrees of recession; and technological changes. Emerging from these problems is a realisation that the continued imbalance between technical and interpersonal/conceptual skills exercised by supervisors has caused poor productivity and increasing resentment from employees.

Proposed restructuring and some actual restructuring have emphasised supervisory role changes. These are based upon introducing or strongly reinforcing existing human resource management. This simply means that managing is concentrated on stimulating employee help and involvement.

Supervisory skills must be balanced to pursue this collaborative philosophy and to cope with the effects on employees of technological change. Since about 1960 writers have expressed concern over the neglect of interpersonal and conceptual skills. Decades ago research findings verified the urgent need, but only recently have the full implications been highlighted through large discrepancies in productivity between competing countries.

Fewer middle managers

Introducing technologies – especially information technology – without appropriate structural change that alters supervisory roles is a serious error. For example, information technology has made desk-top computers common-place therefore ample data are available at all managerial levels. This naturally affects the decision-making process and allows direct access by senior managers to the lowest levels during operations and when information or specialist advice is needed.

This significant change is all-pervading and invites drastic structural reform. Apart from overcoming many communication problems, the change queries the relevance of middle managers as information processors and as linkages in the organisation. Computerised procedures and systems further reduce the need for information finding, processing, and transfer to other levels, which are also at present the province of the middle manager.

Inevitably supervisors assume these roles since they are in the vital place. They give information direct to senior levels, hierarchical protocol seems to disappear, and new relationships emerge – especially in information procedures and systems. Consequently there is the opportunity to flatten the organisation pyramid. However, bearing in mind certain organisational principles (*see* Chapter 3), other middle management roles remain. In the USA there is a trend to reduce the number of middle managers; some concerns are combining middle and first-line management levels to work with both shop floor operatives and administrative staff on all operational aspects.

Employee-centred culture

A further example directly involves employees. Strong competition has forced organisations to streamline the work-force, introduce technological changes in production and encourage employees to be more committed through various devices such as co-partnership, profit-sharing schemes and shareholding opportunities. Such encouragement is insufficient to bring to fruition the productive potential of the remaining work-force. To succeed with such plans a further burden is placed on the supervisors. They must adopt a philosophy – with all the attendant skills and techniques – to build up employee commitment to the company and to achieve more involvement. Firm support from senior management through a genuine collaborative philosophy is crucial.

To summarise, the quality of supervisors and their training programmes are becoming key factors. Neglecting supervisors in future will cause serious organisational malfunctions. An employee-centred organisational culture created by human resource management is essential to gain maximum benefit from new technologies. Hence a collaborative management philosophy is the only sensible way to achieve high productivity levels already enjoyed by communities and companies elsewhere.

This philosophy involves employees at all levels in decision-making, which includes all activities in the concern. Human resources are considered paramount with the aim of establishing employee trust, commitment, loyalty, and industry. To succeed, emphasis on interpersonal and conceptual skills is needed for supervisors who must be given the opportunity to use them.

Supervision and management

Supervision implies operating at close range by actually overseeing, controlling, dealing with situations on the spot as they arise, whereas management implies controlling remotely by using other administrative means. Supervision and management naturally overlap in practice, partly from necessity, where managers show a close personal interest in order to achieve co-operation, and partly from lack of management training.

It is essential to note the difference between the two functions. The supervisory function is concerned with the day-to-day running of the group, which will entail a certain amount of attention to detail depending upon the size of the section. If the section is large the supervisor will need to master the art of delegation, passing on the minor tasks to colleagues, thus providing more own time to plan and control the work effectively. The managerial function, on the other hand, should be concerned with thinking well ahead on questions of policy, programmes of expansion, new products, new markets and so on, thus leaving the detail and less important tasks to managers' subordinates.

This distinction between a supervisor and a manager, although very clear in theory, is frequently obscured in practice when supervisors are inclined to skip essential detail and concentrate on forward planning, whereas managers are seen to be very keen on attending to detail, often in order to compensate for their lack of drive, vision and decision-making ability (*see*

Chapter 7). Hence, managers' and supervisors' views of each other's jobs vary extensively in practice. Attempts to overcome this diversity of opinion and operational fault have included retraining managers, completely removing the supervisory level, and encouraging collaboration at the interface between management and supervision.

Moreover, another factor affecting relationships at this important level is the supervisor's background. For example, if a supervisor were promoted the tendency is to feel a strong link with previous peers but a weaker bond with management. Behaving like a first-line manager, therefore, is more difficult. However, if the supervisor starts a job as a very junior manager, there will probably be a weak link with clerks or operatives but a strong link with management. The supervisor will find it easier to act as a junior manager but more difficult to relate to employees.

In both instances the void between managers and employees is clearly marked and somehow interface difficulties have to be tackled. Bringing the two sides together amounts to managing supervision effectively by using various approaches.

The collaborative approach

As already explained this modern concept means that a new relationship is developed between the manager and supervisor. Both must collaborate together in many of the managerial aspects, such as problem solving, decision making, communicating, and sharing views and ideas, *on an equal footing*. Both need to have their aims clearly in mind: to bring the two structures closer together, to analyse and come up with more acceptable approaches, and to improve relationships generally.

Although the approach needs strong management support, often the supervisor will have to take the initiative, point out the possibilities, and press hard to make the change. Sometimes managers are unaware of the void, fail to recognise it as a cause of many problems, or they simply ignore it. More time has to be spent on promoting a better understanding through the manager and the supervisor working far more closely together than is normally acceptable to management.

The retraining approach

To understand thoroughly the two environments that exist – the management sphere and the working sphere – means considerable education and retraining. Closing or narrowing the gap is a fundamental question which, at discussion stage alone, demands a revision of many basic attitudes and ideologies. Training alone will not solve anything unless both parties are prepared to co-operate, use their knowledge and common sense, and forget old traditions. One of the big stumbling blocks is class, discussed below.

The classless approach

Many countries, including Germany, are proud of their 'classless' society. In Britain many managers give the distinct impression to employees that not only are they proud of being in a seemingly different class, but also they are pre-occupied with status and intent on widening the gap. To the majority of supervisors the division of class structure appears at a level above them. If the line is not made obvious to them a strong feeling persists that they are not part of the management class. Some feel alienated, not being a part of the working class or in the middle class. Some senior managers even consider themselves as upper class, the property owning class, or they aspire towards this level. Seldom do managers see themselves as part of the proletariat, although all are employed by the company except the owner/managers.

The outcome is a variety of class structure models which adds to the confusion and causes people to react mentally and sometimes physically against those considered to be above them.

In contrast, the classless approach encourages managers to spend much less time on elevating their class and demonstrating their so-called superiority and much more time on removing the barriers, fostering sounder relationships, and utilising modern motivating techniques to achieve objectives. Even some supervisors are equally at fault and the same approach applies to them. Further discussions on class are in Chapter 9.

Questions

1 Discuss the possible effect of rapid change in information technology on the role of the supervisor.
2 What are the main factors that cause supervisory role changes?
3 How may the decline in union power affect the supervisor's role?
4 'A common interest exists for all people in an organisation.' How would you attempt to convince an employee that this statement is true?
5 Explain the difference between unitary, pluralistic, and radical approaches.
6 Examine the systems approach and its effect on key supervisory roles and the organisation.
7 Outline the main phases in management thinking that have affected supervision.
8 'An employee-centred culture is essential to exploit the productive potential of a working force.' Discuss this statement.
9 Explain the collaborative approach and its importance in a modern organisation.
10 'Supervising is easier in a classless society.' On what grounds would you agree or disagree with this statement?

Case study 1

'I know all about these new-fangled ideas of supervising but so far as I'm concerned it's "heads down and do a fair day's work for a fair day's pay"; then we'll see better results,' stressed Janet, seated at the coffee table with two other fellow supervisors.

Elsie reacted. 'That's OK for you; I've got teenagers to cope with and if I don't give them freedom to have a chat and a giggle they would "go round the bend" working those blasted terminals eight hours a day!'

'You're too nice to them, Elsie,' complained Paul. 'What you don't realise is that my lads are distracted by your girls babbling away and flaunting themselves around. Concentration is lost and up go the errors.'

'There, you see,' exclaimed Janet, 'Give them an inch and they cause more trouble than the union. We've got the upper-hand now with high unemployment, and it's up to us to take advantage of it.'

'That's a joke, Janet! Your productivity figures are worse than ours,' cracked Elsie.

1   Are there any clear cut answers to these problems?
2   What could management do about this situation?

Case study 2

Andrew was a newly appointed trained supervisor. He was confronted with a situation where the three other supervisors seemed to sit back and allow the sections to run themselves. The general atmosphere was relaxed and cordial between sections. Discipline appeared to be non-existent.

Andrew found this way of operating difficult to accept and after a few weeks decided to see his boss. He explained and thought that although the work loads were completed on time there was over-manning according to his calculations.

To his surprise the manager scowled, sat back, and said, 'So you want to rock the boat and upset everyone? You'll cause a lot of trouble with the supervisors and staff but at the end of the day will it be worthwhile?'

Andrew reacted, 'Yes, I think it will in the long run. It's soul-destroying to work in a department that's out of step with the rest of the organisation!'

1   What can be done in this situation where Andrew obviously lacks his manager's support?
2   If you were Andrew would you consider discussing the problem with the other supervisors?

3 Organisation of work

Organisation design

An old adage is that people make an organisation work, not the design of its structure. Whether this holds true in modern times is debatable. Nevertheless many employees severely criticise organisation design, while many specialists claim it has a partial effect on productivity.

Invariably structures suffer with design faults as growth and environmental changes occur. Everyone has to live with this inherent 'organised chaos' and make the best of it. As Peter Drucker (1955) mentions, 'The best managers are those who think through organisational dilemmas.'

The successful application of behavioural knowledge and motivators depends partly upon various structural aspects of organisation. These are discussed first from the strategic viewpoint of treating the organisation as a whole which is consistent with modern systems theory, and second from the tactical viewpoint which includes structuring, problem areas, organisation criteria, organisation theory, critical organisation principles, co-ordination, and structural designs.

Organisation structuring

The ideal organisation achieves its objectives by structuring and restructuring in such a way that maximum effectiveness is drawn from its members — the employees. This goal should not be superseded by other supplementary objectives often encountered when powerful individuals or groups structure to suit their own personal requirements.

The term *organisation* in this context means structuring activities into operational groups, each of which contain employees who are allocated roles and duties and given varying degrees of authority and responsibility. In brief: the formal organisation.

The way people behave within the organisation is a product of their job description and events which directly affect them during their initial period at work (induction). In other words they are affected by the economic system (their job) and by the social system (interaction with others) which create expectations of the roles they should undertake. This two-fold effect explains why no two people see the organisation in exactly the same way and why the informal organisation is so important.

Formal and informal structures are intertwined and often indistinguishable. Thus organisation is a purposeful social unit. The implications are that each employee possesses a slightly different mental make-up; their attitudes towards events bias their view of the organisation structure, their reasons for staying in their job vary, and they possess differing expectations of roles they and others should play.

Problem areas

Certain fundamental difficulties must be overcome to achieve maximum effectiveness. Here are the most common ones:

1   Formal organisations are structured to conform to an established set of traditional principles set down in most textbooks on organisation and management. These principles do not allow sufficiently for social interaction and modern technologies.

2   So far there is no workable way of restructuring an organisation to suit the modern employee and to replace completely the outdated traditional organisation concept.

3   Although incomplete, there is sufficient evidence to show how people behave in organisations and where improvement areas lie.

4   Organisational change is often traumatic, expensive, and sometimes disastrous at present. Therefore there is some inertia from owners and managers to adopt sound ideas.

5   Industrial unrest causes difficulties in certain trades but not so much in others. Nevertheless organisations are composed of employees who are there to provide other people with a product or service, regardless of the type of industry.

6   Some managers feel, and through experience know, that many popular behavioural theories do not necessarily conform to industrial reality and are not easily installed.

Organisation criteria

To satisfy the individual and the community there are certain essential requirements for high productivity. In some respects the requirements are conflicting but this is mainly due to imbalance between economic and social factors. Balance is attainable when each requirement is allowed to find its own determinable level through the operation of political, technological, economic, and social interaction.

There is little difficulty in listing the criteria:

1   Designing the job to suit the individual.
2   Establishing acceptable performance standards.
3   Appropriate staffing consistent with planned output.
4   Group structuring to satisfy social interaction and maximum participation.
5   Removing class barriers.
6   Structuring all resources (including specialists) to satisfy worker demands and roles.
7   Creating appropriate systems essential for operational and functional effectiveness.
8   Integrating the above criteria.

The above requirements are not flimsy narrow ideas, they contain complex modern concepts conforming to research findings. Figure 3.1 illustrates the criteria and essential factors.

Adverse features

Certain inherent difficulties are often associated with social and environmental influences. With job design (item 1) the concepts and problems are mentioned in Chapter 17 – Employment.

Acceptable performance standards (item 2) are involved because acceptance must be agreed by management, employees, and trade unions. Sometimes conflict commences here. Management may employ and often train work-study specialists who have the capability to assess accurately performance standards for quality and working rate. The calculated time for a task is at a normal working rate but this may not be acceptable to everyone.

Appropriate staffing (item 3) becomes a hazardous task considering problems associated with acceptable performance standards. Indeed manpower planning – a critical feature – is not made any easier. This might lead to disastrous consequences through its effect on corporate planning and policy making.

Group structuring (item 4) is discussed in Chapter 4, and items 5 and 6 – class barriers and human resources – in Chapters 9 and 6 respectively. The latter two are often thought to be the major sources of industrial problems in Britain. In Germany they claim no classes exist; in Japan all specialists – including managers and supervisors – are treated as resources for the workers; in Britain everyone knows their place.

Establishing appropriate systems (item 7) is a controversial subject. A straight-forward administration task becomes absurdly complex when social interaction is considered. This dynamic process of systems integration through communication networks (see Chapter 14) and control processes introduces contingency approaches where refinements absorb a variety of behavioural aspects already discussed.

JOB DESIGN	SELECTION	INTRAGROUP STRUCTURING	INTERGROUP STRUCTURING	ESTABLISHING INDUSTRIAL CLIMATE	ESTABLISHING SYSTEMS	SYSTEMS INTEGRATION
1 Synchronisation with other jobs	1 Manpower planning	1 Use of resources	1 Use of resources	1 Removal of class barriers	1 Social interaction	1 Communication networks to achieve co-ordination
2 Integration with the organisation	2 Use of specialists	2 Role conflict: job role–membership role	2 Demands of employees	2 Optimising conflict	2 Administration specialists	2 Control processes
3 Problems: values, pacing, repetitiveness, unreal objectives.	3 High moral managerial code	3 Norms	3 Conflict	3 Minimising role conflict		3 Rules and regulations (danger of bureaucracy)
4 Role-participation, etc.						
5 Critical organisation principles						
6 Adequate rewards						

Fig. 3.1 An outline of organisation structuring criteria

Certain essential requirements must be considered for behavioural balance and to achieve high productivity. Standards are judged by employees and are accepted as essential. Each factor finds its own determinable level through political, technological, economic and social interaction

Finally, although integration of the criteria (item 8) is an Utopian objective, it should not be ignored. All changes in any of the seven requirements should be treated as possessing interacting effects. Contemplating such changes should be made with integration in mind.

Integration difficulties

When all the roles and tasks are allocated, groups formed, and functions structured, a common dilemma appears. This is because communication networks must be established to achieve co-ordination which means designing forms, establishing rules, regulating control mechanisms, and so on. Without them there would be chaos; with them employees tend to build in rigidity and inflexibility which stifles initiative. In other words bureaucracy takes over: everyone must conform to rigid procedures, forms must be completed, no by-passing is allowed, and there are no exceptions for extraneous circumstances.

In this situation over-all objectives are subordinated to local procedure-dominated aims. Employees are entangled with 'red tape' and roles become blurred.

Role stress

This blurring effect causes stress as expectations are not realised or only partially realised; role playing is not fully satisfied. Role conflict occurs (explained in Chapter 5) and role ambiguity is prevalent as expectations are not fully understood or are misinterpreted.

Typical examples of role ambiguity are generally seen in supervisory jobs, discussed in Chapter 1. The supervisor must bond together primary and secondary groups, but as a superior in one group and a subordinate in another the supervisor's roles are viewed from two fronts. Consequently often it is impossible to please management and subordinates since both groups expect the supervisor's support.

A further example is the secretary who feels a loyalty to the boss and to the company. When the secretary discovers the boss is falsifying petty cash claims she or he suffers with uncertainty, torn between a supportive role towards the boss and a protective role towards the company.

An outline of organisation theory now follows which is complex but essential for supervisors. They must know which type of organisation they are involved in since expectations from management will vary accordingly. Furthermore when organisation changes are proposed or occur supervisors should understand their significance in the job and know how to adjust.

Organisation theory

Organisations were first studied thousands of years ago. Many complex and diverse theories exist mainly due to changes in organisational size and number, and increased complexity of technologies this century. Recognition of dependency among various organisational activities is now an important feature. Such dependency could mean increased harmony, solidarity, and support for the concern. In fact members often resent dependency and react against each other. To counteract this tendency new theories have emerged.

A selection of theories has been chosen to illustrate the main schools of thought and to provide evidence of interest to the supervisor.

Traditional thought

Classical approaches are cold, impersonal and mechanistic. They follow a scientific pattern: establishing all the tasks required, designing a structure to accommodate them, achieving co-ordination mainly through supervision, communicating through the line of command, and controlling by holding everyone accountable for the work performed.

Many principles were established but some are severely criticised on grounds of poor behavioural sensitivity, contradictions, and lack of evidence to prove they are universal truths.

Transitionary concepts

These recognise that organisations are essentially dynamic due to the human element, therefore many control mechanisms and relationships exist. A dynamic base implies feedback into the organisation process, typically methods of communicating, participating, decision making, problem solving, planning and motivating.

This cybernetic trend (see Chapter 22) leads to open–systems and management science.

Balance theory

The idea of organisation equilibrium considers (1) the behaviour of people who decide to join the organisation, remain employed or withdraw, and (2) the balance of inducements to stay and the contributions offered by employees. Therefore there is an actual decision to participate, to stay or leave.

Peter Drucker (1967) emphasises this aspect: 'If an organisation cannot hold or attract people it is doomed.'

Role theory

The organisation is viewed as a number of role performers who are co-ordinated by a role system. Each person adopts roles through certain expectations from others and from themselves. Roles interact with each other and so continuity or co-ordination is achieved.

The systems approach

This concept views organisations as systems of elements (or parts or activities), each contributing to the operation and each being dependent on other aspects of the system for its own requirements. These elements are interdependent, interrelated, and self-adjusting to pressures or disturbances that upset aims.

Systems are common everywhere, especially in the social, physical and biological worlds. A system is generally described as an organised or complex whole: a combination of parts that form a unitary whole. Two types of systems approach are recognised: the closed- and open-system.

Closed-systems approach

Originating from traditional organisation theory, this approach is based upon physical sciences and is applicable to mechanistic systems. It is self-contained and adopts highly rationalistic approaches. The external environment which includes the economic, technological, governmental and other factors is ignored. As expected, this inherent tendency moves the system towards equilibrium and entropy – it runs down.

Open-systems approach

This system adapts continually to the changing external and internal environment by revising sub-systems within its structure. The dynamic process causes changes in all the critical features such as goals, values, technologies utilised, the organisation structure itself, psycho-social aspects and managerial aspects.

The maintenance process is an essential part. It constructs and maintains the staffing establishment, building and plant so that the manufacturing (or servicing) process may function to change the inputs of material into finished products.

Socio-technical systems

This approach emphasises the interrelationships between technology, the environment, sentiments of employees and the organisation form. The simple, broken-down elements of a job are recombined into a larger whole by assigning the reconstituted jobs to groups. Thus cohesive social units of workers and supervisors are established that correspond to meaningful technological units with reasonable autonomy and responsibility for the total job.

The contingency approach

This concept is a refinement of open-systems theory and information technology related to specific organisation structures. Lawrence and Lorsch (1967) maintain there is no one best way to organise since it depends upon choosing the most suitable combination of parameters which include technological factors, the external environment and behavioural aspects.

Empirical evidence supports this situational approach. Here is one important contribution among several.

Production technology

Joan Woodward studied 100 British companies classified into three types of production technological environment: (1) unit and small batch, (2) large batch and mass, and (3) process. The organisation structure, human relations and status were examined. A direct relationship between them and technical advance was discovered.

Interesting features related to the three groups were span of control for first line supervision: 21–30, 41–50 and 11–20 respectively; levels of management were: 3, 4, and 6; and the number reporting to top executive were: 4, 7, and 10. In unit production there were small intimate groups, considerable participation, permissiveness and flexibility in job interrelationships; in mass or batch production there were clear-cut duties, line/staff conflict and poor industrial relations; in process production there were good interpersonal relations and little conflict or stress.

Supervisory roles

Clearly the supervisor's role is related to the type of production environment. The following tendencies are noticeable:

1 *Unit production* the operator expects from the supervisor leadership, pace setting, quality standards, general control and especially technical advice.

2 *Batch production* the supervisor tends to be a disciplinarian or undertakes a more task-oriented role. He or she expects operators to conform to schedules on time and in accordance with specifications.

3 *Continuous process production* the supervisor undertakes co-ordination activities, advises, and concentrates more on interpersonal and conceptual skills.

Critical organisation principles

Although there are many principles, some are critical and their degree of use is often a deciding factor in the type of structure envisaged. In this category are:

- Centralisation of authority
- Authority levels
- Span of control
- Corresponding authority and responsibility
- Delegation
- Unity of command
- Specialisation
- Structural height

Centralisation

Inevitably a designer must consider the amount of authority to be retained at the apex, how much to delegate throughout the structure, and how this spread should be arranged. These considerations determine the number of managers who will be able to commit resources and by how much.

If the spread is wide and deep a highly decentralised organisation is evident. If commitment of various resources rests with only a few at the top the organisation is obviously highly centralised.

Various spreads may be seen in practice. Generally as the organisation grows there is more decentralisation, specialisation, rules and procedures. Decentralisation offers less overload at the top, more rapid decisions; more flexibility throughout, more accountability for budgets, and improved conditions for motivation and participation. There are difficulties, however, such as increased probability of control and communication failure, inaccurate alignment of objectives, inconsistency of behaviour towards outsiders, and the need for a higher number of capable managers.

Authority levels

Considering span of control, production and marketing complexity, and management style, it would appear that the size of the concern automatically dominates the number of authority levels. Generally this is the case but not always. There are choices open to the designer. Certainly the small organisation tends to have fewer levels (about three or four), is centralised and has a wide span of control. This flat type of structure may cause behavioural problems if managers and supervisors have insufficient time to spend on individuals and groups. Nevertheless there should be better communication and improved co-ordination.

In the large concern a tall structure is normal, authority is decentralised, there is a high degree of specialisation, and span of control tends to be narrow. Above a certain size there seems to be pressure to maintain the same number of levels at around seven or eight.

Span of control

This principle dates back to Henri Fayol, in approximately 1906 (*see* Bibliography under Gray, I) and simply means the number of subordinates reporting to a single supervisor. Various theorists have attempted to place precise figures on the minimum, optimum, and maximum span. Graicunas propounded a mathematical formula to provide the exact number by calculating the number of social relationships involved. L. Urwick stated in *Elements of Administration*, 1943 that at the most, six subordinates are sufficient if their work interlocks. More recent surveys have shown considerable variation from ten up to eighty.

Experiments with spans have tended to prove that reductions do not necessarily improve performance and have raised many questions. Some examples are:

1 *Which subordinates should be included*? There is no simple answer considering staff officers, the varying width of close control, and the influence of co-ordinating devices.

2 *Should the superior's capability be considered*? It seems that some supervisors effectively control a large number easily.

3 *Should the subordinate's capability be considered*? Some employees are self-disciplined and self-controlled; they require very little supervision and co-operate without aid.

Obviously the choice of span is complex and demands careful analysis in each situation.

Corresponding authority and responsibility

Any supervisor who is given responsibility for a task should receive commensurate authority. Although obvious, in practice it is not unusual for supervisors to be held accountable for certain activities without having sufficient authority to influence them.

According to L. Urwick, smooth working at *all* levels depends on authority and responsibility being coterminous and co-equal. Unfortunately many committees are allocated authority which tends to cut across this principle as do staff and matrix concepts, discussed in the next chapter.

Delegation

This principle has stood the test of time but is probably the most difficult to apply in practice. Many supervisors fail because they tend to take on too much work even when capable help is available. This often occurs because courage, trust in subordinates, and delicate control are lacking.

The procedure for delegating is simple. However, having sufficient faith in subordinates depends on the supervisor's basic philosophy towards people – see McGregor's Theory X and Theory Y discussed in Chapter 11.

Balancing work-loads

A supervisor should not waste valuable time on (a) routine or simple matters and (b) straightforward decision making which should be made at the lowest level consistent with capability. The aim should be to spread work more evenly, based upon capability, appropriate levels, and fair workloads.

Properly arranged, people will have opportunities to develop, gain experience, and practise co-ordinated responsibility. Thus the subordinate is always responsible for doing the job while the supervisor is responsible for seeing it done.

Inspection

Since the superior remains responsible, the natural consequence of delegation is inspection. Control of work is lost without it, hence the saying, 'Inspection is the corollary of delegation'. The object is to check on the work without destroying initiative and causing resentment. Initiative is a vital ingredient for expanding capability; how to inspect and encourage inspection requires experience and judgment. A saying worth remembering during inspection is, 'People with average intelligence are very sensitive whilst those above average are extremely sensitive.'

A superior showing an interest in the work can give much pleasure and satisfaction to the subordinate. In this manner the art of unobtrusive inspection is developed where checking comes through the normal course of contact. The idea is to keep all operations running smoothly; therefore finding out any unsatisfactory work is only a half-way stage. Action is necessary, which is as delicate an operation as finding out since people's feeling are involved. Tactless treatment is likely to lead to repercussions later, although they may be disguised and seemingly unconnected.

Procedure for delegating

1   Make a list of all the tasks performed and include those that are neglected or omitted through lack of time.
2   Mark each one on an 'importance' basis and rearrange in descending order of importance.
3   Allocate time for each task. Accuracy is unimportant so long as an estimate is made to provide a rough basis.
4   Decide how much can be coped with by oneself, starting from the top, and draw a line across the list at this point.
5   Make sure that each subordinate is assessed for his capabilities, and give the benefit of the doubt where necessary.
6   Allocate tasks below the line to subordinates, as appropriate to their capabilities.
7   Follow up and inspect to ensure they are not in difficulties.

8 Rearrange if vital, but remember that it takes people some time to expand and adjust. A fair trial is essential.

Methodical approaches such as those outlined above make the supervisor's task less harassing.

Unity of command

Coined by H. Fayol (1906) who firmly believed in its critical nature, the principle states that each employee should be responsible and receive orders from only one superior. From the employee's viewpoint it makes good sense; from the superior's viewpoint it avoids divided loyalty and is a discouragement to play one manager off against the other; structurally it seems sound but is not in line with modern situational concepts.

The trend away from the principle when utilising matrix concepts seems to be reverting to F. W. Taylor's idea in 1900 of functional foremanship. This old concept allowed a worker to be responsible to about five foremen, each one being specialised in one particular function.

Specialisation

The natural tendency to specialise is obvious in view of the vast amounts of knowledge, skill and experience required in any main or subsidiary function within an organisation. Marketing, production, finance, research and development, to name a few, are so specialised today that it is beyond one person's capability to cope successfully with more than one element. Indeed, in practice it is often beyond some managers to cope with one effectively.

Although essential, specialisation does cause difficulties but these problems do not negate the use of the concept, they simply point strongly to lack of co-ordination or communication failures.

Within this concept are two related technologies which are experiencing rapid change and affecting organisations in traumatic ways: information technology and management science.

Information technology

The increasing importance of information technology probably influences the structure in two ways. Firstly, information processing systems are complex and demanding on managerial specialisms and expertise, therefore more emphasis on the administrative function is inevitable. Secondly, such systems assume that organisations are open-systems that cope with external environmental uncertainty and work-related task uncertainty.

The degree of uncertainty is dependent upon information which is *not* available to managers. Reducing this uncertainty depends upon using information technology more effectively. Peter Drucker makes the point clearly: 'You can usually get all the figures except those you need.'

Clearly an organisation should be structured to cater for this situation. Without due regard for information technology, a concern soon lags behind and eventually fails. Furthermore, the critical reliance on information for some parts of the organisation has to be recognised and adjustments made accordingly.

Certain fundamental changes are already clear, and modern organisations are adapting rapidly to them. Some examples are obvious: to be effective there must be a match between information processing needs and the internal capacity to provide them; the degree of uncertainty varies in each organisation sector; some organisations can more easily adapt compared with others but for *all* the time factor is becoming increasingly paramount as new concerns enter markets.

Management science

A brief look at the quantitative approach or management science indicates its place in organisation design and the need to consider management practice.

A modern supervisor uses various management techniques which utilise mathematical techniques and operational research (see Chapter 22). Although the use of higher mathematics is very useful in decision making, planning and control, as an aid it does not lessen the importance of behavioural science and should be seen in this perspective. Nevertheless organisation designs cannot be constructed effectively without due consideration for this factor which hinges on high technology in the administrative fields and permeates all organisational aspects.

Structural heights

This concept is included here as it is closely related to delegation, span of control, and authority levels. The tall form is designed by narrowing span of control, increasing authority levels and implies the maximising of delegation. The flat form is achieved by reversing the process, *see* Fig. 3.2.

Tall forms encourage close control and strong discipline, similar to the bureaucratic model which is notoriously tall. Modern theorists are critical of this approach on the grounds that it supports McGregor's Theory X (*see* Chapter 11) and there is a natural reaction from employees to close control.

Flat forms allow for modern concepts of control, increased delegation which facilitates job enrichment, and conforms more to Theory Y with its distinct behavioural advantage in managing the modern employee.

Co-ordination

Dividing work into tasks and allocating them to employees immediately causes communication problems when employees attempt to perform their

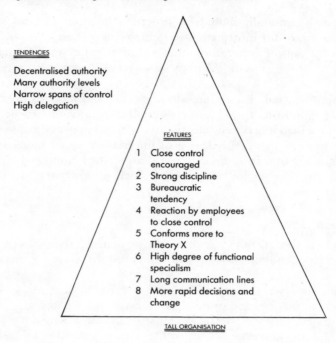

TENDENCIES

Decentralised authority
Many authority levels
Narrow spans of control
High delegation

FEATURES

1 Close control
   encouraged
2 Strong discipline
3 Bureaucratic
   tendency
4 Reaction by employees
   to close control
5 Conforms more to
   Theory X
6 High degree of functional
   specialism
7 Long communication lines
8 More rapid decisions and
   change

TALL ORGANISATION

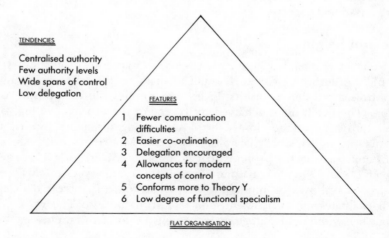

TENDENCIES

Centralised authority
Few authority levels
Wide spans of control
Low delegation

FEATURES

1 Fewer communication
   difficulties
2 Easier co-ordination
3 Delegation encouraged
4 Allowances for modern
   concepts of control
5 Conforms more to Theory Y
6 Low degree of functional specialism

FLAT ORGANISATION

Fig. 3.2 *Extremes of organisation structural height*

The tall form is designed by narrowing span of control, increasing authority levels and – by implication – maximising delegation. The flat form is achieved by reversing the process. Height depends mainly on size, management style, nature of business and production technology

duties successfully. Unlike a situation where there is no division of labour or specialisation – the 'one-man' business or sole proprietor – employees rely heavily on various linking means and devices to overcome co-ordination difficulties. The amount of attention paid to this behavioural aspect partly determines design effectiveness. Employees soon feel isolated and like machines if behavioural means of coupling them together are neglected.

Co-ordination in this context means the outcome of applying successfully all the communication methods and devices needed to couple *everyone* together. Neglecting even one employee may easily cause many operating difficulties. A thorough job is needed with special consideration for the behavioural or human approach as well as the cold, mechanistic aspects. A graphical representation is given in Fig. 3.3, while Chapters 14, 15 and 16 discuss communication in detail.

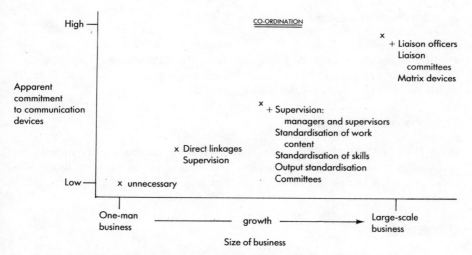

Fig. 3.3 *A graphical representation of communication devices*

Devices seem to develop in phases as communication difficulties arise through growth. Ideally all devices should be used but time and expense work against this concept until co-ordination problems are recognised

Linkage devices

From the behavioural viewpoint there are eight mechanisms to consider:

Direct linkages

Each employee is able to contact his or her co-worker and achieve co-ordination by informal discussion. This mutual adjustment allows people to adapt to each other and hopefully bonds them together. The concept also applies between managers.

Supervision

Allocating authority to an individual who supervises a group should include giving him or her responsibility for the work undertaken. Thus the supervisor establishes links with each subordinate, issues instructions, monitors results, discusses problems, listens to grievances, and presses for ideas.

This supervisory process will naturally occur at all levels of authority.

Standardisation of work content

By establishing such standards each employee knows what is expected by following concise instructions. Depending on the degree of specialisation, a certain amount of flexibility may be built in to allow for job enrichment.

Standardisation of skills

By this means it is possible to train employees so that management will know exactly how they will respond in certain situations. This device is useful when organisations are decentralised among many sites and is really an alternative to following detailed instructions.

Output standardisation

If the expected results of any procedure or system are made known everyone realises their objectives and the anticipated quality of performance. This concept applies not only to production but also to all functions and authority levels.

Committees

This heading covers all the various meetings that may be arranged to improve human relations and communication. The meeting of people in one place immediately assists in breaking down barriers, provided that procedure, size, structure, and chairmanship are adequately considered.

Liaison devices

These are useful when considerable and frequent contact between two people or departments is essential. A liaison officer and standing committees are two examples.

Matrix devices

To overcome problems associated with complex projects a matrix structure may be introduced for a set period. This device is a type of structure which establishes dual authority. In other words a manager is responsible to more than one person and the chain of authority splits at convenient points to accommodate this requirement. Unity of command is abandoned and line managers are equally and jointly responsible for the same decision. This temporary device forces managers to co-operate and reconcile difficulties between them, thus achieving co-ordination. A permanent form is also used when interdependencies between managers are of a fixed nature (*see* Chapter 4).

Structural faults

Management's position

All organisation models have something to offer, but no organisation conforms to all their requirements. It is not surprising, therefore, to hear people say 'It's the organisation that's the trouble!' when problems arise.

Organisation designers naturally know about the main elements of organisation, the co-ordinating mechanisms, the design parameters, contingency factors and structural configurations. Management equally recognises that organisation design is of major importance. Both are limited, however, to designing the formal (or official) structure. The informal (or unofficial) structure lies outside and often through its operations indicates formal deficiencies. Whether management becomes aware of these faults depends mainly on supervisors who should understand structures, be able to recognise faults, and press management to take action.

The supervisor's position

Because of the supervisor's peculiar middle position between operatives and management, he or she can promote the smooth working of formal and informal relationships, or can disrupt these lines of communication completely, whether through wilful lack of co-operation or through ignorance and misunderstanding.

This position in relation to management is discussed in detail in Chapter 7. At this point, however, consideration of the problems met by the first level of supervision, i.e. the chargehand or section head, reveals the supervisor's critical part as the link between the different levels of organisation.

The chargehand or section head must bond together primary and secondary groups, but as a superior in one group and a subordinate in the other, will find that all actions are viewed from two fronts, and it is frequently impossible to please both subordinates and management. Both 'sides' expect support for their view: subordinates think in terms of wages, stability of employment, conditions and participation; management thinks in terms of cost, flexibility, output and productivity. While the task is to control and look after one group's interests as their superior, and at the same time to carry out orders which are frequently unpopular and pass on information for the other group as a subordinate, the chargehand or section head must be adept at conciliation and compromise.

Every supervisor needs full support from management, particularly in the form of status. This status governs the degree and quality of reaction by subordinates to the supervisor's instructions, requests and suggestions. The supervisor, in turn, will mould his or her attitude towards responsibility according to status and degree of management support.

Most members of an organisation are 'status conscious'. They consider status symbols such as rank, position in the organisation chart, wages, bonus, social privileges, dress, size of office or desk and use of own telephone as important, but capability and personality provide the intangible aspect which also influences opinions of a particular supervisor's standing.

Titles such as manager, officer, superintendent, foreman or supervisor do not always convey the true status of executives who are on apparently similar levels.

Moreover, a supervisor may be held in high esteem by the work group as possessing more knowledge, or participating in certain social activities within the company, but top management may be unaware of these factors. The potential status of the supervisor, in these circumstances, will remain unrealised until the facts are transmitted to top management.

Indications of faults

Apart from other main aspects of management and supervision which may contribute towards faulty operational activities, certain deficiencies clearly point to structural problems. Although it may be difficult at times to isolate the organisation as the cause of the problem, the supervisor has to tackle the task by eliminating the other aspects by diagnosis.

Some typical problem areas are now given. Other chapters will clarify some points where two or more aspects appear to be at fault or where there is overlap.

Low productivity

Complaints about other departments where employees seem to have an easier life, coming and going as they please. Decisions appear to be incorrect or unnecessary. Lack of standardised rules and regulations to suit the situation. Low opportunity for advancement and achievement. Lack of opportunity to make decisions affecting work. Too many managers and supervisors, but not enough workers. Overloads of paper-work and petty procedures. Obvious signs of low morale.

Poor communication

Essential information always seems to be missing in emergencies. Conflicting reports arrive from various parts of the organisation. An over-active and unreliable 'grape-vine'. Information received is often incomplete and inaccurate.

Excessive conflict

Employees behave in an aggressive manner beyond normal expectations. Conflicting goals which are not aligned with over-all objectives. Managers are seen to be working against each other. A general state of uncertainty seems to exist.

Poor co-ordination

Lack of teamwork at all levels. Individuals are working in isolation or out of step with each other. Lack of liaison devices. Supervisors and managers seem reluctant to discuss problems and consult.

Weak control

No clearly defined work programmes and directives. Everyone appears to be at cross-purposes with no well-defined priorities.

Low innovation

No project teams, or committees, or meetings to exploit situations. Employees are unsure as to what is expected from them, to whom they are accountable, and how they are appraised. No attempts are made to explore or utilise people's ideas.

Poor delegation

Managers and supervisors are always over-loaded with work. There seems to be no time for solving problems and making decisions by studying the situation thoroughly. Subordinates feel frustrated and powerless to help.

Restrictions

Although the importance of organisation design has been stressed, it is only one aspect of many which contribute towards success. Structural changes cannot easily solve internal political wrangles on many subjects among managers and among employees. Indeed, managers will not quickly alter their views and operating methods through such changes. Neither will employees see the firm in a different light if they hold strong radical views on matters such as giving up autonomy, receiving unequal financial reward or generally feeling exploited at work.

Correct corporate planning and tactical planning, appropriate education and training schemes, sincere participation schemes, the appropriate control of political influences, innovation and allowing for the changing concept of work and work ethics are all essential activities beyond the field of formal organisation design.

Practical steps towards improving organisation

The following rules, which have been discussed in this chapter, should be observed by the supervisor. Where appropriate, regular checks and action should be taken.

1   The over-all objective and the purpose of each part of the organisation must be known by everyone.
2   Know each person's capabilities.
3   Orders must be final and concise.
4   Do not spend, or allow subordinates to spend, too much time on enjoyable tasks at the expense of distasteful or mundane ones.
5   Always welcome suggestions and ideas.
6   Reports must be conscientiously completed.
7   Reports must be used and kept up to date.
8   Plan carefully with the objective in mind.
9   Policy, rules and regulations should be known by every employee.
10   There should be a place for everything, and everything should be in its place.
11   Each employee's responsibilities must be clearly defined and known to him or her.
12   The authority conferred upon an employee must correspond with the given responsibilities.
13   Any changes in responsibility should be made known to everyone concerned.
14   Each employee should be responsible to, and receive instructions from, only one superior.
15   All duties and instructions must be clearly defined and consistent with a person's capabilities.
16   The formal line of command must run from top to bottom of the organisation.
17   A supervisor should not control more than five or six subordinate supervisors, who in turn should not control more than twelve staff.
18   Excessive overloading of work will impair efficiency.
19   Delegate lower-grade work, and spread the workload evenly.
20   Provide a continuous supply of replacements to ensure continuity.

21 Full use of specialisation should be made of people, machines, equipment and processes.
22 Encourage self-discipline.
23 Try to be scrupulously fair and just at all times.
24 Critical words to individuals must always be given in private.
25 Any query on organisation should be carefully investigated and settled quickly.

Procedure

A sound practice is to write down information on the organisation under the supervisor's control rather than to rely upon memory. The over-all position is often clearer on paper; the balance of work-load, possible improvements and any deficiencies can more easily be seen.

A simple method of assessing and improving organisation is outlined below:

Job specification
Note all the duties and responsibilities of each subordinate. This may be elaborated, if desired, to include skill required, mental effort, physical needs, working conditions and any other relevant factors.

Process chart
Draw a diagram, in flow form, from the beginning to the end of each process or procedure using information from the job specifications.

Organisation chart
Draw a diagram showing the lines of authority and responsibility using titles instead of names. Remember to indicate status by using some form of code where misinterpretation otherwise may occur.

The above method may be supplemented to suit particular requirements. The important factor is to put something down on paper, which can be rearranged and improved as a continuous process.

This task is made easier by drawing up a functional analysis, and an ideal organisation chart.

Functional diagram
Draw up a form listing the functions and subfunctions down the left-hand side and the subordinates across the top in columns, so making a space available for each function to be allocated to an individual. Better grouping of functions is immediately apparent when the form is completed.

An outline of functional analysis and appropriate diagrams is given in Chapter 17 in connection with job evaluation and the need to analyse jobs when a concern is growing rapidly.

Ideal organisation chart
Draw the chart with all the improvements which are considered desirable so that as opportunities occur to make changes they can be made with a definite plan in mind.

Questions

1   Describe the ideal organisation.
2   Outline the main problem areas likely to be encountered in an organisation.
3   List organisation criteria.
4   What is meant by integration difficulties in an organisation?
5   Carefully explain the systems approach.
6   Outline the work of Joan Woodward's study on types of production.
7   Discuss the importance of span of control and delegation.
8   Outline a procedure for delegating.
9   Write an essay on information technology.
10   Discuss the role of the supervisor as a co-ordinator.
11   Give a brief description of the main linkage devices that could be used to improve co-ordination.
12   What is meant by natural grouping?

Case study 1

Ruth Remply was worried about the way the staff kept referring to the poor organisation. Every time something went wrong they would pass the same remark: 'It's the organisation – that's the trouble with this place.'

As supervisor she was being subjected to considerable scrutiny from the management. She maintained that the cause of poor returns from her department was due to delays in orders being supplied, but the management seemed to have other ideas.

At a recent meeting with management she was asked whether she kept any records of the delays. She replied that she had not bothered as nothing would be done about it anyway.

1   Comment on the remarks passed by the staff.
2   What should the supervisor do to rectify the situation?

Case study 2

Harry Turnbull's superior was taken ill and he was asked to stand in for him. Leaving supervision to Stan, one of his senior chargehands, he soon found his mind was fully occupied with his temporary position.

After a few days he met one of the employees on the way to work.

'How is everything going, Josie?' he asked.

'Don't ask *me*!' Josie replied and walked off.

Feeling apprehensive Harry decided to have a chat with Stan. When Stan arrived in the office he looked very worried.

'I'm sorry, Harry, but I'll have to back out of this job. The others don't like me and they're giving me hell down there. I lost my temper with young Tim over some work he'd messed up on the first day. I'm sure he did it deliberately.'

What choices of action are open to Harry in these circumstances?

4 Functional aspects of organisation

Structural designs

Many organisations are in a state of tension because of the need to (a) differentiate or specialise and (b) to integrate. Reducing this tension to acceptable limits involves consideration of six main features:

1 specialisation of roles and the degree to which it should be followed in practice
2 whether to centralise or decentralise the main managerial skills, including planning, controlling, problem solving and especially decision making
3 how many authority levels thought to be necessary, considering span of control
4 how much discretion to allow at each level
5 whether to apply considerable standardisation
6 consideration for the appropriate balance between formality and informality

The use of principles already mentioned restricts the designer to some extent as he or she is forced into using a limited range of viable structures. These are now outlined to provide some conception of the difficulties likely to be encountered when working within such structures.

The basic structure

An example of a simple structure is given in Fig. 4.1. This line type organisation represents the first stage of growth from the 'one-man' business or sole proprietor and incorporates the engagement of a line manager to be responsible for, say, marketing or accounts.

The line/functional structure

As functional specialists are needed in, for example, personnel or purchasing, the structure is modified accordingly.

The modified line/functional structure

Continued growth soon causes overloads. These are solved by introducing

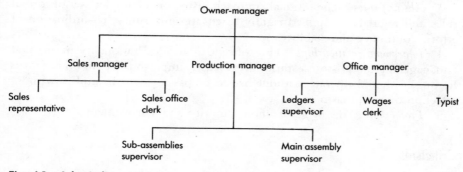

Fig. 4.1 *A basic line structure*

This line type organisation represents the first stage of growth from the one-man business

staff officers; in the example given in Fig. 4.2 they ease the load on the managing director by undertaking to represent him or her – ensuring that policies and decisions are interpreted correctly.

The bureaucratic model

This famous structure was introduced by Max Weber (1947) and represents a rational form of organisation utilising the basic principles of organisation. This ideal construct, however, possesses other characteristics that distinguish it markedly:

1 *Division of labour* This concept implies the use of authority, power, and boundary limitations of the job.

2 *The hierarchy* This principle in rigidly applied, thus each lower post is under the supervision and control of a higher one.

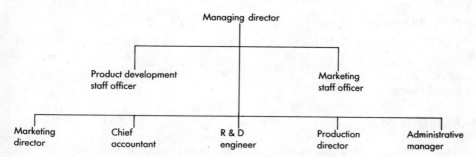

Fig. 4.2 *A modified line/functional structure*

Continued growth causes overloads in certain areas. These are solved by introducing staff officers

3   *Abstract rules*   The rational approach insists on a complete set of formal rules and regulations applied rigidly to ensure uniformity, co-ordination of effort, continuity and stability.

4   *Impersonal relationships*   The concept of an ideal rationality means that a manager should possess a spirit of formalistic impersonality. In other words he or she should operate without hatred or passion which implies without affection or enthusiasm.

5   *Promotion*   This depends upon seniority and achievement.

Criticisms

Most people have experienced bureaucracy and know the frustrations of 'red tape'. The usual observations include inhuman approaches to employees and outsiders, the emergence of the pompous, self-important official, managers lacking in technical competence, arbitrary and silly rules and regulations, an undercover informal organisation, and conflicting roles.

In bureaucracies two popular laws are often quoted:

- Parkinson's Law – bureaucratic staff increase in number in inverse proportion to the amount of work carried out
- The Peter Principle – bosses rise to their level of incompetence in bureaucracies

Modified specialisation structures

Apart from the basic line/functional structure that operates by grouping together common activities there are three other forms of grouping. These are:

- grouping on a geographical format, seen, for example, in transport companies
- by product, which lends itself to companies that produce a number of different articles
- by forming divisions

The latter is particularly useful in large concerns where a number of different articles are produced: the head office retains key functions such as corporate planning, finance, and personnel policy while the divisions operate in a functional role for each article.

Matrix models

The temporary type of matrix structure was explained in Chapter 3 as a means of achieving co-ordination. A permanent form (*see* Fig. 4.3) is also useful when interdependencies between managers are of a fixed nature.

A typical case is where a number of project managers with their own

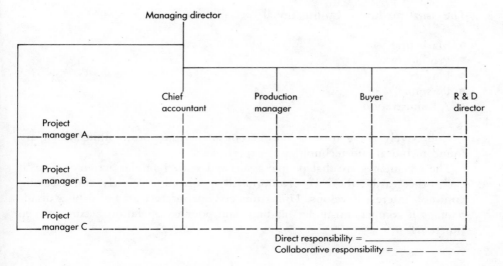

Fig. 4.3 *A typical matrix structure*

A permanent form of matrix structure is useful when interdependencies are fixed between managers. The project managers not only have direct responsibility to the managing director but also collaborative responsibility to all the functional managers. Theoretically this device forces managers to co-operate and reconcile differences between them, thus achieving co-ordination

teams are appointed to be accountable for each sector. They are provided with technological back-up from each functional manager who collaborates with them. Thus a complex matrix is formed which provides project managers not only with direct responsibility to the managing director but also collaborative responsibility to all the functional managers.

A simple example is the development of a new aircraft. Project managers for the body, engine and mainplane will use the resources of the chief designer, production manager and chief engineer. Some criticisms have been aired in recent years but there are also many successful stories. The obvious difficulties are confusion over resource allocation, division of authority, collaboration problems, and divided loyalties.

Being more flexible and more informal, matrix styles suit trends towards decentralisation, more delegation and increased personal accountability. Understandably they create administration difficulties unless the trend to centralise administration is followed and information technology is exploited in the process.

Specialisation

An easily recognised process is the grouping together of similar activities.

The usual method is by functional specialisation:

- Marketing
- Production
- Finance
- Personnel
- Administration

Collectively these form a number of main functions within which are found technical and technological expertise.

The advantages are that people associated with a similar activity relate to each other easily; they see promotional opportunities clearly and a strong common interest develops. Unfortunately this interest may also be a disadvantage if conflict, misunderstandings and poor co-operation occur between functions.

Conceptual skills development

Supervisors should acquire a knowledge of all the activities in a concern. This enables them to develop conceptual skills for the purpose of more effective organisational planning, policy development and systems development. Thus they can apply their influence over wider fields (*see* Chapter 13). They can then deal more effectively with the difficulties arising from specialisation.

Control features and difficulties are outlined in Part Three.

Orientations towards the market

Of particular importance is the relationship developed by everyone towards customers. There are four approaches:

- Market orientation
- Sales orientation
- Product orientation
- Production orientation

Market orientation

This technique concentrates on customers' wants and is often called the marketing concept. The total organisation is geared up to marketing and the customer forms the basis for corporate planning.

Apart from marketing personnel many people throughout the organisation become involved in marketing activities since the customer is considered to be of prime importance and everything must be done to achieve the maximum degree of customer satisfaction.

CORPORATE RESPONSIBILITY

Putting the customer first has always been the prime consideration for the marketing department. Extending this philosophy to corporate level where everyone is committed to this approach demands a major change in attitudes for many. There is no doubt that the introduction of a marketing culture increases marketing effectiveness. The lead must come from the top and supervisors have a strong role to play in planning based upon marketing strategies and forecasting.

Sales orientation

This approach means concentrating on positive selling to persuade people to buy. Thus selling skills are paramount compared with the wants of the buyer. Some insurance companies use this technique.

Product orientation

The quality of the product is considered supreme and the technique relies on the manufacturer knowing exactly what the customer requires.

Production orientation

Production effectiveness, distribution, and price, form the dominant approach to attract customers. A good example is Japanese cars.

Main functions: marketing; production; finance; administration; personnel

Considering that departmentation is recognised generally as being functional in nature the major activities are now discussed: marketing, production, finance, personnel and administration. Note however that other forms exist such as product departmentation seen in some very large companies where the organisation is divided into self-contained product groups; and geographical departmentation where a network of activities substantiates a regional structure. An example of a medium-sized undertaking is shown in Fig. 4.4.

The marketing function

Marketing is a logical starting point since the potential market for a product must be located by research and the want created by arousing customers' interest. When the goods are manufactured they are sold through the efforts of marketing by advertising, sales promotion and direct selling. When sales are completed marketing continues with after-sales service which maintains customer satisfaction through customer relations activities: after-sales help

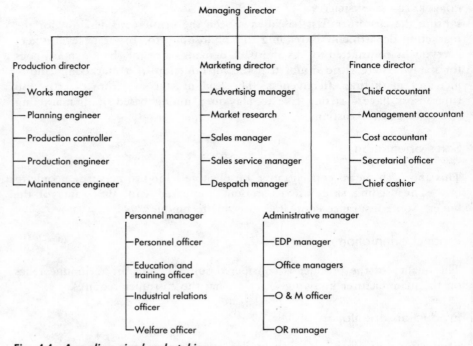

Fig. 4.4   *A medium-sized undertaking*
The most likely main functions and sub-functions are illustrated

and dealing with complaints. A brief survey of the main activities is now given but structures vary dependent upon company size and product.

Market research

Specialists conduct research into current sales of other companies and visualise the future market. Outside groups or individual consultants may be used. The department collects, analyses and communicates the data to other departments.

Typical data include a breakdown of products on offer, where they may be obtained, prices, their uses in households, complaints, suggestions for improvement, and the class of customers. Many sources of such information are available and statisticians analyse and interpret the information.

Marketing strategy is determined and a programme developed which includes resources location, processes involved, the final profile of the product, demand forecasts, and pricing.

Advertising

The object is to inform prospective customers and illustrate the benefits of the product. The advertising department is concerned with design of packaging, sales promotion displays, exhibitions, and distribution of circulars. Critical decisions are made on the choice of media.

Sales

Often a sales manager will be responsible for a number of sales representatives who regularly visit wholesalers and shops to promote the product. Closely associated with this activity is the sales office. Here sales documents are prepared and processed. These include orders, invoices, quotations, and estimates. A separate estimating department is needed where products are of a more unique nature, varying upon requirements.

Warehousing and distribution

Storage of finished goods and distribution are important features since delivery time in accordance with promises made by salesmen is an essential customer service. People are easily irritated when delays occur, often through production hold-ups. Some may cancel the order and become vindictive. Production strikes, of course, easily lose sales.

After-sales service

Problems often start after the sale, for example difficulty in use or if quality does not match requirements. Faults may occur and should be quickly remedied. Complaints have to be treated with diplomacy.

If a customer is not entirely satisfied he or she may easily complain to friends and relatives. Inevitably the company and the product develop a bad name. This point is often overlooked when production operators are not conscientious and fail to realise the long-term implications.

The marketing mix

Marketing strategy is based upon a technique called the marketing mix which is defined as a blend of controllable variables that may be used to achieve an objective in the market. The four variables are easily remembered as the four P's: product, price, promotion, and place. Each sub-divides as follows:

1 *Product* quality, variety, brand name, packaging, warranty, style, service, etc.
2 *Price* gross, net, discounts, credit terms, etc.
3 *Promotion* advertising, sales promotion, sales force, etc.
4 *Place* distribution channels, transport, national/local coverage, stocks, etc.

Choosing the most appropriate marketing mix to suit the proposed market demands expertise. The right balance is difficult to achieve in terms of the product to be offered, the right price, allocation of funds, type of promotion, and the choice of distribution. Timing is also critical.

Market situations change rapidly; a new product may emerge, or competition may withdraw. Proper use of the marketing mix allows for speedy changes in plans but of course there are limits. Often manufacturing and distribution cannot easily change overnight; revised sales campaigns have to be funded, and selling space in the media booked well in advance.

The production function

Production exists to convert raw materials and components into finished goods to satisfy the wants of customers. A typical sequence of activities starts with prospective customers who provide information through market research. This information is passed to Research and Development (R & D). Here any pure and applied research, design and development work are completed. Next, prototypes are produced and if approved they pass to the pre-production stage. Here actual production conditions are simulated. If a successful product is manufactured there is feedback to customers for comments. After discussions, modifications and further trials, eventually production commences.

Production organisation

Various major activities are identifiable in any manufacturing organisation. Understandably there will be different types of structure which depend upon the type of product, degree of mechanisation and automation, emphasis on quality, complexity of R & D, financial importance of purchasing and maintenance, and the expertise of production personnel.

An example below probably covers the sub-functions usually encountered. The works manager or production manager is at the apex. Beneath this person may be a production planner, production controller, production engineer, and maintenance engineer, all described soon.

WORKS MANAGER
In some organisations the works manager is responsible for the manufacturing processes. He or she reports to the production manager who is also responsible for the other sub-functions.

PRODUCTION PLANNING AND CONTROL MANAGER
This activity is often divided into two. Within this section appear planning, scheduling, stores control, purchasing, works orders, progress and quality control. In large concerns some activities are of such size and importance that separate managers are appointed together with appropriate staff.

PRODUCTION ENGINEER

This role may be seen in various activities and is often divided among several specialists, for example R & D, quality control (often shared with other functions), work study, and value analysis. An R & D manager and work study manager may be appointed in the large company. They report either to the production engineer or direct to the production manager.

MAINTENANCE ENGINEER

There is no recognised level for this manager, who might be responsible to the production manager or the works manager. Production engineer responsibilities often cover machines, equipment, plant, buildings, services, and R & D requirements. Being responsible direct to the production manager avoids any undue influence by a particular section. The role is demanding since all production sections need to be operational to achieve objectives.

Conflict with marketing

Although an organisation may adopt the marketing concept, often situations arise that cause conflict between production and marketing. Production employees may see marketing employees arriving late and not conforming to essential rules that ensure smooth production. There is no appreciation that sales people may have been with customers late into the evening.

A further example is where a sales representative on commission is forced to take an order for delivery in, say, seven days, knowing that the amount cannot be manufactured in under a fortnight. This creates a major problem for production and probably excessive costs to produce on time or near the promised delivery date.

Service industries

Although the concepts of manufacturing apply, there are also some unique areas. The term 'operations management' is used in service industries but its importance and purpose remain unchanged. Most operational systems interact directly with the customer; this emphasises the marketing concept and often sales orientation.

The finance function

All the financial and accounting activities in the organisation are included in this function. It involves everyone in accepting responsibility for monetary aspects regardless of any particular specialism. Typical sub-functions are:

1 financial management which takes care of working capital, capital projects, and financial provision
2 financial accounting which records daily all asset and liability transactions

3   cost accounting which determines the cost of output
4   management accounting which gives data to managers for planning, controlling and decision-making activities.

Financial management

Short-term finance for each period and long-term finance for fixed assets are covered by financial management. Sources of cash internally and externally, the justification of expenditure and the feasibility of the funds required, are all debated. Projects are carefully appraised and alternative sources of funds are reviewed to choose the most economic device. Thus the balance sheet is managed and various sources of funds are constantly monitored.

Financial accounting

Managers' requests for funds and external demands from various creditors are centralised here. In addition information is provided to outside parties such as Inland Revenue, Registrar of Companies, and shareholders.

All revenue and expenditure are carefully recorded and analysed to provide the trading position at any time and to give any particular information required by managers. A typical broad coverage would include fixed, current and other assets, current and long-term liabilities, income and expenditure on a daily basis, and manufacturing, trading, and profit and loss accounts.

Cost accounting

The cost accountant is responsible for providing information on total expenditure for a single item or a group of items, or a particular activity. Data are collected from all sources and collated. This activity is very demanding since a clear knowledge of the organisation and the multiple activities is needed to ensure that all expenditure is included.

Management accounting

The management accountant is responsible for decision-making and control accounting. He or she applies various accounting techniques which provide managers with sufficient information. The job demands high expertise in both accountancy knowledge and the business to provide such information partially through interpretation and through the use of appropriate statistical devices.

Control accounting of this nature means providing data at set intervals in a standard format, along with variances or deviations from previous reports so that corrective action is made easier for managers.

Conflict situations

Often production and marketing employees view finance staff as parasites because their role is not understood. Furthermore senior staff view the financial function as a retarding influence since both functions always seem to need more funds than are readily available. From a corporate viewpoint the difficult task of allocating funds among functions is sometimes seen to favour one function at the expense of another.

A financial director may assume too much power through the absence of a senior executive who is capable of effectively balancing funds among functions. When this occurs there is a risk that awareness of functional problems and their effects is not fully appreciated. Inevitably enmity and frustration develop.

The administration function

This function is concerned with communication of information through procedures, handling of paperwork involving data capture, information retrieval, processing and recording data, and proper utilisation of staff involved in these activities. Understandably this function permeates all departments.

If administration is dispersed the true cost of the function may become difficult to assess and enormous savings made possible by a centralised function are wasted. As information technology continues to advance the need for a specialist becomes imperative to structure effective systems and to relieve other functional specialists of this responsibility.

In medium-sized companies the finance manager may undertake this role.

Typical sub-functions

These relate to particular specialisms which are constantly evolving through advancements in information technology. Expertise is essential to ensure free flow of information through networks in the organisation, to satisfy the demands for more information, to determine information requirements and forms of presentation, and to interpret data more accurately.

Professional individuals are developing within narrow spheres and becoming recognised as information technologists in their own right. They are often known as electronic data processing (EDP) managers, corporate planners, long-range forecasters, communication officers, liaison officers, cyberneticists (associated with operation research, or OR), economic intelligence officers, organisation and methods (O & M) managers, management services managers, and chief systems analysts.

Information technology

This science includes first, collecting, analysing, recording and distributing sufficient appropriate information to all organisation sectors; second, operating within a suitable time-scale and using the most suitable statistical form for data according to each manager's and supervisor's capability; and third, providing them with appropriate back-up to solve problems, make decisions and improve anticipating skills in pursuing, adjusting and setting the concern's objectives.

The emerging problems date back to when people first found ways of communicating with each other. Now problems exist in more sophisticated forms due to discoveries in other technological fields, resulting in advanced computers and associated machines and equipment.

Information technology is the prime mover of change and practically every job will be affected eventually. Computers (especially personal computers) have revolutionised systems and organisation structures, and created new skills. Managerial and supervisory roles are changing as networks provide direct access to massive information stores.

The use of integrated systems is essential to provide full benefit and remove old functional barriers. Nevertheless functional specialists remain but with modern wider viewpoints which are vital for corporate success.

The personnel function

The purpose of the personnel function is to provide a specialist who is capable of creating and administering a suitable working environment in a concern which will attract and keep an effective complement of employees.

The personnel specialist must be highly skilled and experienced in such topics as employment negotiations, wages structures, industrial relations, education and training, health and safety, and general welfare services. He or she must be a good communicator, really understand human beings and possess a deep understanding of this function in a concern. If any of these qualities is missing the personnel specialist will quickly gain a poor reputation.

A supervisor cannot be expected to possess the knowledge of a personnel manager and yet all the above essentials of personnel administration are needed to maintain an effective working force. In medium- and large-size concerns such specialists can be afforded and full use of their capabilities must be made by all line supervisors. In the small concern the function cannot be ignored, but by necessity it has to be carried out by supervisors and managers alone. Regardless of company size the functions of personnel work should be clearly understood and practised by all supervisors.

Maintaining a stable force of employees is an economic necessity. The cost of finding suitable employees is continually growing in an age of rapid technological change, housing shortage and rising wage rates. Training individuals is often unavoidable and expensive. They must fit the job otherwise they will be frustrated and probably leave or be dismissed. Careful selection and reasonable working facilities are essential. Good relations between management, trade unions and employees must be created and maintained, otherwise industrial unrest will ruin any attempts to improve productivity. All these factors are part of the personnel function.

The success of the personnel specialist can be seen by improvements in labour turnover, the degree of satisfaction in performing jobs, higher productivity and the advancement of individuals through improved capabilities. The spirit of an organisation should show considerable improvement in the long run.

A closer examination (in the next section) of the activities of a personnel department soon reveals that personnel managers cannot work successfully in isolation. They need full support from management and supervisors in all aspects of their duties. Similarly, those supervisors who cannot see the necessity for using an expert in personnel work will be unsuccessful.

Management of people is recognised today by many concerns as being of equal importance to managing finance, machines, equipment and materials. The strong need for centralising and co-ordinating personnel functions throughout an organisation has resulted in the employment of personnel managers in many establishments but employing a specialist alone does not solve the problem. Top management must be prepared to use him or her effectively which often means that high ranking managers must change and come into line with the personnel policy prepared by the specialist.

Some managers give the impression that they employ specialists to be in the fashion, not because they sincerely believe in the function they perform. Frustrated personnel managers are not uncommon. Management policies and personnel policy must be reconcilable and both ought to be actively pursued.

Naturally there are good and bad specialists in any profession and personnel management is no exception. To some extent it depends upon what management is prepared to pay. The supervisor should try to assess the specialist, noting carefully the effectiveness of the advice offered.

Many personnel departments have been very successful where management has co-operated and the importance of the personnel function will continue to grow at a time when more emphasis is being placed on selection, training schemes and co-operation with unions.

Activities of a personnel department

The activities which are generally recognised as coming under the province of a personnel manager are given below.

EMPLOYMENT

To fulfil this activity successfully it is necessary to begin with consideration of the job itself. Surveys of existing and proposed jobs are needed to plan ahead and to draw up accurate descriptions of requirements.

Further activities cover these aspects: liaison with the sources of prospective employees, knowledge of terms and conditions of employment, understanding of existing and proposed legislation affecting personnel, interviews connected with engagement, transfer, termination and dismissal, procedure for any employee movement, maintenance of personnel records, preparation of personnel statistics, committee work associated with personnel and induction procedure for new employees.

REMUNERATION

The personnel department is responsible for providing accurate information on wages and salaries for the wages section of the accounts department. The wage and salary structure should be administered fairly by careful application of scales of pay, merit rating schemes and bonus systems. Any changes in remuneration must be properly authorised.

Assessment of pay in similar industries and consultation with unions and work study engineers concerning pay rates also form an important part of personnel work.

EDUCATION AND TRAINING

Procedures for training new employees and schemes to improve employees' capabilities form an important part of personnel work with the aims of increasing productivity, increasing employees' pay by improved performance and promoting from within wherever possible. Such training would include schemes for management, supervisors, instructors, apprentices, transferees and newcomers. Encouragement of further education generally would include the use of internal training schemes, Government skill centres, technical colleges and evening institutes. This activity also covers the maintenance of records showing attainments and the publication of information on training opportunities, circulation of educational publications and company magazines and the organising of any special lectures, training in safety, operating suggestion schemes and conforming to the Industrial Training Act 1964.

INDUSTRIAL RELATIONS

The roles of mediating, negotiating and conciliating between employees' trade unions and management form an exacting part of personnel managers' work. They must have a thorough knowledge of collective agreements, conciliation and arbitration procedure, company policy and rules and appropriate legislation.

They must also work to maintain and improve joint consultation, fostering good relationships and making full use of joint committees.

Liaison with unions should include ensuring that personnel policy is clearly understood and that all procedures within the policy are fairly conducted.

These procedures include wage negotiations, complaints and grievances, apprenticeship and other training schemes, application of rules and regulations, dismissals and transfers, redundancy, social activities, and general conditions of employment.

HEALTH AND SAFETY

The promotion and maintenance of good physical health is achieved by attending to working conditions including accident prevention. Statutory requirements under the Health and Safety at Work etc. Act 1974 and related legislation must be complied with. Government health and safety inspectors who enforce the legislation normally work through the personnel manager.

The large concern may employ a full-time nurse and provide certain medical facilities for the well-being of employees. Some companies use the services of doctors and dentists on a part-time basis. This medical service normally comes under the control of the personnel manager who keeps health records, attends to problems connected with hazardous work, arranges for visits to the sick employee and provides for convalescence and rehabilitation.

Further activities connected with safety may include attending accident prevention meetings, inspecting workshops, minimising fire risks, investigating accidents and providing management with accident statistics.

WELFARE

Welfare services and facilities vary considerably from company to company. Some of these, including social facilities, are as follows:

1   various pension schemes
2   savings schemes, benevolent funds and sick clubs
3   co-partnership and profit-sharing schemes
4   financial assistance for house purchase
5   advice and assistance with transport and domestic problems
6   information services such as a library, advice and legal aid
7   a dining room
8   rest rooms and rooms for various types of clubs
9   sports pavilion and grounds
10 dance hall and bar
11 a theatre

If a concern does not employ a personnel manager many of the activities mentioned above are undertaken by other executives as a sideline. For example, the sales manager may look after the canteen while the accountant may attend to any savings and pension schemes.

Personnel policy

Ideally there should be a clear, written personnel policy which is fully supported by management. The personnel manager is responsible for maintaining and interpreting the policy.

An example of a typical personnel policy is outlined below:

1   Fairness and justice should be accorded to all employees irrespective of status, position, sex or race.
2   A fair system of adequate wages and salaries.
3   A merit-rating scheme to compensate those employees who achieve increased effectiveness.
4   All employees should be allowed to develop their own capabilities fully.
5   Suitable education and training facilities, thus enabling employees to progress and have equal opportunity in applying for vacancies within the company.
6   Reasonable working conditions consistent with good health and safety (*see* Chapter 20 for legal requirements).
7   Personnel selection based upon placing individuals in the work situation most suitable for their requirements.
8   Help employees whenever possible with domestic and industrial problems.
9   Conduct all activities between management and employees in a friendly and co-operative spirit.
10 Provide and encourage social activities.

Questions

1   Discuss ways of reducing tension to acceptable limits in an organisation.
2   Consider the disadvantages of the bureaucratic organisation model.
3   What are the advantages of using a matrix structure?
4   Why is the marketing concept important?
5   Give a brief survey of the marketing function.
6   Consider possible conflict between production and marketing.
7   Outline the financial function.
8   Discuss the importance of the administration function.
9   What is the purpose of the personnel function?
10 Discuss how the main activities of a personnel department affect the supervisor.
11 Consider the various ways a personnel manager could help the supervisor.
12 What is the main aim of developing conceptual skills?

Case Study 1

Amanda Pouton was convinced that 'personnel' in Latham Contacts Ltd, a large concern, was an unnecessary financial burden.

'I seem to spend half my time on personnel matters,' she was saying to Ted a fellow supervisor. 'I can't imagine what they all get up to everyday when most of the personnel work is done by us.'

Ted agreed. 'Did you hear of that car rental firm in the States who sacked all the personnel staff and had an "employment girl" for every three hundred employees? She did all the essential personnel tasks and they saved a fortune.'

'Yes, I did hear about that. The comical thing about it was that the president of the company insisted that the girls should never meet, otherwise they would immediately form another personnel department!'

1   Consider this case in the light of all the activities undertaken by a personnel department.
2   Would Amanda's estimate of time spent on personnel work be an exaggeration?

Case Study 2

Paul Mason was a liberable-minded supervisor who tried hard to maintain good relations with his subordinates. On this occasion he was particularly bothered. Karen, one of the young employees, had approached him to see if he would be interested in joining a video club that she had formed in the department. Paul was not interested but he could see no harm in allowing her to go ahead so long as the club operated during breaks.

One of his older employees, with whom he was on friendly terms, casually mentioned the club and told him that the tapes were causing a 'bit of a stir'. Apparently they were a slight shade of purple, according to the rumours.

Paul called Karen into his office and asked her to explain. She replied, 'Well, you didn't ask what they were like and you said it was all right.'

When she was told that the club would have to close immediately Karen became very obstinate. 'I've paid a lot of money for these tapes and I'm certainly not going to lose out on the deal. What are you going to do about it?'

1   What action should the supervisor take?
2   Comment on the original decision.

5 Group activity

Introduction

The urge to belong to and be accepted by a group is commonplace. In companies group membership helps to compensate for poor organisation design which may ignore people's desire to be creative, to do something worthwhile and to receive appropriate recognition.

Group cohesiveness can be very strong, although group membership may range from enjoyment down to discomfort. A member may even go against natural desires to work well if the group's attitude is negative.

Aligning group objectives with organisational objectives should be a firm aim for managers and supervisors. Indeed if group dynamics is understood and applied correctly synergy improves, favourable group norms develop, and – with training – creativeness is encouraged.

Group formation and development

The success of this process depends upon the following:

- interaction
- development of cohesion
- norm formation
- roles
- correct use of power.

Figure 5.1 outlines the main features which are now discussed.

Social interaction

A complex interacting structure exists in any organisation. Establishing formal groups invariably leads to restructuring into informal groups and social groups although the original groups retain their identity. Within a group members influence each other in many ways. Conversations on various subjects affect their opinions and expectations. Fairness and justice are important criteria when decisions affecting the group are examined. If logical and acceptable then rational behaviour follows; if not emotional reactions occur.

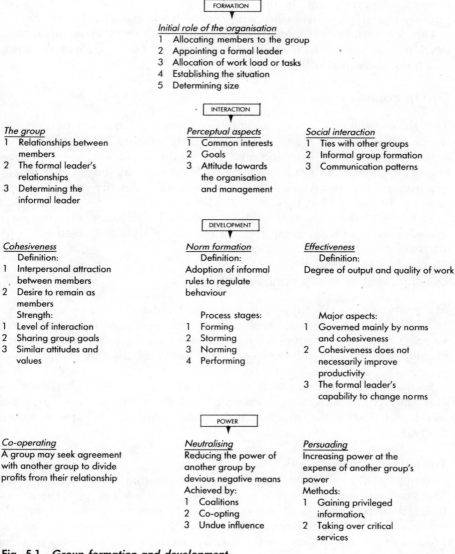

FORMATION

Initial role of the organisation
1   Allocating members to the group
2   Appointing a formal leader
3   Allocation of work load or tasks
4   Establishing the situation
5   Determining size

INTERACTION

The group
1   Relationships between members
2   The formal leader's relationships
3   Determining the informal leader

Perceptual aspects
1   Common interests
2   Goals
3   Attitude towards the organisation and management

Social interaction
1   Ties with other groups
2   Informal group formation
3   Communication patterns

DEVELOPMENT

Cohesiveness
Definition:
1   Interpersonal attraction between members
2   Desire to remain as members
Strength:
1   Level of interaction
2   Sharing group goals
3   Similar attitudes and values

Norm formation
Definition:
Adoption of informal rules to regulate behaviour

Process stages:
1   Forming
2   Storming
3   Norming
4   Performing

Effectiveness
Definition:
Degree of output and quality of work

Major aspects:
1   Governed mainly by norms and cohesiveness
2   Cohesiveness does not necessarily improve productivity
3   The formal leader's capability to change norms

POWER

Co-operating
A group may seek agreement with another group to divide profits from their relationship

Neutralising
Reducing the power of another group by devious negative means
Achieved by:
1   Coalitions
2   Co-opting
3   Undue influence

Persuading
Increasing power at the expense of another group's power
Methods:
1   Gaining privileged information
2   Taking over critical services

Fig. 5.1   *Group formation and development*
This process is a critical factor in organisation design. The degree of alignment of group and company objectives determines the organisation's effectiveness

Joining a group

An individual may change favourably or adversely when he or she joins a group, depending upon previous circumstances. Before, that person may have felt insecure and restricted in outlook, thoughts, and actions, and unable to exercise individuality. In the group he or she may feel a new power, possibly lose some individuality, and responsibility may change.

The new member may influence the group's culture; other members will develop expectations from him or her which will largely govern the roles which the individual will play.

Group cohesiveness

The basic feeling of safety in numbers leads to some satisfaction and increased individual strength and power. Each member needs assistance in some way to do his own job and some tasks require members' collaboration. Certain basic needs are satisfied by the group and there is ample opportunity for social interaction. Feelings of solidarity and increased security are fostered but they may be false in reality.

In Japan workers identify strongly with each other and the company; more leisure time is spent together. In the UK many social schemes fail to attract employees.

Development of group cohesiveness

Management's sincere support is essential. Fundamental requirements are strong interaction, sharing of objectives, and alignment of attitudes and values. Contributory factors are that members must possess various things in common, they should fulfil social and safety needs, and resist adverse pressures.

Such demands in total make it difficult to perceive how cohesiveness is ever achieved if it were not for protection against poor management practices and strong feelings of distrust. Cohesion in this case negates increased motivation.

AUTONOMOUS WORK GROUPS

This approach is mentioned again since various techniques may be applied. One way is to group work tasks to form a logical whole task performed with minimal interference. Another way is called the group technology approach; machines or desks are grouped together based on their contribution to the product or service, not on work similarity. Examples are grouping workers together to make a diesel engine injector or part of a carburettor. The work is so arranged that higher integration and more job satisfaction are achieved through increased autonomy and productive co-operation.

Those who are more instrumentally oriented (financial rewards), do not necessarily welcome such job redesign. Others see it as another management ploy to extract more work for no extra pay. Finding the best fit for technological and social factors is difficult considering high instrumentality and self-fulfilment. This work orientation problem is illustrated in Fig. 5.2.

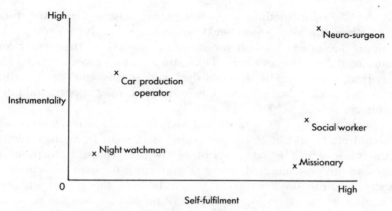

Fig. 5.2 *A work orientation graphical representation*

The extreme concepts of high instrumentality and high self-fulfilment are for illustrative purposes only. In practice most jobs contain an element of both concepts

Group norms

Groups tend to establish their own standards of work-load. One type will expect each group member to produce so much and no more; another will easily exceed an expected work-load. In the former group strong pressure may be applied if a member exceeds the standards set (norms), whereas in the latter increasing productivity is encouraged and pressure is applied to perform well to save group pride.

   Norms are also set for social behaviour. Penalties may be severe if social and work behaviour norms are broken. The ideal for a company is the alignment of its own norms with those of the group. Leadership and other means are used to overcome the differences which exist because the group perceives that its own interests do not coincide.

Norm characteristics

The supervisor perceives norms by witnessing a member's behaviour which may not coincide with the person's feelings or thoughts. Such norms are important to the person and some latitude is noticeable. Consequently a range of acceptable behaviour is permitted by the group within the limits imposed.

Norm formation

These may be identified as a gradual development which passes through various stages and short-cut methods.

The development method uses four main stages. First, the forming process, when the new group seeks information, analyses, orientates and relies upon the leader. Second, the storming process when internal conflict and emotional disturbances occur. Third, the norming process when conflicts are resolved, co-operation is established and norms emerge. Fourth, the performing process when teamwork is recognised, roles appear, and informal problems are solved.

Short-cuts are easily recognised and include: a critical incident which has a profound effect on the group; an explicit statement from management or the supervisor which is taken seriously by the group; a situation which warrants an obvious standard; a strong preference from an influential group member; an ambiguous situation which bothers the group and justifies classification; an embarrassing or emotional problem which can be solved by setting a norm; revising a norm if a developing situation warrants it, such as a trusted supervisor possibly being transferred; and any undue tension which threatens to break up the group.

Norm changes

If a supervisor notes norm changes and attempts to discuss why and how they are enforced, he or she should be able to diagnose more easily the problems within the group. Although this is difficult there are indications. Norms tend to cluster around certain aspects of behaviour which immediately show concern by members. Also they are associated with personal relationships such as particular pairs going to the cloakroom, eating lunch, and taking tea breaks. Sometimes behaviour does not match norms, therefore true norms remain undisclosed.

Roles

Each employee plays a particular role related to his or her own job description and position within the group. The difference between holding a job and performing a role within that job depends upon norms and rights governing the person's eventual behavioural pattern.

Related to the stage, for example, an actor plays a part but the actor's role on stage is far more than simply playing that part. Therefore a role relates to *how* the job is performed, whereas the job involves duties, authority and responsibilities.

Roles are determined by expectations from superiors, peers and subordinates, and by the job-holder's expectations; whereas the job is officially designated with appropriate duties. In other words employees' expectations relate to roles while employees' demands relate to duties.

Formal and informal roles

Typical formal roles are committee membership, chairmanship, secretary, functional advisor, departmental representative and liaison activities.

Informal roles often coincide with personality, knowledge and skills. Some examples are proposing ideas, developing ideas, criticising ideas, supporting proposals, displaying antagonism, disagreeing, testing, acting passively, generating enthusiasm, seeking help, disrupting, introducing humour, and demanding orientation.

Typical employee roles

An employee might assume different roles in different situations – there is no established pattern. Some examples are: short-circuiting procedures to hasten job completion; the good Samaritan; always willing to help solve problems; going by the rule-book; the 'yes-man'; the questioning type; the maverick; the lone-wolf; the rule evader; and the fairness seeker.

Inevitably some roles conflict with each other. For example the trade-union representative may be forced to take a stance which conflicts with his or her role as a loyal employee. Frustration develops as attempts to over-come barriers fail.

Group power

Solidarity and cohesiveness in a group increases its ability to influence other individuals and groups. This may improve group effectiveness but not necessarily organisational effectiveness. This depends on the group's objectives.

Methods to gain power are diverse and devious. Three main ways are co-operating, neutralising and persuading.

Co-operating

Two groups seek an agreement where both benefit in some way. They may guarantee behavioural stability or agree to divide profits from their relationship.

Neutralising

Three ways are possible: adopting coalitions, co-opting other group members, and exercising undue influence. Coalition means joining up with one or more groups; this greatly reduces opposition from an isolated group. Co-opting is commonplace; a member is invited to participate in another group's activities. This move often effectively neutralises the opposition's criticism when one of its own members is involved. Undue influence is achieved by lobbying; it is effective in committee work but may adversely affect decision–making.

Persuading

Often called theft of power this way uses two approaches. First, by gaining access to privileged information which is denied to other groups and is of great benefit when competing for resources. Thus a group can present a superior case. The second, by taking over critical services; a group may dominate if it can withhold or delay a service to another group which relies on it to achieve objectives.

Intergroup activity

To achieve co-ordination the supervisor must understand and influence inter-group activity. Success depends on understanding conflict, diagnosing the causes, appreciating the changes that occur when conflict is reduced, and recognising the tactics and strategies that groups adopt in different situations.

A broad view of intergroup activity covers interaction between individuals from different groups. Consequently interpersonal conflict, intragroup conflict and organisation conflict are included.

Conflict

Organisational conflict is inevitable due to personality clashes, and incompatible pressures or influences. Each member has certain roles, objectives and responsibilities which may be frustrated by others who induce barriers and do not co-operate.

There are many outcomes. Constructively used, conflict may create a more dynamic group that is creative, solves problems more easily, makes better decisions, and is generally more productive.

Unfortunately many adverse effects are seen, such as high mental stress, unco-operative group behaviour, misalignment of goals between the group and the organisation, various stages of group disintegration, irrational and illogical conduct, and communication breakdowns.

Competition between groups

A useful introduction to the competitive aspect is to examine the classical work of Sherif (1953). Although the survey was conducted at a boys' camp in the USA it clearly illustrates the problems. Two groups were formed and deliberately arranged to encourage separate identities. Boys with no particular ties with each other were chosen for each group; they soon inte-

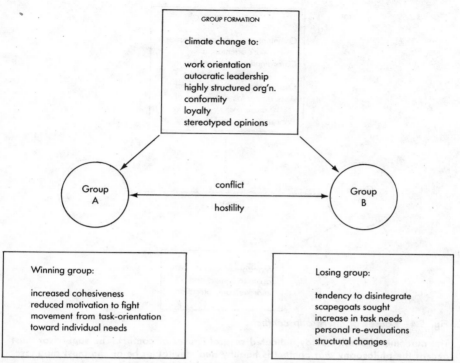

Fig. 5.3 *Sherif's survey of intergroup activity (boys' camp, USA)*

Two groups were formed and deliberately arranged to encourage separate identities. Each group gradually began to view the other as the enemy; hostility increased; both the winning and losing group demonstrated particular tendencies; clearly there were advantages and disadvantages of success and failure

grated, climate changed from play-oriented to work-oriented, leadership became more autocratic and the group became highly structured with considerable conformity and loyalty.

Each group gradually began to view the other as the enemy; this induced hostility and reduced communication which caused negative stereotyped opinions. Figure 5.3 explains the study.

Understandably other considerations must be considered when relating Sherif's work to companies: typically economic and market conditions, the external environment and the existing organisation structure. Two aspects emerge: first, the states of differentiation which include specialisation, attitudes, and managerial behaviour; second, integration in the structure which is the degree of collaboration between departments.

Causes of conflict

An important feature of Sherif's study is the strong indication of several

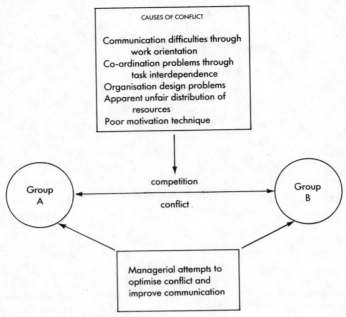

Fig. 5.4 *Causes of intergroup conflict*
The outcome of Sherif's study indicated several causes of conflict. The supervisor must accept the philosophy that conflict is healthy and inevitable; he or she must diagnose the causes, establish rules that optimise and resolve high conflicts by adopting appropriate techniques

causes, namely communication problems through differences in work orientation, co-ordination difficulties through task interdependence, organisation design problems, apparent unfair distribution of resources, and poor motivation techniques. Figure 5.4 illustrates the situation.

Intergroup dynamics

Conflict causes changes in perception, attitude and behaviour in groups and between groups. Favourable changes may occur if conflict is reduced to an optimised level. This achieves higher productivity and improved relationships.

However high conflict levels cause enmity and sometimes vicious behaviour. Examples are sporting activities where players use verbal abuse and even physical violence against each other and a referee – especially if money is at stake.

Intragroup changes

The usual changes within a group during intergroup conflict are: increased cohesiveness, more autocratic leadership to create high responsiveness, increased structural rigidity, more concern for high performance, stronger loyalty towards the group, discouragement of external social interaction, strong control and punishment for deviation from norms, increased formal climate, improved co-ordination, and allocation of specific responsibilities.

Changes in group relations

When hostility rises beyond sensible levels between groups the tendencies are: a decrease in communication, perception distortion, less interaction, over-emphasis of enmity, personal or group goals often over-riding company goals, and a reduction in problem-solving and decision-making orientation leading to an emotional win-or-lose orientation.

Classical examples in the UK are some negotiations between trade unions and companies.

Resolving conflict

There are many ways but choice is difficult and depends upon contingencies, the environment, the technology, and the needs of individuals, groups, and tasks.

Direct action

Redesigning the structure at the trouble spot is one approach. Reducing task interdependence and clarifying task responsibilities is possible, but building-in joint work responsibilities may cause more conflict. Generally the aim is to create self-contained work groups with sufficient resources.

A controversial approach is to bring together both groups and let them sort out difficulties with a minimum of guidance. A fundamental requirement is to have a feel for the situation and to act accordingly.

Indirect action

One expedient approach is to impose a rule which will delay an upheaval and allow time for investigation. Another form is to wait and see if the issue disperses naturally. These are useful if a minor issue is believed to be hiding a deeper problem.

De-escalation techniques

These are attempts to defuse, deflect or smooth-over conflict. Skilful discussion may convince the group that the issue is of minor consequence or that basically both parties' views are similar. This delaying tactic allows tempers to cool and gives the group time to reconsider more logically.

Compromise

Finally this form may work if mature groups are involved. Bargaining is a popular means although criticised because of lack of openness and absence of genuine problem-solving. Another means is to increase contact or communication between warring groups so that stereotyped views disperse. However one school of thought sees increased interaction as providing more opportunity to reinforce negative views. Structuring the interaction to avoid sensitive areas is one answer.

Questions

1 Define group cohesiveness.
2 Give reasons why group objectives may differ from organisational objectives.
3 Explain social interaction in a group.
4 Why are informal groups formed?
5 Explain norm formation.
6 Why should a person change when joining a group?
7 What are the likely advantages of forming autonomous work groups?
8 Discuss the importance of formal and informal roles.
9 How may a group develop power?
10 Discuss the constructive use of conflict.
11 What are the main causes of inter-group conflict?
12 Outline the main approaches to resolve conflict.

Case study

Ralph, unemployed for a year, was pleased to be starting work again at his old factory where business had picked up. He had worked in Main Assembly before, but this time his job was in Goods Inwards. His job was to locate parts and deliver them to the counter. After a while he realised the computer files were incorrect and often found parts supposedly out-of-stock.

Other people in the group were annoyed when told by the fitters, 'Not you, where's Ralph? He always manages to find what we want.' Soon Ralph was shunned, excluded from the usual lunch-break chats and tea-break get-togethers, and generally ignored.

The chief storekeeper noticed and asked Ralph for an explanation. 'I don't know why they're giving me the cold shoulder. I pull my weight and manage to find parts apparently out-of-stock, and the fitters seem happy. I know what it's like on bonus in Main Assembly when you're held up for spares.'

'Ah.' was all the chief storekeeper said, and walked away.

A week later Gloria, one of the Goods Inwards employees who always had plenty to say, approached Ralph. 'Look, mate, you don't seem to get the message. Unless you work like the rest of us you're in dead trouble.'

Ralph lost his temper. 'I don't give a damn for you lot. You haven't worked in Main Assembly – I have. You're just a lazy lot of Reds who don't care for anyone or anything!'

1   Comment on the Goods Inwards group.
2   As chief storekeeper how would you have tackled the problem?
3   Are there any fundamental organisational difficulties apparent from this case?

6 Industry and business

General outline

British industry is complex and difficult to perceive. Its long history with many traditional practices and unique culture has become a disadvantage according to one viewpoint and caused problems, some of which remain unsolved.

A vast range of features exists. Each feature interrelates and interacts with others. This condition causes misunderstandings and difficulties in appreciating the real situation.

Certain topics are of particular interest to the supervisor who may be drawn into discussions with peers and employees. Those selected include:

- historical features
- typical economic difficulties
- types of economy
- types of industry and business structure
- localisation
- government influence
- importance of human assets
- international trade
- Single European Market.

Historical features

The relative decline of British industry is well known and a favourite topic for critics and the media. According to some records the UK's change from super-power status started around 1880; the long decline was accelerated by two world wars and has only stopped recently.

The causes are difficult to disentangle. All participants – management, unions, various governments, the money market, and employees – seem to have contributed to the decline, along with traditional concepts, inappropriate culture, and the educational system.

World War II

Typical situations in World War II illustrate other difficulties.

1   Even during this critical period Britain's performance was poor. The term 'The British Disease' already existed despite government propaganda to the contrary at the time. The so-called magnificent war effort was fictitious. Output compared with Germany was 80 per cent for aircraft and machine tool industries, 84 per cent for coal, and 70 per cent for aero engines.

2   British machine tool industry could not cope with demand from wartime factories. The USA supplied enormous quantities to fill the gap whereas Germany naturally tooled most of her factories.

3   Research and development scientists who invented many famous technological devices often were not familiar with production requirements. The result was many delays and much reliance on supplies of American components.

4   In 1939 education and training in the UK was deplorable and well behind Germany and the USA. Typical examples are: no management or business schools; 700 graduate engineers a year compared with 1900 in Germany plus 2,000 qualified practical engineers; 20,000 in part time further education compared with 1.8 million in Germany.

5   Strikes and stoppages were common place and increased year by year. Walk-outs often seemed to be for trivial reasons. There were strikes in coal mines; there was the aircraft industry's resistance to new technologies; and countless arguments over staffing levels. In the shipping industry, for example, the union insisted that a riveter's mate, who otherwise would be redundant should, on full pay, watch over a riveter when hand riveting was replaced by pneumatic riveting.

Post-war history

The end of World War II marked a drastic change in the financial position of the UK. Before the war a long reputation as a creditor nation had been enjoyed, mainly through flourishing export markets. Owing to the cost of the war, which meant selling many foreign investments, and severe restrictions of exports, Britain entered a precarious phase of financial instability.

Debts amounted to £3,500 million and these were blocked by the government. Aid from the USA included a loan of about £1,000 million which was soon disposed of, and this was followed by a gift of goods, valued at nearly £1,500 million under the Marshall Plan, as part of a scheme of assistance to many European nations, including West Germany and Italy.

The urgent need to increase exports was thrust upon industry under changed conditions where: (1) the workforce had become highly organised and fully employed; (2) greater spending power existed in the home market which tended to distract from exporting; (3) extensive government influence over many aspects of industry had increased.

Half-time Britain

In the late 1940s and early 1950s world trade boomed and tended to hide the UK's industrial problems. The late 50s introduced a new label 'Half-time Britain' when performance was compared with other successful countries. Clearly the weaknesses were persisting; especially noticeable compared with Japan was the inability of government finance and industry to work together to exploit technological changes, and lack of long-term planning.

In the 60s and 70s stagnation continued. Over the period 1955–1973 productivity (output per person-year) in manufacturing industry grew at about 3.2 per cent compared with about 5 per cent in West Germany, France, Belgium, Italy and the Netherlands. The cumulative effect is substantial. Real earnings grew at an average rate of 2.0 per cent in the UK, 8.1 per cent in Japan, 6.2 per cent in Italy, 4.5 per cent in West Germany, and 4.3 per cent in France.

The trend was clear although complete analysis would include other factors, typically output trends, investment, profitability and exchange rates.

Recovery

In the 80s slowly industry began to abandon traditional practices as union power diminished and governmental support increased. Redundancy programmes and plant closures reduced over-staffing of workforce and obsolete practices. Efficiency began to improve as some countries were experiencing recessions. However the devastation created by World War II and post-war policies remained, with high unemployment and lethargic management.

Other countries continued to exploit markets, notably Japan and West Germany. The UK failed to take full advantage of micro-electronics, information technology and other technologies. For example in robotics by 1986 Japan had about 67,000 robots; the USA – 20,000; West Germany – 9,000, and the UK – 3,000. Nevertheless by 1987 a new feeling of optimism was noticeable.

Current situation

Although many reports are extremely cautious there are distinct signs of improvement due to governmental policies and actions undertaken since 1979, and more effective managerial activities.

Estimates from HMSO are encouraging. These show productivity growth based upon output changes associated either with changes in quantity of inputs used (typically employed workforce and capital equipment) or with changes in productivity – changes in output from a given level of inputs.

Productivity is a key factor in the increase of a country's prosperity and demonstrates its influence on a country's international competitive position.

A faster increase improves a country's competitive position unless there are offsetting adjustments in exchange rates or real labour costs.

Productivity growth

UK productivity has been higher so far in the 80s than in the 70s – particularly in manufacturing industry. Growth has been around the top in the international league table in the 80s compared with around the bottom for the 60s and 70s.

Due to the shake-out in over-staffing, the number in employment fell up to 1983. Since then manufacturing productivity has grown by over 4 per cent a year, non-manufacturing by over 1.5 per cent a year, and the whole economy by over 2 per cent a year. The number in employment has increased by over a million, indicating a substantial improvement in productivity growth performance.

Employed labour force

Table 6.1 shows a slowdown in productivity growth in the 70s after the first OPEC crisis. Since 1979 productivity growth in manufacturing has been similar to the rate in the 60s and much faster than that achieved in the 70s. This reflects advances in technology and more flexible working practices.

Table 6.1 Output per head of the employed labour force

	(Average annual % change)		
	1964–73	1973–79	1979–86
Manufacturing	3.8	0.7	3.5
Non-manufacturing*	2.9	0.6	1.2
Whole economy	2.7	1.1	1.9

* Excl. public services and North Sea oil and gas.
Sources: Central Statistical Office and HM Treasury

Relative performance

In Table 6.2 the UK clearly has improved its relative performance considerably in recent years. In the 60s growth though high in relation to the economy's earlier and subsequent performance was towards the bottom of the league. Between 1973 and 1979 there was a general slowdown in productivity growth for most countries and the UK remained near the bottom. Since 1979 the UK's manufacturing productivity growth has been greater than in all the other countries, and the whole economy productivity growth comes second only to Japan.

Table 6.2 Output per head in the major 7 industrialised countries

| | Manufacturing | | | Whole economy | | |
| | | | | | (Average annual % change) | |
	1964–73	1973–79	1976–86	1964–73	1973–79	1979–86
United States	3.4	3.5	2.3	1.6	0.2	0.7
Japan	9.8	4.0	2.7	7.4	2.9	2.8
West Germany	3.9	3.3	2.3	4.2	2.9	1.4
France*	5.4	3.0	2.5	4.5	2.8	1.5
UK	3.8	0.7	3.5	2.7	1.1	1.9
Italy*	5.5	2.5	2.4	5.6	1.7	1.0
Canada	4.3	2.5	3.0	2.5	0.5	0.6
Average of major 7†	5.0	3.2	2.5	3.6	1.5	1.3

*For whole of industry, not just manufacturing.
†Weighted on basis of 1980 manufacturing output, at 1980 exchange rates.
Source: OECD

Major economic difficulties

Attempts to economise effectively takes into account scarcity, choice and supply difficulties. In other words resources are limited; allocating them involves choice; and supply depends upon demand and related price, along with cost of production.

Three questions emerge from this key task. What to produce? How to produce? Who should benefit from the goods? In brief these involve consumption, production and distribution. Any country must attempt to answer these questions and in so doing has to choose a method or system to operate the economy. Choice depends mainly upon political power, attitudes, aims, tradition, and culture.

Effective consumption

This depends upon placing wants in priority order – considering society and the nation – and satisfying them accordingly. Decisions are influenced by: (1) individuals and companies who may act selfishly; (2) the government who considers national problems; (3) other countries who exert political or physical pressures.

Effective production

The full utilisation of each company is essential. Consideration must be given to suitability for manufacturing the product, all work–study aspects, appropriate location of site, and upgrading production by using new technologies, modern designs, and applying economic services.

Effective distribution

This controversial issue implicates the distribution of wealth, equality, ownership, freedom of choice, political outlook, distribution of income, profits, and idealistic concepts.

Types of economy

Various methods have evolved in attempts to economise. Two opposing major systems are a planned economy operated by the state and a market economy where the price mechanism operates through private enterprise. Within these extremes are different combinations of both, collectively known as a mixed economy.

Any economy has market and non-market sectors therefore no extreme type – planned or market – exists in practice. Figure 6.1 illustrates a continuum of planned/market economies. Note that a country may move

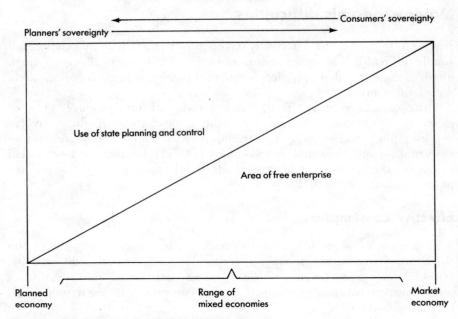

Fig. 6.1 *A continuum of planned/market economies*

A country may move in either direction along the continuum, position depending upon the current economic situation such as a change in government, war, or various economic difficulties

in either direction along the continuum, position depending upon the current situation such as a change in government, war, or a variety of economic difficulties.

Governmental roles

The degree of intervention and ways of intervening are contentious issues among politicians and economists. Roles may be viewed as removing defects of the market system by more planning and control of resources or being limited to the supply of public goods and improving the market system. Public goods benefit everyone, typically national defence, police force, and judiciary.

Roles are very important since the market system has inherent weaknesses and because of the inability of the market mechanism to deliver certain types of goods.

The private sector

In a mixed economy the private sector comprises privately owned firms that are independent of the government. They represent about 70 per cent of commercial firms and about 50 per cent of the economy.

To survive in free enterprise a firm must make a profit so that supply becomes adjustable to price changes. Although profit is a debatable topic it is certainly essential to finance growth, replace obsolescent and obsolete equipment, and compensate investors. The amount of profit is subject to fierce argument.

The public sector and government

Owned by the state and controlled by the government this sector employs about seven million and includes nationalised industries, governmental and local authority services, and various agencies.

These institutions are established to protect the public interest. Typical justifications are natural monopolies, high capital requirements, social essentials, natural rights, general safety, and national importance.

Structures

The government authorises and is responsible for the structural organisations. Distinct forms are the civil service, local and regional authorities, public corporations, nationalised industries, licensed monopoly, and joint ownership.

Monopolies

The Monopolies and Restrictive Practices Act (1948) was passed to counter certain business practices thought to be against the public interest. By definition public interest covers efficient production, sufficient output, and appropriate prices to meet demand at home and overseas.

The Monopolies Commission investigates, analyses and reports on industries where a few large firms dominate the market through assumed collusion. The government may refer a case to the commission and after receiving a report the minister decides on any action.

VIEWPOINTS

This policy directly conflicts with the concept that the market is self-regulating and automatically achieves maximum efficiency. Another view is that it would be better to introduce compulsory intervention by stopping or preventing any firm from dominating the market, regardless of the situation. Anti-trust legislation in the USA is based on this concept which has proved difficult to enforce.

More competition has been encouraged in the UK recently. UK legislation aims to prevent overseas control of key industries, assist in maintaining competitiveness overseas, take advantage of economies of scale, and support more rationalisation to improve efficiency.

Mergers

Under the Monopolies and Mergers Act 1965 the DTI can refer any merger or proposed merger to the Commission provided a monopoly is considered to be strengthened or a monopoly created, and assets exceed £5 million.

Some companies are deterred by the knowledge that the proposed merger will be referred to the Commission, while others pursue proposals by persevering with new schemes if refused initially.

Substantial evidence on the benefits of mergers is often difficult to obtain. Typical justifications are to improve efficiency and effectiveness; and in particular to take advantage of increased size by affording to pursue research and development projects, to use the particular expertise of managers in both concerns, to create more marketing outlets, and to compete more effectively against overseas concerns.

Restrictive trade practices

The Restrictive Trade Practices Act (1956) applied to goods only and established rules for continuance of restrictive agreements, and abolished collective retail price maintenance (RPM). Waves of legislation followed to counter many criticisms of this complex Act. Typically the Resale Prices Act (1964), Restrictive Practices Act 1968, Fair Trading Act 1973, Restrictive Practices Act 1976, and the Competition Act 1980.

Types of industry

The emergence of particular industries in a country is the result of various factors: technical knowledge, availability of trained labour, raw materials and power, the climate, capital resources, stage of economic development, social climate and political organisation.

In the UK during the eighteenth century conditions were favourable for industrial change and expansion. Natural advantages such as climate, geographical position, harbours, navigable rivers and supplies of coal and iron were supplemented by political and financial stability and an accumulation of capital. A gradual development of industry occurred which is known as the Industrial Revolution. The main industries that emerged were textiles, coal, iron, steel and engineering, including railways. Agriculture continued to improve as demand increased.

The introduction of machinery, new techniques and improved communication and transport brought about large-scale production which considerably increased the range and quality of goods. Today the number of manufacturing establishments is about 120,000 and they employ about 5 million individuals.

Business structure

The thousands of industrial concerns in the UK vary in structure as well as in size. The six main types of business range from the 'one-man' or sole proprietor to the nationalised industry.

Sole proprietor

The 'one-man' concern is the oldest type of business and is still quite common, especially among retailers and farmers. The proprietor provides his or her own capital raised either by savings or borrowed from relations and friends. The proprietor is liable for all debts, is responsible only to him or herself, and profits do not have to be shared.

Partnerships

The common form of partnership consists of two or more individuals who agree to establish a business and who generally share responsibilities and profits. The total number of partners is limited to twenty (except solicitors, accountants and stockbrokers) under the Companies Acts 1948–85. The Limited Partnership Act 1907 allows individuals to form a partnership under which a partner's liability is limited, but such a partner is not allowed to participate in the concern's management.

Limited companies

The principle of limited liability means that investors are liable for the concern's debts only up to the amount invested in fully paid up shares in the company. Such a system, legalised in the original Companies Act 1856, has encouraged industry to develop at a phenomenal rate. Large amounts of capital can be raised and companies may expand more easily by raising further sums of money.

Under the Companies Act 1980, companies may be public or private. Both must have at least two members and be registered. A public company must end its name with 'Public Limited Company' or appropriate abbreviations, its Memorandum of Association must state that it is a public company, and its minimum issued share capital must be at least £50 000 of which 25 per cent and all premium is paid up.

Any company not complying with these provisions is automatically private and as such is prohibited from offering its shares to the public.

Co-operative societies

The co-operative movement *in production* has *not* grown, mainly because the employees provide the capital and elect their own managers from within. The restriction in raising capital and the problem of locating effective managers has resulted in the establishment of only twenty-seven concerns who are members of the Co-operative Production Federation. The main lines of production are footwear and clothing; the bulk of output is distributed to co-operative societies.

Consumers' co-operative societies are very popular, with a membership of about twelve million. Each member is a customer who may invest up to £1000 in the particular society, but he or she has only one vote. Interest on the investment is at a fixed rate and the profit for distribution is paid in the form of a dividend on purchases. Any individual may join or leave whenever he or she wishes and there is no maximum number of shareholders. Management is elected by members and the accounts must be published.

Attempts by Labour Governments to establish co-operatives following threatened closures have encountered many economic difficulties. Examples are the Kirkby Manufacturing and Engineering Company, Triumph Ltd at Meriden, and the *Scottish Daily News*. These co-operatives have been severely criticised mainly on the grounds that practically all declining industries suffer from misguided enthusiasm caused by added strains on an already faltering spirit. The result is a further decline which tends to increase in speed. Other criticisms include the inference that backing – in various forms – is insufficient and too late.

Supporters of co-operatives claim that given a viable situation the principle of co-ownership avoids the innate conflict between the two sides – owner and employee – and provides a firm basis for operating industrial democracy successfully.

Municipal undertakings

Local services such as airfields, local transport and water supply are provided by the local authority. Ratepayers are the owners, but the local council is responsible for management.

State undertakings

Within this group there remains at present the Bank of England, coal, electricity, steel, Post Office, Girobank, railways, waterways, shipbuilders, Civil Aviation Authority, water, and London Regional Transport Board.

A committee is appointed by the minister who is responsible for the particular undertaking. He reports to Parliament but the committee actually manages the concern in accordance with Parliament's policy.

Localisation of industry

When an industry concentrates in one area the effect is known as localisation of industry. Many industries in Britain are highly localised; the advantages of this concentration are organised markets, regional division of labour, a pool of skilled labour and development of subsidiary industries.

Organised markets tend to appear in the locally manufactured product. New concerns are attracted and established; a new form of economy emerges where each company specialises in one process or one part of the product. Thus, regional division of labour – like the dividing up of labour within a company so that each person performs a separate function towards manufacturing the product – is extended to the whole industry so that specialisation within each company is achieved.

Full use of skilled labour is possible with localisation as companies will be attracted to areas where such labour is available. Subsidiary industries will also be attracted.

Localisation is not possible in some industries such as public utilities where the service must be near the consumption point because of high transportation costs.

Government influence

The extended government influence today really amounts to the state assuming in many respects the function of top management of industry. Through budgets the demand for goods and services can be varied, growth adjusted, inflation checked, and modernisation programmes can be encouraged. Governmental investment schemes also play a very important part in the economy.

The main current topics of particular interest are now discussed. These include policy on nationalised industries, monetary policy, economic operations, the use of information technology, and share ownership.

Nationalised industries (NIs) and privatisation

The drive to nationalise after World War 2 was mainly ideological and in some cases due to industrial unrest, abuse of a natural monopoly, and trade union influence. Many major industries were nationalised by 1977. They represented by then about eight per cent of the labour force, eleven per cent of total output and 20 per cent of total gross investment in fixed capital.

Government intervention in this extreme form has been subjected to continual political controversy. One view sees nationalisation as beneficial since it stops a small group of capitalists from dominating society by catering for their own interests and ignoring society's interests. An opposing view sees nationalisation as detrimental because it concentrates economic power within one enterprise considering it is better dispersed among many private firms.

Nationalisation problems

Often NIs have not performed in accordance with their main advocates. In some cases they have fallen below levels of their comparable counterparts in private enterprise.

Typical criticisms are that many constitutional problems arise; the concept of monopoly and its faults persists; a tendency to be subsidised if losses occur, thus leading to complacency and lack of market discipline; industrial relations have not improved; a 'take-it or leave-it' outlook and over-caution in decision making develop.

Privatisation

As a whole NIs were performing badly up to 1979 after years of financial problems and subsidisation. The new government decided to return these to the private sector which amounts to sixteen major businesses so far. These include British Telecom, British Gas, British National Oil, British Airways, British Airports Authority, British Aerospace, British Shipbuilders (Warships), British Transport Docks Board, National Freight, Enterprise Oil, and the National Bus Company. For those remaining the government has tightened up financial disciplines, exposed their activities wherever possible to market competition, and generally demanded high standards of management and efficiency.

Now the NI's account for 5.5 per cent of total UK output compared with nine per cent in 1979. They employ 800,000 which is about four per cent of total employees. Labour productivity has risen sharply due to cutting out overmanning and to output increases. This has assisted in reducing grants, subsidies and loans. Management and cost control have greatly improved.

Privatisation has raised about £12b by selling strategic shareholdings. Methods include sale of shareholdings in nationalised industries, disposing of parts of public sector shareholdings in companies, and contracting-out of some local government services.

Arguments for privatisation

Arguments often quoted are that managers are stimulated by the profit motive, they make faster and better decisions being free from governmental restrictions, and they take calculated risks. Consumers benefit through increased competition, wider choice, and the opportunity to buy shares in the companies. Thus the concept of wider share ownership for employees and the community is encouraged, and the funds raised by sales and reduction in loans reduce the Exchequer's burden.

The UK's privatisation programme has stimulated fresh thinking in many countries about the relative roles of the state and the private sector in providing goods and services. General dissatisfaction with the performance of state industries has been one reason for some countries to re-assess the situation. Examples are France, West Germany, Italy, Spain, Netherlands, Turkey, Japan, and Canada. Many governments have sent delegations to the UK to study privatisation techniques.

Monetary policy

The government's monetary policy is central to the control of inflation. A continuous and comprehensive assessment of factors influencing monetary conditions is practised. The exchange rate, narrow and broad money, and other indicators of inflationary pressure such as house prices, are studied.

A complex financial strategy has achieved control of inflation which now averages about 5 per cent, and stable prices. Before the present government's controls inflation peaked at about 25 per cent in 1975, and the general price level tripled between 1968 and 1979, meaning £1 in 1968 was worth only 30 pence in 1979.

This marked improvement in inflationary control has nearly matched rates in North America and Japan, and is actually below the average of other major European countries.

Economic operations

The government has taken a leading part in promoting 'structural adjustment', that is improving the capability of individuals, enterprises and institutions to respond to change by exploiting new opportunities and moving away from declining sectors. The Organisation for Economic Co-operation and Development (OECD) conducted a recent study which showed that industrial countries do not adapt as quickly as they might because their economies are over-regulated and over-protected. This situation indicates that 'structural adjustment' should be promoted vigorously.

The OECD's report showed that economies work best when allowed to operate freely with a minimum of government interference. Using interventions which distort price signals or reduce competition hinders markets.

In the 1980s many governments have substantially opened up their economies to market forces but more remains to be done. The UK government has removed many controls including those on prices; dividends and pay; has improved incentives – reducing income tax rates and raising tax thresholds; removed several taxes including investment income surcharge and national insurance surcharge; encouraged individual ownership of property, and wider share ownership – especially through privatisation programmes and share option schemes; and encouraged the liberalisation of financial markets.

Information technology

The government is now probably the largest user in the UK of IT (computers, integrated with advanced telecommunications and office systems). In 1985/86 spending on IT was about £1,500 million; 20,000 staff are employed, running over one thousand medium to large computer systems nationwide. This approach provides better, quicker and more flexible services to the public; enhancing the jobs of staff; and getting better value for public money.

Departments have developed strategic plans to cope with the changing role of technology in meeting their needs, to build for the future, and to decide priorities with real regard for cost benefits and value for money. They also have top level committees who decide how to use IT. The Central Computer and Telecommunications Agency (CCTA) sits on all these committees. By 1990 about 150,000 terminals are estimated to be in use compared with 30,000 in 1984.

A nation of shareowners

The long-term ambition of the government is to make the British people a nation of shareowners; to create popular capitalism, in which more and more men and women have a direct personal stake in business and industry.

In 1986 a new and radical scheme was launched to encourage direct investment in UK equities – the Personal Equity Plan (PEP). The scheme allows investment up to £200 a month in shares entirely free of tax on reinvested dividends and capital gains. Designed to attract small savers, it is simple and probably favoured by companies.

Human assets

Pushing managers towards a philosophy where people matter most seems to be a dominating thought today. Whether industrial society sincerely adopts this philosophy is debatable. Unemployment and trade-union power reduction may have persuaded managers to feel they now have the right and the opportunity to manage as they wish. Nevertheless many managers are slowly realising that giving human assets priority pays off.

Semi-autonomous groups

Lessons from overseas competitors, research and previous UK industrial catastrophes, are being learned slowly but surely. Furthermore technologies seem to influence and encourage the formation of semi-autonomous groups joined by various forms of matrix models.

This trend is noticeable in large firms and means that classical organisation structures are discounted but not completely, to be replaced by closely co-ordinated groups in loose structures held together by modern IT means.

Social trends

The effects of IT, changing education programmes and new cultures are more noticeable now in people's changing attitudes, wants, beliefs and general outlook. New behavioural patterns are emerging where in the future people will be more interested in self-development and be looking for a more balanced life.

This trend amounts to more dignity, expecting more respect, and not being pushed around easily. Thus fraternal rather than paternal treatment of employees is inevitable. Managers will be severely stretched to cater for demands of such employees and will certainly be in difficulties if they ignore them.

International trade

Unfortunately some of the UK's leading export companies have lost ground over the past twenty years. Many reasons have been proposed for this decline in a country that has probably been exporting longer than any other. Nevertheless the UK's share of world export markets has now stopped falling. Most of the export trade is conducted by a few predominantly multi-national concerns.

There are many managerial qualities that are essential for success in exporting. Examples often quoted are entrepreneurial and innovative outlook, open-mindedness, drive to succeed, positive commitment, adaptability, high capability, and professionalism. These are apart from the technological specialisms of the manager, such as marketing, finance and production.

A selection from the many and diverse topics which also affect success is given below:

1　high degree of employee participation
2　teamwork development
3　sound financial strategy
4　long-term financial support from the money market
5　successful marketing strategy
6　a conscientious workforce with drive, co-operativeness and initiative
7　high product quality and design relative to price
8　a national education and training system geared to the needs of industry
9　adequate reward for highly capable individuals
10　development of industrial respectability to attract high quality individuals
11　good delivery record
12　sound and consistent governmental monetary policies to control inflation and encourage industrial growth

13 investment in, and full utilisation of, current technologies to manufacture the best possible products
14 realistic research and development programmes appropriately funded and supported by the government
15 high flexibility in all organisational operations, unhampered by outmoded pressure groups
16 high welfare provision
17 full regard for human assets

The Single European Market

In 1985 EC heads of government committed themselves to completing the single market programme by 1992. This objective was fixed to eliminate the existing tariff and quota barriers, and other technical barriers between states so that free movement of goods would become a reality.

The 'single market' is defined as an area without internal frontiers in which the free movement of goods, persons, services and capital is ensured in accordance with the provisions of the EEC Treaty. This enormous trade area has 320 million consumers – above the combined total of the USA and Japan. Substantial business opportunities and challenges should mean reduced business costs, increased efficiency, and creation of wealth and new jobs.

The EC is the UK's largest export market and its importance is increasing. Member states accepted about 33 per cent of UK exports in 1972, 44 per cent in 1982, and 50 per cent in 1988 (about £39 billion); the UK accepted 36 per cent in 1972 and 54 per cent in 1988. Understandably all member states will be competing but there is much room for growth.

The Enterprise Initiative

To persuade businesses to take full advantage of the single market the DTI launched the Enterprise Initiative in 1988. This vast programme is a self-help package which provides a valuable source of information and expert resources. Experts are available to help in marketing, design, quality manufacturing systems, business planning, financial and information systems, and export planning. They also assist in linking companies with universities and polytechnics, help to solve technical problems, and provide access to collaborative research projects.

Support services include overseas market data, company information on registration, design testing, patents and trade-marks, small firms assistance, and business development assistance.

European high technology

There is a crucial need for member states to continue developing collaborative research and to improve the capability of bringing new products on to the market. These are essential features for selling competitive products overseas.

Some companies are already strong while there are encouraging signs in others. Examples are: aerospace industry – the airbus consortium which has successfully produced an aircraft to counter US dominance; nuclear energy – fast reactor technology equalling USSR and Japan (world leaders); software industry – beginning to couple into larger groups; weapons systems – heavy export programmes; materials technology – development projects in aerospace programmes; pharmaceuticals, chemicals and biotechnology – a strong position poised for further development.

Collaboration in all its forms provides a unique opportunity for EC industries to become world competitors and face up firmly to competition from the USA and Japan. Getting rid of all the national barriers to protect local industries in member states has been a fundamental problem which should be overcome by 1992.

Questions

1 Discuss some of the effects of two world wars on the UK economy.
2 Why is it essential for a company to achieve high productivity?
3 What effect can government policy have on industry?
4 Discuss the UK's major economic difficulties.
5 What is meant by a mixed economy?
6 Explain the possible adverse effects of monopolies and mergers.
7 List the likely effects if an industry does not keep pace with changing technologies.
8 What are the main discussion topics you would raise with an employee who feels that doing as little as possible for as much money as possible is a sensible approach?
9 Discuss the government's ambition to create a nation of shareholders.
10 'Human assets are of prime importance in any company'. Discuss this statement.
11 Why is exporting so important to the UK economy?
12 Explain the probable opportunities and challenges for the UK in the Single European Market.

Case study

Durajuice Ltd, a company specialising in cartons of apple juice for the hotel and catering industry, ran into strong competition mainly through its higher price and partly because of a new product that maintained a better flavour.

At the factory the situation deteriorated when costs were trying to be maintained. The union insisted on a wage rise well beyond the cost of living increase. Management refused, a strike lasted for three weeks and ended eventually in a compromise: payment of the asking wage and a productivity deal. The outcome was a further loss of business caused by delivery delays and no price reduction.

After two months there was no response to higher productivity comitments and profit deteriorated; the union pressed for a further wage rise. Management decided to renew negotiations with a firm in West Germany for a licence to produce an automatic juice dispenser. If successful the deal would mean 35 per cent of employees would be redundant, survival would be assured and the price could be lowered.

Meanwhile the production supervisors were taken to task for not being able to improve productivity.

The excuses given by the employees were that managers are inefficient and they do not put in a good day's work. The supervisors were reluctant to take up the case with the works manager who spends two afternoons a week playing golf with the managing director.

One morning a rumour circulates that the dispenser may be produced in Germany.

What are the courses of action open to the supervisors when they meet together?

7 Managerial roles

Introduction

The role of a supervisor is generally referred to in terms of the relationship between supervisor and employees, where guiding people is carried out by close contact. Controlling groups by close contact, however, permeates right through the organisation up to the managing director. He or she also supervises a group of senior executives by very close contact. Furthermore, the managing director uses the same techniques and principles recommended to the lowest level of supervision. Obviously this activity forms only part of the job; nevertheless, the supervision of groups commences here and spreads throughout the organisation in a similar pattern. In this sense, a supervisory team exists and the behaviour of each member will be mainly regulated by example set at the top. Generally, supervisors treat their subordinates in a similar fashion to the way their superiors in turn treat them.

All managers who control a group of subordinates directly may be considered as supervisors who, in addition, undertake the heavier responsibilities of thinking far ahead and formulating policy at a higher range of levels to meet set objectives. They control many groups remotely by strength of leadership, communication and the use of management principles. The levels of management are distinguished, therefore, by the amount of policy planning, the total size of the groups underneath, and the amount of problem-solving and decision-making necessary to carry out policy effectively. From this point of view, the management team starts at the top and ends at a point above the highest level of supervision where the emphasis is on problem-solving and decision-making, with a correspondingly smaller proportion of planning and policy-making.

The management team relies extensively on supervision to provide information and make recommendations. Without the aid of supervisors, planning and policy-making become a farce. This reason alone justifies the claim by most managers that supervisors are a part of management. Unfortunately, the recognised supervisory jobs often are considered to be the ladder of promotion for employees but with no further opportunities of entering management. Furthermore, the highest supervisory post is not thought of as the lowest management level.

The fine line between management and supervision – if there is a line at all in practice – is apparent where a supervisor is, in fact, *managing* the department according to definition. He or she may be indirectly controlling more than twenty-five groups and forecasting and planning well ahead, although the policy-making activity may be restricted, dependent upon the business.

To summarise, all management positions contain a supervisory element which decreases as the top is approached; all supervisory positions contain a managerial element which decreases as the bottom is approached. Confused thinking and vague terminology in relation to this situation cause many arguments. The line drawn between management and supervision is purely arbitrary, varying from company to company. A manager in one concern could easily be a supervisor – with no job variation – in another concern.

Achievement of results rests with all members of a company and their ability to work together as a business team, which includes employees, supervisors, and managers. A diagram illustrating the teams and flexible borderlines is given in Fig. 7.1.

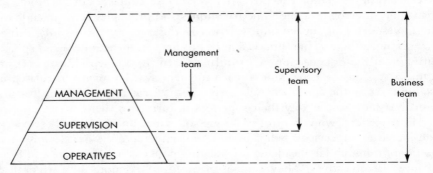

Fig. 7.1 *Management, supervisory and business teams*

The diagram illustrates how the management, supervisors and employees should work together, forming a single united business team

Definition of a manager

A manager achieves objectives at minimum cost by guiding people and effectively using capital. This brief definition could equally apply to a supervisor. A manager must be concerned with the strategic aspect. He or she must visualise the over-all scene now and in the future, up to five, ten, fifteen, and twenty years hence. A supervisor, in turn, concentrates on the tactical aspect of solving mainly immediate problems and keeping activities moving towards objectives in line with over-all strategy.

The supervisor's position

The unique position of the supervisor is the subject of constant argument over whether or not he or she is part of management. Clearly there are three groups involved, namely management, supervisory, and employee; but there are four viewpoints. The fourth viewpoint is that of the disinterested outside observer. General statements are necessary to argue the case.

The management viewpoint claims that supervisors are part of management, but this claim is not upheld in practice. The usual reasons for this attitude are snobbery, social background and confused thinking. The latter is inexcusable, considering that the same managers who persist in divorcing supervisors from their group would think it ludicrous if a blind person insisted upon having his fingers cut off.

From the employee viewpoint, the supervisor represents management and the concern as a whole. They expect their supervisor to represent them to management; but unless the supervisor shows a proper sense of balance (i.e. no particular bias towards management or employee), he or she will fail in this role.

To the outside observer, the supervisor seems to be in an impossible situation, buffeted from both sides, not receiving sufficient support from management and often operating with insufficient information. Management is inclined to ask for information from the specialist departments, so the supervisor then feels that the job's authority and responsibility are reduced and that higher authority does not appreciate the supervisor's problems.

It seems that employees recognise the supervisor as part of management. Most supervisory training programmes stress this point and attempt to place the supervisor as a representative of management in all respects. Managers should also recognise this fact and treat supervisors accordingly, that is, providing them with sufficient information and authority to manage their groups effectively.

Managerial activities

These are usually grouped into seven features: forecasting, planning, organising, co-ordinating, commanding, controlling and motivating. Each one is described in the next chapter. The approach emphasises the managerial process and leadership.

Managerial roles approach

Apart from the above features managers often perform other activities. An example of a broader view is Henry Mintzberg's observations. The list includes:

- figurehead – social activities
- leader
- liaison – communicating internally and externally

- receiving information
- disseminator – passing information to subordinates
- spokesman – passing information externally
- entrepreneur – risk taker
- disturbance handler
- resource allocator
- negotiator

Key business activities

Certain activities are essential. Henri Fayol recognised six key features which represent individuals' capabilities to perform successfully. These are:

1 *Technical*   production or service
2 *Commercial*   distribution and purchasing
3 *Financial*   obtaining capital and using it effectively
4 *Accounting*   providing accurate financial information
5 *Security*   safeguarding assets
6 *Managerial*   forecasting, planning, etc.

To appreciate the significance of all these activities other aspects are now discussed.

Purpose of management

Management's function is to protect the owner's interests by steering the company through channels which lead towards sound goals, and which will enhance and ensure the company's future existence.

To survive in the long run, management must build a reputation for the company of supplying goods or services of good quality at reasonable prices. Profitability in these conditions means that management's purpose includes increasing productivity to a high standard of effectiveness, so that owners, consumers, the community and the country benefit, but not at the expense of one particular group.

Ownership and control structure

To provide cohesion at the top, a pattern similar to the one in Fig. 7.2 is set up in limited companies which form the major part of British industry.

Shareholders

Ownership of a limited company is in the hands of the shareholders who may be members of the public (either directly or indirectly through the various institutions), directors, or employees of the concern. Under the Finance Act 1978, schemes for extending the ownership of a company's

Fig. 7.2 *Ownership and control structures – joint stock companies*

shares to its employees have been encouraged through tax advantages after the schemes have been run for a specified time.

Shareholders are often spread through the country and abroad. Although ownership is vested in the shareholders, control is delegated to the board of directors who are obliged to comply with a large amount of legislation which is designed to protect shareholders' interests.

A great deal of information of both a financial and non-financial nature has to be disclosed in the annual report and accounts to comply with the provisions of the Companies Acts 1948–85.

Public listed or quoted companies are obliged to comply with Stock Exchange requirements which are often more onerous than those contained in the statutes. One example concerns the system of voting at meetings; the Stock Exchange insists on the provision of a two-way form of proxy by way of which shareholders can intimate their acceptance or otherwise of the resolutions proposed. Unquoted companies and private companies, however, are not obliged to circulate proxy forms at all.

Some public companies are controlled by a small group of shareholders. By issuing non-voting shares, a small group will continue to control an expanding concern with no change in the balance of power. More is written about shareholders in Chapter 27.

Board of directors

Over-all control of the company is vested in the board of directors who formulate and approve policy and provide for legal requirements. The size of the board varies considerably. It may consist of full-time directors, working directors and part-time directors who sit on more than one board. Members are generally chosen for their ability; often they hold shares in the concern and, under the Companies Acts, their holdings have to be disclosed in the company's annual report.

The managing director

He or she is elected by the board of directors and normally holds the position of chairman on the board. The managing director conveys company policy to the senior executives and puts forward policy proposals to the board for formal approval.

Policy

Company policy is a guide or principle for the use of management and supervision in order that they may reach objectives by following a set broad pattern of behaviour.

Policies are, by intention, widely defined to allow for individual interpretation in situations which require judgment and initiative. A rigid interpretation destroys policy and turns it into a narrow rule which dispenses with the human approach. A rule has its own place at a lower level in the organisation where policy is interpreted into detailed principles, followed by even more detailed rules for operational purposes. It is essential for policy to be positive and lasting. Detailed principles and rules, in turn, must be more flexible to adapt to rapidly changing situations.

To summarise, a rule is intended to be interpreted in the same way all the time whereas a policy allows for discretion in application.

Policy-making

This multi-stage process may commence with suggestions well down in the organisation structure. Someone has an idea and discusses it with others, who then pass on proposals or information to their superiors, and so on, until definite suggestions reach the managing director. He or she, in turn, receives many suggestions from other sources which eventually are moulded into concrete proposals that are placed before the board of directors. The board after due discussion may formally approve or disapprove the proposed policy.

Alternatively, the process may be two-stage only: a proposal from the managing director and approval by the board.

Essential requirements of a policy

Acceptability

The increasing importance of policy being acceptable to everyone is marked by the persistence of employees who want to know why the policy is made or changed. Adequate reasons must be forthcoming, and management ought to provide supervisors with sufficient information to satisfy queries.

The effect of withholding information which leads to gossip and speculation can be disastrous, causing increased friction between management and employees, upsetting relationships through general suspicion and lowering morale.

Communicated to everyone

There should be no exceptions in communicating policy to employees. In the large concern a group can easily be overlooked, therefore a number of channels should be used.

Convincing people that they were not overlooked intentionally is not an easy task, unless relationships are very good.

Genuine application

It is not unusual for management to declare policy for prestige reasons, such as publicity, and then fail to put the policy into practice. Management's policy, in these circumstances, is to ignore the declared policies. Such complete lack of wisdom is hard to appreciate; not one employee is deceived and the word gradually spreads to all interested outsiders.

Some managers use 'policy' in a negative way, making it an excuse for *not* carrying out some course of action. In these cases policy does not appear in writing and is often made at the time to suit the circumstances. Another practice is wording policy in such a vague way that it can be distorted to fit in with any course of action at the time.

Balanced interpretation

Supervisors who rigidly conform to principles – without due regard for the human situation – would be correctly interpreting policy in their own minds. Something more than correctness is needed in a human society; all the factors, when weighed carefully, might well provide a more balanced interpretation which would not match up with the narrow correct one. Therein lies the art of supervision, which is in no way an abuse of policy.

Alignment with the objective

All policies must follow parallel courses on a broad front towards the objective. If they cross or oppose, collective effect is lost and confusion develops. Misunderstandings are often the cause of the problem rather than faults in the stated policy. This danger highlights the need for careful checking that ambiguity or lack of understanding is not occurring at lower levels.

Fields of Policy

Top policy

Broad policy which indicates the general course the company takes is in most cases the one which people have in mind as 'top policy'. Policy-making is a collective effort and this concept should be communicated to employees to develop a greater sense of belonging. The scheme applies equally in the following two fields.

Functional policy

A breakdown of principles for each function (based upon top policy) forms the next logical step, which is the responsibility of the appropriate senior executive, such as the sales manager, the works manager, or the development engineer.

Departmental policy

More detailed principles are formulated at this stage. This ensures that everyone who is much nearer to the actual operations works within more closely defined limits, with a correspondingly smaller chance of misunderstanding. Some flexibility is necessary so that principles form a guide rather than a hard–and–fast rule. Thus, departmental supervisors are actually policy-makers within their own sphere in this sense, and they are responsible for the effectiveness of such policies.

Managing change

Company survival generally depends both upon management's capability to exploit change and acceptance of change by employees. For this reason managers and employees must thoroughly understand change and its eventual advantages.

Change has no boundaries. If one nation refuses to exploit change for various reasons another nation immediately takes advantage. The result of resisting change on moral, political, social, and other grounds is often not fully appreciated. Sometimes however the result is understood when resistance is used to pull a country's economic performance down to levels that cause unrest and create political situations.

Clearly there is no point in producing unsaleable goods or providing unwanted services. Trying to improve employee performance in these circumstances is a waste of time. The aim must be to improve *worthwhile* employee performance.

Establishing the right climate

As an employee the manager plays many roles, including an economic resource, a professional, as part of a system of power and authority, and as a member of a social group. The roles – if properly conducted – help to establish a climate of trust and mutual understanding of the harsh reality of change and its implications. Unfortunately traditional views handed down from previous generations, the distribution of wealth, and educational levels all detract from managerial efforts.

One strong criticism often levelled at the British manager is that he or she seems to place less value on change, innovation and professionalism compared with the American counterpart. There are many other criticisms which also affect acceptance of change. Ten major topics over which a manager has influence are listed below and are well worth attention:

1   effective recruitment including sound selection techniques
2   removing nepotism and favouritism
3   abandoning the hierarchy of rights involving unfair perks and unearned financial gain
4   improving standards of behaviour by setting a good example
5   abandoning unsound political manœuvring involving political strategies with selfish aims
6   installing modern technologies to keep abreast of change
7   enforcing high ethical conduct with specific reference to sexual harassment and any unfair treatment
8   establishing sound career development programmes
9   sincerely supporting socialisation projects
10   creating mutual trust

Environmental influences

Finally the over-ride effect on productivity of internal and external environmental influences should be considered. They may cause managerial resistance which must be overcome by responding automatically to pressures and changes.

Managers should accept that their efforts will be affected by these influences which are a part of both the sociological structure and political life. In turn they will meet resistance from employees. This takes two forms: established resistance and current resistance. The ideal is to avoid resistance by adopting modern management already described, but this is a lengthy process.

Discouraging established resistance

First there are three major thrusts on which to concentrate; second consideration must be given to various counteraction techniques.

Major thrusts

The three requirements are familiarisation, feedback on views, and positive action. All three depend upon developing close relationships with employees.

1   *Familiarisation*   Spend time with employees and attempt to develop their awareness and understanding of change and its effects. Employees invariably misinterpret information they receive if they do not understand its implications to the company and themselves. Generally this means the change is treated as a threat.

2   *Feedback on views*   Obtain as much feedback as possible on employees' reactions to information. Careful analysis is essential to find out (a) why views are biased, (b) why more information and discussions were neglected if views are based on ignorance, and (c) the possible organisation difficulties.

3   *Positive action*   Recognise that discussion and passing information are inevitably insufficient. Generally negative views are based upon deeper organisational problems and poor managerial practices. These difficulties must be traced, analysed, and corrected as opportunities occur.

Counteraction techniques

Choosing the appropriate technique depends upon capability, the environmental situation, and the philosophy senior management is attempting to develop. Often all techniques may be seen operating in various parts of the company. Degrees of success are difficult to analyse.

Techniques tend to align with styles of leadership. Starting with abdication, the pattern develops to include autocratic or domineering rule, selling proposals by various forms of persuasion, consultation, and finally participation.

Avoiding resistance

Theoretically, the removal of all the threats and suspicions that appear in employees' minds solves the problem. Unfortunately managers are never in full control of all pressures that create threat and often wild pressures cause most of the problems. Much can be done, however, to minimise the effects and, in the case of controllable pressures, to avoid threat completely.

Application of sound management is obviously the answer. The main features strongly associated are:

- to examine the complexity of co-operation
- to create a better climate
- to discuss openly innovation and the risks if ignored
- to recognise the controversial aspects of change related to technology, culture and social structure
- to discuss possible industrial trends and their effects if ignored

The underlying difficulty

Adapting to changes often induces threats, typically risks of permanent and temporary unemployment. Admittedly establishing new industries and increased production eventually help as the economy improves. This is small consolation to those declared redundant especially in later stages of life, hence the importance of state social and welfare schemes.

Questions

1   What are the main differences between a manager and a supervisor?
2   Define the terms management team, supervisory team and business team.
3   Discuss the question of whether or not supervision is part of management.
4   Why is the supervisor's position in an organisation the subject of constant argument?
5   What are the main business activities encountered in industry?
6   What is the prime purpose of management?
7   Discuss the term 'managerial activities'.
8   Discuss the responsibilities of management to shareholders, to the community, and to the employee.
9   Carefully explain the term 'company policy' and state the essential requirements of a policy.
10   Describe the various fields of policy encountered in a business.
11   Discuss the four main functions encountered in a manufacturing concern.
12   Why is managing change essential in every company?
13   List ten topics which, in your opinion, managers should concentrate on to reduce employee distrust.
14   How would you attempt to reduce resistance to change from employees?

Case study

A college lecturer visited a company which had already sent all its supervisors on a part-time one year course over the past few years. Walking round the offices with the managing director and renewing acquaintances she was appalled to discover that no changes had taken place.

The obvious principles associated with ergonomics were still ignored. Simple faults such as bad lighting, poor layouts, no regard for motion economy, no safety provisions, and poor seating arrangements were still evident.

Remembering the excellent projects on work study that had been submitted by the supervisors there, she was puzzled and disappointed.

At the end of the visit she posed the usual question about recruitment and received the following reply from the managing director. 'No, I'm sorry, Madeleine, we're not sending our replacement supervisors on courses any more. As you know times are bad and we have to cut costs wherever possible. We look at every penny these days.'

Give the possible reasons for the training programme failing.

8 Principles and practice of management

Principles of management

All principles of management may be grouped to fit conveniently into seven main aspects of management activity. These are:

- forecasting
- planning
- organising
- co-ordinating
- commanding
- controlling
- motivating

L. Urwick published a logical arrangement of these principles in 1943, in his book *Elements of Administration*.

Forecasting and planning

These activities mean looking ahead and trying to visualise and plan effectively. Certain principles, now described, should be followed from the beginning to cut down the risks of inaccurate forecasting.

Research

Although the value of constant investigation is recognised and attempts are made to carry it out, in practice it becomes too difficult for lack of time. People who are 'pressurised' at work must make decisions, based upon less and less information, with the inevitable consequences. The sight of everyone working at high pitch pleases rather than bothers some managers. If managers are over-worked it is their own fault for not delegating, but there is a limit if top management restricts staff to smaller numbers than is really adequate. Some managers too are unable to assess work content accurately, even after research has been conducted and the information is presented to them.

The following minor principles should be intrinsic to any research.

1 *Cause and effect* A belief that effects can be traced back to particular

causes provides faith and perseverance in pursuing investigations back to sources.

2 *Comprehension*   The results must be measurable and in an understandable form for practical use in forecasting.

3 *Intelligent observation*   Studying an activity requires a certain degree of awareness and appropriate background knowledge before intelligent interpretation is possible.

4 *Recognition and analysis*   Following from intelligent observation, the recognition of similarities is essential for analysing the information and knowing how to proceed to the next stage of investigation.

Forecasting

Armed with sufficient information, the individual must now find a place where it is possible to think without undue distraction. Having found the most suitable place, there he or she must marshal thoughts logically and try to visualise or predict future happenings. Some people call this process intelligent guesswork, luck or being psychic.

Forecasting is often done with very little information in difficult circumstances, hence the phrase 'muddling through'. The unknown factor (the missing information) must be taken into account to maintain balance. Consider the serious punters who attempt to marshal as many facts as possible on the horses in a race. They take everything into consideration, including factors such as the weather and injuries, which make the results unpredictable with any accuracy in order to lessen the odds as much as possible.

The principles of good forecasting may be listed as follows:

- use of all sources of information
- maximum information in the time available
- surroundings conducive to thought
- the unknown factor

Planning

The next step is to determine the targets or objectives and plan a way of reaching these goals.

All industrial activities must be considered in the light of resources available so that plans will be realistic. The good planner will be thinking along lines of economy, which implies that his or her designs are simple, standardised and with due allowance for changes, and weighted dependent upon the importance of the plan. Scientific control is not possible unless a plan is based upon a time scale. Planning on this broad front means deciding *what* shall be done, *where, when, how* and *by whom*. It involves not only readjustment of objectives as new information flows in, but also revision of policies, programmes, budgets, systems, organisation and controls.

Top management's task is *strategic* planning of over-all policies, objectives, finance and control. This is implemented by managers or senior supervisors who are responsible for *tactical* planning of how the objectives are to be reached in the time given.

Supervisors then plan – on a short-term or medium-term basis – the actual achievement of broad plans by using the resources available. This is *process* planning and involves scheduling, progressing, controlling and motivating employees.

The fourth and final phase must logically end on the shop floor or office where employees plan their work (*task* planning) in order to complete the jobs allocated to them within the established time limits.

Organising and co-ordinating

Organising means arranging for everything to be at the right place, at the right time, so that work may proceed according to the plan. Co-ordinating means ensuring that all the formal activities of the concern are combined to form a balanced effective organisation.

The phases which lead to co-ordination are:

1 *planning*, which includes organisation design, or establishing the structure
2 *staffing*, which is completed under the aspect of command
3 *aligning everyone's efforts*, which is the eventual effect of co-ordination

When employees agree to co-operate, and naturally participate willingly, management will be able to co-ordinate successfully. An underlying condition is the ability to lead and motivate people. It is pointless, therefore, for management to complain that employees will not co-operate, when the solution is within its own hands to create the right conditions which encourage and promote co-operation.

Co-ordination is achieved if all the activities are arranged and adjusted in time and situation to ensure smooth economic running and progress towards objectives. Smooth economic operation is an all-embracing term which includes the absence of selfish interests, the balancing of units and adherence to plans.

The problem of balance begins with the co-ordination of main activities or functions by the managing director and continues through to the level of the supervisor who co-ordinates the activities of that section or department with other sections. Balance is made possible by allowing unrestricted input of both information and production assemblies from those who supply the section, and unrestricted output to the receiving sections in turn. If the chain of movement is broken, production is off balance and the co-ordinating effect ceases. In this sense co-ordinating is an intentional, active principle.

Commanding

Commanding (or directing) means giving orders and issuing instructions, *and* deciding when and how subordinates should carry out the work.

Maintaining command includes making decisions concerning priority treatment for jobs and ensuring that discipline is kept at a reasonable level consistent with good working arrangements. Effective leadership is essential for commanding and motivating.

Although organisation and co-ordination are discussed as one because all the principles of organisation are used to achieve co-ordination, in practice command must come between the two for the following reasons. When the design and planning stage is completed, the next step is to appoint competent staff to the positions drawn up in the organisation plan. Upon completion of staffing, when the individuals are assigned to their jobs and given appropriate duties, authority and responsibilities, they will immediately start to issue instructions. Command becomes operational at this point, and its effectiveness will depend upon the ability of managers and supervisors to raise morale by fair and just treatment and to lead in the right direction.

The guiding principles for achieving effective command are as follows.

Alignment of interest

All effort must be directed towards the general interest. Self-interest must take second place, otherwise command has failed.

Staffing

Appointing managers of the right calibre, consistent with company policy.

Morale

The acid test of command is unmistakably the general feeling of all employees, majority and minority groups, towards management and the concern. With so much ill-feeling and friction between the two sides, it takes courage and faith to carry out a long-term programme for morale improvement. A permanent change in management's attitude is essential, otherwise relationships will deteriorate rapidly again.

Adequate payments and appropriate penalties

Adequate payments for services and appropriate penalties for mistakes are two essential principles which should be second nature to the competent manager. Fairness and justice are essential to maintain a good reputation. Any attempt to show favour to one person results in antagonising the rest. Where it is humane to deviate from the rule, the reason must be made known, whenever possible, if the circumstances are not already common knowledge.

Active participation

People must be allowed to expand their capabilities by using their own initiative, criticising and making suggestions openly with no fear of a rebuff. In these conditions they feel more important and develop enthusiasm and drive in response to the progressive atmosphere. These five aspects are all discussed at length in Part Two.

Controlling

Checking performance and taking action to remedy deviations from the plan involves a constant vigil on all stages of the work and the costs incurred.

Effective control demands, *first*, full knowledge of the plans and instructions to proceed; *second*, accurate feedback on operations and results; *third*, a common measure to gauge the amount of deviation from the plan; and *fourth*, positive action to correct the deviations. This subject is detailed in Part Three.

Scientific control is not a haphazard affair; its operation is very demanding and cannot be switched on and off at random.

The board of directors is supplied with control information by the managing director to check on broad policy and programmes, generally from the financial viewpoint. Management accountancy techniques and all the financial control systems connected with them provide the machinery for control throughout the concern.

On the production side, information on labour, machines, materials, quality and output provides supervisors and specialists with control figures. Similarly, information on sales in cash and quantity and all the distribution expenses provides management with control statistics. All the information prepared must 'pay its way' by providing figures at an economic cost for some positive purpose.

Motivating

Each managerial activity is dependent upon all the others, hence the main difficulty of thinking about a particular one in isolation. Managing is a combined operation which demands a wide, balanced, human outlook, tempered with the use of a multitude of principles.

Probably motivation, the inner force which stirs people from lethargic attitudes into dynamic action, is the most neglected aspect of management. Half-hearted attempts to improve matters which are most often abandoned irritate and depress employees; they naturally fail to respond to fresh encouragement and the blame is nearly always laid unfairly on their heads.

Successful motivation of employees requires a complete change in the outlook of most managers who are either unenthusiastic or too cynical or set in their ways to change. Long-term programmes are needed, even though results are sometimes not seen for a few years, to overcome management's faults and misconceptions.

The strong tie between motivation and co-ordination is apparent when the principles involved are considered. These include: job enrichment programmes, constant communication to everyone of all relevant information concerning the business, encouragement of participation and self-discipline, ambitious education and training schemes, joint consultation, personnel counselling, fair schemes of pay, work, and welfare, and sincerity from management.

The skills cycle

Underlying and often permeating the principles described above are certain basic management skills which apply equally to supervisors. By appropriate training it is possible to improve these skills through the repetitive process of practice and adjustment. The development of each skill also depends upon the degree of education in certain disciplines or knowledge areas.

Naturally there is a tendency for the disciplines to overlap into more than one skill and in actual operation the dividing line between some of the skills becomes blurred. For the sake of clarity Fig. 8.1. indicates these skills in sector form to show the cycle effect which operates in a clockwise sequence when logical thought is applied to the work process in any situation. The diagram also indicates some ways of checking on the supervisor's performance as he or she develops. A confusing factor is that during the course of a working day the supervisor will have to cope with many situations and people, which means that a number of these cycles is in operation at any one time.

The diagram can also be used to break down certain principles into component skills; for example, the skills associated with control are to establish suitable standards, to check performance, and to make decisions to correct the deviations that occur. A further use is to locate operating faults; for example, the tendency for some supervisors is to think that so long as employees have been told what is required of them that is sufficient to provide the essential motivating factor. 'I told them what to do but they didn't do it' is a very common saying in industry. Two skills are in fact necessary: first, action to achieve the plan which is the communicating skill, followed by the motivating skill which will decide whether or not the employees will actually do anything although they may know what is required.

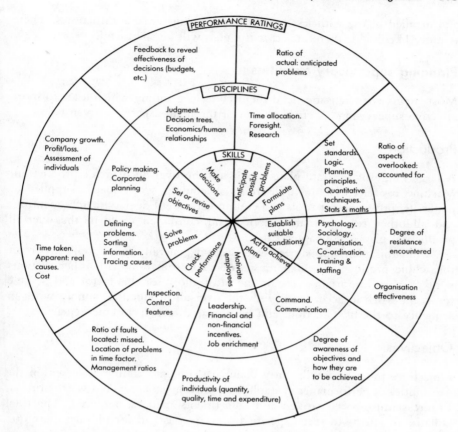

Fig. 8.1 The skills cycle

Note: This composite diagram is not intended to be complete. It represents certain areas of importance among which are many others not mentioned

Planning and the supervisor

Any person who controls a labour force, whether large or small, must plan ahead as far as can be foreseen. Employees expect to work to a set plan and schedule and be controlled in accordance with the plan and changing circumstances. Absence of planning produces chaos on the ground floor. Individuals work from crisis to crisis, frustration develops, and productivity is reduced to a minimum. Clearly the supervisor must allocate time for planning in sufficient detail to satisfy the requirements of subordinates and production. Time spent on planning is never wasted provided the supervisor is reasonably proficient at the task. The extra thought should result in more accurate and detailed plans, with less risk of overlooking possible difficulties. There is more likelihood, therefore, that the plan will be successful.

Planning supervisory activities

Most supervisory activities lend themselves to planning which leads to more effective supervision. A cross-section of the main aspects is given below.

Production

A large range of separate plans makes up the over-all plan for production. Machine capacity, labour utilisation, scheduling work loads, supplies of materials, provision for tools and equipment, safety devices, batch quantities and all other resources are planned and combined to form the over-all production plan (*see* Chapter 25).

Within this plan, the supervisor's section generally forms only a part of the whole production which means that co-ordination with other sections is of primary importance. He or she must allow for this factor and be able to accept work in accordance with the over-all production, supply work in sequence to the next section, and be prepared to help in emergencies.

Objectives

Objectives must be intelligently planned to fit into a time scale within the capabilities of performance. Establishing unrealistic targets is a waste of time. Progress must be controlled and adjustments made as required. The total collapse of efforts to reach specified objectives is bad for morale; therefore, planning with too much optimism should be avoided.

Control

Effective control does not happen by chance. A plan of the particular activity must be drawn up on a time, cost, quality or quantity basis, or some form of standard by which results can be measured. Variances from the plan are now apparent by reference to the data, and control is possible through taking appropriate corrective action (*see* Chapter 22). Planning and control must always be complementary.

Organisation

The importance of planning in connection with organisation has been stressed in Chapter 3. Haphazard growth, rigidity and disregard for organisation principles may be avoided with careful planning. Working towards the ideal organisation and making wise changes when the opportunities occur are made easier by conforming to a plan.

Work study

The introduction of work study can be made easier by planning a careful explanation to employees. The programme may include posters, literature, personal letters, films and introductory talks. Work study can be introduced with a minimum of disruption in this manner.

Planning the actual work to be studied may be based upon those sectors which are:

1 causing hold-ups
2 expensive to operate
3 trouble-spots
4 relatively high labour turnover areas, or
5 where an increase in output is contemplated. Further information is given in Chapters 23 and 24.

Communication

Communication may be improved with experience in running the particular section and a plan of methods, routes and check systems. Suitable improvements may be planned to eliminate weak spots. A simple plan would begin with an assessment of each communication between supervisor and subordinates, thus revealing its importance, the time factor, the cost and the confidentiality factor. It should then be possible to select the best means of communication for each kind of message from the methods available. The objective is to ensure that the right person receives the right message at the right time and interprets it in the right way. All aspects of communication are discussed in Chapters 14, 15 and 16.

The daily routine

Planning the way each day is to be spent is important. Certain daily tasks cannot be neglected and unless the supervisor plans the day, or week, the risk of some vital activity being overlooked is greater. Simple check-lists are useful reminders of daily and periodic tasks which may be easily forgotten. More elaborate activities which extend over long periods may be charted on the wall by using a time base across the top of a sheet and an activity base down the left-hand side to form a grid. Each square may be either ticked or used to enter details if on a larger scale. Pending jobs may be similarly progressed or listed, a pending tray or file being used for the paperwork.

In conjunction with delegation the supervisor should plan to off-load duties as the opportunities occur and use the freed time for more important tasks which have been rather neglected.

Health and safety

Reducing the accident rate and promoting health depend upon detailed planning by management and the supervisor. Planning for safety is an integral part of reducing accidents to a minimum by making machinery and equipment less hazardous and promoting the right attitudes towards safety. The supervisor's social responsibility cannot be fulfilled unless he or she plans to prevent accidents rather than wait for them to happen and then reduce the risk. Chapters 20 and 21 deal with health and safety and welfare respectively.

Maintenance

Planned maintenance is similar in some ways to planned safety. Time and cost may be cut by planning the maintenance of machines to reduce the risk of breakdown. Replacing those components and assemblies whose life is limited before the breakdown occurs ensures smooth output flow. Maintenance is discussed as an aspect of cost reduction in Chapter 29.

Training

Training must be treated seriously as a planned activity to improve productivity by introducing better methods and safer ways of working with less fatigue and frustration. Planned training includes induction training schemes, training employees for new machines as obsolescent models are superseded, training newcomers at weak points where hold-ups are occurring or are likely to occur, and making hazardous operations safer by increasing the skill of the employee (*see* Chapter 18).

Motivation

All that was said above regarding management and motivation applies at supervisory level also. All factors which affect motivation closely interact; therefore, the approach must be on a broad front so that employees can develop their capabilities and enthusiasm simultaneously. The plan must be long-term and sustained in application. New techniques of leadership and supervision, group activity, organisation, human relations and job satisfaction are essentially long-term projects and have a sustained effect whereas financial incentives are short-term and often short-lived as motivators (*see* Chapters 11, 12 and 13).

Human relations

The supervisor who plans successfully also improves relationships with subordinates. They have more faith in a leader who defines objectives, plans carefully, and shows command of the situation. Morale will rise as schemes materialise, and employees benefit by effective plans (*see* Chapters 9 and 10).

The above-mentioned topics are only an indication of the many activities which must be planned by the supervisor. Savings in time and nervous energy are possible by planning any activity. Some guides to better planning are now given, together with the characteristics of a sound plan.

Guides to better planning

1 Planning must not be postponed. Planning is hard work but, without plans, work becomes much harder.

2 Planning must not be selfish. The part played by the section within the organisation must be remembered; therefore, co-operative and co-ordinate elements are essential in plans.

3 Always plan within a time scale. Effective control depends upon measurement of work or a project within a period and, furthermore, employees tend to work within periods related to output, which means they work to time targets.

4 Marshal as much information as possible on employees, machines, equipment, materials and other resources. Use up-to-date information and all resources available.

5 Aim to provide as much detail as possible. There is less chance of overlooking important points and more chance of work proceeding to plan with thorough coverage.

6 Ask for opinions and ideas. Many individuals have something to contribute towards a sound plan; therefore, ask now and avoid adverse criticisms later.

7 Define the problem or objective clearly before planning commences. Look at the whole project and break it down into its constituent parts to ensure full coverage and to provide a working scheme.

8 A sound, workable and economic plan is the outcome of something more than logical marshalling of information into a set routine. Certain intangible qualities must be cudgelled into activity within the supervisor's mind. He must be imaginative and creative, exercise judgment and perception in his ideas, and yet retain an objective, critical approach to the problem.

9 Have the courage to stand by the plan.

10 Check and revise the plan as circumstances change.

The following are ten characteristics of a sound plan:

- Economic, within the financial capabilities of the concern
- Workable, considering the resources available
- Thorough, allowing for most contingencies
- Balanced, to blend with other plans

- Resilient, to cope with unforeseen changes
- Worthwhile, fulfils a desirable purpose
- Attractive, creates interest among all who are concerned
- Detailed, to establish adequate procedures
- Timely, to obtain maximum benefit
- Impersonal, avoids personal prejudices

Problem-solving

Problems and choices are met in all supervisory and managerial activities and must be dealt with, reputations being built or ruined on individual performance. The supervisors often automatically establish standards for a vast number of control aspects connected with problem-solving without fully realising the implications to their subordinates. Human behaviour is a typical example where the supervisors expect a particular code of conduct in many different situations. They are faced with a problem when a standard is violated and if they fail to investigate, find the cause and make a decision, control is lost.

Unfortunately problems do not solve themselves effectively, although some managers will openly admit their belief that if a problem is left for a sufficient length of time it will solve itself. Such managers have not bothered to check on the results of this negative approach which ultimately brands them as ineffectual. A positive approach to problems is essential.

Employees also apply their own standards to many aspects connected with their job. One operator, for example, may switch off a machine immediately a fault is suspected, whereas another may wait until a more obvious sign appears. This range of standards among individuals becomes important from the problem-solving aspect. One operator, for instance, may report that a machine failed to start when switched on, whereas another may state that when the machine was switched on a smell of burning was noticed. Careful definition of the problem in the latter case immediately narrows down the cause of the fault.

The use of standards – in a broad sense – for gathering information should not be ignored. The approach to obtaining the facts as they appear should be made on a basis of comparison to find a common factor or an isolating component within that factor. A line of machines, for instance, may be powered from the same electricity point; if one machine suddenly ceases to run, the fault may be isolated to a particular section if the basis of comparison is applied by stating whether or not the other machines continue to run. Investigating a problem in this way helps to isolate areas quickly where the cause is likely to be found.

The use of standard practice or standard 'set-ups' is common to many facets of industrial activity. Some examples are the following.

1 *The use of raw materials in batches* If faulty work appears it may be isolated to a particular batch which is below standard.

2 *Planned maintenance programmes* When a machine develops a fault it may be possible to trace it from the last maintenance job.

3 *Shift work* A mistake may be isolated to a particular shift or time coinciding with the changeover from one shift to another.

To summarise: problems must be actively solved; the art of recognising and carefully defining problems must be developed; the causes of faults may be more effectively located by looking for common factors and isolating the unusual aspects within those factors, thus tracking down the trouble by a logical step-by-step approach.

Intuition

This apparently simple, rapid method is essential to cope with common daily problems. The cause is often immediately apparent, thus simple and complex problems may be solved effectively in this manner by the experienced supervisor. The obvious danger lies in not appreciating the whole problem through lack of experience and knowledge, and jumping to conclusions. Automatic problem-solving of this nature can also be dangerous when a recurring problem, normally having a standard cause, suddenly occurs through a new cause not foreseen at the time. Nevertheless, full use of this method is essential considering the time-factor.

Analytical thinking

To avoid the dangers of intuitive thinking, logical deduction is often used. The approach is to arrive at an indisputable solution by counting from known factual information. Thus there must be one unique answer which is predictable and the assumption is that the problem has only one solution. For example, if 240 working hours were lost in the typing pool last month, 25 per cent of which were due to absenteeism and 10 per cent through sickness, the answer in hours is 60 and 24 respectively. However, if the question is how to cut down the high absenteeism rate, there are many answers and imagination is needed which is a *creative problem*.

Creative thinking

If things or ideas which were previously unrelated now *have* to be related to arrive at an answer, the individual must use creative thought. To improve creativity there are various training schemes and techniques that may be applied. A popular method is 'lateral thinking' which was developed by E. de Bono (*see* below and Bibliography).

Group discussion

The use of groups for creative thinking was developed in the 1930s. The techniques generally conform to a number of basic concepts which concentrate on breaking down the inhibiting barriers to creativity. Typical examples are: to suspend judgment on other peoples' ideas; to allow everyone to 'free-wheel' so that any ideas – regardless of whether they make sense – are proposed; to produce as many ideas as possible; and to cross-fertilise all the ideas to see if something new emerges. The main barriers are a tendency to think there is only one answer, to restrict thinking within a narrow self-imposed framework, to give answers that sound reasonable, to allow the obvious statements to go unchallenged, and to worry too much about looking a fool.

Brain storming

To stimulate creative thinking this technique is often used. It is based upon the idea associated with value analysis (*see* Chapter 26) and is a way of extracting a large number of ideas from the group in a short time.

A successful session depends upon the capability of the group leader, the experience of the group and the use of the basic concepts mentioned above in group discussion.

The technique is easily adapted to most problems and, apart from creative thinking, is useful to develop interpersonal relationships.

Lateral thinking

This system already mentioned above is designed to escape from vertical thinking (habitual mind patterns) and move into lateral thinking. By using various techniques which are associated with challenging preconceptions and rejecting yes/no thinking it is very easy to convert people into a new way of thinking creatively.

The system has achieved world-wide success but it is essential to read E. de Bono's book, Lateral Thinking (1980), first.

Synectics

This series of techniques in imaginative problem-solving is complex and really should be practised with the aid of authorised practitioners. The body of knowledge is considerable as the techniques have developed over a long period. They include 'right-brain' thinking and sophisticated group behaviour.

Morphological analysis

This form of creativity is based upon the use of a series of dimensions which are examined in relation to each other and to the possible elements within each dimension.

The analysis is complicated and demands a considerable amount of preparation. A typical example is to use two dimensions; products and markets. Elements for each dimension are listed and combinations are established to trigger off ideas.

Logical approach

A logical approach to problem-solving, already discussed (p. 120), may be established as follows.

1   *Set standards*   Establish standards for as many activities as possible. In other words, set your sights.

2   *Measure activities*   Measure actual results against established standards to highlight deviations.

3   *Assess deviations*   A deviation may be favourable or adverse:

(a) *Favourable*: this is a situation (not a problem); nevertheless, the cause should be traced and identified for revising standards and increasing effectiveness.

(b) *Adverse*: this is a problem which is detrimental to the plan. The cause must be located and decisions made.

4   *Carefully define the problem*   A complete detailed description of the problem is essential.

5   *Investigate*:

(a) Judge the time-factor. The supervisor generally has to work within a time scale.

(b) Search for information. Haphazard, intermittent fact-finding is unsatisfactory, but often inevitable. Try to build up a system so that information flows in as a continuous process.

(c) Learn to distinguish between facts, inferences and value judgments.

When assessing information, the source and the number of mouths it has passed through are of prime importance. The reliability of the source and the distortion factor – as information passes from one person to the next – cannot be ignored. The well-known game of making up a sentence and passing it round in a group of, say, ten people often produces bewildering results bearing no relationship to the original sentence. The only sure way to be certain of a fact is to see it for yourself; unfortunately there is seldom time, and also it is impracticable in many instances.

A further confusing point is the inability of some people to distinguish between facts, inferences and value judgements. Each one has its usefulness but the danger lies in mistaking one for another. Here is a typical example of the three: two people decide to walk from A to B along a street which is often very congested with traffic. The lamp-posts are a standard distance apart and as the two people walk at a set pace, one takes the time between two lamp-posts and calculates their speed as, for example, two and a half mph. This is a *fact*. From the calculated speed a further reckoning indicates that they should arrive at B five minutes earlier than they intended. This is an *inference* because any number of situations may arise which will affect their estimated time of arrival and therefore it is a conclusion or deduction from a given fact. One then says to the other, 'It is quicker to walk along this road these days because the traffic is so congested.' This is a *value judgment* because it is an *opinion* based upon a series of events over a period but not accurately measured or analysed.

6   *Analyse and establish the cause*   Draw up a detailed analysis from the information available. Look for indications leading to the source and establish the cause, thus solving the problem. Successful elimination of the cause or avoiding a recurrence depends upon making a correct decision.

Decision-making

Making decisions involves the consideration of a number of conflicting factors such as the objective, degree of ruthlessness necessary, humane treatment of people, cost and effectiveness. The supervisor's reputation is directly affected by the ability to weigh these standards sensibly. The choice is tempered also by two conflicting groups, his or her superiors and subordinates.

One method of making decisions is to use a logical approach by placing each standard in priority sequence. The natural priority is to establish and reach the objective. Having stated this the next priority may be the cost. Assessment is mainly intelligent guesswork based upon considering the courses of action and weighing their probable effect on individuals, general effectiveness and the inevitable undesirable results.

Establishing priorities is a personal matter in which good sense is essential. Choice of decision must depend, to some extent, on morale and the prevailing industrial atmosphere. Ruthless decisions which cause a deterioration in relationships indicate the inadequacy of the supervisor to appreciate hidden costs and the intangible effects of causing frustration.

To complete the cycle of events, new standards must be set to check the effectiveness of the decision, so that variances may be seen and any new problems brought to light for further action.

A logical approach to decision-making may therefore be summarised as follows:

1   Aim to reach the objective.
2   Consider various courses of action.
3   Weigh the factors involved, e.g. individuals, cost, undesirable after-effects, morale, etc.

4 Choose a course of action.
5 Set standards to check after-effects.
6 Follow up and revise if necessary.

Management/supervisor relations

Extra pressures and demands on managers

The qualities needed in a manager are similar in nature to those needed in
a supervisor, but developed to a greater degree because of the manager's
more demanding position. Increasing emphasis is placed on creativeness and
vision as the top of the hierarchy is approached. The burden of responsibility
increases and causes heavier demands on vitality and mental qualities.
Personality becomes more important. People expect a higher standard of
leadership which means a higher standard of conduct and manners, greater
self-confidence and a balanced temperament, together with drive and
strength of character.

High ability is needed to assimilate and put into practice all managerial and
technical knowledge. Good sense in using that knowledge and hard work
are the key factors, in addition to intelligence. The mental and physical strain
of working under the pressure of indeterminable problems and risks is
wearing on the strongest manager. Being in the limelight is not only
rewarding, but also nerve-racking.

Good managers must be ambitious and possess considerable understanding
of people and the world around. They must create the right image and
consistently apply themselves to the job. Such devotion cannot be achieved
by a façade of qualities. Deep sincerity is essential because employees are not
easily deceived. Managers should be judged by results in the short- and long-
term. This highlights the method of achieving results and pin-points the
manager of high calibre.

Present state of management

In the absence of any large-scale surveys, the characteristics of a manager are
discussed from the viewpoint of popular belief. Education is very important
because of the part it plays in creating a good impression, attaining higher
qualifications, and indicating ability. Unfortunately this factor does not take
into account leadership, application to work, balanced personality and experience. Thus, some employees have to suffer under the 'raw' graduate from
university who is placed in a managerial position by virtue of a degree alone.

Buying the right education helps considerably; a public school background
seems to be high on the list of desirable requirements in selection procedures
as it ensures that the prospective manager will not be 'out of place', but of
the 'right type'. A good social background or good family are considered

essential. Furthermore, with some jobs even the prospect's spouse is inter-viewed to assess whether or not he or she will be able to 'mix'.

Naturally, the ideal types will emerge from graduates who possess the additional essential qualities. These outstanding people rapidly rise towards the top; nothing holds them back.

There is also the 'late starter' group, which includes those who fail to reach university and those who do not even reach grammar school level. The handicap of misfortune or late development is eventually overcome through intense drive and a certain amount of luck.

Another characteristic which is not desirable but often seen is the ruth-lessness of the person who manages to disregard certain codes of conduct to achieve a position. This unhappy state in a company is not always a one-sided affair; higher management seems to encourage it, possibly uninten-tionally at times.

A glutton for work is a characteristic which highlights a person im-mediately. Such people seem to attract work and successfully get through a tremendous amount in a short time. They are not necessarily extra bright, but make up for this by using common sense and working at high speed over long periods.

Finally there is the inescapable characteristic of nepotism which is extended here to include friends as well as relatives. Possibly this tendency is so strong because of the misguided idea that a person's loyalty will be with the one who gives him or her the opportunity. There may also be feelings of inse-curity which are eased when friends are nearby for support and encouragement.

From this short résumé of qualities and characteristics it is immediately apparent to those who are directly connected with industry that a shortage of suitably qualified managers exists. Demand is increasing for managers possessing higher qualifications in management skills and more courses for this purpose are becoming available every year.

The present situation is as if someone who cannot read music is conducting an orchestra and expecting the musicians to read music and play well, even though he or she lacks this essential requirement. The resulting discord is easily imagined. There are exceptions, however, in business as in the artistic field, where innate ability and experience compensate for lack of training.

Making allowances for managers

To avoid frustration the supervisor must make allowances for managers. Allowing some latitude for subordinates is easy, mainly because a higher standard is not expected of them, but individuals automatically expect a higher performance from superiors.

In practice it does not always work out that way. Superiors, who are also human beings, have many faults and probably they think that the supervisor acts rather strangely at times too. A sympathetic approach demands culti-vation and an understanding of the problems faced by superiors.

Many managers are untrained. A few have a flair for managing, others may be highly intelligent, but something more than ability is required when dealing with people.

When a properly trained supervisor returns to the workplace to continue operating under an untrained manager he or she will no doubt receive anything but a warm reception. The situation will not return to normal in these circumstances because the supervisor has undergone a change. Instead, frustration will increase. Expanded to national proportions the idea of training supervisors in large numbers, but not managers, is inviting a large pressure group to form with possible disastrous consequences.

The supervisor must not be surprised to receive a negative reaction to a perfectly sound idea. The manager feels rather silly because he or she did not think of it first and responds in the opposite way by displaying indifference, trying to shrug off the idea as unimportant. Probably a few weeks (or months) later, the manager will suddenly mention the same idea as if it were his or her own and expect the supervisor to put it into practice immediately.

Rudeness and offhand treatment by managers must also be expected. Often this form of abuse is due to the manager's complete confusion, lack of ability, or no knowledge of how to deal with a particular situation. Resorting to rudeness is the easy way out, in the short run, amply demonstrating inadequacy and lack of human approach. Bearing such indignities gracefully is difficult; nevertheless, a mature person must be tolerant of others and able to accept conditions as they exist, helping to alter them by example.

The ruthless manager invariably is unaware of other more humane ways of solving problems. Often this type has tremendous drive and when they finally realise that the hidden results of their ruthlessness will offset their achievements unless they modify their ways, they become an asset to the concern.

The supervisor should not expect managers to know everything; they definitely will not, and it is unfair to expect such a high standard from them. They have limitations, make mistakes and suffer embarrassment which they often attempt to hide unsuccessfully. This applies particularly to young managers who suffer with feelings of nervousness, apprehension or, in some cases, over-confidence and elation through experiencing a new sense of power. Without training the process of improvement is long and, of course, some never change.

Some managers have difficulty in facing reality. To achieve an object they resort to various subtle (or so-called subtle) techniques which, in fact, anyone can see through. Consider, for example, trying to force an individual to leave. The farce may begin with silence from the manager. The general pleasantries such as 'good morning' are stopped. The individual's work is by-passed, and some work is passed to other people to create disturbances.

Such practices are not only childish and disrupt the efficiency of the organisation, but are also likely to place the superior in a humiliating position of liability under the unfair dismissal provisions of the Employment Protection (Consolidation) Act 1978. In these circumstances, 'constructive dismissal' might arise when all the facts are considered concerning the manager's 'nit-picking' attitude towards the employee if the employee 'resigns' or walks out for this reason. Whether or not constructive dismissal can be established would be a matter of degree.

Questions

1 How can a supervisor delegate and still retain effective leadership?
2 Outline the various phases of planning.
3 Why does the supervisor have to make allowances for management?
4 Discuss fully any two principles of management.
5 Describe the activities of forecasting and planning.
6 What supervisory activities lend themselves to planning?
7 Advise a new supervisor how to plan effectively.
8 What are the characteristics of a sound plan?
9 Outline the main principles of a command.
10 If you had the opportunity to participate in the selection of a manager what qualities would you make sure he or she possessed?
11 Why is decision-making so important in supervision?
12 Outline briefly the practical steps which are essential in decision-making.
13 Describe the principles you would bear in mind when conducting research.
14 Discuss the phases which lead to successful co-ordination.
15 What are the essential requirements for effective control?
16 Outline a logical approach to problem-solving.
17 What are the main basic management skills?
18 Discuss the skills cycle and how it operates in practice.

Case study

Laura's manager had the habit of walking around her office and speaking with the word processor operators as they were working. Laura had been a supervisor for three months and was still uncertain of herself. One morning after one of these casual inspections she walked around the office and was infuriated to see that Adrian, one of her best operators, was working on material which had nothing to do with his job.

'What's the idea? We don't allow private work – you know that. Pack it up at once!'

Adrian was livid. 'I'm fed up with this dump. First the boss comes round and says "type this for me", now you tell me to pack it up. This is the third time I've typed things for him!'

Laura was taken aback but recovered quickly. 'I'm sorry, Adrian, I had no idea. Leave the typing with me.'

Adrian immediately calmed down and duly handed over the work.

Now that Laura was committed what choices are open to her?

Part 1: Suggested projects

1   Attempt to assess the productivity level in your establishment by surveying the main aspects which affect this topic.

Draw up a list and write an account of the prevailing conditions under each aspect.

Make recommendations for improving the situation.

2   Conduct a survey on the organisation of the Production Department in your concern and suggest suitable improvements. A diagram is required of the existing organisation and the proposed organisation. Tabulate the principles which you consider are misapplied, the proposed changes, and the human problems which are likely to occur during the changeover.

3   Conduct a detailed survey on the authority, responsibilities and duties of two managers and two supervisors in your concern.

Attempt to assess the main differences between management and supervision by conducting your investigation within a framework suitable for this purpose.

Draw up a suitable documentation of your findings and give a careful, detailed opinion of the main differences between the managers' and supervisors' jobs under investigation.

4   Conduct a survey on how supervisors or managers make decisions. The co-operation and assistance of individual superiors will be necessary in preparing a detailed report on the procedure they adopt in varying circumstances to arrive at decisions.

Attempt to tabulate your findings in logical sequence and grouped under various methods. Give an account of your conclusions and recommendations.

5   Trace the price alterations of products in your concern and attempt to find out why the changes were introduced.

Tabulate the price changes and dates and list the possible causes for each change, together with any explanations and your findings.

Attempt to draw conclusions from your investigation.

6   Study the organisation of the stores, including the layout, stores control system and the efficiency of the service. Attempt to plan improvements considering the economic factors involved.

7   Trace the growth of your company over the past thirty years and attempt to discover the main causes of the pattern produced.

Part Two   Creating an Effective Working Force

9   Trying to understand people

The individual

A person's behaviour is unique in any situation. However a supervisor armed with more knowledge about people and with skills development will be able to diagnose and forecast more accurately such behaviour.

Observation of any individual in employment or elsewhere raises many questions which often remain unanswered regardless of effort or study. Certainly extensive but incomplete knowledge on people exists. But their origin remains a mystery and even the reason for their existence is only vaguely guessed – if there is a reason.

Behavioural science

This broad term covers many disciplines which include psychology, sociology and anthropology. Although scientific method is used there remain methodological and validity problems. Concepts are often contested and abandoned as research continues; completely valid theories are not available at present.

The main areas of interest for supervisors are:

- Basic physiological behaviour – limited here to homeostasis, recognition of the individual, and the brain
- Dealing with individual variations
- Recognising mental features associated with personality, characteristics, the distribution curve, and attitudes
- Examining basic mental processes – perception, mental levels and mental experience
- Studying the effects of the working environment on people

- Examining how a person functions within the restrictions of an organisation

Basic physiological behaviour

Three aspects of major interest are now discussed.

Homeostasis

The human body is an open-system (*see* Chapter 3), meaning it is continually subjected to the changing external environment. Controlling these changes internally is called homeostasis which buffers and neutralises through biophysical and biochemical processes.

This control process, often called the *systems approach*, is the basis for modern organisation theory, new management practices, modern economics, and cybernetics. It is related to the individual (homeostasis) and the organisation (open-system approach). The organisation cannot come to life without people who obviously have an impact; it can survive without particular individuals; and adaptations are possible by changing people's roles to overcome setbacks.

Recognition of the individual

One glance at a person is usually sufficient to register the fact that he or she is slightly different from other people. But what is far more important than this visual difference is that each person thinks and reacts slightly differently from others in similar situations. People have inherited and developed certain mental qualities and feelings which make them individuals and therefore an employee requires individual treatment if the right relationship is to be built up between him or herself and the supervisor.

First, true recognition of an individual involves knowing many facets of his or her nature which are difficult to perceive at the workplace.

Only one side of the person is seen, whereas in fact there will be many additional outside interests which affect his or her outlook. Family ties, religion, politics, hobbies and sports all influence the person's general attitude. There is also an unlimited range of traits in people, such as greed, dishonesty, kindness, carelessness, perseverance and patience. Everyone is subjected to many pressures which often confuse and trouble. This may lead to distorted thinking and a tendency to keep other people at a distance. This effect is similar to speaking into a microphone with the switch turned off.

Sympathetic observation and treatment help to reduce the mental barriers, although not many people will allow someone to get too close; hence the so-called 'mask' is always worn which conceals an individual's true feelings in daily contact with others.

Second, true recognition of the individual means treating him or her with respect.

Unless the supervisor believes in people and has a genuine regard for their feelings, their points of view and their potential, he or she will fail to convey this sense of respect. Fair treatment given in a friendly manner does not amount to grovelling or fawning over subordinates. Diplomacy costs nothing, but it has a tremendous impression on employees. Everyone is sensitive to injustice, bullying and offhand treatment. The reaction, whether it be active or passive, is inevitable, and both parties are the losers in the long run.

The human brain

The brain seems to possess an infinite capacity to assimilate information: it constantly seeks data during consciousness, clarifying and tabulating it for future use. This peculiarity coupled with capability form a natural function to acquire knowledge and to use it effectively – if given the opportunity and the right conditions.

This learning process develops a vast range of skills by using various muscles and nervous systems. Such a valuable tendency is often overlooked.

A further aspect is the absurd way the brain will arrive at reciprocal answers unless the individual learns appropriate disciplines and carefully checks. Examples are bragging to impress; shouting to make a point; and grossly exaggerating. Generally they have the opposite effect on individuals who are subjected to these faulty techniques.

Individual variation

Differential psychology concentrates on this aspect by studying stages of growth and intelligence. The aims are to find better ways of measuring the strength of traits so that people may be educated and trained more effectively and are given more appropriate jobs.

Stages of growth

What happens in the very early stages of life governs attitudes to some extent, traits, character, and general outlook. This forms the basis of the well-known saying that people are victims of their environment, and of the view that environmental and educational problems are the responsibility of the community.

Basic attitudes are formed in the first five years. Habits are established and attitudes develop towards parents and other close relatives. These attitudes tend to become models which are used in dealing with people. If attitudes work successfully for the child they gradually become traits which are the core of his or her personality. Examples are aggressiveness, gentleness, greediness, independence, capability, business, noisiness, and cruelty.

Complex phases occur in the sixth and subsequent years. Conscience, personality, repression of emotions, and other features continue to develop.

Intelligence

Three typical meanings are mental ability, quickness of understanding, and capacity to use intellect effectively. Alternatively intelligence means utilising the mental processes of thinking, appreciating, learning, observing, reasoning or problem solving, and perception.

Flair in the successful performance of some tasks such as playing a musical instrument, mechanical aptitude, and public speaking, is a further consideration. Perhaps common sense is also a flair as it involves a certain sensitivity towards the feelings of people, the human race, and the community. Some people possess so-called high intelligence but they seem to lack sound common sense.

Recognising mental features

Substantial knowledge and experience of mental features are essential before a supervisor can accurately note behaviour and analyse findings. Suitable allowances for employees have to be made when they behave in certain ways which do not coincide with their personality or attitude. The supervisor should avoid categorising people based upon his or her own particular values, outlook, likes, dislikes and shortcomings.

The first step in developing recognition skill is to study personality, human characteristics and attitudes.

Personality

Simply described the term is a collection of attributes observed in the individual. Each one varies in strength and is seen as a habit or mode of behaviour. These habit patterns develop in sequence with maturity and are seen as responses to various stimuli.

Any definition includes certain features. First, a person behaves in a consistent and enduring way from situation to situation. Consequently behaviour is predictable in certain situations: if shy today he or she will probably be shy tomorrow. Second, there seems to be a system operating which produces a style of behaviour. Third, each person is unique in his or her behaviour pattern.

Clearly people are predictable in some situations, unpredictable in other ways, undergo change as they develop and continually gain experience.

Human characteristics

Many peculiarities in people fail to match and form a set pattern. Changes are noticed in some while others remain apparently unchanged. Some act like sheep while others are intensely strong-willed and independent.

On the one hand the whole race seems to be very good at killing each other, standing by while others starve, behaving indifferently towards torture and discomfort of others, and lusting for power. On the other hand the human race seems to be moving gradually forward towards higher ideals, a more responsible approach and more consideration for humankind.

Other noticeable features are many likes and dislikes, a wide range of hobbies and ideas, inability to think clearly, faith in the unknown, inability to recognise happiness until later when it is gone, and strong support for whatever they help to create.

The distribution of human differences

If any one physical characteristic of people is measured and plotted on a graph, provided the sample is sufficient, a symmetrical, bell-shaped curve will be drawn, as in Fig. 9.1.

A similar distribution also exists in the hidden and more basic characteristics of people such as desires, ability and disposition. These are exceptionally difficult to measure and considerable training and experience is needed before reasonable assessment is possible. Most people have realised their mistakes later when they have formed strong first impressions of a stranger.

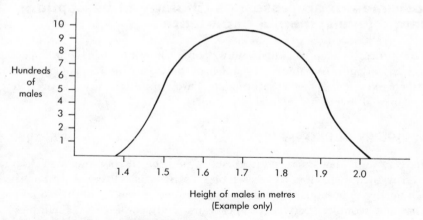

Height of males in metres
(Example only)

Fig. 9.1 *Distribution of human differences*

Distribution curves are normally bell-shaped, since most of the data fall around the average. This is particularly so with natural statistics, e.g. more people are of approximately average intelligence (or height, etc.) than are very far above or far below average

Keeping an open mind and continually observing the person is very necessary to achieve a true evaluation. As opportunities occur for people to demonstrate their particular skills and natural abilities their individual characteristics gradually appear. The supervisor should make sure that such opportunities do occur.

Attitudes

As a concept, attitude is abstract with no generally accepted definition. Certainly it is a form of settled behaviour, a means of indicating opinion, and a settled mode of thinking.

Often three components are stressed:

1 *intention* to act
2 *beliefs* trust or confidence in information being true
3 *values* qualities to be considered as good or bad

These could amount to belief or disbelief, positive or negative feelings, and a tendency to behave in a particular way.

The assumption that attitude tends to lead to behaviour has been strongly contended. According to D. J. Bem in 1970 the opposite applies: behaviour tends to lead to attitude. This idea has led to many motivation theories. Managers tend to blame attitude when employees refuse to conform to their requirements, but obviously attitude is not the only factor that governs behaviour.

Basic mental processes: psychology of perception; mental levels; mental experience

These processes help to explain why people sometimes behave in apparently illogical and unreasonable ways and how they are able to provide meaning to their experiences and environment. Three important features are perception, mental levels and mental experience.

Psychology of perception

The way individuals perceive themselves and the surrounding world largely governs their behaviour. One set of sensations is perceived differently by each person. Consequently this variation in perception creates personal problems and conflict between supervisors and employees. Examples are communicating difficulties; and judging, training, motivating, and assessing performance of employees.

People select, analyse and interpret stimulations from their senses into a framework or picture of the outside environment. The whole process is influenced by their expectations, their needs and incentives offered. A compromise exists between what can be seen and what an individual is conditioned to see, will see, or will avoid seeing. Therefore perception provides a unique interpretation of a situation, not an exact recording or registration.

Sensation and perception

All knowledge accumulated by a person depends upon the senses and their stimulation which are then subjected to perception. These physical senses are hearing, seeing, touching, smelling and tasting; plus so-called sixth senses such as extra-sensory perception.

Perceptual organisation

The perceptual process on receipt of selected data involves many principles. One important feature is given below.

GROUPING
Stimuli are grouped together into a distinct pattern or framework by using the principles of similarity, proximity, continuity, or closure.

1 *Similarity* If stimuli have something in common they tend to couple together into a group. Typical examples are blue-collar workers although each one is different, all shop stewards categorised as a nuisance, and all sales representatives thought of as extroverts.

2 *Proximity* If members of a group are in close proximity to each other they tend to be perceived as belonging together in terms of a characteristic. Examples are: first, a group of sewing machinists in one room may be perceived as all being antagonistic if some of them constantly complain about working conditions; and second, a group of senior secretaries working together in one large office may all be considered as snooty although only two out of six actually are.

3 *Closure* This *Gestalt* principle causes a person to perceive a whole when actually there are gaps and the whole is non-existent. Typically, at a meeting the supervisor may think he or she has complete agreement on a topic whereas in fact there is some opposition.

The cycles

Figure 9.2 shows the operation of two cycles associated with the perceptual process and external observable processes. The first cycle shows the internal data processing activity (perception). The second cycle includes perception and external observable processes: commencing with stimuli and cycling through the perceptual process, resultant behaviour, outcomes, and ending at stimuli.

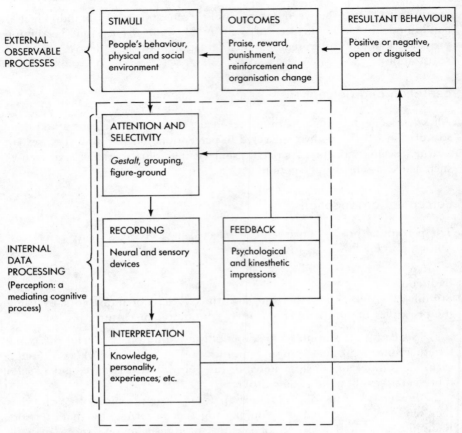

Fig. 9.2 *The perceptual process and external effects*

Two cycles are evident. First, an internal mediating cognitive process (perception); second, an external process starting with stimuli, utilising perception, continuing with behaviour and outcomes, and returning to stimuli

Note the way perception eventually changes stimuli when outcomes impinge on them, consequently presenting a new situation for the perceptual process. A complex series of cause–effect relationships exists.

The perceptual process

Perceptually the process may be divided into four components which form a cycle: attention and selectivity; recording; interpretation; and feedback to clarify and assist perception. These are within the dotted area in Fig. 9.2.

1   *Attention and selectivity*   Initially the person is surrounded by a situation probably including people and many environmental conditions. He or she chooses a feature to concentrate on but may be forced to switch to another

if a change occurs. Examples are: (a) a row develops between a supervisor and an employee outside a manager's office forcing the manager to intervene; (b) the internal telephone rings during a discussion with an employee.

2 *Recording* Sensory and neural devices register the data in preparation for analysis and interpretation.

3 *Interpretation* Neural mechanisms interpret the situation. These are biased by many personal characteristics, for example, personality, knowledge, intelligence, experience, and motivation.

4 *Feedback* Coupling between this and the first component allows for correction of queries on first impressions and feeds stimuli back which are of use to the perceptual process relating to reality. Kinesthetic mechanisms assist in perceiving a dynamic situation requiring rapid adjustment and psychological mechanisms attempt to determine people's intention. Examples are: judging the speed of an oncoming car when deciding to overtake; assessing a manager's mood, or sensing when he or she is joking.

External observable processes

Surrounding the perceptual process is external reality which for this purpose consists of three processes (*see* Fig. 9.2). The first is stimuli – entering the perceptual process – from which attention occurs. The second is resultant behaviour emerging from the perceptual process. The third is outcomes which are the consequences of the behaviour.

1 *Stimuli* They emanate from people, physical situations, and sociological situations.

2 *Resultant behaviour* Typical examples are positive forms of behaviour where helpful actions are generated; negative forms where unpleasant reactions occur; and favourable or unfavourable changes in attitude.

3 *Outcomes* These are the consequences such as praise and reward if behaviour suits the recipient, and punishment if behaviour displeases. Moreover reinforcement may occur (*see* Chapter 12) if the recipient encourages the behaviour pattern.

Perceptual selectivity

An internal filtering process gives priority to vital stimuli. Selection depends upon appeal and compatability through referring to the individual's mental make-up including values, needs, and experience. External factors draw attention through size, intensity, contrast, movement, repetition, and novelty of the stimuli. Thus the whole process focuses attention on particular stimuli and allows for constant changes in attention as desired.

Social perception

This feature plays a vital role in interviewing and the employment situation as it attempts to explain how one person perceives another individual. The major characteristics and features are: profiles of the perceiver and the perceived, perceptual context, attribution, stereotyping, the halo effect, and perceptual barriers.

PROFILES

Perception is strongly influenced by the characteristics of the perceiver and the person perceived. For example if a manager feels pleased with life possibly a favourable impression will be created towards someone who is pleasant and attractive, whereas a manager who is displeased might be unimpressed with an arrogant and unattractive person.

1 *The perceiver's profile*   The perceiver's characteristics affect those likely to be recognised in others. Therefore endeavouring to know oneself makes it easier to see others more clearly.

2 *The perceived person*   The person being perceived also has an effect on the perceiver. Examples are: the person's status; a categorisation into status or role: and noticeable traits.

PERCEPTUAL CONTEXT

The over-all environment in the concern which is created by management also biases particular meanings and values to the employee. Thus communications are distorted to some extent from managers and supervisors. Great care is needed when wording memos and notices, when speaking to employees, and when gesturing to make a point.

ATTRIBUTION

How people explain the cause of their, or another's, behaviour is called attribution. The tendency is to search for causes of behaviour, and when located to the satisfaction of the searcher these causal attributions strongly affect perception.

A typical example is to attribute a new sales representative's performance to the particular territory that was allocated rather than to that person's ability and energy.

STEREOTYPING

Perceiving another person as belonging to a single class or category is known as stereotyping. This error may attribute favourable or unfavourable traits to the individual. Also it implies general agreement on the attributed traits and the existence of a discrepancy between these and actual traits.

Common stereotyped groups are managers, supervisors, trade union members, nationals, and minorities. Examples of stereotyping are: managers are status conscious, Germans are industrious, French are great lovers, and British are conventional.

THE HALO EFFECT

The halo effect is based upon one trait only, not a category as in stereo-typing. Examples of these traits are ability, attractiveness, dependability, and loyalty.

The error is compounded by allowing the single trait to over-ride all other traits in perceiving the individual. Typically, a supervisor may perceive a very good worker as being unco-operative because he or she happens to be reserved; or a manager thinks the secretary is lazy because he or she will not type the manager's private letters.

PERCEPTUAL BARRIERS

A defence mechanism operates when a person is confronted with a situation that is not in accordance with a preconceived idea. This applies when a fact or an event is presented which is unacceptable or perhaps threatening in an obscure way. Typical cases would be between a manager and a trade union representative, or a confrontation between a supervisor and employee's spouse, when the accusation of favouritism is put to the supervisor who is convinced that he or she treats everyone equally.

Mental levels

There are three mental levels: the conscious, the subconscious and the uncon-scious. Some of these have already been mentioned. The supervisor should have some knowledge of the working of these levels so that he or she may show a sympathetic understanding towards subordinates in certain situations such as the examples given below.

The conscious level

Consciousness may be described as knowing what is happening around us and being aware of our actions. Being able to concentrate on a particular task means that a person can successfully block out all those counter-attractions which are happening at the time. If concentration is disturbed by a van passing by, a whistle blowing or any unusual noise, train of thought is lost and an error may occur.

Some people find concentration more difficult than others; the slightest noise which they cannot identify upsets them, or even a familiar sound may disrupt their train of thought. Their work capacity may be excellent, but unless local conditions are satisfactory results will be poor.

The subconscious level

All instructions and information flow into the subconscious mind which retains the messages for recall at any time. Recent messages, which include information and experiences, are easily recalled within days, weeks or months, depending upon the particular individual. Some people find it hard to remember an event after a few weeks, others find it easy. Failing to remember is not a crime; in fact, it is both thoughtless and inefficient to ignore the handicap when it is known instead of making a due allowance for the unfortunate person. The sensible supervisor will avoid placing people with poor memories in situations which call for a good memory where they are likely to fail.

The unconscious level

The subconscious connects with the unconscious mind and passes on all information and experiences for permanent storage. Although all past experiences are stored, it seems that automatic recollection at any time is not possible. Recalling an event at will does not seem to work; often there is a time-lag and suddenly, without any apparent effort, it springs into the conscious mind. A difficult problem may be put to one side and then, without warning, the answer presents itself. Similarly, all manner of information will appear without any conscious effort.

Another effect occurs when a person takes an instant dislike to another for no obvious reason. Psychologists say that this is due to an unconscious connection of the person with someone who caused unhappiness in the past. The danger of allowing first impressions to affect one's judgment is plain.

Mental experience

The actual mental experience associated with awareness involves at any time the interaction of closely knit processes: feeling, willing, and thinking. These are often called affective, conative, and cognitive, respectively. Generally one over-rides the other two although they are also activated. For example an employee notices a mistake in a colleague's work; the first person may feel that the right course of action is to report it, but might *will* himself or herself to take no action, reasoning (or *thinking*) that the mistake will go through the procedure and eventually be spotted.

Coupled with other factors such as the control feature known as sentiments, the influential feature known as disposition, and the complexes associated with them, the subject of mental experience can only be glanced at. There is an extensive amount of material under this heading, but condensed it means that people cannot be held responsible for their nature or temperament. With help, however, they can learn to adjust and become more acceptable citizens and employees. The supervisor should advise employees to seek specialist help when the need is obvious.

Sociology of work

Orientations to work may be classified according to the two extremes: the instrumentally oriented and the expressively oriented employee. One is more interested in financial reward while the other is more concerned with job satisfaction. Within this simple continuum framework various schools of thought have developed about human nature and work behaviour.

The scientific management/human relations school

This style is explained in detail in Chapter 10. The ideas of economic reward as an incentive and that employees tend to slack if given the chance are fundamental. Also, if management relates to each employee and satisfies his self-interest, then full co-operation will be achieved. How individuals relate to each other is vital in this psychologistic style. Participation, participative leadership and development of supervisory skills are key features.

The organic/systems school

This style emphasises the idea of society having an independent and determining effect on the individual. Thus the community which is organic by nature and conforms to a social system really decides how people behave.

The interactionist school

This approach sees the individual and society as being mutually interdependent – not a one-sided deterministic one. Therefore, human behaviour is not caused by internal or external forces but by a process of interpretation of both forces whereby a person constructs his or her own realities through interaction with others.

The social action school

This macro-level approach is involved with the meaningful activity of the person and the grand questions of political, social and cultural change. People are considered to be rational and pursuing certain ends but there is not necessarily a direct relationship between their work and the outcome in terms of social order. People's actions often have unintentional consequences and lead to fundamental conflicts of value, interest and perspective.

The Marxian school

This extreme approach relies on the idea that people achieve fullness of their humanity through their labour. The implication is that the conditions under which labour is performed are crucial. The argument that the worker is alienated is based upon three main assumed points:

1 the owner of a business has sufficient means of subsistence, whereas employees are dependent
2 employees have to put in extra work over and above what is required for their own needs
3 employees are restricted in their striving to achieve creative fulfilment

There are strong economic and social counter-arguments against this line of reasoning.

Class and status

A general belief is that achievement in the job decides promotion prospects. In modern organisations, however, it is apparent that different skills are used in jobs as the hierarchy is ascended, which makes the belief suspect. Probably promotion prospects depend more on a willingness to fit into the power structure and on possessing appropriate cultural, class, status and background aspects which conform to the management pattern. Although there are examples of 'shop floor employee' making good, there is increasing evidence that class-related is preferable to task-relevant criteria.

The 'class' system may also be seen operating in trade unions where antiquated structures lead to competition among unions within companies and in industries. Furthermore, the tendency to emphasise class and status is openly displayed in companies (especially in factories) through the use of notices and rules: 'This door staff only', workers' canteen, and executive staff dining-room. It is usual to find that workers clock-on, staff book-in, while managers simply arrive.

Employees also show concern for status through their sensitivity to differences in wage rates between jobs and, if they are transferred, the level of informal status of the new job. Employees are often subjected to a different type of employment relationship and they often have to adhere to a restricted form of implicit contract. The situation is aggravated when lower rewards induce low trust relationships with managers, when tasks are closely prescribed and executed in accordance with a specific agreement, and when direct control is applied. As the hierarchy is ascended relationships change, the contract and commitment are more diffuse, there seems to be high trust, more discretion and more conception rather than execution of tasks.

Finally, sharp divisions are seen in the distribution of marketable wealth in the UK. According to Inland Revenue statistics (HMSO, 1987), 1 per cent own 20 per cent, 5 per cent own 40 per cent, 10 per cent own 54 per cent, 25 per cent own 76 per cent and 50 per cent own 93 per cent.

Importance of human relations

Unless good relationships exist, most schemes to increase productivity and to motivate people in a particular direction will fall short of their objectives and have no lasting effects. If employees are unhappy, suspicious and generally disgruntled, there will be higher labour turnover, absenteeism and lateness, more risk of waste and accidents, poor work, general slackness, and lack of discipline.

A management policy to improve human relationships must be long-term, as changes do not come about overnight. Deep-rooted distrust and traditional suspicion take time to erase and often the mere act of attempting to improve the situation is treated with doubt. The change must be sustained and genuine.

Employees gradually begin to change their attitude towards work when they see opportunities to use their initiative and abilities to a greater advantage. Feelings of pride and importance in actually contributing something more than the usual day's work, when coupled with the respect received from management and sympathetic understanding from supervision, raise employees well beyond their accepted standards of ability.

Some causes of poor relationships

Traditional treatment of employees

If management in a concern has not moved with the times and continues to treat employees in an autocratic fashion with complete lack of understanding, general resentment grows and possibly leads to increasing friction and strikes.

Lack of understanding by management

Although management may have good intentions, if the true situations on the shop floor are not known and instructions are ineffective its efforts will be wasted. Management must show an appreciation of the situation and relate its instructions to the facts, thus making it obvious to employees why certain courses of action are necessary.

Lack of understanding by employees

Assuming that management's intentions are sincere and the right action is taken, nevertheless employee outlook has to be changed before improvements will be noticed. Management has not altered overnight and it is most unlikely and unsound to reason that employees will change more quickly.

The inherited feelings towards management are tenacious and unfortunately often correct. For example, the argument that management would quickly revert to its old ways if given the opportunity is a difficult one to answer. Any management presenting a new outlook must understand that one false move will convince employees that management is two-faced.

Lack of communication

Unless constant efforts are made to ensure that information reaches all points in a concern, invariably many employees will be neglected. If people are to feel part of an organisation they must be treated as an *essential* part. They want to know what is going on, why changes are made, who the newcomers are. If the formal channels of communication are not used, the 'grape-vine' takes over, creating misunderstandings with unconnected, incomplete items of information which leave much to conjecture. The employees feel that management has no faith in them and that they are of little importance to the company.

Lack of incentive

Without motivation to work well in the form of financial and non-financial incentives severe frustration will appear. (The importance of this factor in human behaviour is discussed further in later sections.) Both forms of incentive are needed and people must be given the opportunity to participate, set themselves objectives and feel they are doing a worthwhile job.

Conflicting viewpoints

The views of management and employees are often opposed on questions of wages, output, working conditions and terms of employment. One group is thinking in terms of profitability, of cost and output, whereas the other group is thinking of sharing the profit by receiving more wages and benefiting from stability of employment. A better understanding of the other party's position in both cases would certainly ease the mutual distrust which defeats many schemes to improve relationships.

A further aggravation is the confusion in employees' minds as to where their loyalty lies. Consideration for the trade union, management, the supervisor and colleagues, poses a bewildering problem to most employees.

Inadequate organisation

The incorrect use of specialists who appear to come between employees and supervisors upsets the desired friendly atmosphere. Similarly, unsound application or disregard of the principles of organisation leads to confusion and agitation when conflicts occur. Working harmony is lost until a sound organisation structure is established and understood by everyone.

Stress

Most people recognise stress in materials and machines because they see a physical effect. A rubber band will break if stretched too far. A fuse will blow if the load is too great. Indeed, stress is occurring long before the result is witnessed, but the cause is accepted when something drastic happens.

With individuals stress also occurs internally and is not recognisable immediately. Some outward signs may indicate problems, but when a breaking point is reached, unfortunately the cause is often not recognised. This difficulty could be due to the fact that people may suffer with *under*loading as well as *over*loading, both being stress conditions.

If a job is enriched it may be difficult to recognise the point where an excessive mental load is reached. Conversely, it is equally difficult to assess when a person is underloaded: working on a conveyor belt might easily cause mental underload. Both situations – it is claimed by neuro-psychologists – have detrimental effects on health and performance. Indeed, stress can affect the state of mind of employees, making them more sensitive to feelings of social dissatisfaction. This complex subject is becoming increasingly important to employers as more are realising that it causes considerable pathological, social, *and* economic problems.

Symptoms

To create a feeling of well-being, the nervous system has to function between particular limits of intensity. If these limits are exceeded the individual soon experiences unpleasant feelings which eventually may lead to a variety of pathological effects such as dyspepsia, headaches, insomnia and exhaustion – in some cases, gastritis, ulcers and coronary disease.

The immediate outward signs of stress may be a sudden reddening of the face, trembling, sweating, hesitant speech, or over-emphasis of a nervous habit. Inward effects are feeling irritated, a thumping heart, sweating uncomfortably, 'butterflies' in the stomach, boredom, anxiety, unaccountable fatigue and loss of appetite.

The causes

Bearing in mind that one form and level of stress may affect one person more than another, the two divisions are physical and psychological causes.

Physical causes include physical work load and physical environment – temperature, humidity, noise, vibration, etc. *Psychological causes* include mental work load and mental environment – danger, confinement, mental atmosphere and general reactions to a variety of problems such as thwarted ambition, personality clashes and lack of job security.

The effects

The results of stress when the optimum level is exceeded in either direction are summarised below:

1 *Overload:* performance suffers in some way and there is risk of pathological problems
2 *Underload:* low performance and pathological risks

Although there is the argument that some people perform better under high stress conditions, they are in the minority (*see* Fig. 9.1 *The distribution of human differences*).

According to some theorists, more working days are lost through stress than through strikes. Absenteeism and sickness brought about by boredom and stress-related illness is said to be considerable.

Problem areas

The main problems associated with stress are given below:

1 Difficult to measure accurately.
2 The optimum level for each person is different and varies depending upon the form it takes and the degree.
3 Each particular situation has different effects on people.
4 Physical and mental fitness can affect the stress level.
5 It is even possible to self-induce stress: a person may deliberately cause someone to react against him or her.
6 Some people manage to cope with stress but they do not necessarily know how to manage it effectively.
7 Considerable research is needed before a better understanding of stress is possible.
8 It is a personal experience which is not necessarily related to success or failure at home or at work.
9 It may prevent adaptive behaviour and cause illogical behaviour.
10 Many people do not recognise it in themselves or in others.

Control of stress

Although the subject is still in its infancy there are already many proposals on how to control stress. Considerable reading material is available and some of the usual suggestions in brief are as follows.

1 Learn about the management of stress.
2 Consider all the environmental conditions.

3 Discuss work-loads with employees and try to make some form of assessment of stress levels.

4 Look for the outward signs of stress and respond accordingly.

5 When poor performance occurs take into account the possibility of a stress problem.

6 Attend courses on the general treatment of stress. These include general information and control through the use of various therapy techniques.

7 The use of work measurement to check on work-loads.

8 The use of work study to reduce overloading and to upgrade underloading.

9 Delegation usually increases stress because routine jobs are handed down which leaves more time to worry about intractable problems.

10 Any uncertainty about an outcome tends to lead to increased stress therefore it should pay to learn more.

11 One way of coping is to avoid stressful activities. These are generally where the outcome is very important to the individual.

General comments

From reading the above list it is immediately apparent that most of the suggestions hinge on good supervision. At the same time some proposals are not feasible; avoiding stress is often not possible and it is very difficult to know well all subordinates and understand their inner feelings. People change too, as do their stress levels. Indeed, it is a lifetime's work to begin to understand people, although of course it is healthier to attempt *prevention* of pathological problems rather than leaving the medical profession to attempt a *cure*.

This sketch of stress may be related to many other supervisory situations detailed elsewhere. There is nothing more stressful, for example, than human presence – meeting other employees and managers face to face, attending meetings, and coping with situational problems concerning people.

Many other general aspects are also involved in stress levels such as diet, lifestyle, workstyle and domestic problems. All these aspects are important in their own right and add up to individual stress levels. In this connection a brief look at the personal aspects of the supervisor and stress is given below.

Stress and the supervisor

Symptoms suffered by the supervisor probably are aligned more with shop-floor ailments than with those of executives. A surprising fact is that major stress ailments such as coronary disease, peptic ulcers and hypertension are more common in people at the base of the organisation. The general impression is the opposite.

Even minor discomfort and pain mars supervisory performance. The basic problem is often associated with bad habits: sitting or standing for long periods, too little or too much exercise, and taking an excess of mild drugs or stimulants (cigarettes, alcohol, coffee, aspirins). The need to keep physically fit and healthy is often neglected by individuals. Generally employers also overlook the need to emphasise this point to employees and to take positive action to help solve the problem. Rapid cures are possible for many of the minor ailments but many people suffer from inertia and need a strong mental push before they will take any remedial steps.

The mental stress concept

There are many viewpoints on stress which should be of personal interest to the supervisor. A study of the subject is worth while and in some cases essential for those who aspire to managerial positions and who feel they are suffering unduly. The main contributors who could be of help are J. Deese, W. T. Singleton, H. W. Magoun, N. H. Mackworth, J. Parrot, A. Fassina, M. Carruthers, and J. V. Brady.

Stress research project

One example is now discussed of a typical research project that has received considerable publicity. Friedman and Rosenman (1959) studied two groups of managers.

Type A – showed a high competitiveness, quick thought and action, and were conscious of time and deadlines. (Typical description would be: thrusters, extremely competitive, aggressive, hasty, restless, impatient, hyper-alert, tense, and feels under pressure.)
Type B – the reverse of Type A. (Typical description: free of habits, no Type A characteristics, no time urgency, no free-floating hostility, does not flaunt accomplishments, plays it for fun, and relaxes without guilt.)
Result – Type A suffered more than *six times* more heart attacks than Type B.

Recognising type A

There are many characteristics that distinguish this type of manager. Some typical examples are listed below:

1 Explosively accentuates various key words in speech.
2 Brings discussions around to topics he or she likes.
3 Always urging people and asking if they have finished a task.
4 Does everything in a hurry.
5 Tries to do several things at once.

6 Thinks about other subjects when people are talking.
7 Feels guilty when relaxing and doing nothing for a while.
8 Suffers with a chronic sense of time urgency.
9 Tries to do things faster than other people.
10 Suffers from obsessions.

Recognising type B

1 Listens to others patiently without interrupting them.
2 Concentrates on one task at a time.
3 Creates a placid atmosphere.
4 Possesses an unhurried approach.
5 Has the knack of taking the heat out of situations.
6 Relaxes when the opportunity occurs.
7 Reads books that require concentration.
8 Enjoys his food and takes his time over meals.
9 Has absorbing hobbies.
10 Lives by the calendar not for the day.

General recommendations

There seems to be a tendency for managers and supervisors to take on Type A characteristics. For those who wish to avoid this trend there are a thousand and one pieces of advice being offered from a variety of sources. Many suggestions are simply common sense and come naturally to most people if they *stop and think*. Referring to the description and recognition of A and B should give ample clues without listing pages of recommendations.

The broad headings of advice range from practising how to still the mind, adjusting attitude and behaviour, avoiding excessive smoking, alcohol and food consumption, exercising, avoiding stressful personal relationships, learning how to relax, down to (or up to) solving domestic and marital problems.

Questions

1 How would you establish desirable superior/subordinate relationships?
2 'Every individual is different.' Explain this statement and how it affects supervision.
3 Why have human relations been neglected in industry?
4 'Human relations and higher productivity go together.' Give your views on this statement.
5 How would you proceed to improve human relations in a department where poor relations existed between supervisors and employees?
6 Can the viewpoints of managers and employees be reconciled?

7 What is meant by 'divided loyalty' in connection with management/ employee relationships?
8 Explain the importance of understanding human instincts as a means of improving the *industrial climate*.
9 What advantages can be gained by a supervisor who recognises the fact that each subordinate is a separate individual?
10 Discuss fully the problem of trying to understand people.
11 How would you deal with a situation where employees complain about a colleague who sits next to them and suffers from BO?
12 How would you react if a subordinate 'pulls your leg'?
13 What action would you take if a subordinate complains that *your* superior ignores him or her?
14 If a subordinate offers you a gift of fifty cigarettes and says they were a gift but that he or she does not smoke, what would you do? Explain your action.
15 How would you cope with a situation where a subordinate is continually critical of your actions but does not make constructive suggestions?

Case study

Terry Browning had been leading a comfortable working life as a supervisor for some years. His group of nine maintenance engineers were co-operative and worked well together. Two chargehands controlled the work loads, one of whom had retired three months ago and was replaced by a good worker, Paul Cummings.

When Paul took over he declared he would start studying supervision. Within two months his behaviour changed and he began to air his recently acquired knowledge among his colleagues at tea breaks.

Initially Terry, the supervisor, could see no harm in it until one day Paul raised the subject of conflict in industry. He outlined various frames of reference which might be used in analysing industrial relations issues. Finally he dealt with the radical framework, stressing certain points such as capitalism and its reliance on rhetoric of social equality and rewards, whereas in reality, he claimed, there is inequality in distributing rewards and in opportunities for advancement. He also raised the questions of unequal distribution of wealth, control of workpeople, issues associated with freedom, choice, independence and autonomy.

Terry could see the group was impressed. Paul said, 'I couldn't understand what it was all about before, why I felt the way I did about going to work for someone else – but I do now.'

The group broke up and Terry suddenly felt very concerned about Paul's successful manipulation of the group. Within weeks he was plagued with problems and it became obvious that the employees' behaviour had changed drastically towards him.

Paul simply smiled when he tackled him and said he could not understand what had gone wrong. The other chargehand was also having difficulties and complained that Paul was indirectly causing discontent.

What could Terry do in these circumstances?

10 Improving human relations

Practical aspects

Before the supervisor can deal effectively with people, he or she must be able to appreciate the stresses and strains within individuals which affect their daily working life. These emotional problems are discussed in more detail below, together with sections on the emotional range of normal people, the problems of resistance to change, and the various types of individual encountered. The importance of group activity is then discussed with illustrations of research into this aspect. The chapter concludes by describing the fundamental problems of human relationships, and lists the many methods of improving relationships on the shop floor.

Emotional problems

Emotion is much deeper and more pronounced than simple feelings associated with 'drives' since it involves environment, training and temperament, among other factors. Three responses occur with emotion: some *physical or organic change*, accompanied by *an impulse* to do something active about the situation, and a *feeling* which hastens the process of action.

A person's temperament is recognised by the way he or she controls emotions, moods, outbursts, and by his or her general emotional maturity.

Further detail of this complex topic is outside the range of this book, but the supervisor will already be able to recognise the problem employee who is emotionally unstable because he or she will be spending more than the usual amount of time with that person. This unhappy employee has problems which cannot be solved in the usual way because of an inability to adjust easily. The signs are antagonism towards management, the group and certain employees, ill-health and absenteeism, generally miserable mood, frequent and trivial complaints, and in extreme cases complete breakdown, violence and excessive drinking.

Attitudes of normal people

A normal person's attitudes are formed by arriving at personal balanced opinions which are, under suitable conditions, open to adjustment through the acceptance of logical reasoning and provision of sufficient information to justify the change.

Although people may behave in different ways tending to suit their own particular needs or best interests, they are all acting normally. Each person has his own method of dealing with problems depending upon his emotions, reasoning and past environment. Moreover, what seems to be an abnormal or extreme reaction may be caused by further factors unknown to the supervisor.

Resistance to change

Any new scheme or change will instinctively be examined from the selfish aspect and, if it pleases, acceptance follows generally. An element of doubt will create the tendency to reject the idea, or to demand more information or assurance.

To some people security is very important and, if this seems to be threatened in some obscure way, a form of guarantee is necessary before the change visualised becomes acceptable. Any proposed alteration affecting wages, safety, working conditions or methods needs clarifying in the employee's mind to remove resistance. Perfectly healthy people will resist change from outside as already pointed out. Individuals do change, however, as it suits them. The process of living requires continual adjustment to social and industrial environment, although it is often a slow and laborious task. The fortunate ones adjust quickly; to others the problem is insurmountable and they require special treatment before their minds can accept a change. An example is where a person suffers a bereavement and cannot face up to the drastic change in family life.

The supervisor should accept the fact that people do change their habits, outlook and attitudes and have the capacity to improve. He or she should be able to recognise the ill-adjusted employee by a variety of indications, including nervousness, difficulty in concentrating, ailments, misunderstandings, unusual behaviour and poor general attitude towards work and people.

The supervisor and emotional problems

This simple classification of people with emotional problems (and their responses under industrial conditions) defines three classes of people: normal, emotionally troubled, and convalescent.

Normal people

This group adjusts readily to problems, provided that the supervisor treats each person with proper understanding and sympathy when emotional stress is evident. The industrial climate must be right, with a friendly atmosphere throughout the organisation, a feeling of belonging and support from superiors.

Emotionally troubled people

There are many different types of people who feel unhappy and suffer generally. Their working efficiency is impaired and relationships with others are often unsatisfactory. They are misunderstood and their problems are aggravated further through general ignorance of their complaint. Trying to understand these people, who are fortunately in the minority, is wearing for the supervisor. They take up a lot of time; often they cannot express themselves adequately; they do not make sense of situations; and they are generally looked upon as a nuisance. Making the effort to understand them is worthwhile for the supervisor; it saves time in the long run and greatly assists them. Some of the types are given below.

The insecure person

Insecurity is apparent when the need for praise is exaggerated to a point where any sign of apparent neglect, although unjustified, will cause the person either to react strongly against the supervisor or to resort to sulking for long periods. When approached he or she will possibly state that there is nothing the matter, or may pick on little faults and grossly exaggerate their importance. This person is commonly known as difficult or touchy and needs regular strong assurance of his or her usefulness and capabilities.

Over-dedication to the job

The person who places too much importance on the job at the expense of outside interests will find job satisfaction increasingly difficult to achieve unless that person is able to advance in step with his or her aims.

Because of an unbalanced outlook, it is most unlikely that this person will possess the right characteristics for promotion. Frustration generally appears as demands are thwarted. Possibly the supervisor may be able to persuade him or her to take up other interests in the social activities of the company.

The temperamental person

This 'time-consuming' type is continually pestering the supervisor with a whole range of problems, registering dissatisfaction, making excuses, and generally being a nuisance. This person appears to be suffering from a number of emotional problems openly expressed through continual upsets with colleagues and authority.

The supervisor should try to refrain from making a direct reproach and attempt to help the subordinate by seeking the cause of the trouble. This method is easily written about but hard to practise as the supervisor also has feelings and emotions which can stand so much provocation and no more.

Within this group are the types who are often absent and have accidents fairly regularly. Developing group spirit so that these individuals feel a stronger obligation towards their colleagues may help considerably.

The convalescent

Due allowance should be made for the person who has suffered a long illness or a breakdown and now wishes to lead a normal life again. The supervisor should treat the matter straightforwardly, informing subordinates of the person's return and making it plain that the convalescent will be expected to be treated as an ordinary employee with no special concessions. This should provide the right atmosphere which might otherwise cause embarrassment if too much fuss were made on the employee's return. Most people are naturally sympathetic and understand the person's feelings on these occasions.

Group activity

This topic was introduced in Chapter 5 and is considered to be an important feature in improving human relations. Further explanation here emphasises recognition of different types of social groups and research in human relations which established the need for group spirit and autonomous work groups.

Types of social groups

There are many types of social group which all tend to merge into each other. Three main types can be distinguished:

- the gathering or crowd
- the club
- the community

First, the gathering of people at a football match, theatre or public meeting occurs when they have something in common. They are guided by events and are inclined to act as a body impulsively and emotionally with no real objectives in mind.

Second, the club type of group is formed through active participation in sports and social activities, welfare or religious work. Club members have definite objectives and generally possess strong sentiments which create the desirable group spirit.

Third, the community type of group is a powerful, complex and stable organisation of individuals with strong common interests and high motivative potential. It is formed by force of circumstances and members play an important part in its organisation, daily operations and objectives. Each member has particular responsibility and exercises self-discipline; group loyalty provides a spirit often known as *esprit de corps* and this stabilises the group. The individual identifies directly with the group which allows the member to assert him or herself through the group structure and satisfy basic needs.

Although something near to the community type of group is very desirable in industry, it is not frequently seen; the crowd type is more familiar. Some of the essential requirements for building up community groups in a concern are:

1 forming the right organisation within each group of individuals and relating each correctly to other groups on soundly based principles
2 creating stability, i.e. a low level of movement of group members – conditions must be such that labour turnover is minimised
3 reaching that stage of development in the industrial climate where each employee feels part of the concern and has a pride in belonging to that particular group, which is recognised by management

Research in human relations

The early pioneers of scientific management, such as F. W. Taylor and F. B. Gilbreth, had concentrated on improving productivity by studying the operator, the job, tools and equipment and working conditions. Although outstanding improvements were achieved by the introduction of financial incentives, new methods, time and motion study, rest pauses for workers, new types of tools, improved layout and specialisation, these innovations did not always achieve the visualised targets.

In 1924 the Western Electric Company near Chicago decided to call in Elton Mayo, a professor of Harvard University, to study human behaviour. The company had already installed the systems of Taylor and Gilbreth, but the results were not up to expectations. Apparently productivity depended upon other factors that remained unknown.

The basis of the investigation was to test the effect of various factors on productivity by altering working conditions. Two equal groups (A and B) of female operatives were formed and studied by Elton Mayo and his colleagues over a number of years. Lighting intensity was increased with A group and, as expected, output increased in sympathy. For no apparent reason B group also increased its output, although the lighting was unchanged. The lighting was returned to its original intensity in A group and output increased further instead of falling back in sympathy.

In view of this unusual result a whole series of experiments was conducted over a period of five and a half years. Two voluntary female groups were formed and observed by the research workers who worked closely with the operators. All changes – which were made regularly every few weeks – were communicated to the operatives who had the opportunity of commenting, asking for additional information, seeking advice and airing any grievances.

This particular series of investigations was carried out in the Relay Assembly Test Room at the Hawthorne plant. Communication was ideal as information was allowed to flow freely in both directions. The supervisor had frequent conferences with the women, their views were requested and in some cases they were allowed to veto a proposal. The women had complete freedom to voice their thoughts and to decide their own working conditions.

A happy working group developed. The women worked freely and confidently with very little anxiety. A supervisory relationship was established which allowed them to feel a new sense of responsibility for their work. On the social side they seemed glad to be together in outside activities and enjoyed themselves through a sense of group solidarity which reflected itself in both the social and work environment.

Group spirit

This series of experiments and many others became known as the Hawthorne Investigations. They provided sufficient evidence to prove that other factors beside wages and working conditions have a significant effect on output.

When employees are in the limelight they feel important, they begin to feel part of the organisation – and a vital part when their opinions are requested – and the climate is improved to a point where group spirit can freely express itself.

Self-discipline is established because a new feeling of responsibility emerges in a group which has freedom to develop its potential, make decisions, and take pride in its achievements.

Autonomous groups

Developments emerging from research following the human relations school have produced a strong emphasis on the creation of autonomous work groups.

Briefly, when changes are contemplated, a technology is *not* designed and then the social organisation fitted to it. Essentially, both technology and organisation are used alongside each other jointly to optimise the two when designing work groups.

One outstanding example illustrates the point. Trist and Bamforth (1963) of the Tavistock Institute studied the effects of mechanisation at the coal face. Results showed that the technical innovations failed to provide social and psychological satisfactions expected by miners in British mines, therefore productivity fell. The reasons were that new occupational roles and shift arrangements destroyed the closely-knit groups, the relative autonomy they enjoyed, and the variety of skills they used in small groups.

A different approach produced a better 'fit' by using the new machinery but allowing retention of the traditional social and cultural factors. Work tasks were grouped to form a logical *whole task* performed with minimal interference. Thus the criterion is to form the smallest group that can perform a whole task which at the same time will satisfy the social and psychological needs of its members.

This technique is known as job redesign, the group technology approach, work restructuring, the cell system, flexible working teams, and group working schemes. It fits into the socio-technical system and complies with new thinking that employees (and organisations) will not operate effectively if counter-productive management practices – considered by many to be necessary and unavoidable – are continued.

Criticisms

The supervisor should note that there are possible problems.

1　Instrumentalism was mentioned in the previous chapter and it could be argued that employees in this category would not welcome job redesign.
2　Employees may contend that it is just another management practice to extract more work for no extra pay.
3　Some authorities claim that engineers cannot work with social scientists to achieve the best 'fit'.
4　The concept inhibits division of labour and specialisation of tasks.
5　In some situations there could be expensive changes involved before installation, and possibly productivity would fall before picking up later.

Whole tasks

An example is a change from the conventional assembly-line – say ten metres long, with short job cycles and operatives spread well apart – to a small working group with longer job cycles. The five employees in this group were given the job of building an automatic programme selector in a television receiver. The entire job (a whole task) included assembling, inspecting, and correcting faults. Group members worked at their own pace, performed a larger job than before, and were trained to perform all the jobs. The group was able to undertake new tasks such as inspection, repair, drawing materials and accounting. It could choose and decide on the distribution of jobs according to individual preferences and successive operations were taught to each other.

Some fundamental problems of human relationships

Selecting and training employees

Every employee must be able to do the job sufficiently well to achieve satisfaction and develop a feeling of pride. The responsibility of management for ensuring that this is possible is twofold: it rests with those who must select the suitable personnel for each job and with those who are responsible for training personnel to perform their tasks properly. Encouragement, patience and tact are needed by the supervisor to see the employee through the training period.

Selecting and training supervisors

Management must appreciate the importance of providing each group with a carefully selected supervisor who is trained in the art of dealing with people. A plan which includes continual search for supervisory ability within the company is essential, coupled with effective education and training schemes. Such a plan demands expenditure and often a change in management attitude towards supervision and its importance in industry.

The position of management

The type of outlook required by management to establish good working arrangements with employees has been stressed already. This fundamental change of attitude is hard for senior and long-established managers to accept and in some cases it is totally unacceptable. Similarly, breaking down the traditional outlook of employees towards management is exceptionally difficult.

Company loyalty

Employees should be able to connect the company, its products or service and its aims with themselves in such a way that they feel the job is worth while. They should feel proud of the concern, otherwise the correct attitude towards work will not follow.

Trade unions

Harsh supervision is often said to be the cause of the rise of trade unions. The modern supervisor recognises that collective bargaining is an essential part of developing human relations and that training in the art of consultation is needed. True recognition of the union and its influence does not exist until consultation becomes a regular, acceptable form of communication. When the union, management and employees work together as a team the problem of loyalties falls into the background. Many managers recognise the practical use of the union for negotiating with employees where the majority are members. All three groups have a similar interest in the company's prosperity and amicable co-operation solves problems and speeds progress.

Divided loyalties

To many employees the industrial situation is confusing and irritating, especially to those who are conscientious and strongly desire satisfaction from work. Loyalties seem to lie in opposing directions: to colleagues, the group, the supervisor, management and the union. Other pressures complicate the problem, and it is not surprising to see some people reach a state where they are prepared to submit to anyone's schemes, thus abandoning their own principles, to secure some peace of mind. Others withdraw from industry and seek employment elsewhere.

Understanding each other

Being able to understand each other is probably the biggest problem. Simple conversations are misunderstood, people's words are easily distorted; in fact, very few individuals manage to be really in tune with each other all the time. Some people try very hard to get on with others without much success while the fortunate few find it an easy task, but everybody finds that a large degree of tolerance and self-restraint is necessary.

Working conditions

Good working conditions are an essential background to good relationships. The atmosphere created by poorly decorated premises which are not cleaned regularly is depressing and degrading to employees. Such poor conditions hardly match any attempts to show personal regard for workers. The contrast of bright and airy offices for higher grades of staff in the same company aggravates the situation.

Ways of improving human relationships

1   Supervisors must show a genuine interest in other people, and display this interest openly, but they should not try too hard to impress in an attempt to win subordinates' interest.

2   They should ensure that the conversation is directed towards the subordinates' interests as these are most important to them. The company's interests can be more fruitfully discussed when good relationships are established.

3   Remember the futility of arguing. The other person thinks he or she is right regardless of the supervisor's viewpoint, otherwise there would be no argument. Although the supervisor may win the argument, the cost of upsetting the bond which existed between him or her and the other person far outweighs the supervisor's own satisfaction; hence the saying 'You cannot win an argument.'

An argument should not be confused with constructive discussion. Where people put forward their opinions – which must be respected – and intelligent discussion follows, obviously only good can result.

4   Try to imagine the other person's viewpoint, feelings and divided loyalties which tend to distort and confuse his or her reaction to a situation. Thus the supervisor will not be so ready to criticise or blame a subordinate; in fact, if the supervisor gives the subordinate a good name to live up to, this objective may help the subordinate to clarify thoughts and realign aims.

5   Do not make promises that cannot be kept. Straightforward talk is much safer and avoids misunderstandings. Always clarify instructions with subordinates and check that they have clearly understood the meaning of statements. People tend to put their own interpretation on what is said and unless care is taken to explain carefully, with illustrations where necessary, the wrong impression is given.

6   Find time to have a good talk with each employee periodically. However, the supervisor should avoid giving the impression that he or she is delving into private affairs. Attempting to give advice on private matters may be dangerous as the supervisor will possess only that information which the subordinate cares to divulge.

7   Supervisors should not attempt to bluff their way out of situations where they are at fault. There is nothing clever in concealing mistakes, which may cause more trouble and expense to correct at a later stage of development. Admit an error or inadequacy and most people will immediately feel sympathetic. Any admission of mistakes should be followed by prompt action to correct the fault.

8   Avoid direct criticism wherever possible. A better way is to make a constructive comment and so avoid an argument with someone who is probably already agitated by the situation. The supervisor will not necessarily appear too easy-going as one may expect; instead the individual will appreciate his or her sense of understanding and tact and working harmony will be kept.

9   Always give a subordinate the opportunity to speak; it does not matter if he or she complains so long as a person's thoughts can be aired, and criticisms will become more constructive eventually with a little prompting as the person realises that the supervisor is consulting, instead of insulting by ignoring his or her ability. Where changes are necessary, less friction will occur when the subordinate has taken an active part in suggesting ways of altering the system.

Subordinates should be encouraged to talk about themselves and their problems. The supervisor must be careful to give them undivided attention, or the supervisor's advice and sympathy will not be sought again.

10   The supervisor should be pleasant and try to develop a friendly atmosphere. Resentment and misunderstandings are caused by abruptness and putting on a tough front. Always use common courtesies such as 'good morning' and 'good night'. Avoid addressing employees by their surnames only; remember there is a handle to the name – always *Mr* or *Ms* Jones. Try to have a few words with each employee every day.

11   If an employee is doing well, then he or she should be told. Do not allow praise to go unspoken; always show appreciation actively. Supervisors are often quick to complain but slow to praise extra effort.

Continually impress upon employees that their jobs are important. The desire to feel important and be appreciated spurs people on when they see recognition of their efforts, but not in financial terms alone.

12   Try to allocate the right jobs to the right people. The supervisor should always make sure that he or she knows what is involved in a particular job before assigning it, otherwise an unnecessary burden may be placed on someone. Make sure that the subordinate also understands clearly the instructions.

13   The reason for policy and rules of organisation should be carefully explained and discussed. If employees are not satisfied, endeavour to find more information or obtain explanations from management.

14   Try to be a patient listener to grievances. Supervisors will have even less time available later if they allow problems and complaints to remain unsaid and repressed. Gain confidence by showing sincere interest and taking positive action where necessary.

15   Supervisors must be particularly careful in their dealings with employees of the opposite sex. Avoid being familiar, and bear in mind the emotional relationships which may exist in groups consisting of men and women. Words should be chosen carefully, the correct approach being essential. Someone nearby will always be ready to misinterpret a supervisor's intention and pass on the incident and conversation to everybody – suitably distorted, of course.

16   Be just and fair in all dealings with subordinates. The danger of being easy-going should be borne in mind, as this will retard the supervisor's efforts to treat everyone in the same way. The supervisor must have facts right so he or she should be continually on the lookout and not trust to chance. Action should be timed well and alertness to situations will ensure that the slackers do not escape reprimands.

Fair treatment is essential at all times and standard ways of dealing with subordinates in similar situations will show objectiveness or lack of personal bias. Avoid having favourites; these are guaranteed to upset all efforts to improve relationships.

17   Stress the permanence and security offered by management to employees. Any feelings of insecurity such as rumours of redundancy will

immediately affect morale and output. Of course it is management's responsibility to provide the right climate before security can be impressed upon employees.

18   A good rule is to question every action involving employees to ensure that their self-respect is not affected in any way.

19   Promotion should be open to everyone. Opportunities for advancement should be well publicised and when appointments are made the reasons should be stated clearly to those who are unsuccessful; thus resentment is minimised.

20   Make sure that the members of the group are not in conflict. Although people of different temperaments will work together happily, some will be antagonised through conflicting beliefs, e.g. racial, political or religious ideals. Where a clash occurs it is cruel to force such people to work together; they must be separated, otherwise the group will suffer unduly.

Questions

1   Discuss the various types of emotional problems that an employee may have to face at work.
2   How would you recognise the emotionally troubled employee and what would you do to help?
3   What is meant by the term 'a normal person'?
4   'People don't change.' Discuss this statement.
5   What is meant by 'resistance to change'?
6   How would you deal with the insecure individual?
7   How would you explain the change in an individual when he or she joins a working group?
8   Discuss the various types of social groups, illustrating your answer with suitable examples.
9   Write an esssy on the Hawthorne experiments and include your personal opinion on the unusual effects that were discovered.
10   What is meant by 'group spirit'?
11   Why are selection and training important factors in the problem of establishing good relationships with subordinates?
12   'Traditional outlooks tend to thwart attempts to improve management/employee relationships.' Explain this statement.
13   Discuss the various ways of improving human relationships.
14   On your first day as supervisor, an employee makes a rude remark as you go by. On the second day a similar remark is passed by the same employee. What would you do?
15   If your best subordinate receives permission to attend a relative's funeral and on your journey home you see this person leaving the local football ground, what would you do?

16 How would you cope with a situation where an employee complains that colleagues refuse to speak to him or her?

17 An employee suddenly becomes very quiet and has nothing to do with colleagues. Outline the action you would take.

18 How would you deal with the following types of employee: sensitive, casual, aggressive, constantly grumbling?

Case Study 1

Irene Tavist, aged 26 years, joined Angle Superstore as a sales assistant four years ago. She was successful and liked her work. During a slack period her supervisor lost her deputy in a redundancy programme and she was not replaced. Later business picked up and soon the supervisor was overloaded with work. She decided to ask Irene to help her as she thought Irene was well-liked and she was pleased with her performance which exceeded many of the 'old hands'. They were not informed as she thought it might upset them.

Irene was given the stock-level reports to complete and this meant checking with other sales assistants. Next day she was absent and it was not until the third day that she reported back. To the supervisor's surprise Irene handed her the reports and declared that she preferred not to be involved. After several attempts to seek an explanation the supervisor gave up.

By chance she overheard the end of a conversation between two of the older sales assistants: '. . . and that soon fixed Irene, lording it over us!'

1 What were the likely causes of the problem?
2 Could the situation be rectified at this late stage?

Case study 2

The Truesome Tyre Company was an old-established firm with a good reputation for ethics and loyalty. Robert, the sales office supervisor, had studied hard and was conscientious at work. He knew the present office manager would retire soon and from chance remarks he thought he would certainly be a strong contender.

One week-end he attended a sailing course at Brighton. On Saturday evening the small group decided to pub-crawl in the town. At a crowded bar Robert bumped into his sales manager, Sam Townsend. Looking very embarrassed he acknowledged Robert and elbowed his way from the bar. It was unlike Sam to be off-hand.

The following Monday Sam called Robert into his office and apologised for his abruptness. 'You know I would be obliged if you don't mention to anyone about seeing me with Pauline. I was supposed to be at a sales conference in Bradford. I'll do the same for you one day.'

Robert reddened uncomfortably. 'Of course, Mr Townsend, but in fact I didn't see your secretary there.'

The following month Sam was promoted to sales director. During a coffee break someone mentioned that Sam very nearly did not get the job because of some discrepancy over expenses.

Six months later to Robert's dismay he was passed over for the office manager's job. To everyone's surprise it was given to a supervisor with a poor reputation. Robert was convinced that his failure was due to Sam and his connection with the incident at Brighton.

In fact, Sam thought Robert *had* seen him with his secretary. The managing director had queried his expenses but knew nothing of the relationship with his secretary, and Sam had not recommended Robert for the post.

Robert decided to see the managing director and complain. He explained everything and waited impatiently for a reply.

1   Consider the question of loyalty and trust in this case.
2   What would you expect the managing director to do?

11 Motivation

Introduction

Motivation is a basic psychological process in human behaviour. Motivation should not be confused with behaviour; the former being simply a theoretical explanation of how peoples' minds operate, which results in the latter – behaviour. Thus motivation cannot be seen operating but behaviour can be observed. The supervisor should attempt to understand how and why people are motivated in the employment situation.

So far there are no exact laws of motivation psychology; however certain theories, principles and tendencies are proposed. As already explained, the nature of psychology and physiology insists on individuality. Thus people are predictable in terms of how the majority will behave in particular circumstances, but unpredictable for determining how each individual will react in a similar set of circumstances.

Without complete knowledge the probability of arriving at the right conclusion as to the cause of anyone's behaviour is very low. For example, an employee suffering from exhaustion through sleepless nights with a newly-born child could be labelled as lazy if he or she did not disclose the problem. Similarly a wrong word from the supervisor may unintentionally upset the employee and cause erratic output, or a change in working position may cause the employee to feel unsettled and affect the quality of his or her work.

Factors affecting motivation

The main factors which affect motivation of people are the job itself, the company environment, external pressures on people, internal human pressures, individual capacity and over-ride features. There are many aspects within each main factor (*see* Fig. 11.1). Furthermore, there is no way of accurately assessing each factor, or aspect within that factor; therefore the idea of calculating which mix is suitable for motivation is strongly suspect at present. In other words, it seems that the priorities and correct mixtures of factors vary with each individual.

There are many different ways of grouping all the aspects to form main factors; this particular approach in Fig. 11.1 takes into account the various

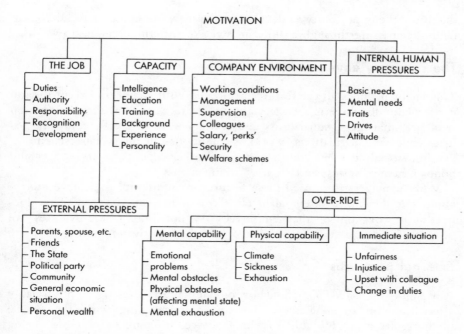

Fig. 11.1 *The main factors affecting motivation*

current theories, but at the same time adds other factors which are often not mentioned when a certain concept is considered. Each factor is now discussed before continuing with the various concepts.

The job

The breadth of the job undertaken by an individual seems to have undergone a cyclical effect. Craftsmen possessed a very wide job breadth a few hundred years ago. Gradually the breadth has diminished: in fact a policy of job narrowment has been adopted over the past seventy years up to a point where a factory employee will simply turn a spanner, for example, many hundred times daily. The story is similar in the office.

Now the vogue is job enrichment, which means not only continuing the cycle by increasing the job breadth, but also ensuring that the individual actually gains genuine achievement in the tasks, gains recognition for this achievement, has a definite interest and responsibility for the job, and is allowed to develop so that he or she may advance to even more complex jobs.

Management, it may be assumed, has not thought much of this factor as a motivator during the twentieth century. Possibly the job width cycle is due to a natural process of production development alongside technological advancement. This trend may give the employee of a few generations into the future the opportunity to develop in a narrow but complex technological field after passing through an interim stage of suffering very narrow jobs.

The company environment

This factor includes all the features associated with a concern except the job itself. Naturally there is a large variety of features such as the organisation structure, managers, supervisors and colleagues at all levels, company policies, rules and regulations, working conditions, all the welfare schemes – pension, social facilities, clubs, 'perks' and other benefits, salary, wages and bonus schemes, status, and security arrangements.

Many managers have used these features in an attempt to achieve motivation, but they have often fallen far short of projected targets. This does not mean, of course, that employees do not think these features are important. The question is whether or not they motivate employees.

External pressures

A person is subjected to a whole host of external pressures which presumably affect behaviour to some extent. The strong desire to mix with other people often results in an individual seeking advice, listening to opinions, being subjected to political views and generally being indoctrinated. The main sources and features are parents, spouse, friends, relatives, the state, political parties, the community, colleagues, superiors, the economic situation, various advertising media and the amount of capital in his or her possession.

The effect that some people have on others is frightening: sheer strength of personality is sometimes sufficient to make an impressionable person go against logical reasoning and behave in very odd ways. The element of confusion caused by many external pressures also should be taken into consideration. If this factor plays an important part in motivation it then becomes the responsibility of everyone in a country to ensure that their influential powers are used to encourage motivation. The well-known chain effect now applies because someone, in turn, needs to take the responsibility for ensuring that each individual is capable of exercising this responsibility.

It should not be forgotten that an external pressure such as an ambitious spouse, can motivate, if he or she can use subtle powers of persuasion which appear to the other person as an intense inner desire on their part.

Internal human pressures

These pressures come from within the individual in the form of basic needs, mental needs, traits, drives and attitudes. Some of these features are an inherent part of the person – he or she is born with them – while others depend partly upon many external features encountered during growth.

Whether or not it is the responsibility of everyone to know oneself and make certain adjustments which will favourably affect one's behaviour is debatable. Again the chain effect may apply where, for example, it could be the responsibility of the Department of Education and Science to ensure that people receive sufficient education in particular disciplines which would allow them to benefit by self-adjustment.

So often people enter business with very little knowledge of what it is all about: a completely new environment is encountered with no real understanding of the importance of co-operation, co-ordination, self-discipline and self-control. The 'do this, do that' type of environment soon moulds people into attitudes involving suspicion and antagonism towards management. Frustration soon sets in as management's emphasis on certain features becomes obvious and the opportunities to satisfy higher needs become more and more remote. Such a situation tends to force a person into behaving irresponsibly, not necessarily because his or her attitude is at fault but rather through a healthy reaction to an unhealthy situation. Resorting to highly absorbing hobbies and arriving at work absolutely exhausted could easily be a symptom of low satisfaction from the employment situation.

Capacity

Capacity is closely coupled with the previous factor. The main features are education, training, background, experience, and intelligence. The extent to which capacity affects behaviour depends upon matching the individual with the job not only from the 'square peg, round hole' aspect but also from the individual's ability to develop within that field.

Although it is healthy to stretch a person's mind, over-reaching the limit of his or her capability will cause frustration. Conversely under-utilisation is just as dangerous. The need in these circumstances for rapid detailed feedback on performance and careful adjustment of the job based upon results is vital. These aspects were emphasised under *Stress* in Chapter 9.

Over-ride

For want of a better name the so-called over-ride factors upsets the effect of all the previous factors regardless often of their combined strength to motivate. Over-ride comes into play on the spot: it has an immediate, powerful and dominating effect on motivation by altering behaviour through some mental incapability, physical incapability or sudden change in the situation surrounding the individual.

From the mental aspect an emotional problem, a mental obstacle or a physical obstacle can suddenly appear which may completely throw the employee off balance and produce erratic behaviour. Similarly, from the physical aspect, feeling off-colour, sustaining an injury or suffering from a physical disability may produce unpredictable behaviour. A sudden change in a stable situation such as unfair treatment, an injustice or a change in the environment without due consultation will again induce a similar effect.

All these features associated with over-ride tend to destroy a great deal of effort to motivate in other factor areas. Indeed, their effect frustrates many managers who abandon perfectly healthy schemes for the wrong reasons. In these cases employees are often branded as being lazy, which really means either that they are suffering from some mental or physical incapability or that they are reacting strongly against some unfairness or injustice. The use of the word 'lazy' should be avoided as it immediately highlights the superior's complete inability to diagnose the individual's problem, as will be seen from the next section.

The psychology of motivation

The remaining aspects for analysis are those associated with internal and external motives, and the various obstacles that prompt particular forms of behaviour.

The motives that dominate behaviour may be subdivided in various ways such as grouping them into basic needs and mental needs. Another method of subdivision is to group them into internal motives such as the wish to satisfy hunger or thirst and external motives such as taking shelter if a gale is blowing or lighting a fire if it is cold.

Motives may also be divided into known and unknown. The actions of eating and sheltering are obvious and would group conveniently into known motives, but other actions such as suddenly punching someone on the nose could be due to an unknown motive, unknown often both to the aggressor and to the victim, the real reason being obscured by an apparent reason. Motivation in this sense is essentially a force that comes from within a person, or, put another way, an internal cause produces motivation. Understanding this aspect is most important.

These known and unknown needs vary in strength along similar lines to the main factors and features of motivation outlined in the previous section. Some needs are easily satisfied while others, unfortunately, are subjected to barriers or obstacles. If these are not overcome the individual suffers some disappointment and frustration. The barriers are divided into two groups: external and internal obstacles.

The process

The basic psychological process of motivation is often said to conform to a 'need–drive–goal' cycle. This concept is generally acceptable and the three factors are considered to be interdependent and interacting.

Actual behaviour is more involved because of many managerial and environmental issues. Nevertheless this theoretical framework is a useful intro-

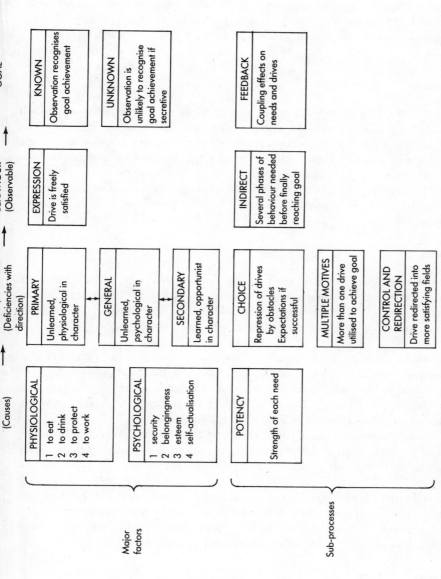

NEEDS
(Causes)

DRIVES/MOTIVES
(Deficiencies with direction)

BEHAVIOUR
(Observable)

GOAL

PHYSIOLOGICAL	
1	to eat
2	to drink
3	to protect
4	to work

PSYCHOLOGICAL	
1	security
2	belongingness
3	esteem
4	self-actualisation

PRIMARY
Unlearned, physiological in character

GENERAL
Unlearned, psychological in character

SECONDARY
Learned, opportunist in character

EXPRESSION
Drive is freely satisfied

KNOWN
Observation recognises goal achievement

UNKNOWN
Observation is unlikely to recognise goal achievement if secretive

POTENCY
Strength of each need

CHOICE
Repression of drives by obstacles. Expectations if successful

INDIRECT
Several phases of behaviour needed before finally reaching goal

FEEDBACK
Coupling effects on needs and drives

MULTIPLE MOTIVES
More than one drive utilised to achieve goal

CONTROL AND REDIRECTION
Drive redirected into more satisfying fields

Major factors

Sub-processes

Fig. 11.2 *A simplified motivation model*

Major factors and sub-processes are indicated within the need–drive–goal cycle. The rectangles should only be treated as building blocks

duction to motivation, illustrated in Fig. 11.2. Initially the three factors are examined. Analysis is easier if homeostasis and other processes are recalled from Chapter 9. The idea that human behaviour is instinctive has now been abandoned except as an explanation for a few activities which seem to be unlearned. The term motivation is interpreted as meaning an *internal* force that pressurises or moves an individual to take action towards achieving a goal.

Needs

A need – the first factor – is often described as an *internal deficiency* which is created through homeostasis when a physiological or psychological imbalance occurs. Types of physiological needs are to eat, drink and work. They are explained as a deprivation condition in a cell. Psychological needs include security, love, esteem, and self-actualisation. Specialists – some of whom tend to disagree – have drawn up a large range of needs. The existence of a hierarchy of needs was propounded by A. Maslow whose influential theory is discussed later.

Drives

A drive or motive is established to satisfy a need. These drives are often defined as *deficiencies with direction* because they are action–oriented and pressurise the individual into taking action which achieves a goal.

They are often grouped into three categories:

1 Basic or primary drives which are not learned and possess a physiological character such as thirst, hunger, sex, sleep, and pain avoidance.
2 General drives which are again not learned but more psychological in character. They often include achieving competence, curiosity, manipulation of objects, being active, and seeking affection.
3 Secondary drives which are learned and tend to take over from primary and general drives if the opportunity occurs such as enjoying higher standards of living and general educational development.

Drives may appear in the conscious mind and force the individual into taking a certain line of action which he or she might not have taken if given time to think. If one of the drives is suppressed, frustration may result, causing loss of energy unless an adjustment is made.

Goals

The cycle ends with the achievement of a goal. Any attainment that reduces the drives and relieves a need is termed a goal. Considering homeostasis, the psychological and physiological balance is restored and the drive is cut off.

Examples are actually eating food, drinking, being accepted by members of a club, and passing an examination.

Motivated behaviour

The above theoretical model is only observable through behaviour. Whether motives may be accurately inferred from behaviour is doubtful for several reasons. Motives often are seen in various disguised ways and more than one motive (or drive) may be expressed through one act. Individuals may act in several different ways with the same motive in mind, or 'unlike' motives may be seen in similar behaviour.

Furthermore behaviour may take on several forms in expressing a motive. *Instrumental behaviour* is a typical example where an act only indirectly satisfies the need; if an employee joins the company's sailing club he or she may be a good yachtsman and is seeking recognition. The act of joining is instrumental in nature. If another employee joins he or she may be seeking friendship, not being particularly interested in sailing. Thus a form of *substitute behaviour* applies. Finally if an act directly satisfies the need, then consummatory behaviour *is* apparent such as eating a meal.

Drives are now discussed in more detail because of their strong effects on behaviour.

The complexity of drives

Drives or motives and their effects are illustrated first, by giving five examples of secondary drives which differ from others because they are learned; second, by examining various outlets for drives; third, by considering the concept of motives and barriers or obstacles that frustrate motives; and fourth, by outlining the behavioural patterns that emerge in reaction to obstacles.

Examples of secondary drives

- Aggressiveness
- Acquisitiveness
- Self-assertion
- Constructiveness
- Gregariousness

Aggressiveness

The drive to be powerful expresses itself in general hostility, awkwardness, and being generally quarrelsome; in extreme cases the use of physical force, shouting and banging the table violently. The drive is very close to the desire to escape when confronted with an intolerable situation. In proximity these two drives sometimes force a person into an unhappy state of mind when he or she may want to attack a manager and leave the concern because of a feeling of unfair treatment. If outside commitments restrict the person from taking this course the resulting conflict causes severe stress. The results often seen are day-dreaming, constant complaints and poor productivity. A popular individual may even gain support from colleagues whose productivity also drops.

Clearly all employees should have the opportunity to develop so that they feel they are not just cogs in a large, impersonal machine. The chance to study and expand the job with equal opportunity to be selected for higher posts naturally needs stressing, as does the need for a policy of fairness and justice and strict adherence to the policy by all managers.

Acquisitiveness

The desire for protection and possession is directly associated with this drive. Sometimes it develops as a strong desire to control and possess power over others. Satisfying this drive means a manager should ensure that company policy adequately protects employees by including secure employment, insurance, superannuation and other welfare benefits.

Factors such as full employment, State benefit schemes, State retraining schemes, powerful trade unions and staff associations, and the general feeling of job security all contribute towards the state of mind of the employee. Satisfying this drive, however, does not necessarily mean high productivity, since this factor is only one of many to be correctly adjusted.

Self-assertion

The drive to be important is closely coupled with constructiveness. Receiving due credit for creating something is essential but when a product or a system is divided into many jobs the feeling of importance lessens because there is no direct association with one individual. To compensate for this remoteness from the end product an employee may turn to the group within which he or she is a member and enjoy group spirit if it is strong. Thus group dynamics must be considered; this depends on the people in the group and the amount of attention given by management to this factor. Consistently fair and just treatment, careful counselling of each person's problems, development schemes for employees and a human approach all help to foster a keen group spirit.

The aim is to make each employee important. Trying to make a person feel important is not enough because the feeling soon disperses as reality becomes obvious. Each employee must be placed in a such a position that he or she *is* important and, knowing this importance, can actively demonstrate it to colleagues.

Constructiveness

The strong drive to create probably causes more trouble in business than any other drive because in so many jobs the opportunity to create is omitted from job requirements. The effect is severe frustration yet the whole concept of manufacturing processes and office work in general is based upon narrowing jobs down to relatively simple tasks.

People satisfy the urge to create by suggesting improvements, having job flexibility, preparing and discussing ideas, and knowing they actually participate in decisions affecting their jobs. Recognition of their contribution combines with self-assertion; they know they are important and they are actively contributing towards the success of the business. The disastrous effects of frustration if this drive is ignored are discussed later.

Gregariousness

Another drive which is associated with group behaviour is the urge to belong to and be accepted by the group. Throughout life the tendency to group together is seen everywhere and people will go to great lengths to be included in various social groups.

The need to unite is probably close to mating and parental drives. Banning a person from a group is particularly harsh and inhuman. The victim may be driven to near-panic and there are many dangers.

Outlets for drives

Driving forces which compel a person to take action in specific ways must be relieved or released through activity. If for any reason they are blocked the effect is rather like an excess of steam that cannot escape inside a boiler; sometimes the pressure builds up until breaking point is reached and the boiler explodes.

The three main outlets to satisfy drives are:

- expression
- repression
- control and redirection.

The supervisor should be able to recognise symptoms which will indicate which outlet is operating and in some instances he or she will be able to assist by redirecting a person's energies.

Expression

When the drive is freely satisfied by an activity directly connected with it the term expression is used to describe this normal outlet. An artist painting a picture and a strong-willed individual being appointed chairman of a social club are typical. A distinction is noticeable if examples of aggressiveness are taken such as murdering an individual and publicly speaking for increasing the pensions of senior citizens. One could be called a barbaric or primitive approach to satisfying the drive, and the other, a civilised or cultured approach. When free expression is very difficult and the person feels restricted he or she may unthinkingly repress the drive.

Repression

To avoid nervous tension when an impulse is restrained the drive may be repressed unconsciously and transferred out of the conscious mind. Unfortunately this process of forgetting about it or banning it from conscious thought is unhealthy or harmful because confusion and a weakening of energy occur. Also the painful experience continues at another level and generally the outcome is only a temporary repression. Suddenly the drive will break through, often at the most inopportune moment which causes embarrassment and an even more painful situation. Partial repression of this nature causes various forms of perversion in certain circumstances.

Many difficulties experienced in business are the direct result of repression. The supervisor has a clear social responsibility to avoid placing employees in situations where repression may occur. Typical symptoms are poor co-operation, apathy, disinterest in the job and the company, maladjustment, antagonism, and low concentration.

Employees should not be forced into situations where there is no choice but repression. Inevitably verbal or physical violence will result as a retaliation against a supervisor or, indirectly, the concern. A much better approach is to control and redirect the outlet.

Control and redirection

For those individuals who possess a well-balanced personality there is ample opportunity to recognise the nature of the drive within them. With appropriate knowledge and experience they redirect their natural urges into more satisfying fields. Similarly the manager should ensure that supervisors can recognise drives and appropriate symptoms in their staff with a view to encouraging employees to adjust by redirecting within the job and in other social pursuits within the concern.

In the majority of cases redirection or sublimation occurs unconsciously. Consequently someone with a strong constructive drive with no opportunity to exercise it at work may become involved, for example, in building complex model aircraft. Similarly, someone with a high aggressive impulse may be engaged in clerical duties at work, but in social life outside will be running a tennis club, organising help for senior citizens, or chairing a local residents' association. Such redirection is quite healthy and desirable. Unfortunately the chances are that in similar situations another individual might develop unhealthy alternatives such as pursuing criminal activities, bullying, or perversions.

The motives concept

Often the term motive is used as an alternative to drive. Generally three divisions of motives are mentioned to illustrate behaviour.

The first division is straightforward and divided into two groups. One consists of basic or of satisfying needs such as the desire to eat, drink and work; the other satisfies higher or mental needs and includes safety, esteem, self-fulfilment or creativeness.

The second division is related to internal motives similar to satisfying basic needs and higher needs; and external motives dominated by outside factors such as temperature changes, other climatic conditions, dangerous elements like fire, water in connection with drowning, and so on. An external motive forces an individual to take action such as running away from an approaching flood or putting on extra clothing if the temperature drops.

The third division is more complex and often difficult to analyse. The group of known motives is relatively easy to distinguish when actions occur such as ceasing to write through cramp, sitting down when the legs ache and removing a coat if the temperature rises. The group of unknown motives is troublesome. Sudden inexplicable actions are confusing to all who are involved, including the one who may be acting in an illogical way. In the extreme such actions are violent while other symptoms may be non-co-operation and sullenness. Often the real reason for this conduct is obscured by surface reasons.

There is also a favourable side of action resulting from unknown motives. A sudden upsurge of enthusiasm and willingness to co-operate are typical examples where a change has induced the person to act in a different way. In both favourable and adverse actions the driving force has emerged from within the person; although an internal cause has motivated him or her to take a line of action the reason may remain obscure. Sometimes it is difficult to assess whether the motive is known or unknown.

Certainly the reason will be connected with satisfying the needs already outlined, but the strength of these needs varies with each individual. Indeed, some needs are easily satisfied with certain individuals while in others there is great difficulty in satisfying them.

Obstacles

When needs are not easily satisfied the barriers or obstacles cause disappointment or frustration if they are not overcome. The effect is various patterns

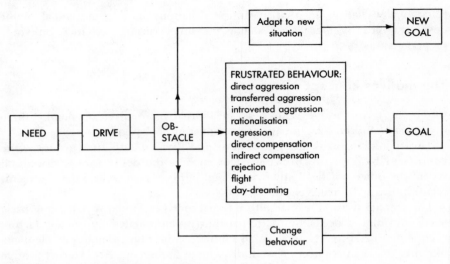

Fig. 11.3 *Behaviour patterns reacting to an obstacle*

Three choices are available: change behaviour to reach the goal, adapt to the new situation and establish a new goal, or react and adopt frustrated behaviour

of behaviour illustrated in Fig. 11.3. To understand this reaction the obstacles are examined by dividing them into two groups: internal and external.

Internal obstacles

An impressive array of internal barriers restricts a person from achieving the aims and needs he or she feels are desirable. A self-assessment of capabilities may mislead the person into believing his or her limitations are much higher than the true ones. Personal traits might cause inner conflicts when associated with both physical and mental restrictions. The person may lack the right degree of confidence and inhibitions could restrict desires. Often the way people see themselves differs from the way other people see them. This situation is misleading and faults are not readily accepted even when they are explained to people.

Inability to self-analyse accurately causes internal conflicts which confuse; generally upset stability; and encourage mental exhaustion, apathy and a non-co-operative outlook.

External obstacles

The main groups of external obstacles are people, society, and objective restrictions. The barriers people raise may be direct or indirect in intention. Where enmity or clashing interests are involved there is often a direct restriction which is obvious, but occasionally this may not be known, as devious means of raising barriers are employed. Such devious treatment is bewildering as well as frustrating; unfortunately people like to use this technique.

When people satisfy their own desires and inadvertently stop or restrict someone else's efforts, an indirect intention occurs. The natural tendency to compete in an insensitive manner savours of jungle law which is mainly completely impersonal and often depends upon being in a certain situation at a certain time. Another factor is the effect of family and friends. In some circumstances they can apply restrictions which are difficult to overcome without causing an upheaval in domestic affairs.

Closely associated with this factor are the restrictions applied by the type of society within which the person has to live. Society pressurises to conform to certain codes of conduct which result in sanctions being applied if broken. The codes are learned through upbringing and education, but if they are unacceptable the resulting conflict may cause change, the erection of insurmountable barriers, or eventual adjustment.

Finally the obstacles associated with objective factors include changes in the economic situation, international problems, governmental policies and even changes in the weather. All these aspects, plus many more not mentioned, cause people to react in various ways which are now described.

Patterns of reaction to obstacles

Reaction to obstacles takes on many different forms and combinations of forms. These frustration symptoms may be grouped into characteristics. When the characteristic is recognised the type of obstacle remains as an important feature in determining the course of action. The main characteristics are now discussed.

Direct aggression

The usual symptoms which precede direct aggression are depression, sourness, sullenness, and displeasure. A selection of these may be expressed at every opportunity. Such tendencies are caused by a weakness which blocks needs and may suddenly express itself in physical violence and emotional outbursts. This primitive reaction is often seen in children and animals; more refined versions are displayed by adults who may shout, swear violently, use sarcasm, and generally act in an over-excitable fashion.

Calmness, judgment and logical thought are affected; whenever possible it is better to fight against the tendency and attempt to control it. When dealing with people suffering in this way it is advisable to give them time to 'cool off' before reasoning with them.

Transferred aggression

When aggression is transferred to a false barrier it is generally because the true barrier is unknown or it would be dangerous to use direct aggression against the barrier. In one sense the irritation is controlled compared with direct aggression. It may be recognised through symptoms of peevishness, pedantry, constant complaints, criticisms, and a negative outlook.

The false barrier is generally of a weak nature which gives the person the opportunity to bully or vent feelings freely, often with disregard for the harm this might cause. The supervisor should be aware of the possibility when dealing with complaints concerning the employee's colleagues.

Introverted aggression

A sense of failure or some failure may cause a poor energy level, depression, poor initiative and self-accusation. This failure results in self-punishment – the anger being diverted inwards and causing introverted aggression. Examples are failing an examination, not being selected for promotion, or through rejection by the opposite sex. Self-denial of this kind normally rights itself in time, but in some abnormal cases it may even result in suicide.

Rationalisation

When people have acted in a silly way or find themselves in a humiliating situation they may unconsciously twist their motives. For example, an employee fails to operate a machine properly after instruction and pretends not to care whether he or she can operate it or not. In another case the person may blame the mistake on someone else by insisting it is not his or her responsibility to check for errors.

When someone's self-respect is hurt this emotional reaction must be expected: the person rationalises to justify his or her behaviour. It becomes more difficult to solve problems logically because the real causes are not acceptable at the time. Later the person may admit the fault when self-respect and esteem have recovered. Admission is not the aim; it is better to help the individual by not dwelling on the mistake but advising on how to avoid a similar recurrence.

Regression

When behaviour becomes less practical than may be considered normal probably the person is retiring into earlier primitive habits. Consequently he or she neglects later-acquired, more adaptive habits. This regression tendency is noticeable when, for example, a person insists on being incapable of performing a task but it is perfectly obviously that this is not so.

Initial symptoms are the inability to use knowledge, techniques or skills, along with signs of vague thinking, slovenly dress and the tendency to lose control easily. Generally the normal work-load becomes more and more difficult to cope with since interest wanes and concentration becomes increasingly difficult. Often there is difficulty in locating the barrier before help is possible.

Direct compensation

When all the person's efforts are concentrated on trying to defeat the obstacle it is known as direct compensation. The barrier is generally internal and caused by a weakness or lack of some requirement. Good adjustment is possible if these efforts succeed and are socially acceptable. However overcompensation occurs if the individual assumes an arrogant and over self-confident manner to cloak shyness and an inferiority feeling.

Exaggerating and stiffness in behaviour are general symptoms. Fixation is another form which means the person's energies are too strongly concentrated, resulting in a continual return to the same lines of thought or narrow thought patterns. Such patterns are illustrated by stubbornness, unresponsiveness to logical reasoning and a tendency to argue with no firm foundation. Uncertainty underlies this form of behaviour which is a desperate attempt to protect self-esteem.

Indirect compensation

If a substitute goal replaces the original one which is unachievable, an obsession to reach the substitute often occurs. This means all the person's efforts are aimed in that direction.

Although indirect compensation is a form of frustration high performance often results if a domestic or outside social upset is traumatic and forces the individual into over-emphasis on his or her employment. This imbalance is unhealthy. Other signs are wearing clothing unsuitable for the job and expressing absurd opinions.

Rejection

Casting aside past unsuccessful efforts and trying to forget the problem as if it never existed are known as rejection or repression. To protect self-esteem and self-respect unpleasant memories are forced into the back of the person's mind, thus making the conscience clear and uncluttered with humiliating thoughts.

In the subconscious mind these memories persist and affect behaviour and dreams. The symptoms are very little courage, poor energy and projection – possessing a fault but refusing to admit it. Alternatively the person finds that the fault with which he or she is suffering is very noticeable in others, and continually refers them to it. The reason for this strange behaviour is that the person's own desires and failures are projected onto other people's behaviour. Consequently if the person sees this same weakness in others he or she will feel more secure.

Flight

As the term implies, an individual may physically retreat from an obstacle. Examples are leaving a job if there is no prospect of promotion, or transferring to another department to avoid a supervisor's criticism. Flight may be considered a good adjustment if the change is successful. If the change worsens the individual's position, then bad adjustment applies.

Internal obstacles may be subjected to a form of flight such as resorting to alcohol or drugs which only provide temporary relief. Persistent absenteeism and lateness are also symptoms. A more potent form is recognised when a person 'gives up' or shows resignation in the working situation. This condition unfortunately is contagious to colleagues and may cause low morale.

Day-dreaming

Near to flight is resorting to fantasy. Examples are being frustrated by petty irritations and apparent insurmountable problems. Day-dreaming is a blessed release because immediate removal from the obstacle is made possible and time is available to regain control and drive.

Provided day-dreaming is not preferred continually to reality, there is very little maladjustment; many people day-dream. Maladjustment is noticeable when continual errors occur for no logical reason and there is no drive to develop further. When questioned the individual tends to lapse into blank expressions, staring out of the window, and in extreme cases seems unable to find words to express him or herself.

Solving frustration problems

The probable conclusions from the above brief survey of frustration caused by motives being blocked either internally or externally are:

1 Considerable attention is required to ensure that employees are placed in suitable jobs appropriate to their capabilities.
2 A careful check is essential to monitor progress to avoid frustration if the employee cannot cope with the job.
3 Continuous assessment is needed because people change through various internal and external circumstances.
4 The opportunity to develop further should be open to everyone.
5 Employees need help in their jobs and in the social side of employment.
6 Restructuring jobs to avoid frustration through boredom must be considered.
7 There are many needs to satisfy; concentrating on one group alone will not avoid frustration.

8 Employees are subjected to a wide range of pressures which easily upset performance. Their way of life does not coincide with sustained high performance; people naturally are affected at work by external upsets and internal problems.

9 Suitable organisation arrangements are necessary to cope with human problems. Everyone has off-days and suffers with some form of frustration.

10 The study of human problems is just as important as the technical problems of a supervisor's job if he or she is to be successful.

Behavioural theories

The two main theories associated with an understanding of basic needs, motivation and job satisfaction are process theory and content theory. Research findings in these fields so far have been found to be inconclusive.

The process or *mechanical* theories attempt to explain the processes involved which lead to choices among alternative courses of action, the amount of effort expenditure, and persistence over time.

Content or *substantive* theories try to specify the substantive identity of the variables that influence behaviour, such as rewards, basic needs and incentives.

Process theory

Various theories under the general heading of process theory attempt to postulate a formal explanation for the direction, amplitude and persistence of behaviour. The main ideas, in sequence, leading up to these theories are as follows.

1 In earlier centuries, it was thought that rationality and free-will decided behaviour.

2 Early twentieth-century concepts retained rationality for people but animal behaviour was thought to be a mechanical response set in motion by instincts. Darwin's evolutional model introduced biological explanations which led to the idea that instincts explained behaviour. McDougall (1908) gave the term *instinct* respectability but its use was stimulated beyond acceptable limits. A proliferation of instincts emerged and became difficult to manage experimentally, resulting in Woodworth (1918) creating a new concept: *drive*. He defined drive as a unitary concept which represented an over-all activity level.

3 Mid-twentieth-century ideas assumed that people make choices among behavioural alternatives on the basis of their knowledge. Thus people consciously calculate the relative pleasures and pains of various outcomes provided by alternative actions and seek to maximise their total pleasure.

Within this concept there are three major determinants of action: reinforcement, drive (a need) and incentives. Either singly or in combination they formed the major motivational models which were developed up to 1960. Simplified, reinforcement means the effect on the individual of learning habit-forming activities. Thus habit strength is dependent upon the situations that the individual has been subjected to in terms of magnitude and frequency. The energiser or motivational component, drive, indicates the general level of pressure for activity. Incentive represents the pulling effect of rewards.

Within the process theory concept lies the expectancy theory which attempts to explain the reactions of individual behaviour by arguing that they depend upon the discrepancy between what the environment offers and what the person expects, or has adapted to, at the time. In other words, a person will be expecting a particular outcome when he or she performs a particular act. If expectancy fails there may be a pleasant or unpleasant surprise, possibly with emotional reactions.

Content theory

Theories under this heading attempt to suggest the specific identity of variables discussed in general terms by the process models. The history of content theory is located in the theories of instincts which fell into disrepute at the beginning of the century as a result of the propensity to postulate a specific need for almost any human act. They achieved respectability again, however, when they were changed in concept to one of needs being acquired through the learning process.

Content theories are more concerned with specific rewards, the basic needs that may be identified, and the strengths of incentives on offer. For example, considering job performance a theory may attempt to classify the strength of achievement possibilities, recognition, responsibility, promotion prospects and salary increases. Another theory may propose a different list.

Conclusions

So far the motives which govern behaviour are seen to be extremely varied and capable of complex classification. The barriers which tend to destroy motivation force people into reacting in a variety of ways which are known as forms of frustration. Knowing the terms associated with frustration does not help unless the supervisor has the time to think and to analyse employees. The supervisor can assist in promoting emotional stability with the aid of further information and with the idea of trying to help employees adjust to situations often outside their control.

A vast amount of information on motivation is available; in the following section some of the main authors and their work are discussed by way of an introduction only. An essential requirement for understanding the work of behavioural scientists is to read their books and papers.

The behavioural scientists

A cross-section of the best-known behavioural scientists includes Abraham Maslow, Frederick Herzberg, Clayton Alderfer, Douglas McGregor, Chris Argyris, David McClelland, Saul Gellerman and Rensis Likert. The main features of their research findings and concepts are given below.

Abraham Maslow

In 1943 Maslow wrote a paper on motivation ('A Theory of Human Motivation') which put forward what has become the most widely accepted theory on the subject. He maintained that the process of satisfying human needs is continuous; as soon as one need is satisfied another one takes its place. This implies that needs form a hierarchy of importance and that when one need is satisfied it no longer acts as a sustained effective motivator. Maslow subdivided needs into the following groups: physiological needs – hunger, thirst; safety needs – security, order; belongingness and love needs – affection, identification; esteem needs – success, self-respect; and self-actualisation needs – desire for self-fulfilment. These groups are in ascending order of importance commencing at the lowest level.

The hierarchy breaks down when all the needs are developed; the needs remain, but energy is spent differently on a continually changing basis as an attempt is made to satisfy all or any one of them. Furthermore, if a lower need is at risk a higher need will be given up as the hierarchy reasserts itself. All the needs stay with a person regardless of whether he or she is at work, at home or at play.

A slightly adjusted arrangement of these motivation levels in Fig. 11.4 illustrates that when lower needs are satisfied increasing those factors such as wage rates, working conditions and fringe benefits will have only a slight effect on motivation. If a person is suddenly deprived of air, however, the immediate effect is to motivate the individual to satisfy this vital need, thus over-riding the higher levels temporarily. This reverting effect applies in varying degrees of strength at other levels dependent upon changing circumstances.

He also pointed out that in some circumstances people would reverse the stages and ignore some completely within the hierarchy of needs. Typical examples are the starving artist who could buy oils in preference to food, the struggling composer and the 'resting' actor. These people will often willingly give up basic needs for self-fulfilment, although they are the exceptions. Many individuals are satisfied with lower levels of achievement and

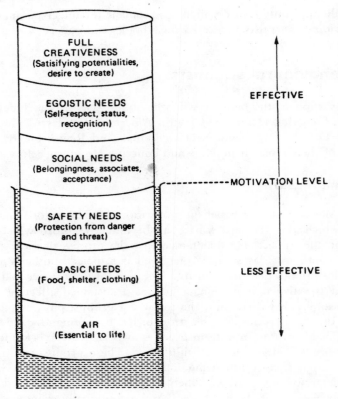

Fig. 11.4 *Motivation levels*

Imagine the tube contains the needs of an individual arranged in a series of levels.
The tube is situated inside the container of liquid. As each need is satisfied in
ascending order, the one above becomes the need most urgently requiring fulfilment.
The previous need, being satisfied, submerges the tube below the motivating point.
Only those needs above the liquid level are effective motivators, unless a lower one is
at risk

some, with low levels of ambition, are quite happy with the basic needs of
life.

Higher standards of living and increasing social legislation affect the
motivation level up to a point where social and egoistic needs become more
important. If these are neglected, individuals will tend to be indolent and
unwilling to accept responsibility and to behave in an unreasonable manner.

Concentrating on one motivating factor alone has, at the most, only a
temporary effect if it is already sufficiently satisfied. All factors connected
with motivation closely interact with each other, and management's
approach to motivation must cover all areas if the knowledge, intelligence
and enthusiasm of employees are to be released into channels conducive to
higher productivity.

Maslow's theory was first published in the *Psychological Review*, Volume 50, 1943. He also wrote many other papers, including 'A Preface to Motivation Theory' in *Psychosomatic Medicine, Vol. 5*, 1943; and various books, among which was one in conjunction with B. Mittleman, *Principles of Abnormal Psychology*, published in 1941.

Frederick Herzberg

How the needs described by Maslow actually operate has been studied by Herzberg who has drawn certain conclusions which have received much publicity and achieved popularity in Britain. He has analysed the main factors which result in either satisfying or dissatisfying experiences at work and has arrived at the conclusion that satisfaction and dissatisfaction are not attached to the same factors.

Satisfaction, Herzberg says, is induced through the job itself by the adjustment of achievement, recognition, the work, responsibility and professional growth; these are the motivators. Dissatisfaction is induced through the environment by adjusting company policies and administration, supervision, working conditions, interpersonal relations, money, status and security. This environmental aspect Herzberg refers to as 'hygiene' and he considers that, although the hygiene factors are important and that dissatisfaction should be kept to a minimum, only a fair day's work is possible if management concentrates on the environmental approach. Approach through the job itself, however, seems to have a larger and more lasting effect. Concentrating on job design or job enrichment provides more satisfaction to the employee and in turn increases productivity.

For a full appreciation of this motivation – hygiene theory there are two books written by Herzberg that should be read. They are *The Motivation to Work* and *Work and the Nature of Man*. Herzberg is Chairman of the Department of Industrial Mental Health, Case Western Reserve University.

Many criticisms have also been published. The research undertaken by Herzberg was concerned mainly with accountants and engineers. Often it is suggested, therefore, that his specific findings should be treated with discretion when dealing with shop-floor employees and clerical staff.

Alderfer's ERG model

Clayton Alderfer examined more recent evidence which caused him to reformulate Maslow's theory into three basic needs and refine Herzberg's two-factor or motivation-hygiene theory:

1 *Existence needs* Desires for material substances that are in finite supply. Typically food, shelter and money are included. The implications are that one person's gain is another person's loss; existence needs are not insatiable; and that people reach a satisfaction level which is thought to be sufficient therefore no-one loses in times of plenty.

2 *Relatedness needs* The mutual sharing of thoughts and feelings with others. This assumes people desire to inform others and to expect them to reciprocate. The communication should be open and accurate regardless of any unpleasantness.

3 *Growth needs* The interaction of the person with the environment to develop ability and capacity along lines which are most important to that person. This assumes that people seek to change their capacities according to their perceived requirements.

Needs continuum

Alderfer felt – like Maslow and Herzberg – that there was value in categorising needs, but he viewed them more as a continuum. He disagrees with the ideas that a lower need must be satisfied before a higher need and that deprivation is the sole way to energise a need. A good example is growth needs that may intensify the more they are satisfied.

This model is compared with Maslow's and Herzberg's in Fig. 11.5.

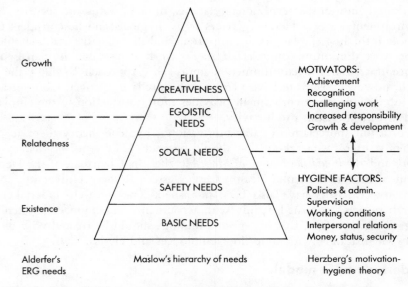

Fig. 11.5 *Relationships between Maslow's, Alderfer's and Herzberg's concepts*

Douglas McGregor

McGregor's work was based on his idea that effective leadership depended upon a manager's assumptions of the nature of management and about people in general. This idea was the keystone to his best-known contribution – Theory X and Theory Y.

Although the reasoning behind these two theories is in fact very subtle, it does have the appearance of being simple. This misconception has resulted in a tendency to oversimplify McGregor's thoughts; to be sure of the correct concept it is essential to read his books *The Human Side of Enterprise* and *The Professional Manager* (1960).

McGregor stated there were two sets of assumptions about people; since then these assumptions have been interpreted in many different ways. Briefly Theory X and Theory Y – the terms given for these two assumptions – attempt to account for the way a manager can deliberately influence the behaviour of an employee. This influence is exerted through an underlying philosophy which is communicated by the use of all the techniques associated with contact between two people such as speech, written notes, gestures, tone of voice, atmosphere, expressions, and so on.

Theory X is a philosophy where a manager sees employees as inherently disliking work, being unimprovable, needing to be coerced, controlled, directed and punished, avoiding responsibility whenever possible, and generally being unambitious.

Theory Y involves coaxing people through reward, praise, permissiveness and attention; it assumes that people will work naturally, will exercise self-discipline and self-control in certain circumstances, and will have potential for further development.

Both theories assume that productive work is an unnatural form of behaviour and that some form of pressure is essential to achieve it. The strategy behind Theory Y not only involves coaxing but also demands the structuring of work so that opportunities for further achievement and personal growth are possible.

Some people incorrectly interpret Theory Y as completely abandoning the limits or boundaries associated with discipline and control. In other words, people are allowed to do as they wish with no pressure to conform. This interpretation really amounts to anarchy, and unfortunately when such an approach is tried employees tend to take full advantage of the situation.

McGregor's work clearly anticipated the present vogue of job enrichment; he thought that trust should be established by a collaborative effort where mutual support encouraged high motivation. He was Professor of Industrial Management at Massachusetts Institute of Technology.

Chris Argyris

According to Argyris apathy and lack of effort are due to healthy reactions by normal employees to an unhealthy industrial situation which has been created by management policies. He feels that most people are naturally motivated to act responsibly and to be self-reliant and independent. Most jobs are structured, however, to create a childlike role and as a result lead to frustration which is demonstrated as a defensive manoeuvre, indifference and contempt so that the individual preserves his or her self-respect.

Argyris feels that people must have a sense of pride and accomplishment at work, but management still concentrates on financial reward, job security and fringe benefits. Thus employees find little stimulation or dignity in work and employment becomes a necessary evil partially compensated by applying for more wage increases as a penalty payment to offset lack of job satisfaction.

He also points out the difference between happiness and motivation. Making people happy does not necessarily motivate them. Conversely a motivated employee is not necessarily happy.

A further aspect examined by Argyris was that of interpersonal relationships which are the characteristic way of perceiving and dealing with each other. Apparently there is a tendency for managers and supervisors inadvertently to filter information and to have difficulty in giving their real views. This lack of interpersonal competence can be improved, he says, by sensitivity training or T-group training.

The method involves placing people in a unique situation which encourages openness and risk-taking but discourages defensiveness and mistrust. Thus their behaviour should give them the opportunity to improve their communication effectiveness, to reduce the barriers affecting relationships with other people, and to remove the filters that tend to distort information flow.

This unique atmosphere is created by operating very informal sessions without a chairman or an agenda. When the session commences, the participants soon realise that a framework is needed where each individual plays a predetermined role if anything is to be achieved. The learning occurs as the group copes with this problem, each person seeing the effect of their tactics on the others, observing the personal bias effect and noting the distortion of information flow between them.

Argyris emphasises that T-group training does not solve management problems and that he would not recommend its use in certain cases. Evidence shows that this training helps to make a person a better listener and that he or she becomes more receptive to information from other people.

Argyris has written many articles and books; the best known books are *Organisation and Innovation, Interpersonal Competence and Organisational Effectiveness* and *Integrating the Individual and the Organisation*. These should be read to appreciate his work, including his analysis of executive behaviour patterns. He is Beach Professor of Administrative Science at Yale University.

David C. McClelland

According to McClelland, most people feel they have an achievement motive. Research, however, shows that in the USA only about 10 per cent are strongly motivated for achievement.

McClelland's definition of an achievement motive is 'the tendency when you are not required to think about anything in particular to think about ways to accomplish something difficult and significant'. Apparently a person with a strong achievement motive is likely to surpass the accomplishments of an equally able but less strongly motivated person, especially if he or she is employed in such occupations as sales and marketing or management or is an independent business executive.

People with a strong achievement motive possess three major characteristics: first, they set their own goals; second they prefer moderate goals; and third, they prefer immediate feedback on their progress. They have a high opinion of their value in the form of wages, but it is questionable whether high reward makes any difference to their output as they normally work at peak efficiency. It would seem to follow, therefore, that monetary incentives have more effect on weak achievement drives. McClelland stresses that achievement motive is not the only source of high achievement; other drives can also play a part in different occupations.

There are reserves of achievement motive which can be utilised by introducing into jobs more achievement characteristics such as personal responsibility, individual participation in selecting production targets, moderate goals, and rapid feedback of results. Thus many standard supervisory practices are not appropriate and may even hinder employees' performance.

McClelland's best-known books are *The Achieving Society* and *The Roots of Consciousness*. He is Professor in the Department of Social Relations at Harvard University.

Saul D. Gellerman

According to Gellerman, it is possible to make some generalisations on motivation from research findings. These are that many motivational problems stem from the method of managing an organisation rather than the reluctance of employees to work hard, that managers have a tendency to overmanage by narrowing employees' jobs and by making too many decisions at too high a level, and that studying the employees' environment indicates reasons for their behaviour.

Gellerman's principle of psychological advantage explains that employees are motivated by their own desire to get by in the best possible way in the kind of world they think they live in. Thus employees are less susceptible to the influence of other people and more susceptible to their own drives which presumably are partially governed by the standard of education, degree of independence and the demand for what they have to offer. Managers can play a part, therefore, by ensuring that these desires can be satisfied by offering a change in the role an employee can play rather than concentrating on financial reward alone, although it is important.

Gellerman recommends three approaches which have a positive motivational effect. These are to 'stretch' the employee by giving him or her more difficult duties above the level normally considered suitable, to apply the principles of management by objectives, and to encourage participation by asking the employee for opinions before making decisions affecting the employee's work. These and many other concepts are given in Gellerman's books entitled *Management by Motivation, Management of Human Relations, Motivation and Productivity* and *People, Problems and Profits*. He is President of the Gellerman Kay Corporation.

Rensis Likert

The research undertaken by Likert is particularly interesting to supervisors. His findings indicate the importance of quality of leadership and that certain basic patterns of supervision give the best results. According to the data, supervision and leadership style usually influence productivity far more than attitudes towards the company and job interest.

Likert states that supervision is always a relative process; a supervisor must adapt his or her behaviour to allow for the expectations, values and interpersonal skills of subordinates, colleagues and superiors. He maintains that there are no specific rules of supervision which work well in all situations, but broad principles do apply to the supervisory processes and provide useful indicators to behaviour. These principles should always be used bearing in mind the situation and the employees involved.

A fuller understanding of leadership styles and Likert's research work and empirical tests is very useful and these can be studied in his book *New Patterns of Management* published in 1961. He is Director of the Institute of Social Research, University of Michigan.

Conclusions

Even a brief study of motivation theory as propounded by the above authors is sufficient to indicate the complexity of the science. There is a tendency for managers and supervisors to hear about a theory or a technique, try it, and abandon the idea for the wrong reasons. This is mainly due to misinterpretation of the theory or arriving at apparent causes of failure instead of the real causes, or failing to appreciate other factors that over-ride the behaviour of people in certain situations.

The social organisation in concerns is another important aspect affecting productivity. Society is rapidly changing and it is not easy to maintain close touch with reality. People are reacting more strongly against undue pressure and general unfair treatment by management, and the trend towards satisfying the more sophisticated needs is increasing along with more opportunities to develop a higher educational standard. The strong demand for management to adapt to these changes is obvious and cannot be ignored if attempts to motivate are to succeed and people are to be relieved of the multitude of senseless obstacles that frustrate them in many companies.

Questions

1   How would you recognise high motivation and what are the essential factors that are needed to achieve it?
2   What part should management play in promoting high motivation?
3   Discuss the methods open to the supervisor for developing group spirit.
4   In your opinion how important is the human factor in connection with motivation?
5   If an employee accuses you of always giving him or her the difficult jobs and it is not true, what conclusions would you draw and what action would you take?
6   How would you explain the fact that employees may receive wage increases, but no difference in their attitude towards work is seen?
7   What would you do about a situation where your group starts openly to 'carry' an employee for no apparent reason?
8   'Behavioural Science is based upon the assumption that behaviour tends to lead to attitude'. Discuss this statement.
9   List the main factors that affect the motivation of people.
10   Outline the internal and external barriers that may stop an individual from satisfying his or her needs.
11   List the ways that people may react to obstacles which thwart their needs.
12   Write brief notes on the work of Abraham Maslow.
13   Discuss job enrichment.
14   Distinguish between a need and a drive. Explain their importance in analysing behaviour.
15   What is the difference between instrumental and substitute behaviour?
16   Give three examples of secondary drives and describe their significance in motivation.
17   Discuss the three main outlets to satisfy drives.
18   Describe Theory X and Theory Y. Give your opinion of their validity in modern industry.

Case study 1

Maureen, the electron gun room supervisor, was responsible for twenty young women. The room was notorious for word-slanging matches. Some people refused to enter since they would be unmercifully treated with a barrage of ribald comments.

The work was exacting and demanded concentration, but consistent high productivity with a good quality record puzzled other supervisors. No-one argued with Maureen; she was tough, ruled harshly, and considered to be fair. One morning the works director walked in unannounced. The workers had never seen him before and immediately he received the full treatment. Howls of laughter and whistles followed him as he left hurriedly.

Maureen left the following week with no explanation. A new supervisor, Dan, arrived from outside; he was 30 years old with modern ideas. Within a week the workers were out of control. There were fights, materials were continually being thrown around, and the room was in an uproar. In desperation Dan appealed to the works manager who rather hastily decided to sort the workers out. Instead they sorted him out with a few well-aimed shots at his face. He retreated to the personnel manager's office.

1 Analyse the situation from the information provided.
2 What can the personnel manager and the works manager do now?

Case study 2

Malcolm Candy had been supervisor of the hardware department in a well-known store for twenty-eight years and was due to retire within one year. In his department there were twelve employees, but no deputy supervisor. They muddled through when he was away. The store manager decided that a deputy should be appointed and told Malcolm to put forward some proposals.

The situation as Malcolm saw it was that his department always seemed to be the busiest in the store. New models, especially in electrical goods, were continually coming along which were very demanding on him and his staff, as the store's policy was that the staff must know how their sales products operated, but everyone seemed to get on well together and it was unusual to receive complaints. Pay was reasonable even though there was no union recognition. From the employees' viewpoint there was no one like Malcolm and the current comment was 'We're going to miss him.'

In Malcolm's opinion there were three candidates:

1 *Tom Janson:* the department's joker, well-liked, not serious minded, work was exceptional, fifteen years with the company and 35 years old;
2 *Susan Bagley:* quiet, a good worker, rather reserved, but with a talent for organisation, experienced background, seven years with the company and 42 years old;
3 *Gary Wittering:* the natural leader, wastes time, work just acceptable, respected, twelve years with the company and 36 years old.

If you were Malcolm what proposals would you put before the store manager?

12 Further aspects of motivation

The remaining features are often discussed in view of their strong relationship with motivation theory and general management thought. Included are:

- The behaviourist approach
- Financial incentives
- Managerial aspects
- The group
- The individual and human relations
- The job itself
- Employee participation

The important features of leadership and power are covered in the next chapter.

The behaviourist approach

This theory studies the behaviour of an employee and attempts to identify causes by varying the environment which precedes and follows it. Although often considered under motivation theories, it differs fundamentally because thoughts, beliefs, attitudes, and feelings are ignored. In other words instead of focusing on inner aspects or inner motives it concentrates on past and present features of reward and punishment, assuming these determine behaviour. The idea is that behaviour is controlled by its immediate consequences.

Further reading on learning theories and on memory factors is essential to appreciate the full background. The two main techniques – organisational behavioural modification and social learning theory – are outside the scope of this text. However the main behaviourist principles are given below since many supervisors relate them immediately to practical situations.

Stimulus-response relationships

In the employment situation these relationships occur between superior and subordinate, between peers, and between employees and associations. Typically a supervisor asks a subordinate to undertake a task (a stimulus); if the performance (response) is acceptable and the supervisor congratulates him or her (a further stimulus and reinforcement), the response is strengthened. Consequently reinforcement not only strengthens the response that preceded it but also increases the possibility of the response occurring again.

Success is measured by noting whether future behaviour responds favourably to this particular stimulus. If it fails another type must be tried. A classic example is the use of money as a reinforcer. If it produces improved performance more frequently, this type is successful, but until tested there is no guarantee. If it fails another form of stimulus is tried and compared.

Types of reinforcement

The forms of stimulus or types of reinforcement are generally classified under four headings: positive reinforcement, negative reinforcement, extinction, and punishment. Within each heading are a number of choices; they are viewed as *contingently applied* for positive reinforcement and punishment, and *contingently withheld* for extinction and negative reinforcement. These are diagrammatically presented in Fig. 12.1.

The difference between the four types may be clarified initially by examining the aims, ways of achieving the aims and effects of each one. Positive

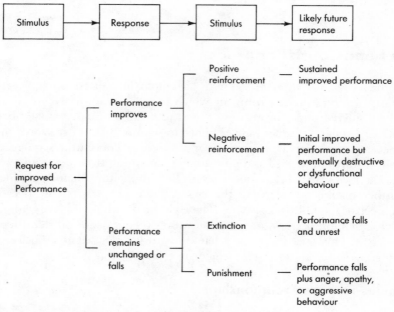

Fig. 12.1 *Types of reinforcement and their effects on performance*

The four types of reinforcement are: positive, negative, extinction and punishment. Positive is most successful since it indicates clearly rewards for desirable behaviour. Negative is unpleasant such as harassment or a reprimand. Extinction means stopping positive reinforcement for only mediocre performance

reinforcement strengthens response and increases probability of repetition, as does negative reinforcement. The positive reinforcement way is to use presentation of a desired consequence, while the negative reinforcement way is by terminating or withdrawing an undesired consequence.

Punishment differs from negative reinforcement by using a negative consequence to weaken response; it suppresses and implies that if an individual has a choice between punishment or no stimulus he or she would choose the latter. Extinction differs by stopping positive reinforcement for only slight increases in performance; it tends to make the undesired response disappear whereas punishment tends only to suppress.

Positive reinforcement

This is a pleasant or desirable stimulus such as financial gain, praise, more attention, a visual sign of approval, or expressions of affection. A positive reinforcer is immediately applied when performance improves, the effect being to strengthen response and increase the possibility of the response recurring. Provided the appropriate positive reinforcer is chosen by the supervisor success is assured, as already explained.

The principle is to stimulate when there is any movement or response which indicates an improvement, not to wait until an acceptable performance level is reached. Consequently the supervisor must be made aware of any favourable change immediately and time must be found to apply the stimulus.

Backing this approach is the *law of effect* by E. L. Thorndike. Dating back to 1911 it has stood the test of time and most behavioural scientists accept its validity. Briefly, the law states that of several responses made to the same situation, those accompanied or closely followed by satisfaction in the form of reinforcement will be more likely to recur; those accompanied by or closely followed by discomfort in the form of punishment will be less likely to occur again.

One danger with positive reinforcement is to apply it when inappropriate behaviour is occurring. For example a supervisor may neglect to give employees sufficient attention when they are working well on the grounds that a busy schedule does not allow for back-up of this nature. When something goes wrong and the cause is traced to an employee whose behaviour has dropped for some reason, the supervisor sees him or her and adopts a patronising approach by attempting to boost morale. The supervisor may say that the employee is doing a grand job and avoid the true reason. The employee knows the real reason for the interview and may feel he or she is receiving attention (positive reinforcement) when behaviour standards drop and subsequently adopts a similar pattern in the future.

Obviously the way to encourage undesirable behaviour is positively to reinforce it. The problem is to find time positively to reinforce for appropriate behaviour. This aspect is discussed later.

Negative reinforcement

An unpleasant or undesirable stimulus such as harassment or a reprimand is withheld or removed if performance is acceptable. Thus the employee avoids being constantly badgered or pestered and behaviour improves. Unfortunately if productivity falls and harassment begins, frustration and anger are created with inevitable results, since the technique savours of social blackmail.

Sometimes confusion arises between negative reinforcement and punishment because both may apply together: if a supervisor is discussing a topic with a group of employees and one is obviously not paying attention, a situation may develop when the supervisor asks the offending employee a question. The person does not realise this until attention turns to him or her as the rest await the reply; this person's attention is now focused as the supervisor repeats the question or asks if the question is clear. Embarrassment causes the person to pay attention after the incident, thus punishment is administered through embarrassment and negative reinforcement is applied at the same time by strengthening attention level.

Extinction

Stopping positive reinforcement for only mediocre performance levels is called extinction. This situation may occur due to a policy change or in a recession. Behaviour generally decreases and the risk of unrest is increased unless a revised positive reinforcement programme is introduced in an attempt to improve productivity.

If there is no external or internal reward such as financial reward, praise, or job satisfaction, the tendency is to extinguish the particular behaviour. Consequently an employee who suddenly suffers extinction by not receiving praise for his or her efforts, mediocre though they may be compared with others, will respond with lower efforts. This emotional reaction caused by cutting positive reinforcement may also induce attitude changes towards colleagues, general dissatisfaction with the company, and other forms of adverse emotional behaviour.

A common fault in managers is to adopt a stance where silence is intended to convey approval and praise to an employee when performing well. This high-handed approach is often accompanied by strong reaction from the manager if a mistake occurs or if behaviour of some description does not suit. An employee has to be very understanding and mature not to react according to extinction. Generally the outcome in the long-term is to seek attention by adverse behaviour, thus the manager is reinforcing lower performance tendencies.

Punishment

Harassment and reprimands are applied for only moderate behaviour. The outcome is generally decreased productivity, anger and apathy, and some-times aggressive behaviour. Although severe punishment may stop a behav-iour, inevitably it seems the long-term side effects set in.

If resorting to punishment it should be combined with some form of reward or praise for a favourable response as a result, and it should be applied immediately. Another way is to use *informative punishment* by illustrating how adversative consequences may be avoided. A vital point is always to ensure that the punishment is associated with the unfavourable response, and not confused with other responses. Punishment tends to concentrate on the nega-tive side by indicating that something should not be done rather than on the positive side by indicating what should be done.

Conclusions from research

Positive reinforcement is most successful because it clearly indicates to the employee the rewards to be received for desired behaviour. Extinction and punishment do not illustrate to the employee what is expected from him or her as they only show that poor behaviour is undesirable; however this claim may seem unacceptable because most people are fully aware that a company seeks higher performance levels.

Negative reinforcement may increase behaviour, but it also creates some negative feelings because the employee knows that if the desired behaviour ceases he or she will be subjected to harassment. Obviously negative rein-forcement and punishment are both negative control devices although they have an opposing effect on behaviour.

Applying reinforcement

The two classes of reinforcement, namely primary and secondary, are considered before discussing applications. *Primary reinforcement* satisfies a physiological drive such as hunger, therefore examples are food, water, and flight from pain. *Secondary reinforcement* is learned, acquired through prior association with a primary reinforcer, and cannot directly satisfy a physio-logical drive. Typical examples are financial reward, praise, encouragement, and opportunity to participate. Secondary reinforcers applied by supervisors are typically money, approval, affection, and attention.

Considering financial reward (secondary reinforcement) first, although the immediate application of rewards is desirable for positive reinforcement, scheduling may be continuous or partial in practice. Continuous application is costly and difficult to maintain over long periods as it requires supervisory and administrative time. The alternative is *partial reinforcement* which applies rewards from time to time. Although less effective as the desired behaviour takes longer to achieve, it is more economic, sensible and less cumbersome.

Four ways of application are at fixed intervals, variable intervals, fixed ratios, and variable ratios. These terms are self-explanatory. Briefly, a fixed time is arranged, say a week or a month, for payment of reward, but the tendency is towards uneven levels of performance. Variable intervals are of a random nature, thus the employee is unaware of the next payment date and the outcome is more consistent performance. Fixed ratios are simply based upon a number of output units and often high performance levels are achieved, provided payment is immediate. Finally variable ratios are similar, but the number of units is based upon a variance around a set average of productivity.

Further considerations

When considering such reinforcers as praise, an essential practice is to determine carefully the behaviour to be reinforced. When using extinction and punishment one approach is to treat these techniques as devices to stop or reduce undesirable behaviour, thus providing an opportunity to use positive reinforcement since the behaviour has improved. This amounts to a two-phase approach.

Choosing between extinction and punishment is difficult. Using extinction immediately indicates to the employee that something is wrong and provided the person is sufficiently sensitive towards the low performance and the situation he or she will connect the two changes. Such performance change must occur fairly recently and be noticed quickly otherwise the employee may not connect the two. If the supervisor has neglected to act quickly or was unaware of low performance which presumably has continued for a relatively long time, he or she may resort to punishment and rely upon positive reinforcement later.

Financial incentives

The desire to work is strongly coupled with the desire for financial reward through the very nature of society and the need to satisfy basic urges or drives. The degree of influence financial incentives have on output, however, depends upon many factors such as the wealth of the individual, the standard of pay already being received, the relative influence of social factors, the strength of the greed trait, general character and intelligence. If wages are high, the effect of a further increase may be negligible – perhaps a short burst of effort followed by a rapid fall to the original output level.

Two strongly opposing views are often heard in connection with financial incentives. One view is that a fair system is one where people are paid for what they produce; in this way the slackers are not supported by the energetic workers. Another view is that this system upsets human dignity when people have to jump for the so-called 'jelly-beans'. The emerging questions are: why do some people *want* to slack, and how are scrupulously fair schemes arranged and operated?

Successful motivation in non-financial terms eventually overcomes the first problem; the second question, however, does conform to a number of conditions that must be satisfied before non-financial forms of motivation can be applied. The main aspects are that management must be completely open with its intentions, and be fair when operating the scheme; employees' acceptance is essential and they should have confidence in its operation by possessing a complete understanding of the system; substantial incentives, promptness of payment, just penalties for poor work, and prompt attention to queries are all necessary.

Methods of remuneration – manual employees

The main types of wages schemes are day work, measured day work, graded day work, graded level day work, piece work or premium bonus schemes, the points system and bonus schemes.

Day work

Day work is a simple, easily understood scheme where the employee is paid a standard rate or flat hourly or daily rate. This method is also called 'time work' and is suitable where standardisation of work is not possible and quality is important. The method may include a lieu bonus where employees are working near others who receive an incentive bonus.

The method is also used when it is not considered economic to introduce an incentive scheme or when output is not governed by the operator. Strong leadership is needed to make up for the lack of incentive.

Measured day work

A flat rate is provided, as in day work, but performance is also measured and used to assess the payment of annual increments. This method thus provides a form of competitive incentive.

Graded day work

Another variation is to base payment upon a graded structure according to ability. The pay level is reviewed regularly and is partly subjective in nature through the application of merit rating if increase in skill is the yardstick. Alternatively length of service may determine the increases, or output levels may be determined over the period under review and used for appropriate increases.

Graded level day work

This is a more sophisticated scheme utilising work measurement. Payment is based upon a graded structure of proved performance levels. Advancement depends upon the employee demonstrating the ability to perform at the next higher level for a probationary period. The scheme is operated on a basis of mutual trust: the employee undertakes to work at a determined level while management guarantees a wage level regardless of any change in circumstances.

Piece work

Where operators need rewarding for exceptional ability straight piece work is suitable. A fixed amount is paid for each unit of work produced of a set quality, payment being directly proportional to output. This sum is calculated by timing the unit of work at a reasonable speed of operation and relating it to the wage rate, plus an allowance to give the operator the opportunity to earn a bonus.

Setting rates may pose problems; the rate must be fair and should be fixed with great care, as any change contemplated because of an error in the original rate-fixing may disrupt good relationships. Some agreements are made not to pay less than the basic rate. Close inspection for quality is essential, but close supervision is not so necessary as the scheme provides a strong incentive.

Signs of overstrain should be borne in mind and the scheme must be run fairly. Clocking-off the job may be necessary if delays occur and certain rules are needed to clarify situations where additional tasks are involved which are outside the rate set. Normally allowances for fatigue and incidental tasks are built into the rate.

Other forms of piece work are simply variations such as differential piece work which provides steps in the earnings to accommodate increased or decreased rates at certain levels. Many geared schemes may be used to make payment regressive or progressive at appropriate levels where, for example, quality falls off rapidly or more enthusiasm is needed to reach a level where a higher bonus becomes operative.

Premium bonus schemes

The basis of all premium bonus schemes is to share the savings provided by working faster than the set standard time to do the work between employees and the company. The three main schemes are the Halsey, Weir and Rowan systems, although there are many schemes in operation which are the offshoots of these three.

One-third of the saving is given to the employee under the Weir system, whereas half the saving is given under the Halsey system. The proportion of saving is variable under the Rowan system which allows a bigger bonus for small savings compared with the other two. When half the time is saved, however, the Halsey and Rowan systems give the same bonus. The Rowan system also limits the increased earnings to nothing more than double.

A prerequisite of any system is the careful use of work study to determine the best way of doing the job and to set a reasonable time for its performance (*see* Chapters 23 and 24).

Points system

The job is carefully evaluated on a points basis to provide a set number of minutes in which an operative working at a reasonable speed could complete the process. A point usually represents one minute, as in the Bedaux system, and an average operative is assumed to work normally at a speed of sixty points an hour.

A basic rate is guaranteed and the bonus is calculated on about 75 per cent of the time saved.

Bonus schemes

The remaining schemes involve either a group of employees who work as a team and are paid a bonus on group output or various ways of distributing a proportion of company profits to all employees.

1 *Group bonus* Financial reward is based upon the combined output of the group. The effect is to bring each employee's work under the scrutiny of the rest of the group. Employees become dependent upon each other's work and, where they can help each other within the group, the group spirit grows and output should improve.

Precautions are needed to ensure that the group does not suffer unduly when a member is absent. Group size becomes critical and the bonus schemes should be so arranged that *all* groups have *equal opportunities* to earn more at the same differential of payment.

A degree of flexibility or allowance is essential so that those employees who naturally work quickly are not restricted. Group incentives also seem to induce a better standard of quality compared with individual bonus schemes. Close supervision is not so necessary as the group attends to the lazier members automatically. The system is essential where individual effort is difficult to measure, as in the case of track-laying teams.

2 *Profit sharing* There is a variety of profit-sharing schemes which are extensions of the group bonus system. Generally all employees are included provided they have completed about two years with the concern. The object is to build up a collective effort, though some individuals cannot correlate their own work with the over-all concern.

The bonus fluctuates because of other factors besides employee effort which some people consider unfair. Ideally profit–sharing should at least join the interests of employees with those of the company, and provided the scheme is operated fairly with full disclosure of figures there should be more confidence in management.

Payment by results — wages

A study of the above schemes indicates that the quality of work could be in jeopardy as employees strive to increase output. The use of the scientific management approach with PBR may well induce conflict between quality and productivity. The safer alternative is to use contingency management with emphasis on participation and quality circles (Chapter 26). In Japan, for example, emphasis on employee control has always been avoided and substituted by more modern approaches.

Considering instrumentalism discussed in Chapter 9, the importance of PBR should not be underestimated. Some people are prepared to accept monotony for high wages but others with higher skills may become frustrated if their efforts are thwarted through hold-ups of materials, tools or assemblies, trade-union restrictive practices and poor rate-fixing.

Methods of remuneration — staff

For employees other than manual operatives it is more usual to pay an annual salary. This amount is then subjected to either irregular or regular increases and fringe benefits. The figure is set by senior management generally in conjunction with the personnel department and the staff association, or the union. The criteria include internal and external economic factors such as company policy on the going rates, demand and supply of specialist staff and company profitability.

Fixed annual rate

This category is set generally through some form of legislative requirement. It is not subject to regular increments and is normally restricted to high-level posts.

Annual rate

Most staff come within this scheme which may be subjected to regular or irregular increases which are listed below.

Incremental schemes

Job grades are established (*see* Chapter 17) covering all the staffing levels. Within each grade a series of steps is listed and, provided the employee is efficient, he or she may ascend the scale one step each year. Generally the scales overlap for promotion purposes, and for exceptional performance more than one step may be given.

Merit rating

Also described in Chapter 17, the scheme allows for extra reward based upon various levels of performance. Sometimes the concept may be applied more than once a year when appraisals are conducted.

Cost of living increases

Some companies adjust their salary scales once a year dependent upon the change in the inflation rate or some other similar assessment.

Bonus schemes

Typical examples are based upon annual profit share, commission on sales, success of special projects, or co-partnership shares in the company.

Overtime payments

Although arrangements vary considerably, in general overtime is paid below a certain job grade. Sometimes a set number of extra hours is expected to be worked before eligibility.

Payment by results – salaries

Staff who perform well naturally expect higher rewards; however, in some cases these rewards do not necessarily mean immediate financial gain but probably improved long-term promotion prospects. For the unambitious and the instrumentalists the system may seem unfair. Even merit rating schemes suffer with inertia although regular fair performance appraisals partly overcome the difficulty.

Unlike shop-floor work, if performance drops after the award the enhanced salary is generally maintained. Hence the tendency with some individuals to work hard, achieve permanent reward and then relax until the next opportunity.

Management

Relationship with employees

The employees' reliance upon management is fundamental. Management ought to appreciate the employees' desire to be proud of their managers; they should be right and look right in employees' eyes. To reach such an exalted position managers must possess and display a number of qualities. Sufficient knowledge of management principles, organisation, motivation and human relations is essential; managers should know what life and work are all about. They must be vital and dynamic to a point where their enthusiasm becomes infectious. Managers' achievements are measured in growth and financial success, but they must conduct internal affairs in a human way and not by ruthless methods.

The organisation should be treated as a community where a network of human relationships seethes with activity, controllable only by sensitive understanding and a high degree of skill.

Supervisors should be allowed to develop employees' capabilities so that ambition and self-improvement are considered normal and a sense of opportunity is felt by everyone. Appointments should be conducted on sound scientific lines for the most efficient deployment of labour, and with impartiality and fairness to maintain good working relationships.

Finally, objectives and information on performance are just as important to employees as they are to management, and these should be communicated fully and promptly to every member of a concern.

Management by objectives

One method of motivating both managers and supervisors is by using a technique called management by objectives (MBO). The title is misleading considering that everyone normally works towards given targets. Management by *acceptance* of objectives is more accurate.

Briefly the technique of persuading subordinates to accept objectives is achieved by:

1 allowing them to clarify their job by establishing their own ideas of its content and purpose
2 coming to a mutual agreement with them on their responsibilities
3 allowing them to decide what their targets for a given period should be and agreeing them with their superior
4 letting them work on their own as much as possible during the target period, asking their superior for professional advice (rather than direction) whenever they feel the need
5 conducting an appraisal of personal performance at the end of the period with a view to improving their effectiveness by further training and general assistance as required

Successful application of the scheme depends upon using the appropriate strategy. This is based upon modern methods of influence and control which allow people to feel unrestricted and free to develop and improve their performance according to their own ideas. Naturally there is a degree of restriction according to company objectives and economic factors.

The group

Successful handling of a group depends upon supervisory skill and adequate knowledge of group activity. This was discussed earlier in Chapters 5 and 10 and a brief summary here is sufficient.

Group behaviour

Within the group every individual invariably supports its activities, finding security in it and working to a common goal. The peculiarities of group behaviour are, first, that the group is very sensitive towards the treatment of its members. Second, the group is stronger than the sum of its members, more emotional and open to ideas, but it takes longer to change and therefore seems to be more set in its ways. Third, when aroused to achieve an objective, its driving force can be tremendously strong and sustained. There is a definite connection between productivity and group activity.

The supervisor's job is to satisfy the group's natural desire for solidarity which gives individuals a sense of security and importance.

Social activities

Adequate accommodation and financial support for social activities encourages the development of group spirit. Although some managers have been bitterly disappointed at the lack of enthusiasm or wavering interest in such schemes, no doubt they should look elsewhere for the cause rather than blaming employees entirely.

If employees suggest the facilities required and organise the activities themselves, there should be more personal identification and hence more satisfaction. Managers should actively support but possibly not take any part in controlling the proposed programmes.

Supervisors should also be active and enthusiastic. They can often recommend certain employees whom they know have a flair for sport and other interests. The sphere of recreation allows supervisors to gain a better understanding of subordinates outside the working environment.

There are many opportunities open to social clubs to represent their company in the outside community, e.g. joining local sports leagues, assisting in charitable work, taking part in parades, holding joint dances with other companies. All are ways of encouraging pride in the group and the organisation and enabling employees to appreciate their role in the community as a whole.

The individual and human relations

Although the importance of the group should be recognised, and techniques used to develop this motivation factor, similar emphasis on the individual is necessary to provide employees with a balanced outlook.

As mentioned previously, people are too complex even for expert psychologists to understand completely. The supervisor can with perseverance, however, use certain techniques effectively. Being more objective in the approach towards people and finding out as much as possible about them will produce the desired results.

Any supervisor who attempts to apply principles in isolation without considering the human factor will inevitably receive a poor reaction from a subordinate. The chances of choosing an effecive course of action based upon principles alone are remote. Human factors can easily over-ride the most elaborate plans. An obvious method of increasing employee motivation may produce a negative reaction because an equally obvious human factor has been ignored. Negative reactions must be accepted as a failure to weigh up the true interpersonal relationship. Reasons for failure must be thought out and new approaches tried with more emphasis on human relations. Understanding people, therefore, is a vital part of successful motivation.

The job

The job itself plays a part in providing the employee with sufficient scope for motivation. A thorough knowledge of job content (i.e. duties, status and line of command as laid down in the organisation plan) is essential otherwise the difficult task of matching a suitable individual to the job becomes impossible.

The job should be kept sufficiently broad to give the employee some flexibility and initiative. A very limited job may rapidly produce boredom and frustration as the opportunity to contribute is reduced.

Committees, conferences, suggestion schemes, competition and personnel counselling provide further outlets for active participation once the familiar barriers of lack of time and reluctance to accept responsibility are broken down. Some of these activities are discussed in more detail below (*see also* Chapter 16 and 17).

Meetings

The right atmosphere at committees and conferences is created by the chairperson who should be well versed in the art of persuading all the members to make some contribution to the discussion. Often employees are reluctant to speak in front of their supervisors, especially if they disagree with their views.

The purpose of a committee is defeated if one side dominates and all the parties concerned do not contribute and share information, opinions and ideas.

Suggestion schemes

Many employees are already aware of better ways of doing their jobs. Others are capable of thinking about the problems and coming up with ideas which would save the concern a great deal of money. A well-organised suggestion scheme combined with good relationships provides encouragement for employees to put forward their ideas.

Everyone gains under a fair suggestion scheme. Relationships are improved, an excellent outlet for participation is provided, and employees are able to identify themselves more closely with the concern. Even generally inactive employees are known to have submitted excellent proposals as the impetus to take part catches on. The element of competition and the chance to be recognised incite people into action.

Launching the suggestion scheme

1 *Publicity* A full-scale campaign is essential to diffuse information through every part of the concern. Posters should be prominently displayed and supported by letters to employees; supervisors should be carefully briefed to give any additional information that may be required.

2 *Boxes* Suggestion boxes should be placed in well-chosen positions and accompanied with a supply of forms. The conditions of the scheme should be clearly stated on the form and it should be brought to the attention of the employee where the signature is required.

3 *The supervisor's position* The attitude of the supervisor is most important in generating a successful scheme. He or she should understand that suggestions are not personal reflections on the supervisor and should encourage and stimulate interest in contributing ideas.

Operation of the scheme

A manager should be given the responsibility for operating the scheme. Finer details of the system will depend upon circumstances, but the essential points are that collections should be made regularly, recorded, and acknowledgements sent promptly. If privacy is requested, notification through the outside mail to the employee's home address could be used.

A recording system is necessary to avoid errors. Each form should be numbered and a file raised to accommodate the correspondence and findings. A sorting scheme is essential to cover all the areas of likely suggestions, each area being represented by an executive who can study and investigate fully each proposal before recommending a course of action. Possibly a committee should finally approve or reject the suggestions and award appropriate sums.

A rejection requires a carefully prepared and adequate explanation. On occasions a similar idea may already be in hand; in these circumstances proof is needed to show the employee that he or she was not the first to think of the proposal (one very important reason for keeping careful records).

The amount of award varies considerably from about 10 to 50 per cent of the savings for a year. Suitable publicity of awards should be given and additional benefits such as a free summer holiday, attending special functions or theatre visits could be given periodically to all award winners.

The main reasons why the scheme may fail are: long delays in administering the system, poor rewards, inadequate reasons for rejecting proposals, poor supervisory support, or that suitable relationships were not established before commencement.

A successful scheme demands time, expense and additional managerial effort. The gains are mainly twofold – financial economies and higher motivation of employees.

Periodic comparisons of the number of submissions and acceptances give an indication of the trend, and for this purpose the following formulae may be used:

$$(a) \quad \frac{\text{Total suggestions submitted}}{\text{Average number of employees}} \times 100 = \frac{\text{Submission rate per 100}}{\text{employees}}$$

$$(b) \quad \frac{\text{Total accepted suggestions}}{\text{Average number of employees}} \times 100 = \frac{\text{Acceptance rate per 100}}{\text{employees}}$$

Competition

Fostering a competitive spirit between individuals and groups provides them with an additional interest in the job. The easiest way to stimulate rivalry is to give everyone all the information on production, including employee and group performances on output, quality, economy and productivity.

The information should be presented with some highlighting effect to arouse interest and, after a while, followed up with targets which should not be unreasonable. A production drive for one month to achieve a delivery date for a particular order is a typical example. The output targets should not be over-demanding. The drive needs staging properly with, say, an opening ceremony and well-publicised daily progress.

The scheme may be extended into the fields of quality, waste prevention, absenteeism and accidents. Suitable rewards for efforts could include extra privileges besides financial gain.

Job satisfaction

The effect of experiencing differing job satisfaction levels seems to vary, depending upon the particular individual. The main areas of thought are worth mentioning although they lack clarity, are sometimes conflicting and difficult to reconcile:

1 Improved job satisfaction increases happiness and contentment but not necessarily productivity.
2 Motivators will often improve productivity and job satisfaction.
3 Elements such as resources provided, financial rewards, relations with co-workers, and comfort may improve job satisfaction but not necessarily productivity.
4 Improved productivity generally implies higher rewards which together should improve job satisfaction.
5 Improved job satisfaction generally leads to higher morale which should make (a) the application of motivators easier and more likely to succeed, and (b) possibly improve mental and physical health.

Employee participation

Probably the biggest step forward in recent years in trying to understand people and the way they behave is the upsurge of interest in various ways of involving employees in their work and work organisation. The participation concept admits that employees are not just 'pairs of hands', that they have a considerable amount to contribute, that their needs have to be considered, and that their wishes and expectations are important factors in determining the success of changes.

Within this concept there are many interpretations, ranging from consultation, quality circles, autonomous groups, motivation theories, leadership style, consultative bodies, through to employee control in industrial democracy.

The background

Scientific management – meaning direct control strategies – is still widely practised. Moreover, in sectors where technical change involves deskilling it is increasingly utilised successfully. The danger is that costs may increase eventually through employee opposition. When this danger point is reached management tends to introduce a variety of responsible autonomy approaches to moderate the adverse effects of direct control.

Taylor (of scientific management) recognised the importance of work groups and sought to remove the solidarity they represented. The human relations school used an alternative approach by integrating the work group to achieve easier control. Structural design was not touched but the training of supervisors became popular. The concept of employee-management to humanise marginally was encouraged.

As the neo-human relations school developed the suggestion of structural redesign is noticeable by emphasising self-actualisation (Maslow), job enrichment (Herzberg), and group integration (Likert). Eventually job redesign dominated through socio-technical systems, innovation conforming to the autonomous work-group.

The philosophy

The *achievement principle* is widely accepted in society. It means that people feel the distribution of rewards is fair because they believe it is related to what is actually achieved at work or related to the qualifications obtained to enable them to do the work. Thus the philosophy of participation is strongly imprinted in people's minds and may conform to any of the three basic approaches outlined in Chapter 2: unitary, pluralistic and radical philosophies. These may be tied to the various choices (or levels) of participation below, remembering that they are rival frames of reference attempting to explain work relations.

Levels of participation

The range may be divided into three main levels. Starting at the organisation base the first is a consolidation of consultation, job enrichment, and quality circles. These coincide with the unitary philosophy by reorganising work to increase its scope for the satisfaction of employee needs *and* to improve the company's efficiency, in the national interest.

The second moves up the line to include participative leadership, consultative bodies, works councils, and Whitley Councils. These conform to the pluralist philosophy by establishing structures and operating techniques that go with a situation where unions are sufficiently powerful to contest management who treat them as a loyal opposition. Thus management is willing to compromise in the interests of harmony and unity.

The third level is associated with board representation for policy making, worker control, self-management and worker co-operatives. Here the radical philosophy applies where major inequalities and imbalances of power are accepted by management and the trend may be gradual or revolutionary. The Bullock Report (*see* Chapter 19) explains the position in the UK regarding opinion and legislation.

Conclusions

Considerable publicity has been given to successful schemes. In Japan the use of quality circles has proved to be worthwhile. Throughout the EEC employee participation is a reality in terms of political, legal and social aspects. Sharing in the capital and profits is often created by collective agreements, and in France by legal obligation. The scope of collective agreements is increasing and includes economic policies of companies and the organisation of their industrial and commercial affairs. Co-determination in Western Germany is well-known.

There seems to be a danger that the characteristics of the situation – socio-cultural and socio-technical – may be incorrectly assessed when participation schemes are introduced, resulting in failure. Such inaccurate assessment does not mean that the concept is wrong. Similarly, lack of adequate preparation before introducing the scheme and insufficient attention to education and training programmes may also cause problems.

Questions

1 Explain the behaviourist approach and comment on its degree of realism compared with motivation theories.
2 Outline the types of reinforcement and their effects on performance.
3 Explain and give your opinion on the principle that forms the basis of positive reinforcement.
4 Discuss the difference between negative reinforcement and punishment.
5 Explain primary and secondary reinforcement.
6 'Employees are just "pairs of hands" with little to contribute.' If you were given this opinion by a supervisor colleague how would you react?
7 'My job's boring. If you must know, the reasons I come here are for the money and because its difficult to find work elsewhere.' If your best worker confronts you with this statement, what would you do?
8 Discuss fully financial incentives and give your personal opinion of their effectiveness.
9 How would you organise a suggestion scheme?
10 Do you think a suggestion scheme is worthwhile? Explain your viewpoint thoroughly.

Case study 1

Cynthia was relating to her friend the situation at her office. 'This girl Daphne actually sits there most of the day knitting and on senior secretary's pay. Her boss is nearing retirement *and* he says that so long as she gets his work done that's all he cares about. We're working flat out to keep up, but she never offers to help. In fact she said to Mandy who was over-loaded, "More fool you. Find a slack boss like mine and you're home and dry."'

Cynthia continued, 'My boss doesn't open her mouth. I take in the work, she signs it, hands me another tape, and reaches for the 'phone. I started to complain about the office, but as soon as I mentioned Daphne she cut in, "Later, not now, I'm busy. You're already behind with that tape."

Angela said she got the same treatment from her boss. She said she never gets a word of thanks. When she mentioned Daphne he scowled and told her it was none of her business and not to mix work with petty politics. We hear on the grape-vine that Daphne is related to the company secretary and she's been seen out with her boss.'

Cynthia concluded, 'We feel we get punished for working hard while she's protected for doing nothing. It's unbelievable what goes on.'

1   Analyse this case with specific reference to the behaviourist approach.
2   What further evidence would you need before arriving at any conclusion?
3   What could the secretaries do in this situation?

Case study 2

Abraham Smithson, a managing director, spent Saturday afternoons on the golf course. During a round his golf partner, a company director, explained about the works council he had established recently. 'It keeps the employees quiet because they think they have a say but really it's the same old thing as the joint consultative committees we used to hold years ago.' He continued, 'We simply apply delaying tactics if we don't like the recommendations and after a few meetings they've forgotten what they proposed anyway. Gives them a chance to let off steam, you might say.'

'It sounds good,' Abraham replied. 'Of course I've read all about participation and the Bullock Report but we don't need it. I rely on my production manager who holds meetings with the supervisors and they sort out all the difficulties. It's just another management gimmick that will be out of fashion in a couple of years.'

'It works well in Germany and Japan and after all they're our major competitors,' a third partner cut in.

'Maybe, but they're not British!' Abraham snarled. 'Their unions co-operate and they don't understand attitudes like "I'm all right Jack". You can't escape the fact that it's them and us over here and you've got to make the best of a bad job! Participation won't solve anything!'

Comment on the attitudes displayed by the directors and relate your main points to the philosophy of participation.

13   Developing leadership and power

Introduction

Leadership is one of the main factors determining group behaviour. When it is correctly applied, each employee actually enjoys feeling a strong commitment towards achieving organisational goals. The willingness or eagerness to follow a leader apparently relates to people perceiving that their own needs will be satisfied.

To determine actions and assess needs, the supervisor should possess sufficient knowledge of leadership and develop leadership skills. The essential requirements are now outlined.

Definitions of a leader

Simple definitions are:

- capability to energise a group
- ability to relate various skills so they emerge as a driving force
- making people feel responsible
- inducing a dynamic common purpose to magnify the wills of employees, to inspire enthusiasm and to influence positively individual behaviour

Advanced definitions are:

1   a dynamic activity within a group where one person influences all the other members voluntarily to contribute towards achieving established tasks and goals in a unique situation
2   an outstanding member of a group who has the capability to create conditions within which all members feel a strong commitment towards achieving accepted objectives in a given environment

Clearly, leadership is a much wider concept than management, considering these definitions.

Leadership effectiveness

Over the centuries the qualities of famous and notorious leaders have puzzled researchers. No acceptable list of traits – or whatever – seems to fit them all. Certainly *what* they do is clear, but *how* they do it and *why* they are so successful is conjecture.

Modern thought sees leadership effectiveness as a composite skill and includes style theories, trait theory, and contingency approaches. Indeed, it is unfeasible to isolate one leadership component and attempt to relate it to all good leaders, their success rate, or its particular importance.

One approach is to accept the main factors and their implications. The main factors are: ability to inspire, to take action that improves behaviour, and to be sufficiently sensitive towards individuals' differing motives and the situation in which they find themselves. The implications: leaders are born with certain advantageous qualities – they have the good sense to acquire knowledge on human behaviour, and sufficient ability to develop appropriate leadership skills.

Leadership behaviour alone does not highly correlate with leadership effectiveness. Other factors play important parts. Consider, for example, two leaders placed in an identical situation. They may behave similarly, take the same steps, but achieve different results.

An effective leader finds the right balance between concern for people and concern for production. This means the supervisor is responsible for doing the work which is actually done by employees who should receive sufficient consideration for their development. Achieving this balance might persuade a supervisor to think less about himself or herself and more about employees.

Types of leader

Five main types of leader are identified. The first three are of academic interest while the next two are significant to supervision.

The charismatic type

Personality traits enable this well-known type to excel easily. Such examples as Churchill, Kennedy and Hitler indicate the class.

The traditional type

Position is conferred by birth: typically kings and queens. Obviously the class is severely restricted and many are doubtful leaders from the managerial viewpoint.

The situation type

This type is limited to circumstances where the leader is able to exert considerable influence due to his or her unique knowledge and experience. Generally such leadership is only temporary.

The appointed type

Most managers and supervisors are classified under this heading because their influence is exerted from their positions held in the organisation. Some confusion often arises when they expect to exert power through their appointment and fail to see the difference between power, authority, and leadership.

The functional type

This category utilises modern contingency theory which concentrates on what a leader does and discounts what he or she is.

Major theories

Six main categories have emerged over the past fifty years:

- the trait approach – personal qualities ensure success
- the situational approach – a particular type of leader satisfies the immediate perceptions of people
- style theories – concentrate on the behaviour and philosophical outlook of a leader towards employees
- contingency theories – emphasise adaptive leadership behaviour which varies, depending upon the situation
- Path-goal theory – incorporates expectancy motivation theory and use of power
- a normative model – attempts to illustrate how a leader should act in a number of given situations

The trait approach

Up to about 1950 most studies tried to identify leadership traits probably because in early times great men seemed to possess exceptional physical, mental and personality characteristics. These were perhaps essential to survive in battle and to dominate relatively ignorant communities.

Findings of research tend to disagree on a set of traits or qualities that distinguish leaders from followers. Nevertheless research has indicated significant correlation between certain traits and effective leadership. Examples are intelligence, dependability, conscientiousness, social well-being, and socio-economic status. Other traits often mentioned are supervisory ability, initiative, self-assurance, broad social interests, maturity, respect for others, and an interest in people.

The situational approach

Fresh ideas were sought when trait theory was discredited. Notorious leaders like Hitler and Mussolini led researchers to introduce a theory relying upon a unique situation demanding a particular type of leader. Thus the belief arose that leaders are the product of a given situation.

Castro and Roosevelt are good examples since they diagnosed the people's perception correctly and began programmes which appealed to them.

Style theories

These concentrate on the behaviour and philosophical outlook of leaders towards employees. To appreciate the theories four basic styles are explained. First, the dictatorial leader uses the philosophy of fear. Second, the autocratic leader directs and expects compliance; this type is forceful, positive and dogmatic, and exerts power by giving or stopping rewards and punishments. Third, the democratic leader consults, encourages participation and uses power with, rather than power over employees. Fourth, the laissez-faire leader allows a high amount of independence; employees set their own objectives and decide how they achieve them.

The use of authority forms the basis for these styles together with a philosophy variance ranging from fear, single authority, decentralised authority, through to complete freedom from authority. Many models have been submitted by writers and institutes based upon particular research findings. These fit into three groups: authoritarian versus democratic styles; concern for employees versus concern for production; and socio-emotional leader versus task leader. Their complexity demands considerable reading in separate literature mentioned in the Bibliography. A brief survey is now given.

Authoritarian versus democratic styles

McGregor's work on this concept is discussed in Chapter 11 since it is the foundation for many motivation theories. His Theory X and Theory Y clearly demonstrate the two opposing assumptions about behaviour and the supervisory stance adopted.

Likert's work in 1961 classified styles into four groups. These are based upon certain characteristics of the company: degree of freedom which employees feel about communicating with managers, and the amount of confidence and trust they feel the managers have in them.

The groups (ratings) are:
System 1 – exploitative authoritarian leadership

System 2 – benevolent authoritarian leadership
System 3 – consultative leadership
System 4 – participative leadership, based upon teamwork or participation which demands confidence and trust.

Research findings indicated a strong connection between System 4 and sustained high productivity.

Likert stresses the application of three principles:

1 Full use of the concepts and techniques of motivation.
2 Development of a tightly knit organisation of work groups committed to achieving organisational objectives. These groups should be interlinked by employees who possess overlapping membership in two groups.
3 Establishment of high aims for managers and employees, and clarification with them of the aims they are expected to achieve.

Finally an example of a continuum of leadership behaviour (Fig. 13.1) is given by Tannenbaum and Schmidt. Underlying these styles is the thrust to adopt a democratic style.

Personal relationship versus task accomplishment

Concern for people as well as production is the theme. Various grids and

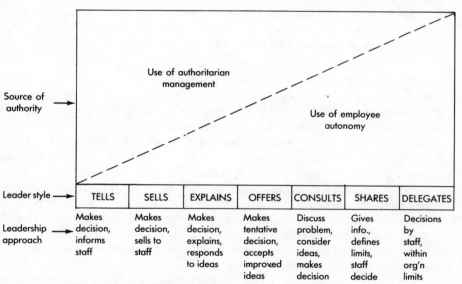

Fig. 13.1 *Continuum of leadership behaviour*

(adapted from Tannenbaum and Schmidt, 1957, Harvard Business Review)

The range of styles is expanded by Tannenbaum and Schmidt into a continuum of behaviour. Underlying these styles is the thrust to adopt a democratic style and to emphasise the importance of a leader's behaviour

frameworks are constructed to indicate where a supervisor fits in relation to his or her bias towards group members and tasks. The four studies of interest are by Blake and Mouton who developed the managerial grid; The Survey Research Centre at University of Michigan; The Ohio studies prepared by the Bureau of Business Research at Ohio State University; and the 3-D theory introduced by Professor Reddin at New Brunswick University.

Socio-emotional leader versus task leader

Harvard University identified two distinct groups of leaders in small-group behaviour. These were essentially mutually exclusive as in the heading above.

This aspect is interesting since it agrees partly but not wholly with research findings on group dynamics. Some leaders were found to be task oriented, others were democratic; some were both task-and relationship-oriented; while others seemed unconcerned about either.

Contingency theories

The following two approaches are based upon the application of adaptive leadership behaviour which varies dependent upon the prevailing situation. They differ from trait and style theories since the multiple dimensional factors are taken into consideration.

Functional leadership

The concept was developed by J. Adair and is often called action-centred leadership. The model is illustrated in Fig. 13.2 and it utilises three components: individual needs, team maintenance needs, and task needs. These components are related to the over-all situation. The leader in these circumstances must be aware of the needs within the three components and must possess sufficient skill and training to meet them in accordance with the priorities of the particular situation.

Action-centred leadership is an apt description of the approach, which avoids emphasising personality, incorporates concepts in other theories, distinguishes between concern for individuals and concern for groups, and stresses the importance of acting in accordance with situational priorities. The obvious examples in practice are the introduction of a computer in an office, the introduction of a new engine involving changes in assembly and bonus schemes, and emergencies; each case utilising individual needs, group needs and task needs respectively.

Individual needs or maintenance functions should include counselling to understand the person's feelings, outlook and expectations; dealing with

Fig. 13.2 *Action-centred leadership*

This model was propounded by Professor J. Adair. The three components are related to the over-all situation. The leader must be aware of the needs within the components and possess sufficient skill and training to meet them in accordance with the priorities of the situation

personal problems; assessing capability and training as required; and encouraging.

Group needs or maintenance functions include counselling with the informal leader, building team spirit, aligning aims and goals, communicating effectively, setting fair standards, encouraging training, and liaising with other groups.

Finally task needs or functions are directed towards planning, setting objectives, defining the tasks, allocating work and resources, and controlling.

Leadership contingency model

F. Fiedler propounded this approach which views group performance as being contingent upon the leader adopting the most effective style to suit the relative favourableness of the situation. According to Fiedler the three major parameters which seem to determine the leader's effectiveness are:

1   leader–member relations
2   degree of task structure
3   the leader's position power

The first two tend to coincide with consideration for people and consideration for the task, both of which appear in style theories; while the third is a combination of the leader's suitability for dealing with the situation, situational theory and task concepts.

Path-goal theory

This modern approach incorporates expectancy motivation theory and the use of power to smooth the employee's path towards achieving a goal.

Development of the theory was by R. House and M. Evans who both wrote papers on the subject. An adequate explanation includes a version of the four leadership styles, and identification of two situational factors, and a description of the influencing technique.

Choice of leadership styles

The four versions to choose from are outlined below.

DIRECTIVE LEADERSHIP
Specific directions are given and people know exactly what they are expected to do. The leader schedules the work, maintains standards of performance, and encourages standard rules and regulations. No participation is allowed.

SUPPORTIVE LEADERSHIP
A genuine concern for employees is shown by being always approachable and friendly. Employees are treated as equals and a pleasant, enjoyable atmosphere is encouraged.

PARTICIPATIVE LEADERSHIP
Suggestions are encouraged and used but after due consultation the leader still makes the decisions.

ACHIEVEMENT–ORIENTED LEADERSHIP
Challenging goals are set for employees who see an open display of confidence in their capability to perform well and achieve these goals. Trust is essential and personal responsibility is encouraged.

The inference is that different styles should be employed by the leader in different situations, consequently the approach differs from others in this respect. To provide guidance on the choice of style two situational factors are employed.

Identifying two situational factors

The first is an assessment of each employee's characteristics which include ability, needs, and locus of control.

ABILITY
If an employee perceives his or her ability as low it is possible that directive leadership will be acceptable but if high probably unacceptable.

NEEDS
The mental make-up of the individual – taking into account needs, drives and personality – may also influence the style which will be acceptable. For

example a strong drive for achievement would cause a favourable response to achievement-oriented leadership.

LOCUS OF CONTROL

If employees view what happens to them (or their future) as being under their control, this is termed internal locus of control. Therefore a participative leadership style would be acceptable. However if the opposing view is held the employees feel external locus of control is operating, which means events are determined by influences outside their control. In this case directive leadership is more acceptable.

These characteristics are assumed to govern the degree of satisfaction and future satisfaction which is biased by the style of leadership applied.

The second factor is an assessment of the employee's environment which will decide the coaching, guidance, support and rewards which he or she expects before effective performance is likely.

Theoretically the leader's behaviour will be motivational if his or her assessments are correct and the appropriate style in each circumstance is chosen. Thus the employee's perceptions are influenced and motivated which provides a smoother path through role and goal clarification and increased satisfaction.

The working environment is divided into three categories: employee's tasks, the formal authority system, and the primary work group. After an assessment the leader must decide on an appropriate style. This must give sufficient direction and support to compensate for the lack of motivational features.

The influencing technique

House and Mitchell designed six steps for the leader to follow in order to accomplish motivation.

1 recognising and/or arousing subordinates' needs for outcomes over which the leader has some control
2 increasing personal payoffs to subordinates for work-goal attainment
3 making the path to those payoffs easier to travel by coaching and direction
4 helping subordinates clarify expectancies
5 reducing frustrating barriers
6 increasing the opportunities for personal satisfaction contingent on effective performance.

The accomplishment of each aspect still depends upon appropriate choice of style. The complex theory is very demanding but successful leadership behaviour is possible.

A normative model of leadership

Vroom and Yetton have attempted to establish a specific normative model illustrating how a leader should act and how decisions should be made in given situations. Other theories avoid these approaches which have a limited use at present.

The most recent complex model uses five leadership styles, seven decision rules, seven situational dimensions and fourteen problem types. A separate study in depth is essential to appreciate the use of the decision tree and all its components.

Many managers find the model an interesting and informative approach, but so far there are insufficient research findings to validate it and encourage its use.

Leadership objectives

These are generally assumed to be aligned with supervisory and organisational objectives. Unfortunately in some situations the assumption may be partially false when a supervisor pursues personal ends.

Typical situations include practices associated with the 'rat-race' and 'empire-building'. Whether or not they contribute in any way towards achieving organisational objectives is debatable and depends upon the long-term outcomes which will vary in each particular case. Presumably top management is aware of the practices and agrees with them; or disagrees but is powerless to interfere; or is unaware and out of touch with reality.

Influencing behaviour

Clearly an effective leader is not necessarily an effective supervisor when he or she uses leadership to pursue personal goals. Leadership in this context is broader than management which is considered to be a form of leadership with the aim of achieving organisational objectives. Thus leadership is exercised at any time when a person is trying to influence behaviour.

The complexity of the scene increases when the number of authority levels, group objectives, and formal and informal leaders, are also considered. Group leaders may visualise a number of different objectives. Choice becomes difficult and is partly influenced by the strength of top management, partly by power, how it is used, and how it contributes to ultimate ends.

Supervisory power

There is a noticeable trend towards developing supervisory power and influence as a way of improving co-ordination and because of its strong advantage in achieving effective leadership. Such power does not mean bullying, malevolence or deceit. Benevolent power is implicit, which means influencing by encouraging and heartening the employee by exhibiting goodwill and some humanity.

If successfully applied the employee feels a strong desire to follow and work more willingly towards achieving goals. Probably he or she is influenced towards more responsible behaviour which in turn generates more power that elates and encourages improved performance.

Power-seeking

Power struggles among people are inevitable and cause revulsion among those who have experienced its misuse. Therefore the use of power should be learned with long-term effects in mind. The likely reaction from certain individuals should be expected. Power certainly satisfies some higher needs; therefore attempting to stifle drives to gain power is understandably frustrating and causes adverse reactions.

The supervisor's intentions may be numerous when he or she is power-seeking. They could be for self-interest, self-development or self-advancement, or to benefit the company, or combinations of these reasons. Inevitably managers and employees soon recognise intentions and possibly constructive conflict emerges which aids decision making.

Reputation

Clearly the supervisor's reputation heavily depends upon the method and use of power and how he or she develops it. One belief is that the authority given to the supervisor equates with appropriate power, but considering a definition – the ability to get things done – this idea is suspect. Indeed relying on authority means depending on the superior who may easily increase or decrease support. Such conferred power also needs employee support through fear. In this situation reward and sanction predominate, and possible reaction – especially with trade-union support – could be disastrous.

Authority power

If a supervisor relies on authority power – or position power – he or she might be successful for a while, provided the situation allows it. Therefore eventual change will be difficult to control and long-term effectiveness is low as reaction occurs.

This effect could be dangerous if the 'successful' supervisor is promoted in the short-term and a replacement finds reaction setting in. Therein lies a selection problem when people are promoted on quick results or on the immediate favourable behaviour of their staff.

Employees' degree of acceptance of position power depends upon many factors related to managerial prerogatives. Typical features are traditional contention, employee attitudes and culture, trade-union influence, and company climate.

Personal power

In a sense this form is the opposite to authority power because support comes from below the supervisor. Through charisma and the use of appropriate leadership styles he or she relies upon building respect and appealing to employees' needs. This volatile situation depends on legitimate power, referent power and expert power. The supervisor must have a legitimate right to influence behaviour (legitimate power), employees must perceive the supervisor as a potential leader (referent power), and he or she must possess sufficient expertise (expert power) to convince employees of this right.

Always there is the possibility that the situation will change and employees will no longer support the supervisor for some reason. He or she relies heavily on ability to motivate them and theoretically effective leadership over the long-term is possible if the supervisor is successful in adjusting to inevitable changes in each individual's needs and group needs.

Methods of developing power

Many common methods of developing power are witnessed every day. Typical examples are:

- attempting to dominate by using oral eloquence
- exerting mental pressure by using charisma
- developing friendships with powerful superiors and using these links to influence subordinates
- seeking alliances with peers to exert group pressure
- using an association by accepting a post and exercising influence through the automatic support of its members
- developing expertise in a new technology or discipline which is recognised as a critical feature for company survival or development
- seeking weak points in the organisation and exploiting them in a variety of ways
- achieving effective performance by working hard, developing new roles and proposing new ideas
- establishing strong relationships with influential people outside the company who are able to exert pressure in some way
- creating a better impression through a variety of means such as improving speech, education, technical and social skills, dress, manner and social work.

The effects

The use of a particular method may have varied effects on employees. These would include fear, submission, obedience, capitulation, motivation, antagonism, or retreat. Being able to forecast the response from superiors and subordinates is understandably difficult in practice. Choosing the appropriate methods improves the probability of advancement since organisations are political arenas, healthy conflict reduces the risk of stagnation, and the role system regenerates. Thus power-seeking is considered in one respect to be essential.

Exercising power can be equally destructive if used solely for self-development by ignoring the over-all effect on the company. Some examples are destroying someone's career by devious means, empire-building, causing disruption between departments, and restricting information flow.

The power game

The concept of the power game is often interpreted as a means by which the supervisor can impose personal status or image, and gain employee support and dependence. Winning power battles is essential for prestige since many of the supervisor's superiors and subordinates also will be engaged in power struggles and be watching closely for weak points. Those who are not actively involved will feel some frustration, but the process of winning also helps the supervisor's subordinates by often automatically elevating their power.

Careful planning of strategy and tactics in playing the power game allows the supervisor to establish certain objectives and make concentrated attempts to win battles that are essential. Losing those of minor importance may be tactically sound in circumstances where a subordinate's prestige is enhanced but the danger of upsetting another subordinate must be remembered.

Rules

Whether people play according to rules of moral conduct hinges back to the reputation they hope to achieve or maintain. As power develops and advancement follows, some people change the rules to suit themselves, but of course everyone recognises this and opinions alter. The practice is hazardous since it becomes lonelier as the hierarchy is ascended and enemies tend to increase in proportion to the degree of rule bending. Some specialists argue that when the unhappy day arrives when the supervisor looks for support which is not forthcoming this is all part of the power game and is a healthy process.

Many rules for playing coincide with developing good human relations already discussed and come naturally to those who wish to develop a good reputation. Other rules have no boundaries and many techniques of an under-handed nature are employed by the ruthless individual looking for success at the expense of others. Debatable aspects are the effects on employee performance, the 'cut-and-thrust' of business life, managerial ethics, moral codes of conduct, acceptable practices in other countries, and company survival.

Power development concepts

A modern view of power places it within the realm of organisation politics. This term is interpreted by S. P. Robbins as any behaviour by an organisation member that is self-serving. Other definitions of organisation politics are the structure and process of the use of authority and power to influence objectives not agreed by top management; ways to advance in the organisation; and a dynamic process that uses power to improve career prospects.

Types of power

In addition to legitimate, referent and expert power already mentioned, J. French and B. Rowan include reward power which means possessing the capability and resources to reward employees, and coercive power – the capability to punish. The five types of power combined together become a strong composite political power when applied by those with appropriate authority and capability. The outcome is an organisation that differs drastically from theoretical notions. The distribution of power among organisation members is generally biased in certain directions, often inducing callous treatment of some employees. Coalitions emerge, disappear, and re-emerge in different forms, causing competition for resources and protection of certain individuals.

Political strategies

Many political strategies for developing power have been proposed. A well-known example is by A. Du Brin who drew up a list extracted from literature on the subject. Strategies of divide and rule, avoiding decisive engagements, progressing slowly – one step at a time, forming and maintaining alliances with powerful individuals, taking counsel with caution, are well-known examples. Others are making a quick reputation by concentrating on one task immediately to gain attention; and collecting and using IOUs, which means doing favours but letting it be known that something in return is expected later. A long list of strategies was also compiled by R. H. Miles, while J. Pfeffer included managing uncertainty, building alliances, and controlling resources.

Probably political manoeuvring and power-seeking features have always been present in organisations. Possibly the mere presence of people and groups is sufficient to trigger-off such processes. Recognising, understanding and using politics and power seems to be an essential requirement for the successful supervisor. Whether he or she is more effective is debatable at present since research is still continuing.

Leadership development

Armed with sufficient knowledge and theories of leadership the potentially effective leader should be able to apply a straight-forward approach to developing leadership skills. A logical and recognised programme for developing any social skill is:

- attempt self-analysis
- to spend more time on trying to understand group members
- to develop a better understanding by concentrating on improving inter-personal relationships

These three features are discussed shortly. There are many adverse influences – sometimes of a powerful nature – that upset a programme. These are mentioned and discussed elsewhere. However the leader must accept the situation and concentrate on the over-all philosophy.

Developing self-analysis

This stage relies partly upon acquiring the information given in Chapter 9 to convince supervisors that perception is important. How supervisors are perceived by others and how the supervisors see themselves are major considerations. The effects of interaction, reaction, and acceptance should justify the need for self-analysis.

Self-opinion ranges from a low level of inferiority and opinion up to a high level of confidence and opinion. Most people crudely rate themselves somewhere on the range, but self-analysis to confirm their opinion or regrade themselves is unusual. The tendency is either to over- or under-rate, sometimes excessively. Indeed very few analyse themselves to discover their strengths and weaknesses. Many tend to live in the past, picking on good or bad times, and convincing themselves that if it were not for a particular circumstance they would be following a totally different career – generally one well above their present occupation.

Many also blame a relative, or an individual, or a concern, for the problems they face (or reject) through previous experiences which have affected their career. To overcome such prejudices and excuses a supervisor should find time for self-analysis or self-awareness and attempt to be more self objective. The exercise also helps to improve home and social life. Two techniques are now outlined.

Compile a personal record

Having acquired sufficient knowledge on human beings, the next step is to check with a friend, relative, or colleague, and list features that are obvious and those discovered through personal contact. From this material the supervisor builds up a personal dossier. Included initially are features similar to those used for interviewing and selection. More details are added as ideas occur. Areas demanding special attention will inevitably be highlighted as the leader diagnoses problems encountered with employees.

For those supervisors who are inexperienced in personnel selection techniques, two well-known examples to consult are the seven-point plan published by the National Institute of Industrial Psychology and the five-fold grading scheme by J. Munro-Fraser.

Useful initial headings are: impact on other people, abilities, capabilities, drive, enthusiasm, temperament, prejudices, confidence level, introvert/extrovert tendencies, physical make-up, special aptitudes, interests – intellectual, social, and general, disposition, and so on. A crude framework would be to start with behavioural, mental, physical, and emotional headings.

Diagnose strengths and weaknesses

This technique demands courage and honesty. Approach others for information if the climate is right. Developing rapport with the right people who are willing to help takes time since they are often unwilling to be honest because of possible consequences. Usually someone's confidence will eventually provide some new and often vital information. Suggesting a mutual exchange of information is often helpful.

Improving an understanding of employees

The second stage is simply an extension of self-analysis concepts applied by the leader to others within the group. They are no different from the leader in many ways although each one will vary to some extent, as already explained.

Each person requires a particular approach, has certain expectations, and so on. In this way there is an increased chance of gaining a better understanding. Individual treatment to cater for expectations can only be based upon detailed knowledge and experience. Building up such information is time-consuming and costly but this must be expended considering the benefits. Span of control is another important feature since it becomes increasingly difficult to know each group member sufficiently well as numbers increase.

Developing interpersonal relationships

The third stage depends upon the results of the previous stages and the leader's acceptance of other influences over which he or she has no control. Negative pressures from power groups such as militant shop stewards and belligerent informal leaders must be expected, not used as an excuse to avoid the exercise.

A fundamental belief in people is essential. This philosophy should be made known through the leader's behaviour, remembering praise where necessary and counselling. Adequate explanations of unpalatable actions which occur as company goals or survival take precedence are a part of the programme. Whenever participation is feasible it should be used, but there are inherent dangers.

Inevitably the leader's actions will sometimes cause adverse reactions. The secondary effect is to cause a further reaction from the leader which aggravates the situation. Logically this hostility cycle must be broken immediately, therefore the leader's response has to be favourable or acceptable.

Such a reversal of the leader's natural emotional retort when an employee reacts badly is exceptionally difficult, but it is the only way to break the syndrome. Most people react to rudeness, for example, by reciprocating the rudeness. Avoiding this retaliation demands strong emotional control, self-discipline, and an understanding that pride and status are not lost by allowing an employee's reaction to pass. Of course there are limits beyond which disciplinary procedures apply. Attention to all the obvious requirements of employees is all that is required. Most reasonable people know this. Making the effort and spending the time reaps its own rewards.

Questions

1 Discuss whether it is possible to develop leadership skills.
2 'An effective leader finds the right balance between concern for people and concern for production.' Explain this statement.
3 Outline the main theories of leadership.
4 Explain functional leadership.
5 Write an essay on leadership styles.
6 'Leadership objectives are assumed to be aligned with supervisory and organisational objectives.' Discuss the significance of this statement.
7 'Power struggles among people are inevitable.' Is this statement a valid reason to develop supervisory power? Explain your viewpoint.
8 Define the term benevolent power.
9 What are the dangers of relying on position power?
10 Outline the methods of developing power.
11 Write an essay on the power game.
12 Explain reward power and coercive power.

Case study

Two supervisors – June and Mavis – were tipped for promotion to the vacant office manager's job. In terms of age, length of service, education and qualifications there was nothing to choose between them. June was smart but inclined to be short-tempered. Mavis was more homely, with a good sense of humour and an excellent conversationalist.

June used her assets well, developed appropriate relationships with managers and was known to get her own way. She could sense weak points in the organisation and several times turned them to her personal advantage. Sometimes she was called a gold-digger.

Mavis used her strengths to develop good relations with the clerical union and with staff. Several of her ideas had been accepted by management and she had continued studying. Sometimes she was criticised for being too casual.

Both performed well in their jobs, they had a clean record and were hard workers.

1   Consider the difficulties likely to be faced by the selection committee.
2   What advice would you have given to June and Mavis five years ago, considering the use of power?

14 Introduction to communication

Importance of communication

Successful communication of information between employees, fellow super-visors and management is an essential part of the supervisor's job. Achieving effective communication is always a problem in any situation, mainly because the topic is generally underrated. Despite many well-known exam-ples of disaster through poor communication it receives insufficient attention and training. Nevertheless communication is frequently discussed at all organisation levels, many employees recognise its failings, misunderstand-ings occur frequently, and often it is one of the major difficulties facing management.

Numerous ways of improving communication are available. A worthwhile aim is to improve the industrial climate and so reduce suspicion, distrust and antagonism which are severe barriers. The six main aspects affecting employee performance are the scope of communication, types of channels, networks, methods, the communication process, and communication flow.

Effects of poor communication

Poor communication will have a drastic effect on production and individual relationships. Continual misunderstandings lead to confusion, mistakes, wastage and accidents. Employees become frustrated and morale drops, resulting in lack of motivation and low productivity. When changes occur and reasons are not communicated, unrest and possibly strikes follow. Very little information flows upward to managers who are unaware of the situ-ation as the complaints, grievances and trouble spots reach the lower levels of supervision, and stop there. The general feeling of dissatisfaction spreads and poor co-operation is general throughout the concern. Employees leave and labour turnover increases until the situation is recognised by manage-ment and attempts are made to improve communication. Many of the symp-toms mentioned are measurable so trends should be watched and appropriate steps taken.

The scope of communication

There are distinct communication classes:

- basic mechanical aspects – often called information theory and systems theory
- interpersonal communication
- organisational communication

These are now discussed.

Information theory and systems theory

The scientific study of communication is becoming increasingly important as research into operational faults and disasters mainly reveals errors caused by a low comprehension of information theory and systems theory. Information theory is a scientific approach involving probability theory of mathematics. The main thrust is a study of the transmission (encoding) and reception (decoding) aspects, but also considered are functional roles and their contributions towards improving performance. Emphasis is placed upon using statistical data to encode messages, employing electronic devices to transmit, and selecting appropriate channels.

Interpersonal communication

This class is behaviourally oriented and concentrates on transferring information from one person to another. The ramifications are: establishing a basic method of effecting behavioural change, accounting for psychological and sociological features, using language and non-verbal communication, and developing the art of listening.

The interpersonal process is subjected to many influences within the individual (perception, learning and motivation), within the organisation (intra- and inter-group activities), and externally from the outside environment.

Organisational communication

This dynamic approach is a continuous transactional process since everyone is sending and receiving messages simultaneously. All members are involved in encoding and decoding activities, and they influence and affect each other.

Traditionally the structure was visualised as a series of linear information flows, similar to a telephone network. Information consisted of commands, directives, reports, enquiries, and requests operating through the chain of command. Now the systems approach accepts all the external influences which disturb, make demands and cause operational difficulties. These receive little or no attention in traditional approaches.

Communication channels

A wide range of formal and informal channels is available. More than one channel may be used to reinforce the message, while choice depends upon personal preference based upon the supervisor's knowledge of the individual (the receiver), experience and the environment. The channels form patterns or networks which are interconnecting lines between people who may be grouped in various ways with one- or two-way communication facilities.

Formal channels

These are easily recognised by the strong relationship with military practice and direct authority lines identifiable on an organisation chart. Not so evident are the functional and staff channels explained later. These supplement the scalar process (operating a formal line of command from top to bottom of the organisation) and ease overloads.

Formal channels are connected with many official activities: joint consultative committees; discussion groups; personnel interviews and counselling; liaison with trade unions; company journals, posters and literature; policy publications; direct letter; notice boards; conferences and suggestion schemes.

Informal channels

These operate unofficially through the grape-vine, discussions with trade-union officials, consultation, contacts with outside sources and services, and airing grievances and complaints. The channels work effectively because most organisation members want to contribute by passing on gossip, scandal and rumour as well as factual information.

The three major informal channels are horizontal, ad hoc, and line by-pass which are discussed soon under the heading *Communication Flow* since they are essentially spasmodic and operate as required. Nevertheless they are critical and bind the structure together to form an effective working unit.

Using formal and informal channels effectively

Formal channels of communication operate through the lines of command throughout the organisation. The effectiveness of these channels is probably measurable by assessing the time factor, the accuracy of the message, responsiveness of employees, and the cost per unit of manufacture. The time taken to achieve a good response from employees is the important factor. The quickest way of passing information and making decisions is a one-way communication process from supervisor to subordinate. The amount of response, however, depends upon the supervisor's influence and powers of persuasion and the amount of consultation and participation in making decisions, involving two-way communication which slows down the process.

Other factors must also be taken into account when dealing with communication problems and the correct balance must be achieved between speed of transmission, accuracy and effectiveness, depending upon the particular circumstances.

Employees should be given as much information as possible. Information flows in from a number of sources. Some of these are very unreliable and unless the sound, official sources of information operate effectively, people are given wrong impressions that cause considerable harm to relationships. The easiest and quickest way to squash rumours is to publish the facts and demonstrate by positive action the truth of the issued statements. This method cannot work in circumstances where poor communication blocks the upward passage of information in the organisation. The supervisor should bear in mind that executives cannot make statements explaining away rumours until they are aware of the situation.

Some supervisors have the mistaken idea that withholding information demonstrates power to subordinates. The reverse is the case as employees will find out through other sources and, if it is obvious that the supervisor was aware of the information, he or she will be despised and distrusted.

A similar situation will occur when the supervisor withholds any information from a superior. Regardless of whether the superior will be pleased or annoyed at receiving the information, it is better for it to come from the supervisor rather than from another source.

No manager or supervisor likes to be in the position of being taken by surprise. He or she would much rather learn about problems and mistakes from a subordinate than first hear of them in the form of complaints or reprimands from a superior, since early information will give the supervisor the opportunity to investigate and correct the trouble and prepare an adequate explanation.

The grape-vine

This informal channel of communication operates through all members of the organisation. They pass on gossip, scandal and rumour to each other during their daily contacts at the workplace, in the canteen and during social activities.

When used properly the 'grape-vine' is a quick way of assisting the formal channels and it provides a guide to the effectiveness and accuracy of other channels.

Dangers of the grape-vine

Management is usually to blame if the grape-vine plays a dangerous part in the communication system by betraying confidential information and spreading rumours based upon odd scraps of information and conjecture. Invariably the leaks may be traced back to managers' lack of circumspection: e.g. careless remarks over the telephone, leaving confidential papers lying around, imparting information to close associates without authority to do so. Few people are able to keep confidences *completely* 'under their hats'.

Subordinates expect their supervisors to know the facts about any rumours which are circulating. If supervisors do have confidential information they are then placed in a difficult position where they must either deceive employees, antagonise them by withholding the information or betray management's confidence. Management should prevent such situations by issuing statements in advance or ensuring that no leakage is possible.

When any instructions are issued without acceptable reasons, or when breakdowns in formal channels occur, the grape-vine promptly takes over and creates the information which is lacking. If the facts are not available from official or unofficial sources, someone always gives an opinion which is accepted as fact until proved false.

Employees want to know about the concern, any current news which may affect them, proposed changes and development of existing programmes. If information is withheld, the inevitable rumours will quickly destroy good relationships. Rumours cannot be stemmed unless management understands the situation and provides sufficient information for supervisors to pass on.

Uses of the grape-vine

1   As a control check to ensure that information reaches everyone in an undistorted form.

2   As an informal means of supplementing formal channels of communication. Certain employees have a reputation for always being 'in the know'. Many are informal leaders of groups and are usually good workers with a genuine interest in their job. The supervisor should make sure that these people are supplied with the right information to pass on. Often this method of passing information is more effective if used properly because individuals pay more attention to those employees 'in the know'.

3   As a means of keeping up to date on events so that further information may be obtained from management and passed on quickly to subordinates before rumours can develop.

4   To counteract rumours. Management should supply the facts and demonstrate the truth whenever possible by definite action.

5   As a means of locating the malicious gossiper. There are generally one or two employees in a concern who try to ruin personal reputations and lower morale by continually running down managers and supervisors. The slanders can be discredited quickly if the true facts are fed into the grape-vine. An interview with the person responsible is essential to find out why he or she acts in this manner and disciplinary action may be necessary to protect others against his or her spiteful activities.

Communication networks

Choice of network is dependent upon the degree of centralisation envisaged by management. Centralisation in this context means formal power to make decisions within the network. Thus 'centralised' means one person has the power, while 'decentralised' means the power is dispersed among members. Perhaps concepts of participation, democracy, decision making, control, and bureaucracy may appear to dominate choice, but the main thrusts are behaviour and communication factors. Consequently other issues emerge: specialisation, co-ordination, and direction.

Co-ordinating decisions

Undoubtedly centralisation is the easiest way to co-ordinate decision making, all decisions being made by one person and enforced by direct supervision. Snags may arise, however, if the person becomes overloaded due to the development of an excessive number of decisions. The only answer is to decentralise using appropriate specialists, dividing the activities, and supplying information as required. This action speeds up decision making; the structure becomes more sensitive to change, response is quicker; and more people are motivated through increased responsibility and achievement.

When an organisation contains many networks it is impracticable to describe it as centralised or decentralised, since some parts may be centralised while others may not. Probably to describe centralisation in these terms might mean comparing one organisation with another by commenting that one is more decentralised than the other.

Power distribution

Decentralisation is easily described as a dispersal of power among members in a network. However to be more specific – considering the principle operating at organisation level – means augmenting it with other organisation principles such as the use of specialists and delegation. In most organisations decentralisation through specialisation and delegation is usual. More unusual is decentralisation through power distribution to network members which raises issues of industrial democracy.

Networks

Degrees of power distribution occur by altering the design of networks. A. Bevelas is well-known for studying these 'communication nets'. Some examples and comments are given in Fig. 14.1. Note that the centralisation tendency is high in fan and wheel nets. Communication restrictions are high in fan, chain, radial, wheel, and Y nets. Decentralisation is high in circle and all-channel nets where power to communicate is shared equally and conforms

FAN

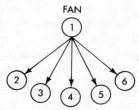

Power = 1
Centralisation tendency = high
Communication restrictions = high

Y

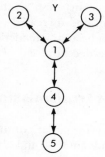

Power = 1
Centralisation tendency = intermediate
Communication restrictions = high

CHAIN

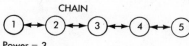

Power = 3
Centralisation tendency = intermediate
Communication restrictions = high

RADIAL

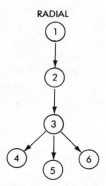

Power = 1
Centralisation tendency = intermediate
Communication restrictions = high

CIRCLE

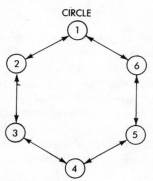

Power = equal
Centralisation tendency = nil
Communication restrictions = intermediate

WHEEL

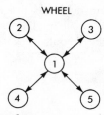

Power = 1
Centralisation tendency = very high
Communication restrictions = high

ALL-CHANNEL

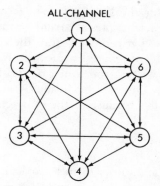

Power = equal
Centralisation tendency = nil
Communication restrictions = nil

Fig. 14.1 *Formal communication networks*

to democratic structures. Both tend to suffer with more noise, slower communication, and increased errors. Research with small groups by M. E. Shaw (1964) indicated a tendency for centralised nets to cope with simple problems while decentralised nets cope better with complex problems.

Methods of transmission

There are many means of communication between individuals in a concern. Each has its advantages and disadvantages and particular uses. The main methods of transmission discussed are: speech, writing, signs, actions, silence, and general behaviour and attitudes.

Speech

Although oral communication is direct and more personal than written instructions, great care is needed in choice of words and expressions. The message should be given a little thought before it is prematurely announced to someone, otherwise the risk of misunderstanding is increased. Wherever possible use simple words and state the message slowly and distinctly.

After all precautions have been taken, the risk of misunderstanding is still high, therefore always check to be sure that the employee understands clearly. Remember that absolute concentration is difficult in noisy conditions with other subjects on the mind at the same time.

Written communication

From the sender's viewpoint, writing is more difficult as he or she must make up for the lack of face-to-face contact which affects the tone of the message. Facial expressions and gestures are missing which means that much of the impact is removed from the communication.

Being able to express a message clearly in writing demands practice. The danger of writing too much or too little is always present. The receiver is inclined to jump to conclusions – nearly always the wrong ones – without checking first because of the remoteness factor.

Signs

Signs and indicators form a particular class of visual communication where the loss of impact is a special problem. Notices such as 'No Smoking', 'Danger', 'Handle With Care', 'This Way up', 'Press Here', 'Keep within the white lines', are examples which are often ignored. The usual excuse is that the sign was not noticed. Similarly the use of flags, coloured lights and mechanical devices also has limitations because concentration is necessary.

People need constantly reminding, otherwise they tend to forget or overlook the most glaring signs.

Actions

Positive demonstration by actually doing something is the best means of communication; it is immediately recognisable by everyone and is the least likely to confuse. The effectiveness of an individual's various senses is not the same. The sense of sight is about 87 per cent effective, hearing 7 per cent and smell, touch and taste about 6 per cent. A well-worn saying 'Actions speak louder than words' makes good sense in communication.

Silence

The use of silence is probably the most subtle form of communication, but when misused is the stupidest form. As a means of showing displeasure because a particular code of conduct has been ignored it is very effective and harsh. Sending someone 'to Coventry' causes the offender feelings of uneasiness and frustration, followed eventually by near panic in some cases.

Another example occurs when an employee is given a thirty-minute job five minutes before time, by a supervisor who does not bother to enquire if the employee wishes to stay late. The employee's silence may be accompanied by a facial expression which is more than sufficient to indicate his or her feelings.

Some of the effects of silence on people are: annoyance, indifference, disgust, hurt feelings, fear, suspicion, distrust, amusement and antagonism. They form an excellent list of feelings which must not be generated in employees. The danger of allowing false impressions to develop generally outweighs the effectiveness of silence and this approach should be used with great caution.

Non-verbal communication

Non-verbal communication (NC) may emphasise a message, clarify, or cause misinterpretation. It may be consciously or subconsciously recognised, depending on the people involved. Culture, class levels, age, sensitivity, sex, education, training, and experience are significant features in interpreting NC.

NC signals are classified in various ways. Here is a typical grouping.

1   *Body movements*   these include facial expressions, eye movements and gestures. Facial 'give-aways' are well-known and recognised by expression, crying, blanching, blushing, dilating and contracting of pupils, and changing gaze direction. Blink rate, narrowing and widening eyes, gaze, and eye

movements convey a variety of messages, typically to interact, relate, sexual interest or disinterest, deploring conduct, surprise, or anger. Many gestures are commonplace and have universal recognition.

2   *Proximity signals*   people stake out their own 'territory' through space and distance between them. They tend to back away or retaliate if their territory is violated and take offence. Animals behave in a similar way by marking territory.

3   *Body contact*   touching (in many forms) is easily misunderstood, may invite violent reaction, and has strong sexual meanings. Touching is personal and should be avoided since a reputation of being a 'pawer' is easily gained.

4   *Appearance*   clothes, cosmetics, perfume, wigs, jewellery and trinkets tend to convey a variety of meanings and are often misinterpreted. Probably people dress in certain ways to either convey how they feel or to project an image.

5   *Physical characteristics*   these convey particular meanings through stereotyping and experiences with various categories.

6   *Time frame*   people are often grouped through punctuality, a hurried or leisurely approach, and applying rituals. Establishing rapport may depend on synchronised time frames especially when cultural aspects apply.

7   *Environmental features*   often people are assessed through their general surrounds, typically a tidy clean desk, appropriate furniture and decor.

The communication package

People are influenced by *all* methods of transmission in the form of a total package. NC is an important feature and worthy of more study. M. Argyle (1975) outlines the practical applications.

Managerial receptiveness

Poor managerial receptiveness is a common complaint from employees. Often excuses are made by managers who realise they are at fault: typically lack of time, performing an urgent task at the same time, and apologising for being easily distracted. Other managers do not bother and may perform other tasks while the employee is speaking, such as reading a letter or memorandum, dialling a telephone number, speaking to a secretary, chatting with another manager, displaying boredom or disinterest, or adopting a blank expression.

These practices are guaranteed to increase the class gap, frustrate, irritate and cause general distrust and suspicion. Indeed, the busy manager will find he or she is firmly establishing an even busier future.

Process models

Interpretations of a communication process vary. Typical views are: a course of action starting with the sender and ending with the receiver; a series of operations from an information source to a receiver; a series of changes involving information passing through many stages, being utilised for action or attitude change, and finally returning to the source to augment the original information; and a dynamic continuing series of transactions leading to co-ordination.

The process concept insists that the sender must allow the receiver to influence or persuade him or her to change the message in such a fashion that it becomes more acceptable to the receiver. Consequently misunderstandings or rejections are avoided. To operate this concept feedback loops are vital.

Effective feedback

Although feedback is treated as part of the process it can also be envisaged as a communication process in its own right, hence it will suffer with similar difficulties when the supervisor applies feedback to the employee. Typical features will be parallel with process stages, along with other aspects which are critical. These apply because of the sensitive nature of feedback in operating conditions such as checking performance and behaviour, constructive criticisms, correcting deviations, and counteracting inaccurate instructions.

In these circumstances adopting certain practices may avoid ill-feeling.

Some examples are:

1 *Objectivity* to ensure the receiver appreciates the reason for feedback such as avoiding a bottleneck in production or avoiding wastage.

2 *Comprehension* sometimes the supervisor can misunderstand very easily especially when a subordinate is attempting to explain a complex situation.

3 *Purpose* the aim of feedback must be specific, not vague or general, otherwise further complications arise and frustration may develop.

4 *Acceptability* provided the information is useful and helps, trains, pleases, or encourages the receiver there should be no problem.

5 *Accuracy* if feedback is inaccurate it will certainly antagonise, irritate, or cause some emotional reaction. At the same time some accurate information can be hurtful if, say, it reprimands, therefore due care and sensitivity are essential.

6 *Timing* as already explained in chapter 12 immediate comments, criticisms or reinforcement are essential. Delay may cause insecurity, surprise, confusion and resentment.

Communication flow

Communication flow lines permeate the whole structure and must be fully utilised. Probably the two most important factors are speed of communication flow and relevancy of information in the flow lines. The main problems are distortion and noise.

The supervisor always needs appropriate information on time without excessive overload. This depends upon:

1 being able to state requirements
2 the systems specialists' capability to provide them
3 effective communication flow.

Consequently the supervisor should be able to solve problems, make decisions and accurately assess employee performance.

Flow lines

The six major flow lines are:

1 *Downward communication* traditional authoritarian flow conforming to lines of command.

2 *Upward communication* the reverse of downward flow, conforming to formal lines and operating on a 'subordinate to superior' basis.

3 *Horizontal communication* flow between peers who are accountable to the same superior.

4 *Ad hoc communication* flow between colleagues in different sections or departments.

5 *Line by-pass communication* flow between a superior in one section and an employee in a different section at a lower level in the hierarchy.

6 *External communication* flow between any organisation member and outside people including customers, suppliers, and other companies' representatives.

Informal flow lines

Item numbers 3, 4, and 5 above are illustrated in Fig. 14.2 to demonstrate their operational uses.

Downward communication

This classical authoritative flow line suffers with delay, distortion and loss of information as it descends the chain of command. Adequate feedback is needed to overcome perception problems and to confirm that the information is actually read.

According to the systems view, this flow line should be treated as a 'superior to subordinate communication' which is a transactional process.

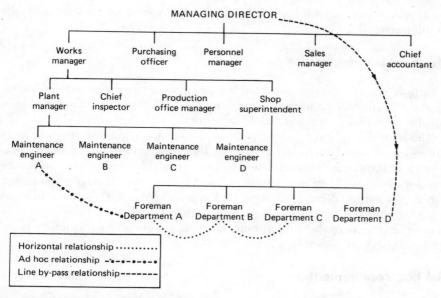

Fig. 14.2 *Informal communication flow lines*

This diagram illustrates the three informal relationships that bind the organisation together to form a working unit

Thus emphasis changes into a two-fold feature in which downward and upward communication are intertwined. The downward part provides:

1 instructions and directions
2 information on administration procedures and systems
3 the rationale of the subordinate's job
4 the subordinate's performance level
5 the company's policies, ideas and general thinking in an attempt to induce a better understanding of the organisation's objective and goals.

Upward communication

This part of the two-fold feature explained above depends upon trust and confidence felt by the subordinate towards the superior. If a sound relationship exists the supervisor should receive full support, ideas for improvements, early warning of difficulties, participation, receptiveness for change, and more acceptance of change.

A vital factor for co-ordination is the supervisor's desire – and positive action – to pass on information further up the line with a minimum of bias. Even adverse information that may damage the supervisor's image (in his or her eyes) must be transmitted. Supporting this flow line could be suggestion schemes, counselling, committees, the grape-vine, complaints and grievance procedures, termination interviews, an open–door policy, and the ombudsman.

Horizontal communication

This flow line is strongly connected with group activity explained in Chapter 5. Poor horizontal communication may divide a team; the danger applies equally to management and employee groups.

The high risk of inter-group rivalry and cussedness in these circumstances causes group members to feel apart from the larger system outside their own. Therefore the system boundary will be less permeable. Rigidity of this nature develops into an urgent problem as organisations grow. Sharing information, problem solving, decision making and resolving conflict, become increasingly difficult. Group performance will probably be low and the supervisor is obviously at fault, bearing in mind the supervisory role of fostering intra-group activity discussed in Chapter 5.

Ad hoc communication

The supervisor should encourage staff to expand ad hoc relationships with employees in other sections since this time-saving activity is vital. A situation where all messages pass up and down the line is anathema and must be avoided.

Staff should know that they cannot commit their immediate superior on questions of policy or decisions affecting others. One way of encouraging ad hoc communication if there is a difficulty is to ask staff to contact each other after the supervisor has discussed and agreed the practice with the other employee's superior. Such sensible arrangements bring the organisation to life.

Line by-pass communication

This flow line is very useful to avoid trouble-spots growing into major upheavals. Often managers further up the line are not made fully aware of difficulties because managers at lower levels either do not pass up any information which personally affects their image, or they distort the information. If it is accepted that the person nearest the adverse situation is the one who knows most about it and who will provide a less distorted impression, the logical approach is to by-pass intermediaries and go straight to that individual.

Should a manager feel dissatisfied with the way a situation is developing, doubts certain information, or if change does not occur as expected, he or she will often not hesitate to use this approach. Any sensible, trained manager or supervisor located between the two parties communicating in this way will appreciate the need to adopt such action.

External communication

This flow coincides with general systems theory and its importance has already been stressed. Although some employees may not be directly contacting outsiders they are invariably associated through domestic situations, clubs, and other gatherings. Often vital information is transmitted by this means especially when managers meet their counterparts in golf clubs, social activities, and various professional associations.

Causes of misunderstanding

Problems of expression

Educational level and experience

Allowance for an employee's level of education and amount of experience is essential otherwise a message can be so worded that it goes completely over that person's head. Embarrassment may prevent the individual from querying the message in these circumstances. The situation is not revealed until later when a problem arises because no action was taken by the employee. This problem requires careful treatment when it seems that a subordinate has deliberately ignored an instruction. It is always wise to ask first if the message was clear.

Interpretation of words

Words that have definite meanings such as those describing buildings, furniture, tools, machines and work benches are easy to understand. Confusion occurs, however, when the word describes an object of which there is more than one. Additional words of description are essential in cases where misinterpretation is possible.

Words that have vague meanings should be avoided whenever possible when describing the degree, condition or manner of things. Otherwise they must be explained or their meaning demonstrated.

Some examples of vague words are given in the sentences below.

The job will be finished *soon*.
Give the end of the tool a *light* tap.
Hold the wire in the cutters *gently*.
Slowly withdraw the assembly from the furnace.
This job is *urgent*.
Fix the bolt *securely*.
Make sure the nut is *tight*.
When the liquid is *hot* dip the assembly in and out *quickly*.

Press the valve in a *little* bit.
Mix well before replacing the cap *firmly*.

A moment's thought will show how these instructions could be made more clear and precise.

Abstract terms

Words which describe qualities or intangible things should not be used carelessly as their meaning varies from person to person. Abstract words are often used when people wish to avoid being precise or have not thought about exactly what they mean. The tendency to be vague is because people feel more secure when they do not commit themselves and it requires less mental effort. The effect on subordinates is frustrating because they do not know where they stand.

These are some carelessly-used abstractions: democracy, virtue, peace, morality, responsibility, conformity, truth, liberty, honour, religion, power, poverty, standard, progress.

Technical jargon

Although the use of technical terms has its place this practice should be avoided in communications intended for those who are not acquainted with the terms. The full meaning is seldom conveyed and often completely misunderstood. Using jargon becomes a habit and some people even think its use makes them appear superior.

Gobbledygook

This American word describes the style of speaking or writing which confuses through its complexity. Too often a number of words are used where one would do, or long and uncommon words are used instead of short, simple ones. Here is an example of gobbledygook:

'The general arrangement in the drilling section has now been made untenable from the risk of fire point of view. The positions of the benches and drill stands have been altered considerably from the previous working layout which allowed the fitters, drillers, and female assemblers free access from the gangways to the emergency exit which was installed three years ago in case of fire.'

A suggested revision is:

'The rearrangement of benches in the drilling section has blocked the emergency fire exit.'

Problems of reception

Company size

As a concern grows the problem of communication and misunderstanding increase in proportion. More specialists are introduced, each with their own problems of communication. When dealing with others who are unfamiliar with their function, specialists are often misunderstood and so misused. In the growing concern information passes through many more hands and remoteness becomes a danger as keeping in touch with everyone gradually becomes more burdensome. People are less familiar with the whole situation, thus it is easier to misunderstand information.

Poor organisation

If people are unsure of their own authority, responsibilities and duties in the concern as well as those of their colleagues, inevitably there is considerable uncertainty concerning instructions, official backing and the importance of a message. Surveys show that poor organisation is common and that many misunderstandings stem from this which could be improved rapidly by clearly defining everyone's function.

Previous environment

Memories of past treatment at home and in industry shape the attitudes of employees. If they have suffered injustices or harshness before they will be on the defensive. They are often suspicious and prejudiced against their superior's intentions although the communication may be clear. This inherent tendency to distort the message to suit the individual's attitude towards the sender should be recognised.

Class consciousness

Some people seem to thrive on continually emphasising how much better they are by standards of bank balance, blood line, residence, previous schools, culture or accent. Such people are bores, and some are unaware of the gulf they create with colleagues and subordinates by their immature attempts to assert themselves. This form of assertion is short-sighted, since other people's reaction is more likely to be dislike, jealousy or contempt than admiration. Such feelings will distort messages received and misunderstandings are inevitable.

False reasoning

Reasoning must follow a set logical pattern, otherwise it is easy to fall into the trap of associating a statement of fact with some item of knowledge or another factual statement assuming a connection and jumping to the wrong conclusion. An example of reasoning by deduction, using logic, is given below, followed by a statement of ridiculously obvious false reasoning:

> All dogs have four legs;
> An alsatian is a dog;
> Therefore, an alsatian has four legs.

> All dogs have four legs;
> A cat has four legs;
> Therefore, a cat is a dog.

Although the second example is obviously false, people are inclined to reason along similar lines confusing facts with possibilities. A cat *may* be a dog on this basis, but without further information one cannot be sure. Always be particularly careful to check the sense of a statement when it is based on the relationship of two connected statements or facts in this way.

The wrong context

When conversations are overheard a misunderstanding may occur because the opening remarks which clarify the subject and throw light on the meaning are missed. An example of how the wrong impression can be caused is given below:

> He was inhaling oxygen, when suddenly the supply was cut off and he was dead a minute later.

The correct context was an incident in an operating theatre, but it could have been in an aircraft flying at forty thousand feet or in a space capsule on the moon.

Thinking in terms of extremes

Some people develop a habit of judging or thinking in terms of extremes at each end of the scale and not appreciating that problems and situations are multi-sided affairs. Not many events are so clear-cut and simple that they fit conveniently into a set pattern. There is a whole range of sides to a problem, each requiring separate consideration. For example, if a machine breaks down because a fuse has blown, the fuse could be replaced immediately. An engineer, however, might reason why the fuse burned out, make several checks on the machine before replacing the fuse, and so save the concern money and wasted time on future delays.

Difficulties of the sender

The sender must be able to assess the outlook, problems of understanding and particular interests of the receiver. The right approach produces a more positive reaction and a better response to the message. Every person needs individual treatment which means that judgment plays an important part in successful communication. A friendly approach and giving information form only part of a far more complex programme discussed under human relations and motivation.

The idea that communication is simply passing information from one person to another is quite common, and some companies spend large sums of money with this thought alone in mind. Negligible results are achieved because the full process of communication must include motivating employees by modern leadership. This concept encourages self-discipline through persuasion and consultation and aims at convincing employees that management and society want them to develop fully their capabilities.

Questions

1   Explain the term *communication* and its importance in connection with production and human relations.
2   Discuss the main channels of communication and how the supervisor should use them.
3   Discuss the existence of the grape-vine as an essential channel of communication.
4   Consider some of the common causes of misunderstandings and how they can be overcome by the supervisor.
5   How would you assess the effectiveness of communication in a concern?
6   Why is communication so important in business?
7   Outline the means of communication and the possible dangers involved, if any, with each one.
8   How can a supervisor use the grape-vine effectively?
9   State the advantages and disadvantages of one-way communication and two-way communication.
10   Why is it essential for formal channels of information to be supplemented by informal channels?
11   'Withholding information unnecessarily can be dangerous.' Explain this statement.
12   Discuss the effects of silence as a means of communication.
13   What advice would you give to a supervisor who cannot understand why employees ignore signs such as 'This way up' that are arranged for display at various points?
14   Why do subordinates and supervisors easily misunderstand information?
15   Outline the main communication networks and their uses.
16   What are the dangers of using non-verbal communication?
17   Why is feedback so important when communicating?
18   Outline the major communication flow lines.
19   Give some examples of non-verbal communication and their uses.
20   Discuss the process concept of communication.

Case study

The introduction of a typing pool at J. L. Conway, a medium sized company manufacturing fishing equipment, had worked well. All managers used the scheme although there was a tendency for the same typist to be allocated to the same manager each time as this approach provided some continuity. Strict devices were exercised to control output and to balance work-loads. The supervisor spent considerable time on ensuring there were fair work-loads.

Three incidents occurred one Friday afternoon. First, Julie caught her finger in the cloakroom door and injured it sufficiently to slow down her typing speed. Second, Anna who worked mainly for the personnel manager had helped in the preparation of material for a week-end training course and was invited to assist because his deputy had a domestic problem. Third, a rush job came up unexpectedly which meant that with a full complement of staff they would have to work on Saturday to complete it in time.

When the supervisor explained to the typing pool about the urgent work, Julie complained that her finger felt worse. Anna then mentioned her 'invite' to attend the training course. The supervisor became annoyed and said: 'Anna, your job is here. You can't go to the conference and that's that!'

Comment on the conduct of the personnel manager, the supervisor and Anna.

15 Communication: practical applications

The art of listening

The ability to listen with genuine interest and concentration is an essential part of supervisory skill in communication.

As thought is faster than speech it is easy to be inattentive and let one's mind wander ahead. Much of what is said is missed and the real message is not absorbed. If the speaker senses inattention, then the desire to communicate is lost and communication breaks down in the early stages.

The use of rules for better listening can improve performance considerably if they are followed with persistence.

1 *Maintain undivided attention* Use the spare time caused by higher thought speed to sift what is said into important and irrelevant points, examine them for validity, try to classify them and decide what is missing. Try to imagine what is coming next and link it with the change of mood or actions of the speaker. This flexible technique will fill the spare thought time and ensure that the mind does not have the opportunity to wander.

2 *When practicable, find a place with a minimum of distractions and interruptions* Noise and disturbances will ruin the continuity of a message for both parties, and lead to mutual irritation.

3 *Show a positive interest* Some supervisors deliberately pretend not to be interested, but this should only be done when some diplomatic action is called for, e.g. to discourage a request which will cause resentment if refused. Intelligent questions and comments in appropriate places help to convince the speaker that he or she is being heard with interest and understanding. The atmosphere should improve and the sender is more likely to gain confidence and expand on thoughts. In other words, listening should be dynamic and magnetic.

4 *Make due allowance for distortion* This applies both to supervisors and subordinates. Supervisors must recognise that they are capable of distorting information as they receive it and of discarding those parts that do not fit into their own outlook. Supervisors should try to treat the message objectively and ignore any personal feelings towards the speaker which might influence their reaction to the message. (This does not mean that the personal approach of being friendly should be discarded.)

5   *Be co-operative: allow the speaker to hold the floor and say everything on his or her mind*   Anything left unsaid grows and nags soon after. Check to ensure the full story is given.

6   *Do not rely on memory in a long conversation*   Recognise that memory lets a person down later when a number of points have been raised which demand some action.

Make a written note and give the reason for doing it. This also reassures the speaker.

7   *Improve the art of listening by practising*   There are many opportunities for experimenting away from the workplace such as trying to decipher a relative's conversation at home, using the radio and television and listening to conversations on buses and trains. Attempt to determine the main topic by sorting the major points from the side-issues and padding. Look for particular techniques in emphasising the subject matter and note the words which arouse particular feelings and emotions. If there is time write a summary and check on the facts for correctness and ambiguity. Look for ideas from facts and reason out why there is an objection to certain words or phrases.

How to communicate effectively

Any plan for communicating effectively should conform to a scientific or logical method. A general approach is suggested below, which may be applied to most types of communication, including orders, reprimands, grievances, policy, rules, induction, interviewing and information passing.

The twelve main steps which the supervisor should practise are as follows:

- Clarify the purpose of communication.
- Classify the type of communication.
- Obtain the relevant information.
- Assess the individual (the recipient).
- Determine the best means of communication.
- Decide on the channel or channels to use.
- Assess yourself (the sender).
- Make any necessary arrangements.
- Transmit the message.
- Check that the message is clearly understood.
- Listen carefully.
- Follow up.

Clarify the purpose

The question to be asked is: what should be the result of the communication? Care is needed to avoid stopping short of the real objective by shallow thinking. For example, if a reprimand is necessary the true purpose of the communication is not to reprimand the individual, but to point out the error. Assist by trying to help the person readjust, if necessary, and by showing fair play to other subordinates. The purpose cannot be achieved unless it is correctly identified at the beginning.

Classify the type

The means of achieving the purpose may now be decided and the type of communication chosen, e.g. an order, a reprimand, a discussion, a report or an interview. The communication will often consist of more than one type and the particular points which apply should be studied before proceeding further.

Obtain the relevant information

Although the time factor is nearly always against supervisors, they must make an attempt to gather as much information as possible on the topic. Information is often more easily obtained informally by talking to the people who are close to the trouble-spot or situation and their information will contain less distorted material. After the information is found it should be examined and classified. Unnecessary information should be discarded and the remainder translated into simple, straightforward language for easy transmission.

The receiver's viewpoint must be borne in mind; if any vital piece of information is missing, the 'grape-vine' will fill the gap. The supervisor ought to check that the message is complete, otherwise he or she is deliberately or unintentionally creating a distorted picture in the receiver's mind.

Assess the individual

Make sure that all aspects have been considered when assessing the person who is to receive the message. The individual's job, background, education, experience and present social and domestic life all mould outlook and account for present mood. Past history should be taken into account and any possible past injustices and problems noted. Many factors will affect the person's reaction to the message and knowledge of the individual helps in the choice of the best method of communication.

Determine the best means

Choosing the best means of communication depends upon such factors as speed, security, accuracy, impression on the recipient, need for a permanent record and the complexity of the message. When the information is complicated, the answer is to combine different means by using speech, diagrams, notes and visual aids such as files and charts. Further considerations are the type of impression it is desirable to make and the cost involved. In a large company information may be announced through a public address system, or in a small company the general manager may call the employees together and speak directly to them as a group. Naturally some personal contact is lost but in some circumstances, such as a threatened strike, it may be justified to speak to employees as a group instead of individually. The best means to use will vary as each situation varies.

Decide on the channel

The choice depends upon a variety of factors such as the number of people involved, the importance of the information, status of the individual or individuals concerned and the time available.

If one person is involved and the message is important, a face-to-face discussion through the formal line of command may be needed. Unimportant information can be passed verbally through a third party or a note may suffice. A number of channels could be used simultaneously if many people are involved and they should all receive the information at about the same time. This may be essential to maintain good relationships when union officials and fellow supervisors are concerned with the information. When in doubt it is wiser to use many channels to avoid the repercussions if someone is overlooked and the dangerous effects when individuals resort to the grape-vine.

Assess yourself

Being honest with yourself is not easy. Self-analysis means recognising your own faults and personal prejudices and your good points. You are influenced by your own background and experience in exactly the same way as other individuals. Consider your objectives and what you will gain or lose by your intended actions. These factors will determine your tendency to understate or overstate your case.

All these points add up to you as a person. Unless you are familiar with your own bias you will be unable to counteract the tendency to twist information you receive and transmit. A common fault is to allow your particular specialisation to distort your outlook which means that you fail to see other specialists' points of view.

Make the arrangements

The timing depends mainly on the type of communication. With reprimands or the discussion of grievances promptness is essential, but there is often more latitude with other types of communication. There may be unavoidable delays if arrangements have to be made for another person to be present such as a union official or a superior, in which case the delay must be explained to the individual as soon as possible.

If the message is important and requires emphasis timing again must be given some thought. A message given two minutes before lunch break will obviously get a half-hearted reception with little or no response from the receiver. Notification of appointments for important communications, e.g. interviews, new policy announcements or reprimands, are communication problems in themselves and similar principles apply.

A further aspect is the question of privacy and lack of interruptions and distractions. Although very important and essential with some types of communication, these requirements are often out of the question in some establishments owing to pressure of work and poor working conditions. Tact is vital in such situations.

Transmit the message

To minimise distortion there should be a friendly atmosphere, clear simple language should be used and a genuine sense of security created so that the receiver responds without fear or suspicion.

A careful note of instructions or promises is essential so that future communications on the subject agree with the original statement. Although a mistake made later may be unintentional, the supervisor will have difficulty in convincing subordinates.

Check that the message is understood

Do not assume that the message is understood. It is only too easy for people to take it for granted that they have understood. Some nod their heads indicating that they understand although they have only partially heard the message; others do not understand but cannot be bothered to query it.

Effective communication implies that checking is an integral part of the process. Failure to check is like setting the hands of a clock correctly and forgetting to wind the spring. A further advantage with the check is that in the process of repeating it the message is impressed more deeply on the receiver's mind.

Listen carefully

Although the point was stressed as the beginning of effective communication it is listed again here as an essential step in checking that the message is received and acted upon as desired.

The advantages to be gained by listening far outweigh the satisfaction received when transmitting information. People respect those who are prepared to listen attentively. The person who listens is nearly always up to date because individuals will go out of their way to speak if they are sure of a sympathetic hearing.

Follow up

Any promises made by the supervisor should be put into action quickly just as the supervisor expects, and he or she should check that subordinates take note of the communication without delay. The immediate effect on the individual and colleagues should be noted. A careful check on the long-term effects is essential until it is apparent that no trouble-spot is developing.

Try to visualise the possible problems which may arise; be ready to spot danger signs and attend to them quickly.

Order-giving

The main purposes of giving orders are as follows:

1 To stir people into action to achieve an objective – by giving them information on a situation which demands attention.
2 To indicate that a particular person is held responsible for performing a task – by approaching the subordinate, discussing the situation and arousing in him or her a strong desire to deal personally with the particular situation.
3 To give the superior the opportunity of contacting the subordinate and issuing instructions – in a way which will be most acceptable.
4 To give the subordinate the maximum opportunity of consulting and participating in the situation – so that the person may develop capabilities fully and display potential qualities for promotion.

To achieve these purposes the supervisor must treat order-giving as a continuous process of passing information, checking and controlling. True assessment of each individual's capabilities is not possible otherwise.

Types of orders

Although it is possible to classify orders into six types according to method, there are many combinations possible based upon the words used, the tone of voice, facial expressions and gestures.

Four other factors also must be borne in mind:

1 *The job to be carried out*   The order must be modified to suit the circumstances; these may involve dirty work, difficult tasks perhaps with risks, disagreeable work, actions which may have a detrimental effect on future relationships, or work of high importance.
2 *Personalities involved* whom the subordinate may find difficult to approach or deal with.

3 *The type of subordinate* who is receiving the order.

4 *The relationships* which exist between supervisors and employees and the general industrial climate.

The six common methods of giving orders are:

- command
- request
- suggestion
- open order
- mutual effort
- volunteers

The command

A direct or autocratic order is essentially one-way and will get a job done quickly provided it receives an acceptable response. Simple or straightforward tasks carried out by normal people under favourable conditions are especially suited for this type of order where there is little to discuss. Such phrases as 'Leave that and do this', 'Help them now', 'Do this', 'Get that', are typical examples.

The sensitive individual will often be antagonised by a direct order, whereas the lazy worker may be jolted into action. The order is emphatic and useful when the diplomatic methods fail. The unreliable or troublesome employee may respond to this treatment and, of course, in emergencies immediate response from direct orders is essential.

The request

The request is more personal and tactful, arousing a friendly atmosphere of co-operation. The emotionally unstable employee is less likely to take offence as the request softens and displays understanding and sympathy. Examples of opening phrases are 'Could you look into this one?' 'I wonder if you could arrange for . . . ?' 'Would you mind having a look at . . . ?' 'How about having a go at . . . ?' 'Do you think you could find out . . . ?'

The request is particularly useful for dealing with subordinates who have made mistakes. Generally they are aware of the error and even when they do not know, it is soon obvious after the request. Some ways of opening the request are 'Would you mind correcting it?' 'Perhaps you could have another look at this?' 'Maybe you could go over this one again?' 'Possibly you could improve on this?'

The suggestion

This is the mildest form of a request. Mentioning the subject is sufficient to the reliable experienced person who immediately sees the implication and acts accordingly. There is no demonstrated weight behind the order which is really thinking aloud, e.g. 'Lateness seems to be on the increase', 'The floor is rather dirty', 'There are more rejects this week', 'I have not seen the new assembly yet.' This technique allows the receiver to develop his or her capabilities but the sender should remember the importance of follow-up in case the remark was not fully understood. A further danger is obvious if this method were used on a new inexperienced employee.

The open order

This type gives the receiver the maximum opportunity to experiment and develop his or her capabilities. The supervisor gives information on what is required but leaves an adequate allowance for the individual to work out how to perform the tasks. The degree of allowance depends upon the subordinate's experience and ability to perform the tasks within a time schedule and the ability to deal effectively with any problem that may arise. The open order provides guiding principles together with additional essential information such as deadline dates. This type of order is particularly useful for developing potential leaders.

Mutual effort

This advanced type of order is only practicable under conditions of high morale and active participation in a concern where everyone is pulling in the same direction – towards the company's objectives.

The order takes the form of discussing the situation with employees and the union when they have a common objective in view. It takes longer to arrive at a solution but the results are more effective and permanent. This form of 'combined operations' uses everyone's knowledge and experience and the actual order is unnecessary. All concerned already know what has to be done and they go ahead and solve the problem without any persuasion. The basis of this technique is called the *law of the situation* which means that the situation itself demands action determined by mutual discussion, thus reducing personality problems and depersonalising order-giving.

Volunteers

Asking for volunteers is useful when it is obvious that choosing a subordinate will upset relationships and when the task is particularly unsavoury or detestable. The call may arouse in someone the desire to be important, though the same person would probably refuse if approached directly. The danger of receiving no volunteers should not be overlooked when morale is low.

Causes of low response to orders

Poor approach

If the supervisor adopts the old approach of being the boss and completely ignoring modern methods of leadership he or she will receive negative reactions. Today's employees are more independent, more aware of their rights, possess increased power and will not tolerate harsh, illogical methods of supervision.

Lack of information

If insufficient information is provided by management or passed on by the supervisor, the chances are that the receiver will not fully understand the order. Errors may occur and subordinates are less likely to react properly to a situation.

Poor assessment of the individual

Unless the true attitude of the receiver is known and his or her experience is used through genuine consultation the supervisor will not be able to communicate with that person or gauge the response accurately. Poor assessment stifles the individual and wastes his or her knowledge and capabilities to the detriment of other employees and of the company.

Low morale

A good response to orders is not possible when morale is low. Human relations need improving as well as communication before any results will be noticeable.

Apart from sensing morale by atmosphere, variations can be measured through productivity, the amount of information flowing to the top, the number of mistakes, complaints, grievances and strikes, wastage, labour turnover and the degree of co-operation.

Although morale is difficult to define accurately most people know what is meant by the term. State of mind, outlook, enthusiasm, collective attitude, sensitivity and co-operation all add up to morale. Building up morale takes a long time but knocking it down is easy and rapid.

Causes of low morale have all been mentioned before. They are:

1 poor leadership
2 very little fairness and justice in all aspects of industrial life, which includes wages, promotion and working conditions
3 no chance to display initiative
4 no satisfaction from the job
5 no feeling of importance

Discipline

People tend to think of discipline as a system of rules and appropriate punishments when they are disobeyed. This system is quite common. Other forms of more sophisticated discipline demand high morale and enlightened management which, of course, go together. The problem employee who is instinctively hostile towards authority calls for reprimands based upon a fair standard of rules and punishments; therefore, such a system is essential and cannot be removed entirely.

A higher form of discipline emerges automatically if employees are well-trained and are allowed to take more part in their work than the simple performance of tasks.

Self-discipline

When employees are given the opportunity to develop their capabilities the group spirit and general working arrangements with supervisors foster a personal driving force within each individual. This drive is often called *positive discipline* which urges employees to conform to rules and unwritten codes without restricting their enthusiasm.

The application of negative forms of discipline such as penalties or fear of dismissal fall into the background as people find new outlets for their energies through creativeness, sense of belonging and greater freedom to develop their abilities. The supervisor must be sensitive to the degree of change as individuals begin to practise self-discipline and the organisation structure fosters it. The application of consultation and participation is a long process which means that both types of discipline have to be varied in proportion to suit the situation as it progresses. This process does not give the supervisor the opportunity to shirk responsibilities for the group he or she controls. A superior must continue to use authority to make unpleasant decisions which someone will probably disagree with at times. A policy of fairness and justice includes imposing penalties not only to correct the offender but also in fairness to those who are conforming to regulations.

Reprimanding

Negative or imposed discipline uses the system of punishments which may be rebukes or penalties. The reprimand can easily destroy good relationships unless it is acceptable to the individual and the group as a whole. Although basically acceptance depends on high morale, the way the supervisor handles the actual reprimand will be the main deciding factor in individual cases (*see* Chapter 12).

A number of questions must be satisfied before the offender will feel that he or she has received a square deal. The person must understand clearly the reason for the rebuke, why the offence demands a reprimand and, even more important, must be aware that other offenders have not been allowed to 'get away with it'. Provided he or she receives a fair hearing and is not emotionally unbalanced, the reprimand should be acceptable.

Some basic rules are given below but supervisors should remember that they are also individuals with good and bad points. They should try to assess and develop their own good points so that their technique in dealing with these awkward situations is improved.

Basic rules for reprimanding

1 Be impartial. Treat everyone alike.

2 Make sure the information on the case is correct and complete.

3 Be human. Remember that rules and regulations are guides for the supervisor who should not interpret them too rigidly. Sympathetic understanding of other people's actions is essential.

4 Always check the information. A good opening is to ask the offender for facts, the offender's views on the case and his or her opinion of the rules. This technique gives the employee's 'safety valve' a chance to blow a little and may avoid an emotional outburst later. The person's feelings are made known to the supervisor early in the proceedings which is an advantage.

5 Do not allow your temper to interfere with the discussions at any time. Although the employee may make outrageous remarks about the system and the company, remember that he or she is under stress and also that the individual is entitled to personal views, especially if you have asked for them.

6 Most people have a sense of fairness and are conscientious. If they commit an offence they expect repercussions; therefore, it is pointless to prolong a reprimand by lecturing on the subject. This just encourages feelings of antagonism and disgust to develop in the employee.

7 Be straightforward. Tell the offender what you think has occurred, why you think it must not be overlooked, and the consequences if it occurs again. Make sure that he or she is aware of all the facts.

8 Try to help the employee. Find out why the offence happened; perhaps something may be bothering the person and unless you can win his or her confidence the true cause will not be found. Avoid arguments and listen carefully to all comments.

9 When all the information is known, try to be constructive by doing something positive whenever possible. Avoid any form of threat as this will immediately arouse aggressiveness and fear.

10 Another good opening is to praise the employee. Generally there is something you can praise such as good timekeeping, consistently high output or low absenteeism.

11 Never be sarcastic. Some people do not realise they are being sarcastic until someone points out the fault. The habit easily develops because it inflates feelings of self-importance. Unfortunately, the receiver is sadly deflated and intense dislike, lack of confidence and insecurity soon follow.

12   Although timing is important do not hold up reprimands without good reason. Allowing reprimands to accumulate amounts to shirking responsibility and when a supervisor eventually loses patience the offender will be astounded and puzzled. He or she will have the excuse that nothing was said on previous occasions.

Some sense of proportion is essential, however, otherwise the supervisor may be continually rebuking which is pointless.

13   Always think in terms of the offender's feelings, not your own. Avoid lowering his or her prestige in front of the group, thereby forcing the person to retaliate to save face. In brief, make sure that any unpleasantness or difficulties are discussed privately out of sight and hearing.

14   Do not be offhand after the reprimand. You have carried out your responsibility and your relationship should continue to be firm and friendly. Only immature supervisors hold grudges after they have reprimanded and subordinates quickly recognise the fact.

Procedure for reprimanding

A suggested logical approach to reprimanding which uses the basic rules above would be on the following lines:

1   Get your facts right. Check with the employee.
2   Listen carefully to his or her views and any special circumstances.
3   Explain the rule, why it is necessary, the reprimand for breaking it and penalties for further violation.
4   Weigh and decide in the light of evidence, previous cases and the human aspect.
5   Make the reprimand in a straightforward manner and in private.
6   Ask the employee if he or she has anything further to say; allow the 'safety valve' to blow a little.
7   Give any help the offender may require. If you feel that you have not really got through and there is something bothering the employee, follow up until you are satisfied.

Types of reprimand

The type of reprimand given for an offence is to some extent at the discretion of the supervisor, especially for a minor offence, but will also depend upon disciplinary procedure laid out in union and/or company agreements.

1   Probably the mildest form of reprimand is a disapproving look or a few short words to remind the employee of the code of conduct expected from him or her.
2   The straightforward reprimand would follow the procedure outlined above when an offence is committed. Depending on the nature of the offence, the reprimand may be given and forgotten officially, or a note may

be given to the next level of authority, or perhaps a written account will be made on the employee's record card.

An indication of a routine would be as follows:

First offence – Verbal reprimand.
Second offence – Written reprimand.
Third offence – Written reprimand, mentioning that the works manager has been informed and a note has been entered on the employee's record card.
Forth offence – Written reprimand and three days' suspension.

Such routines vary considerably depending upon existing agreements and company policy.

3   Some offences may warrant a reprimand and an immediate three days' suspension. Care must be taken to conform *strictly* to any management procedure or trade union agreements in this connection.

4   After a number of reprimands for a similar offence, the question of terminating employment must again conform to official procedure and to statutory requirements (*see* Chapter 17).

Serious offences

Although the supervisor may be sympathetic towards an employee who has committed a serious offence, he or she must not shirk social responsibility in these circumstances. Such cases as gross carelessness which endangers life, malicious damage to property, indecency, stealing, violence or insulting behaviour must be severely dealt with in fairness to other employees. Invariably this form of offence leads to instant dismissal.

Grievances

A grievance is any situation or act which is unfair in the eyes of the complainer. The cause may be the act of a manager, a supervisor or an employee or a situation which is allowed to continue and develop. The grievance may be held by an individual, a group, a section or even a department, and the complainer may be personally involved or may act as a representative for others. At this stage whether the grievance is right or wrong is unimportant. The point is that the employee *thinks* there is a legitimate complaint; other factors are by the way.

The supervisor's role is essentially active, seeking out employees with grievances and solving the problem quickly in the most effective way. Knowingly allowing employees to seethe for weeks is inviting disaster when the upheaval occurs.

Basic causes of grievances

Some knowledge of the reasons why employees complain and the causes of their complaints will help in minimising grievances. Early action ensures that the grounds for complaint are prevented from appearing. Sufficient information should be passed to satisfy any suspicion concerning a particular action to avoid a complaint in a few days' time.

Employees complain for two main reasons: either because they are emotionally unstable or because they feel there is some unfairness or injustice.

The problem employee

The problem employee is easily recognised by the continual waves of complaints, mostly settled by carefully explaining the truth that is distorted in his or her mind. Unfortunately some of these employees are beyond the stage where the supervisor can help. When readjustment is not possible, replacements may be necessary and every effort should be made to persuade the individual to seek medical advice.

The inexperienced supervisor may easily confuse the problem employee with one who has a deep legitimate grievance which is hidden by a steady stream of petty complaints. These minor grievances are a symptom of a more basic grievance which does not emerge until the employee has full confidence in the supervisor who should listen carefully with sympathy and understanding.

Lack of understanding

The second basic cause of grievances covers all those activities of management and supervision which, for many reasons, are unacceptable to employees. This could be summed up as lack of training and understanding of people by managers. In more detail the problem includes poor communication when breakdowns occur in both directions, poor organisation which is aggravated by violation of principles, unsound policies and rules, general lack of fairness and justice, poor working conditions, overloaded supervisors who do not have sufficient time to assess subordinates and ensure smooth running of the section, inability of supervisors to assess subordinates, favouritism which may be intentional or unintentional, poor training schemes for managers, supervisors and employees, jealousy between individuals and sections and rumours and gossip. There are many more causes but the above cross-section indicates the depth of the problem which faces the supervisor.

Recognising grievances

A grievance is recognisable in two stages. First, when the event occurs which causes the grievance to materialise in the person's mind and second, when the person voices the grievance to someone in authority. The second stage does not require any effort from the supervisor except to listen initially, but by this time the complainer has been turning over the grievance in his mind for some time with obvious effects.

The real problem of recognition occurs at the first stage. Such recognition is very demanding on the supervisor who must be continually on the alert, watching for the danger signs to appear. He or she should be looking for: changes in attitude in seasoned employees, antagonism, suspicion, indifference, carelessness, day-dreaming, rudeness, slacking, absenteeism, frequent cloakroom visits, gossiping and general carelessness.

Successful discovery of a grievance in its early stages is time consuming; the supervisor must be continually in close contact with subordinates to assess the situation. He or she must know each individual sufficiently well to notice changes and be able to identify the likely causes. When the supervisor has gained the employee's confidence, the employee feels able to ask the supervisor immediately for more information, for reasons, or for fairer action and the natural tendency to hold back complaints and suffer unnecessarily is lessened.

In the long run time spent on observation and settling of complaints in their early stages is economical compared with the adverse effects and long sessions spent later in sorting out and trying to solve grievances that have reached a complex stage of development.

Solving the grievance

Each supervisor should gradually develop a personal technique of solving grievances as he or she becomes more experienced in understanding individuals. How to assess their problems and their reactions to suggestions and advice must also be considered. Some basic steps are useful as a guide and they indicate the main stages in any investigation of employees' complaints.

Knowing the individual

The supervisor should attempt to know as much as possible about the individual. This essential requirement includes studying the employee at work and on the social side, knowing his sentiments and his background, and his attitudes and outlook generally. Accurate assessment is a long painstaking process. A proportion of the supervisor's time must be allocated for this purpose to avoid an increasing amount of time being spent later on grievances.

Watching for change

Being constantly on the lookout for changes in individuals is habit-forming and becomes a sixth sense after some practice. A change may be due to any number of reasons outside the working environment, such as a domestic upset, and is often indistinguishable from a work problem. The change is difficult to correlate with a particular type of problem unless the individual is well known and responds in the same way each time. For example, a close colleague could sense when a friend has had a row with his or her home partner, particularly if they occur fairly regularly.

The supervisor may find it useful to connect events with individuals. Instructions, change in work-load or any alterations in conditions might cause complaint. If the alteration coincides with some change in a subordinate's behaviour the cause is probably self-evident and the supervisor is provided with some form of opening topic to discuss with that person.

Analyse change and any information

Attempt to assess the change and what it means in connection with other close associates. Perhaps one subordinate looks distinctly unhappy while another looks very happy, both being unusual for the two people concerned. The whole group may be antagonistic and this may not be apparent until several people within the group are contacted. A study of the information available and some attempt to couple events with people could give a clue to the problem. A word with other supervisors might help if the situation is puzzling.

Consult with the employee

Do not delay in approaching the employee. Take the initiative and try to persuade the person to talk about the grievance. Ask appropriate questions and lead on to those topics which may be the cause of the change in attitude. Remember to listen with sympathy and openly show that you understand. If you do not understand ask more questions until you are sure that everything is clear.

Presentation of grievance by the employee. If the employee takes the initiative before the supervisor has the opportunity or because the situation was not known, remember that the person is already emotionally aroused. Allow him or her to give full vent to feelings and keep your temper in check. If there is an outburst, let it subside before proceeding along the lines stated above.

People often have difficulty in explaining their thoughts clearly and they may be embarrassed or nervous because of this problem. They may not be sure of the real cause of the grievance themselves until the whole question is talked over carefully and calmly. A combination of events at work and at home may eventually arouse the person into action. People are complex and easily upset. They need help, friendly advice and often seek it from a supervisor who creates the right atmosphere. A small irritation often becomes a large grievance in the employee's mind and it must be treated as it appears to that person.

Treatment

Some grievances can be solved by patient listening and showing a complete understanding of the complainer's feelings. If the employee's position is sincerely appreciated and consolation is given, although no action is possible, it relieves the tension and emotional disturbance. The employee may then feel the position is understood and the grievance is solved. Similarly, genuine praise for good work and an assurance that all the conditions under which the employee works are known and understood relieve the complaint.

Other grievances demand some positive action – not reassurances or promises that cannot be kept. Shallow promises are fatal and highlight the weak supervisor. If a supervisor cannot deal with the situation because it is outside his or her authority, the facts must be reported *objectively* to the superior. The risk of distorting the story to cover any error on the supervisor's part is not worth while. If the superior interviews the employee and if that story does not agree with the supervisor's report the supervisor's position is not an enviable one.

Often a grievance is solved simply by providing the employee with information, in which case, where the supervisor has not withheld the information, a check should be made on the breakdown in communication.

Finally, some grievances are beyond the solving point. Sometimes there is no way out and unfortunately the problem ends in termination or perhaps a transfer. Possibly the cause can be traced back to poor interviewing for the job or a drastic change in the individual's outlook through no fault of the concern.

Follow-up

No sound grievance-solving procedure is complete until some form of follow-up and checking is made at intervals after treatment. If the treatment has been unsuccessful another discussion is necessary, and so it goes on until a more acceptable solution is found. Patience, understanding and courage to take action are the essential requirements.

Group discussion

The supervisor may decide to hold a group discussion to talk over a grievance, a problem or a situation. The supervisor assumes the role of discussion leader and preparation for the discussion is normally his or her responsibility, defining the objects of the meeting and outlining the main topics in some form of order for discussion.

A careful selection of members is essential and should be restricted to those who will be able to contribute their knowledge, experience and ideas on the particular subject. Choosing the right number is generally based upon the inclusion of those who have a direct interest in the problem. About five or six is a good number for ensuring that each member has the opportunity to participate.

Any information which may be needed to supplement the discussion should be provided. Without essential information, valuable time is often wasted arguing over opinions instead of being spent in intelligent discussion based upon factual information.

Conducting the discussion

Introduction

Establish a friendly relaxed atmosphere and remind members of the purpose of the meeting. Generally, notice of the purpose and main points for discussion should be distributed well in advance to give members sufficient time to think over the problem and make a few notes.

Continue with the background information and hand out any further details. Do not expect members to hold figures or complex information in their heads.

Stating the case

When the members have settled down a lead should be given by mentioning the controversial or important aspects and asking for opinions or ideas. Perhaps a question could be put forward to stimulate the group or, if this fails, the group leader's opinion may be stated to bring out any reaction.

Controlling the discussion

When the discussion is under way the leader must control carefully, keeping to the point, but not stopping any member from having a say. The reluctant member should be encouraged to give an opinion because the best ideas do not always come from those who have most to say.

When the discussion warms up, control becomes more difficult as personalities become involved and feelings run high. The tension may be removed by summarising at appropriate points and clarifying a person's remarks to make sure that he or she is not being misunderstood.

Conclusion

When everyone has had the opportunity to speak and fully discuss the problem the leader may reach a conclusion and recommend certain actions.

He or she should note any further comments and thank the members for attending.

The work of committees is dealt with in the next chapter with other aspects of communication.

Questions

1   State how the supervisor can improve his or her performance in the art of listening.
2   What are the main purposes of giving orders?
3   What factors should be borne in mind when giving orders?
4   Discuss the main ways of giving orders and suggest suitable situations for their use in each case.
5   In what circumstances would a supervisor resort to a direct command and when should its use be avoided?
6   'Many supervisors blame their subordinates when they receive a low response to their orders.' Comment on this statement.
7   How would you encourage self-discipline among your subordinates?
8   When should a supervisor use negative forms of discipline?
9   What precautions should be taken before reprimanding a subordinate?
10   What advice on reprimanding would you give to a newly promoted supervisor?
11   Suggest a logical procedure for dealing with a reprimand.
12   What action would you take as a supervisor if you saw an employee who was not in your department deliberately damaging a machine?
13   How can a supervisor use subordinates' complaints constructively?
14   Discuss the basic causes of employees' complaints and the role of the supervisor when dealing with this problem.
15   How would a supervisor recognise the symptoms of a complaint before it is aired by the employee?
16   Outline the basic steps in solving a grievance.
17   How would you conduct a group discussion?

Case study

Sarah Pringle had been employed as an office supervisor for twelve years in the typing pool. Recently her office manager, without warning, told her that two XYZ word processing machines were being delivered next day.

Sarah met the training adviser who arrived with the machines. She explained that part of the deal was a three-day free training scheme for three typists. Sarah picked the best workers and told them they were going on a course.

When they returned all three insisted they could not work the new machines because they were too complicated and made their backs ache. One threatened to leave if forced to use the machine. The other two were equally hostile and said they were going to see the staff representative.

1   Consider why these reactions could have been foreseen by Sarah.
2   Comment on the manager's approach to installing new machines of this nature.

16 Communication: further aspects

Interviewing

Whenever the supervisor is conversing with another person and information is being exchanged, he or she is interviewing or being interviewed. The broad concept of an interview goes well beyond the general impression that interviews are solely connected with employment. A wide range of interviews takes place every day on topics such as induction, training, grievances, suggestions, wages and merit rating, discipline, policy, regulations, operating problems and personnel counselling. *Interviewing* in this sense becomes an active two-way process of exchanging information, ideas and opinions between people, while the term *communication* forms the passive link between people throughout the concern. The exception which illustrates the difference is a *direct order* which is one way, not an interview but nevertheless a communication.

Although experience is invaluable in the art of interviewing, the supervisor should also take full advantage of books written by specialists on the subject (*see* Bibliography). Reading soon dispels any common misconceptions that interviewing is easy and that individuals can be assessed accurately at first sight or in thirty minutes.

The inherent problems of interviewing are: making people feel at ease, knowing the right questions to ask, recognising faults and elaborations, being able to size up people and not allowing personal prejudices to interfere.

Interviewees tend to create impressions of what they think they are or would like to be, which of course is natural but misleading to the interviewer. Similarly, when individuals pass on information, the tendency to give favourable impressions of themselves causes them to slant the information to conform with this pattern.

Types of interview

There are five types of interview used in various situations, including the application for employment:

- closed
- open
- self-controlled

- group discussion
- board or committee

Closed interviews

This type follows a set pattern of asking questions which are planned to cover all the requirements of a particular job. Considerable skill is required to overcome the stereotyped approach. Learning the questions and being able to vary their order helps to break up a rigid or formal effect.

An advantage is that all the essential information is gathered together and the interviewee is also given sufficient information to make a decision. Careful planning is needed to cover all the aspects of the job and, whenever particular skills must be demonstrated, the interviewee is passed to a specialist who checks the requirements personally.

The closed interview can be very impersonal unless the right atmosphere is established by the interviewer.

Open interviews

This type offers more scope for the skilled interviewer to make a better assessment of the individual. Although a job specification and information on the concern is used, the object is to put the interviewee at ease, draw him or her out on the subjects under discussion and steer carefully on to new topics.

The open interview is closely coupled with the closed type as both have a certain object in mind, that is, to obtain and give particular information.

Self-controlled interviews

When suggestions, complaints or grievances are presented, the self-controlled interview allows the interviewee to express him- or herself fully without worrying about time limits. The interviewer plays a 'near passive' role by listening sympathetically and agreeing periodically with the interviewee.

If the interview starts 'drying up', the interviewer must be sufficiently skilled to encourage the interviewee to gain confidence and air thoughts openly.

Group discussions

A well-conducted group discussion is an excellent way of exchanging information and fostering new ideas. The right atmosphere of co-operation and enthusiasm must be induced.

The discussion may be conducted with a specific subject in mind or as an open discussion to see what may develop. The group approach was discussed more fully in the previous chapter.

Board or committee

This technique subjects the individual to a number of interviewers who are known as a board or committee. The interviewee will probably feel very nervous when confronted by, say, six people who in turn ask questions based upon their own particular experiences.

Facing up to such an ordeal is part of the technique, but there are variations; for example, where the individual is interviewed privately by each member of the board. The opinions of each member are then examined and analysed by the board and if agreement is unanimous the choice is made.

Employment interview

The interviewer must have a sound knowledge of the job, including the degree of authority and responsibility and the duties involved, to form a clear picture of the personal qualities required. A questionnaire should be designed which includes all the information needed from the applicant. In addition, the applicant will be interested in the company, its policies and regulations, the products, working conditions, social activities and pension schemes. All this information should be available and accurate.

Various plans have been designed to assist the interviewer in assessing the candidate and his or her suitability for a particular job. The Seven-point Plan of the National Institute of Industrial Psychology is one example. This plan was devised by Professor Alec Rodger and used in vocational guidance work by the Institute. There are seven headings and each one contains a number of questions, as detailed below.

The seven-point plan

1 *Physical make-up* Has the candidate any defects of health or physique that may be of occupational importance? How agreeable are appearance, bearing and speech?

2 *Attainments* What type of education has the person had? How well has he or she done educationally? What occupational training and experience has he or she had already? How well has the candidate done occupationally?

3 *General intelligence* How much general intelligence can the person display? How much general intelligence does he or she ordinarily display?

4 *Special aptitudes* Has he or she any marked mechanical aptitude? manual dexterity? facility in the use of words? or figures? talent for drawing? or music?

5 *Interests* To what extent are the candidate's interests intellectual? practical–constructional? physically–active? social? artistic?

6 *Disposition* How acceptable does the person make him- or herself to other people? Does he or she influence others? Is the candidate steady and dependable? self-reliant?

Table 16.1 The Five-fold Framework

		Grade E (bottom 10%)	Grade D (lower 20%)	Grade C (middle 40%)	Grade B (upper 20%)	Grade A (top 10%)
Impact on others		Dirty clothes and sullen expression. Difficult to understand with manner causing avoidance by others whenever possible	Rather scruffy in appearance with local accent and limited vocabulary. Manner rather off-putting through lack of self-confidence	Undistinguished in appearance while speech and manner attract little attention. Difficult to call to mind after interview	Well turned out. Expresses self with enough confidence to meet most situations	Very pleasant to talk to; shows interest in what one says. Has considerable attraction in other ways
Qualifications and experience	General education	Incapable of normal education; school for educationally subnormal	No recognised qualifications in examination passes. Lower-streamed classes	GCSE Grades D–G	GCSE Grades A–C to 'A' level	University degree from pass to Honours level
	Vocational training	Left to pick up the work alone	Unsystematic on-the-job training, limited to work to be done	Systematic training at work with part-time classes, but no publicly-recognised qualifications	BTEC National or Higher National or similar standard at local college	Equivalent to a university degree at polytechnic or similar institution
	Work experience	Unskilled work on simple tasks that call for a minimum understanding	Semi-skilled on jobs that have been pre-planned and are carried out to set standards	Work calling for varying levels of skills and knowledge. Mainly routine involving little planning or decision-making	Middle or supervisory management posts, responsible for day-to-day operations	Higher management, mainly concerned with long-term planning

Innate abilities	Mentally subnormal	Slow in understanding and tending to reach over-simplified interpretations	Capable of taking in everyday affairs but has difficulty in understanding new or complex ideas	Above-average intelligence, but lacks the extra spark that would push the pendulum into grade A	Quick and active mind capable of taking in all sorts of information, interpreting it effectively and thinking up new ideas
Motivation	Incapable of supporting self and completely dependent on other people	Lacks initiative to find means of applying effort satisfactorily. Tends to rely on others to organise work and spare time	Motivation adequate for routine work provided someone is available to deal with unexpected problems	Hard-working, with enough initiative to overcome day-to-day difficulties	Very high level of drive and enthusiasm; always succeeds in finding outlets that provide self-realisation
Emotional adjustment	Incapable of adapting to normal social roles and frequently requires special treatment	Has difficulty in meeting the demands of normal roles and tends to be found 'awkward' by colleagues	Fits into normal roles acceptably but may become emotional when anything unforeseen crops up	Tends to be accepted in central roles as others find they can depend on candidate in difficulties	Capable of social roles that involve continuous stress; remains calm and rational in the most difficult situations

7 *Circumstances* What are the person's domestic circumstances? What do the other members of the family do for a living? Are there any special openings available for this person?

A development of the Seven-point Plan was introduced in 1950 by John Munro Fraser. This plan is called a five-fold framework and Table 16.1 (*see* pages 278–9) illustrates the main features. An assessment for each grade is based upon the distribution of human differences which was mentioned in Chapter 9.

The final arrangements which should be made before the interview are to ensure that:

1 all the questions to be asked are clear
2 sufficient time is allowed to complete the interview thoroughly
3 the applicant is notified of the arrangements

The introduction

Reception arrangements and appropriate accommodation are important aspects for establishing the confidence of the applicant. Every attempt should be made to put the individual at ease. Naturally he or she is nervous and time should be allowed for the candidate to settle down. Any quick assessment should be avoided and the interviewer must be extremely careful not to give the wrong impression because the applicant will be judging the interviewer as well during these critical early stages.

A short chat on any topic which is familiar to both parties helps to relieve the tension and establish a friendly relationship.

Exchange of information

As the interview develops information will flow in both directions. The interviewer should be seeking attitudes as well as facts which can only be found by listening carefully to assess pauses, evasiveness, embarrassment, over-elaboration or sketchiness.

The interviewer is not there to impress, nor to show personal feelings. True assessment demands concentration and, if there is a doubt, the topic should be clarified by asking further questions until the position is clear.

The interview must be controlled smoothly and scientifically.

The conclusion

The interview will gradually draw to a close quite naturally and sufficient time should be allowed for this to happen. Both sides will run out of questions, but the interviewer should allow the applicant a little time to think of any further points which are often forgotten under the stress of the interview.

The applicant should be thanked courteously for attending and should be allowed to bring the interview to a conclusion if possible. No doubt should be in the applicant's mind about the job or the company. He or she will then feel that the interview has been fair with the fullest opportunity to state a case for obtaining the position.

The new employee

The importance of communication to the new employee is often neglected because most existing employees take their surroundings for granted and fail to see the strange picture presented to the newcomer. First impressions tend to mould attitudes towards individuals, the concern and the job. These attitudes remain fixed and are very difficult to change, hence the increasing interest in induction schemes which help the newcomer to adjust rapidly to surroundings and which create more favourable impressions.

The main points to remember are as follows:

- First impressions are important.
- Be friendly.
- Try to put the new employee at ease.
- Show him all the amenities.
- Have patience when teaching him the job.
- Praise him when he does a good job.
- Check for any problems periodically.

The question of induction is discussed in Chapter 17.

Appraisal interview

Bearing in mind the principles already mentioned above, the first stage is adequate preparation. Ensure that all documentation is available including the employee's personal file, the job description, previous appraisal and a plan of the main points to be covered at the interview.

Give the employee plenty of warning so that he or she may have sufficient time to consider views before the interview and remind the person in advance of the reasons for conducting appraisals.

The actual interview obviously should be conducted along the lines already mentioned for maximum contribution and co-operation. After the meeting it is essential to write up the results and obtain agreement as soon as possible. Any misconceptions should then be corrected and a time-scale drawn up for any follow-up meeting to overcome problems, training schemes, possible transfer or promotion.

Meetings and committees

The object of committee work is to provide an opportunity for people representing the functions or sectors which come under the committee's sphere of activity to meet and act as a group. Under the guidance of a chairperson, information and ideas from each sector can be pooled and discussed in order to reach more accurate and balanced decisions. Provided the meeting is conducted properly, closer co-ordination between sectors should automatically follow.

A good chairperson is essential. He or she must conduct the meeting firmly, using the correct procedure and planning carefully throughout the life of the committee.

Members must be conscientious to a point where their own and the group's interests are subordinated to the common interest, that is the objective set for the committee. The chairperson can control this factor when it is obvious, but unfortunately self-interest can be shielded when specialists are drawn together. Besides problem-solving, the meetings help people to appreciate other points of view and so broaden their outlook. As the body of knowledge grows, people have to specialise on narrowing fronts which increases the problem of trying to understand the over-all picture and the problems of other specialists.

The type of authority given to a committee affects its status and procedure.

The first type is *direct* where members vote and are responsible as a committee for the decisions implemented.

The second type is *advisory* assisting the manager who is chairing the meeting. The chairperson gathers the knowledge and experience of members and proposals are discussed; then he or she makes the decision and is responsible for it.

The third type makes *recommendations* to the manager who is not the chairperson. The manager considers the proposals later, and either accepts or provides the committee with an adequate reason for rejection.

Committees also are held for other purposes such as *consultation*; for example, where representatives of management and employees are brought together to give their views, and 'communication by committee' ensures that information is received by all interested parties.

To summarise, ideally committee work is an excellent means of supplementing the organisation framework, providing a meeting-ground for individuals from different parts of the concern who normally would not have much direct communication. Purposeful control and suppression of self-interest are difficult to achieve, and as a result some committees have a poor reputation and become known as 'time-wasters'. However, much invaluable work is done at meetings to co-ordinate activities and to improve the effectiveness of the organisation.

Attending meetings

The main points to consider when attending meetings are as follows:

1 Study the constitution of the meeting which gives the rules for conducting proceedings.

2 Enquire from the secretary for suitable dress.

3 Study the previous minutes of the meeting, the agenda and any information forwarded in advance.

4 Prepare any facts or figures which you will need to state your views.

5 Send a written apology or telephone the secretary if you are unable to attend as soon as you are aware of the fact.

6 Plan to arrive five minutes before the meeting commences.

7 During the meeting always address your words to the chairperson unless directed otherwise.

8 Think carefully before you speak as you will be judged by your words and ideas.

9 Make your speeches clearly, slowly and with brevity.

10 Do not take offence at criticisms of your views. They are probably made with as much sincerity as your suggestions. Remember the object of group discussion is to discuss the best solutions to problems by team effort which means constructive criticism, putting forward ideas and arriving at several conclusions.

11 Listen attentively and use the spare time to think over proposals.

12 Criticise constructively and tactfully.

13 Ask questions if you are uncertain about any point or if you do not understand clearly the decisions reached.

14 Avoid any comments and suggestions after the meeting. The time to speak is at the meeting and failure to comment until later indicates that you are uncertain of yourself.

The meeting as a means of persuasion

On some occasions the supervisor may have difficulty in persuading management to take an obvious and essential course of action. When these circumstances are known to everyone and management remains indifferent, it is possible to ask for a meeting to be arranged to discuss the question.

In many cases this will be agreed and, by the time the meeting is held, the chances are that management has already acted to avoid embarrassment.

Report writing

An efficient communication system has to rely, to some extent, upon the conscientious provision of written reports. Neglecting to render worthwhile reports has resulted in disastrous blunders, poor decisions and wasted time.

A report is a written account of an event or situation, together with relevant facts, figures and recommendations where required. The purpose is to provide information to those who are concerned with or responsible for taking some action on the matter.

Every supervisor who is responsible for a number of subordinate supervisors soon realises the importance of the reports received from them; but this person, in turn, must attach a similar importance to the report he or she conveys to superiors. The supervisor will expect the reports received to be clear, accurate, concise, logically arranged and on time, and he or she must conform to similar standards in making reports.

Readability

The report must be easy to read and understand otherwise the reader will be distracted by the wording. One method of calculating readability is called the Fog Index, which increases in value as the writing becomes 'foggier'.

The index is calculated in the following way.

1   Work out the average number of words in each sentence in a passage of about 100 words by dividing the total number of words with the number of sentences. The final sentence in the passage should be included or excluded depending upon which word count is nearest to the 100 word total.

2   Count the words containing three or more syllables in the passage, but excluding proper nouns and easy compound words, i.e. words beginning with a capital letter and words such as 'extend' or 'repress' when they appear as 'extend*ed*' or 'repress*es*' should not be included.

3   The results of 1 and 2 are added and multiplied by 0.4 to give the Fog Index.

A passage with an index of six is very easy to read, while an index of seventeen is extremely difficult. Any figure above twelve is considered to be difficult to read. The Fog Index may be improved by restricting a sentence to about two ideas and eighteen to twenty-two words, keeping sentences short but varying their length and structure, linking and relating sentences to each other and using short-syllable words wherever possible.

Other points to note are: use adequate conjunctions (and, but, with, that, etc.), avoid lengthy prepositional phrases (for the reason that = because), wherever possible use short-syllable familiar words, and avoid passive verbs ('The rollers' position is changed to . . .' becomes 'The rollers move to . . .').

Types of reports

One method of classifying reports is to split them into their main types:

1   personal accounts
2   routine reports
3   special reports

The first two are fairly straightforward accounts of incidents or events including facts and figures. Personal accounts include presenting information, as witnessed at the time, on events such as accidents, social disturbances and disciplinary action. Routine reports include all information passed to control points on topics such as production progress, machine breakdowns and idle time, which are everyday occurrences.

The third type is for unusual events which are generally far more involved. The report includes investigations and analysis of information illustrating the significance of findings and often recommending courses of action. Careful planning and a logical approach are needed, otherwise the reader will spend considerable time wading through the material in an attempt to sort out the sequence of events and the points to be noted.

Procedure

A recommended approach is detailed below:

1 The object of the report
2 Preparation–method of investigation, area, etc.
3 Collecting information
4 Collating the report
5 Revision

The object

Make sure that the aim of the report is perfectly clear. Any ambiguity or uncertainty in the terms of reference should be clarified before proceeding further. The terms of reference must give sufficient detail to establish accurately:

1 the topic of investigation
2 the limitations, if any, of the enquiry
3 the purpose of the report

Preparation

Before enquiries and the collection of information commence, it is essential to prepare a framework of investigation. Work can then proceed to a flexible plan which may be revised as necessary when fresh information becomes available. The plan should be based upon such factors as assessment of the likely difficulties, the time factor, amount of co-operation from employees, degree of secrecy, amount of detail required, known availability of facts, possible repercussions from certain individuals, and any special requirements for the report.

The reader must be considered when drawing up the plan. An assessment through personal knowledge, previous experience or by discreet enquiries will enable the writer to decide how much detail is needed depending on what information is already known to the reader, whether technical jargon or plain language should be used, and the reader's likely reaction to the significance of the findings as they may affect him or her.

Collecting information

Collection of information and ideas should proceed according to the plan. The sources of information are found by personal knowledge, or by using the 'chain method' of asking one person who suggests another and so on. Careful observation, reading and experiment form part of the technique.

Notes should be made immediately whenever possible and in sufficient detail for very brief notes are often difficult to decipher later. The use of rough sketches assists the writer in refreshing the memory. An important precaution is always to identify the source of information.

Collating the report

The first draft of the report should be written within a suitable framework, usually made up of headings such as the ones given below:

- The subject
- Introduction
- Findings
- Conclusions
- Recommendations
- References
- Summary

The report must also be dated and signed.

1   *The subject*   Terms of reference should be stated in full. In some instances the source and date of directive should be given, especially if copies are to be sent to various departments.

2   *Introduction*   The method of conducting the investigation should be given, together with any major difficulties which were encountered. Any major gaps in the report must be mentioned and an assessment of their importance given. If background information is considered to be of use it may be mentioned at this stage. Any relevant information which does not fit conveniently into the rest of the framework of the report may be included in this section. Examples are: the general attitude of employees towards the subject, degrees of secrecy, explanations of courses of action, or necessary technical jargon.

3   *Findings*   This section forms the main body of the report which includes all the facts presented in logical sequence and in an unbiased manner. Whenever possible it is a good plan to tabulate the facts; this has the advantages of clarity to the reader and easier preparation for the writer.

4 *Conclusions* An analysis of the facts and all the inferences and value judgments should be included in this section. Adequate explanations of conclusions drawn from the facts are essential, otherwise the reader will be unable to assess their value. Logical conclusions based upon a number of facts are generally straightforward and immediately acceptable, but if experience and judgment are included in the basis this should be stated.

5 *Recommendations* Recommendations are based upon the findings and conclusions. If there are a number of choices available they should be weighted with arguments for and against each one. Some of the important factors may be: the cost, time, disruption of production, human problems, availability of supplies and space.

6 *References* References to any documents or books should be listed in this section. Sufficient information should be given for easy location. Naturally this section may be omitted if there are no references mentioned.

7 *Summary* A brief outline of the report is essential for some people who have insufficient time to read the full story. Care is needed to ensure that the correct meaning of each section is conveyed. Figure 16.1 gives an example of the layout of a summary page.

```
                          TITLE           Page 1

Terms of reference ......................................................

Introduction ............................................... Date ..................

Summary of findings
1:
2:
3:
4:
5:
Conclusions ....................................................................

Recommendations .............................................................

                                          Signature
```

Fig. 16.1 *Summary page of a report*

A single-page summary is necessary for those who will not have sufficient time to read the full report, and is also convenient for those who have. Clear, logical layout is important, and the figure shows a sample layout and the points to be included

Revise

Whenever possible wait at least a few hours before attempting to revise the first draft. A slight change of mood provides sufficient variance of insight which helps considerably in rendering a more balanced report. The document should be read critically and objectively. Try to be ruthless and remove all unnecessary words.

If a person can be found who will give an honest constructive view of the report, the second draft should be submitted to him or her for comment.

Essential requirements of a report

- On time.
- Accurate, concise and clear.
- Tactful and unbiased.
- Logically arranged and complete.
- Depth of investigation consistent with importance of subject.
- Conclusions and recommendations aligned with the facts.
- Illustrations used where words are inadequate.
- Stimulates interest otherwise no one will read it.

Project reports

Some examination boards, including NEBSS, require course members to investigate a problem or situation by collecting appropriate information, analysing it, arriving at logical conclusions, and making suitable recommendations. Apart from using information preceding this section, further notes are given now on the choice of subject, the investigation, and the report.

Choice of subject

Four main phases are recommended.

1 *Write down immediate ideas* Rather than agonise over whether a situation or problem is suitable simply write down the immediate difficulties being experienced or the obvious faults surrounding the job, taking into account procedures, systems, control, etc. Note that there are inevitably hundreds of suitable subjects in the immediate vicinity.

Choose subjects that appear to be straightforward, of sufficient depth to warrant investigation, demonstrate obvious improvements immediately, and are considered worthwhile in terms of savings, improving efficiency, or increasing effectiveness.

2 *Consider the work involved* Add to each idea a rough plan of the possible work involved, bearing in mind interviews, studying the immediate situation, guessing at possible avenues to be traced away from the workplace, assessing the people to be contacted, and forming a general impression of the project's breadth.

Note: even simple situations and problems become complex when investigated in their entirety; often that is why they exist.

3   *Decide on the category*   Sort ideas into categories: problem solving, procedural rearranging, cost saving by simplifying, and so on. Use work study techniques to categorise. When complete, consider which one suits available knowledge and experience.

4   *Select two or three*   Write a framework of ideas for each one. Discuss with the manager for opinion. Discuss with tutor for opinion and approval. Decide on the most suitable subject.

Investigation

The following points are worth bearing in mind.

1   Always be diplomatic towards the people who are involved. They may feel apprehensive and even hostile if there are obvious improvements they have ignored.
2   If hostility is met and there is no improvement, consider an alternative project rather than create an incident.
3   Avoid any personal prejudice. Try to present facts not opinions unless there is no alternative.
4   Information may be obtained by asking someone, and by observation and research. Use all three to confirm if there is any doubt.
5   Seek permission before overstepping any sectional boundaries.
6   Revise the plan as new evidence indicates, to provide balance and pertinent information.
7   Try to identify effective lines of enquiry to save time, especially if generalisations are appearing.
8   Consult the manager if advice is needed. Two purposes are served: he or she may be flattered and will not be taken by surprise at the end if made aware of progress.
9   Revise what is hoped to be achieved if there are difficulties.
10   Use work study techniques.

The report

The following points are often of use.

1   Make several attempts before choosing an appropriate arrangement.
2   Avoid very brief headings; convey their meaning plainly. Example: avoid 'stock', use 'finished goods stock'.
3   Avoid including information that is not strictly relevant. Ask yourself:
(a) Does this particular information lead to the conclusions and recommendations proposed?
(b) Is it of use to justify the recommendations proposed?
4   Emphasise significant information to avoid doubt as to the validity of conclusions and recommendations.

5 Try to provide balance by minimising space on minor subjects and maximising on major factors.
6 If recommendations are controversial indicate how the proposals will harmonise with other sections.
7 Include details 'of alternative proposals that were abandoned and give reasons. Thus questions will be anticipated.
8 Remember to include acknowledgements, especially help received from the manager.

Questions

1 Discuss the importance of developing a good interviewing technique in connection with supervision.
2 Describe how you would conduct an employment interview.
3 'The importance of reports is often overlooked.' Discuss this statement.
4 Outline a logical approach in preparing a written report.
5 Discuss the essential requirements of a report.
6 What advice would you give to a colleague who is going to attend his or her first meeting as a member of a committee?
7 Put yourself in the place of a new employee and describe your feelings and what information you would hope to receive from your supervisor.
8 Outline a logical method of communicating effectively.
9 Discuss the importance of external aspects of communication in connection with the supervisor's role as a leader.
10 Outline the various types of interview.
11 Discuss the Five-fold Framework, illustrating the main features of the plan.

Case study

Sally Newton, young and single, was warned about the men in her department of a well-known travel company by her superior before she took over the supervisor's job. The caution was expected as the eight men, most of them young, enjoyed a reputation as teasers and for not tolerating favouritism.

On the first day Sally soon found herself attracted to Bob, a popular man in the group. She could not keep her eyes off him and inevitably it took only a few days for the other men to notice. She deliberately spent a minimum of time with him, knowing the risks. Bob soon became aware of Sally's interest and made it obvious, it seemed, that he was equally attracted to her.

Sally, being no fool, was sure that the other men were wise to the situation. She was uncertain as to whether Bob was setting her up, or genuinely interested in her. Several weeks passed and everything went smoothly in the department. Package holiday bookings boomed beyond their previous high levels, and there were very few hitches.

Her superior was delighted, praised her and added, 'Incidentally, Sally, what are you going to do about Bob?'

1 How would you answer if you were Sally, after you had recovered?
2 How would you account for the successful running of the department from the information given?

17 Employment

Certain topics under the general heading of employment are of particular interest to the supervisor who will be concerned with them either directly or indirectly.

These topics are job tasks, activity analysis, job evaluation, job design, engagement, the employment contract, equal opportunities, induction, performance appraisal, transfers and promotion, terminations, redundancy, lateness and absenteeism, remuneration, and manpower planning.

Job tasks

A surprising number of tasks and the time element are often forgotten and neglected unless an attempt is made to record all the details on a daily basis. A useful addition is to summarise the details on a weekly basis which, although time consuming, is worth while. A simple example for an office is given in Fig. 17.1. In conjunction with activity analysis and job evaluation explained below it provides a sound framework for employment purposes, control and work study.

Job title:			Name:	
Section:			Day:	
Time			Task	
Start	Finish	Minutes		

Fig. 17.1 *Daily task sheet*

Activity analysis

To achieve a comprehensive picture all the activities of a section should be analysed by tabulating all the tasks. Included in the survey should be an appropriate title for each activity, the time spent, the employee's name and any other useful data.

An appropriate form may be easily drawn up. The layout will depend on the circumstances, but a typical example is given in Fig. 17.2 as a guide.

Section:								
Week commencing:								
Activity	Superv.	Hrs	Clerk A	Hrs	Clerk B	Hrs	Clerk C	Hrs

Fig. 17.2 *Weekly activity form*

Job evaluation

Job evaluation is a systematic approach to the problem of determining the value of a job in relation to others so that a fair wage scale may be applied. A scientific basis of assessment of *all* factors involved in a job is essential. Although personal bias or opinion cannot be eliminated completely, new techniques are being developed which will eventually place job evaluation on a more scientific basis.

Judging the relative values of jobs is difficult even within the same department and becomes exceptionally difficult when applied to different industries. With sufficient experience the superior should be able to make a reasonable assessment. Opinions vary among supervisors, however, and a determined attempt to be as objective as possible is recommended.

Successful introduction of job evaluation depends to some extent on the ability of supervisors to make sound assessments and on the careful compilation of the wages structure. A good scheme should result in a reduction in labour turnover and an increase in morale and output. Correct placement of employees in suitable jobs is made easier and publication of the job classifications clearly indicates the duties, authority, and responsibilities of each employee.

Procedure

The scheme is generally based upon particular standards which provide a fair comparison between various jobs. The main factors under consideration are as follows:

- Physical and mental effort
- Education and training
- Experience
- Degree of authority and responsibility
- Particular skills and aptitudes
- Working conditions

A detailed examination of the job is essential. A suitably designed form should be completed for every job and the findings then carefully assessed on a comparative basis. When all the jobs are assessed they are arranged in sequence of value and related to the wages structure by using the most logical method possible.

Methods of evaluation

There are four ways of evaluating jobs, but the two main methods are called points rating and ranking.

1 *Points rating* This system attempts to rate each factor of the job by allocating an appropriate weighting of points. Each factor may be assessed within a range of 0 to 10 points, or 0 to 20 points if a wider choice is desired. An example of a form using the points rating system is given in Fig. 17.3. The total number of points is calculated and matched against a wages table which is designed on a points wage-rate basis.

2 *Factor comparison* This is a variation of the points rating system. The main difference between the two schemes is that only five factors are used for factor comparison. These are: mental, physical, skill, responsibility and working conditions.

Key jobs are chosen to represent various wage levels and the wage for each job is proportioned among the five factors. From this information a value can be placed on each point and an appropriate rate may be calculated for those jobs which come between the key posts.

3 *Ranking* This is the other main method, which involves judging each job as a whole and attempting to assess its relative value by ranking a whole job against another whole job. This simple system includes preparing a job description and grading the levels for allocation of wages. The system does not indicate the degree of difference between jobs which is a disadvantage for the large company where a wide variety of jobs usually exists. In the small business this method is likely to be more suitable because of its simplicity and the reduced range of jobs is probably easier to define.

```
┌─────────────────────────────────────────────────────────────────────┐
│                         JOB EVALUATION                               │
├─────────────────────────────────────────────────────────────────────┤
│  Job title................................................................  │
│                                                                       │
│  Name.......................................  Clock No..............  │
│                                                                       │
│  Department..............................................................  │
│                                                                       │
│  Responsible to..........................................................  │
├─────────────────────────────────────────────────────────────────────┤
│  Job summary                                                          │
│                                                                       │
│                                                                       │
│                                                                       │
├──────────────────────────────┬──────────────────┬───────────────────┤
│                              │                  │     Points        │
│        Job requirements      │    Assessment    │     (1-10)        │
├──────────────────────────────┼──────────────────┼───────────────────┤
│  Education                   │                  │                   │
│  Experience                  │                  │                   │
│  Learning period             │                  │                   │
│  Responsibility              │                  │                   │
│  Physical conditions         │                  │                   │
│  Hazards                     │                  │                   │
├──────────────────────────────┴──────────────────┴───────────────────┤
│  Job grade......................  Signature............................  │
│                                                                       │
│  Total points...................  Title................................  │
│                                                                       │
│                                   Date................................  │
└─────────────────────────────────────────────────────────────────────┘
```

Fig. 17.3 *Job evaluation form*

This shows the layout of a typical job evaluation form, using the points rating system

4 *Classification* This is a method that may also be seen. Before the jobs are ranked this scheme determines the grades and salaries within which prepared job specifications are fitted. Personal judgment is employed to group and rank the jobs.

A job grading scheme

Although the four ways of evaluating jobs mentioned above obviously need considerable personal judgment they are often called scientific methods.

An example of a job grading scheme which clarifies the levels in office work is offered by the Institute of Administrative Management.

Grade A Simple or closely directed tasks requiring no previous experience to perform them.

Grade B Simple tasks requiring only a few weeks' training, closely directed, carried out within a small number of well-defined rules, checked and following a daily routine.

Grade C Routine tasks following well-defined rules, requiring a reasonable degree of experience (or a special aptitude), amounting to a daily routine and subject to short period control.

Grade D Tasks requiring considerable experience, some initiative, pre-determined procedure and a slightly varying daily routine.

Grade E Tasks requiring a significant amount of discretion and initiative (or a specialised knowledge), and responsibility for the work undertaken.

Grade F Tasks demanding an extensive amount of responsibility and judgment or the use of a professional technique, such as legal work, accounting or engineering.

Merit rating

A number of steps is normally incorporated within each grade mentioned above. Staff are placed on a particular step depending upon their expected performance. Adjustments are made in a number of ways such as annual increments, further qualifications and merit. A typical merit rating scheme submitted by the Institute of Administrative Management is outlined below.

Merit grade	Classification
1	beginner
2	qualified
3	experienced
4	superior
5	superlative (ready for promotion)

Flexible working hours

An attempt to overcome the timekeeping problem has been made by many companies by offering flexible working hours. A standard scheme sets core hours from 10.00 am to 4.00 pm when everyone should be present; outside these hours the times are negotiated individually.

The disadvantages are serious with flow line production but in most other cases the problems may be overcome with careful planning. The advantages claimed are that timekeeping improves, overtime is reduced, and a more even flow of work is maintained. Furthermore, the scheme is favoured by employees who can avoid rush-hours and reconcile their social programmes.

Functional analysis

In connection with job evaluation, the supervisor may feel that a complete or partial revision of the activities within each job is required. This situation often arises when a company is growing rapidly or has developed on a 'stop-gap' basis. The analysis may be conducted in two stages.

Stage 1: functional analysis

A complete survey of all the activities conducted within a department is recorded. The two main details noted are the particular activity and the employee who is responsible for it. In many situations a number of employees will be performing similar activities. A typical example of a form which may be used for analysis is given in Fig. 17.4.

| | Activity | FUNCTIONAL ANALYSIS | | | | | | | | | | PACKING OPERATION | | |
| | | Operator | | | | | | | | | | | | |
		A	B	C	D	E	F	G	H	I	J	K	L	M	N
1	Assemble packing carton														
2	Pack carton														
3	Check contents														
4	Seal carton														
5	Label carton														
6	Weigh carton														
7	Load on pallet														
8															
9															
10															
11															

Fig. 17.4   Functional analysis of all activities (Stage 1)

This form is used to record all the activities conducted in a department as the first stage of functional analysis. Each activity and the employee responsible is noted

Stage 2: job analysis

The activities can now be rearranged to form a more logical pattern among the employees. The knowledge and experience of operators will be taken into consideration, along with any other relevant factors which will affect the allocation. Fig. 17.5 illustrates the type of form which can be used for this purpose with a simple example. This information provides valuable data for the preparation of job evaluation forms.

This analysis forms part of a procedure for assessing and improving the organisation described in Chapter 3.

Job design

Successful job design embraces two major features:

- satisfying personal and social aspects
- satisfying technological and technical aspects

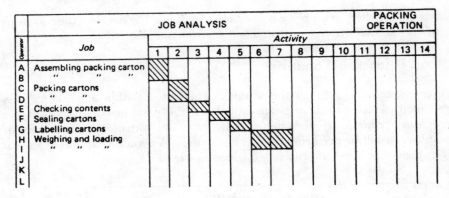

Fig. 17.5 *Job analysis form (Stage 2)*

The latter is fairly straightforward since there is generally available a large body of technological data continually up-dated by concerns. However, many difficulties arise to satisfy the former (humanising the job), consequently this feature is often neglected. A useful analogy of this situation is the absurdity of building a space probe for a ten-year journey and then considering accommodation for the astronauts.

The way jobs are designed has a critical effect on behaviour and satisfaction. Good design may make employees feel happy, comfortable and motivated. Poor design can induce the opposite. The reasons for these effects are now examined and recommendations suggested.

Human problems

Many managers and supervisors are fully aware of the human problems associated with job design: the effect of differing values, forced uniform pacing, repetitiveness, very short cycle times, poor working arrangements, unreal or distant objectives, difficulty in communicating with colleagues, and so on. These problems have a critical effect on productivity and job satisfaction.

If these problems exist, and managers are made aware of them and their effects, the reasons for not pursuing job redesign programmes must be interesting to discover.

The industrial climate

A variety of features make up the industrial climate in a company. These include boardroom policies (mostly unwritten), personnel policies, acceptable managerial and supervisory practices, job grading and evaluation schemes, class and status boundaries, shop-steward practices, and many worker-group practices. Combined they form an influence on a manager or supervisor which will no doubt persuade him or her to adopt various stances which may well affect the outlook on job redesign.

In brief, the social tools in companies are there, but the appropriate climate may be missing. Consequently there is a deadlock, perhaps with a few successful attempts to overcome the difficulty. Latest theories on job design, however, seem to be gradually focusing more on these problem areas related to the complete role of the individual in a productive type of organisation. This role encompasses many recognised ways of improving job satisfaction and behaviour; typically, Herzberg's concepts: self-control regulations, encouraging self-discipline, and creating a new culture.

Modern job design

The new approach is to include in design not only personal needs of the individual, sociological aspects surrounding the job, and the organisation structure which correlates with these two aspects, but also adjustment of the technology which is treated as a variable factor rather than a fixed configuration around which other aspects are manipulated. Thus modern job design in Britain is often known as socio-technical systems studies which have already been mentioned in Chapter 3.

The aim is to develop a more responsible autonomous job by adopting the following concepts.

1   To work at a pace that suits the individual.
2   To enlarge or enrich the job either by adding more operational tasks, or by including such activities as drawing materials, setting-up machines, servicing machines and plant, inspecting the work, some accounting operations, and rotating jobs.
3   To make the individual (or the group) responsible for a cycle of activities needed to complete, say, (a) a particular assembly, or (b) a sector of work, or (c) the whole product, depending on circumstances and technological feasibility.
4   To place responsibility at its lowest level (not supervisory level) for rate of working, output, quality, and material wastage.
5   To encourage the interdependence of the employee (or the group) on other groups for effectively progressing a cycle of activities.
6   To encourage autonomous behaviour by every means possible. Typically, developing self-regulation, self-evaluation, self-adjustment, self-establishing of individual or group objectives, self-discipline, and participation in all discussions that may affect the working group.

Current changes

The six aims given above indicate the complexity of change and the urgent need to continue with research. Eventually hypotheses and prescriptions to validate redesigning jobs may become more acceptable and workable within the framework of the technology, the individual, group activity, and other influences.

The old, and even some new concepts of management and organisation, may have to change drastically to mesh successfully with new techniques.

Engagement

The supervisor is often asked to interview a prospective employee to assess his suitability from the technical aspect. Generally the personnel manager conducts an initial interview to check details and assess personal qualities. The newcomer is then passed to a specialist or supervisor who assesses the individual for a particular function. Usually the supervisor also makes a general assessment which is compared with the personnel manager's opinion and a mutual agreement is reached. (Interviewing techniques were discussed in Chapter 16 as an aspect of communication.)

Where no personnel department exists, either the departmental manager or the supervisor engages employees. Such an arrangement is wasteful – unless a check is kept on all vacancies – as suitable employees may be available in other parts of the concern. Moreover, planning for future vacancies is virtually non-existent.

The employment contract

The Employment Protection (Consolidation) Act 1978 requires that an employee be given written particulars of terms of employment within thirteen weeks from the date of commencement.

The written statement must include the following:

1 The names of the parties to the contract of employment.
2 The date of commencement. If the contract is for a fixed term, the date of expiration should be stated.
3 The scale or rate of pay, or the method of calculating remuneration.
4 The intervals of payment, i.e. weekly, monthly, etc.
5 Hours of work, including any terms or conditions associated with this aspect.
6 The terms and conditions relating to holiday periods and holiday pay. These should include calculations for accrued holiday pay and rights to pay during sickness and injury.
7 Length of notice the employee should give and which he or she is entitled to receive.
8 The name of an individual whom the employee may consult and to

whom the employee may apply for redress of a grievance, the procedure to follow and any relevant details.

9 A statement of any works rules and a statement of the title of the job.
10 Details of pension rights if any.
11 Whether a contracting-out certificate in respect of the state pension scheme is in force.

Any changes made after commencement of employment must be given in writing to the employee within a month. If the employer fails to provide any of the above information the employee may apply to an industrial tribunal to establish the missing details. These particulars will then be recorded and deemed to have been given by the employer.

Employee records

Many companies now keep employees' records in a computer. These records must comply with the Data Protection Act 1984 which is detailed in Chapter 21 on Welfare. The inherent dangers in a computerised record system are well-known.

Equal opportunities

Discrimination in employment on the grounds of sex or marriage is prohibited under the Sex Discrimination Act 1975. This applies to interviews and other selection procedures, benefits such as opportunities for training and promotion, and any action which may be detrimental to employees such as short-time working or dismissal. The Act goes further by stating that discrimination is unlawful in relation to membership of, and benefits and facilities provided by, trade unions and any other organisations (such as professional bodies) which substantially influence the possibility of an individual carrying on an occupation. Any pressure exerted on another individual to discriminate unlawfully and the publishing of discriminatory advertisements are also prohibited.

The Equal Opportunities Commission (EOC) was established to promote the objectives of this Act and the Equal Pay Act 1970. It can carry out formal investigations into discriminatory practices and issue 'non-discrimination notices'. Breach of such a notice may be enforced by injunctions in civil courts. The Commission carries out research, advises the government on ways in which the legislation may need to be improved, and may assist and represent individual complainants.

An individual feeling discriminated against in employment on the grounds of sex can make a complaint to an industrial tribunal. A conciliation officer of the Advisory, Conciliation and Arbitration Service (ACAS, *see* Chapter 19) will attempt to settle the problem. If this fails the complaint will be considered by the tribunal which has the power to declare the complainant's rights and/or award compensation against the employer and recommend action which, if not complied with, could lead to increased compensation.

The tribunal may also declare a case of general discrimination which can then be made the subject of a formal investigation by the EOC.

The Act provides for exceptions in certain posts where a person's sex is a genuine occupational qualification. The criteria are as follows:

- For reasons of physiology or authenticity.
- In social and personnel work where teams of both sexes are essential.
- In a predominantly single-sex institution where members of one sex are legitimately important to the character of the institution.
- On grounds of propriety and privacy which would be affected if the appropriate opposite sex were employed.

Induction

The importance of introducing the new employee correctly has already been discussed in Chapter 16. First impressions form a permanent mark in the newcomer's mind and, if they are unfavourable, it takes a long time to change the individual's outlook towards the company.

The personnel department has the opportunity to create a good impression from the beginning if given a free hand. In view of the high cost of labour turnover and the importance of first impressions, it is surprising to see some personnel departments housed either in huts tucked away in the most unattractive part of the concern or at the end of long, bleak corridors.

The personnel department's part

A list of information which the personnel department normally provides for a new employee is given below:

1 Organisation charts and an explanation of where the particular job fits into the over-all plan.
2 A booklet on terms and conditions of employment. The personnel officer should explain any items which are not clear and mention those which are likely to be altered in the near future.
3 A clear statement of the authority, responsibility and duties of the job and the job title.
4 An outline of possible channels of promotion.
5 Details of the concern's education and training schemes and the name of the training officer.
6 A plan of the workshop or office showing all the usual facilities which should include cloakroom, washrooms, medical services and the dining rooms.

7   The names of the immediate superior and the superior in charge of the department.
8   Full details of commencing salary or wage rate, the scale of pay increases and any financial incentives which are in operation. Personnel should make sure that the new employee understands the pay scheme properly.
9   An outline of the social activities and the name of the welfare officer or the individual who arranges such activities.
10   The hours of work, including tea/coffee break times, lunch times, starting and finishing times. Any allowances for clocking and times for washing should be explained, if relevant.
11   The general amenities such as bicycle sheds and car parking arrangements.
12   Information on the trade unions and where to locate the union representatives.
13   Advice on safety and a copy of the company's written safety policy.
14   Background information on the company, its achievements, products and objectives.

As well as providing all this necessary information, the personnel officer should carefully point out that the new job will no doubt mean some amount of adjustment to new surroundings, new colleagues and work methods. He or she must emphasise that the personnel department is there to assist and offer advice whenever anything is bothering the new employee.

Further it helps to create a good impression if employees' legal rights are made known. For example, legislation on health and safety (*see* Chapter 20) and industrial relations (*see* Chapter 19).

After a formal introduction to the supervisor concerned, the personnel department officially hands over the newcomer.

The supervisor's part

The next step of induction begins at this point and preparation by the supervisor for this time is just as important as planning for induction in the personnel department.

The supervisor should make sure that the following arrangements are made.

Preparation

1   *The individual.* Know all essential information such as the employee's name, clock number, job, background, education, experience and assessment.
2   *The section.* Pass on the necessary information about the newcomer to colleagues and other individuals who may contact him or her.

3 *The workplace*. Make sure the place where the newcomer will be located is tidy and clean and that all tools and equipment which can be obtained beforehand are available and in good condition.

4 *Procedure*. Make all the arrangements beforehand which may be needed for special passes, forms for social activities, beverage and meal tickets and any hand-outs which are not covered by the personnel department.

Arrival

Give the newcomer a warm welcome. Show that you are pleased to see the employee; you probably are, so why hide the fact? Introduce him or her to all colleagues in the group and mention in passing any special interests. This will give the newcomer an opening for future conversation with colleagues.

Try to put the person at ease by conversing on general topics but without giving the impression of being too interested or over-inquisitive about personal affairs. If you feel the newcomer is reacting against your approach take the initiative and proffer some information about yourself and your own interests.

Provide the new employee with as much information as you feel can be assimilated at first. Do not expect him or her to remember everything. Be prepared to repeat information several times on different occasions. This technique may seem tedious, but remember that strangeness is caused by lack of information on people, the job and surroundings.

Make sure that his or her authority, duties and responsibilities in the job are clear; also make sure that the newcomer knows the person to whom he or she is responsible. Explain the job in greater detail and question the person to see if everything has been clearly understood. The learning and teaching period is covered as a separate topic in the next chapter.

Supplement earlier stages of induction by discussing the terms of employment and regulations in more detail. This procedure is essential as there may be small but important variances due to local conditions which the personnel department could easily overlook. The employee is also given a further opportunity to clarify any queries which may have arisen since the interview with the personnel officer. Matters such as transport problems, holidays, insurance schemes, social activities, pay problems and working arrangements often require additional on-the-spot advice.

Naturally there is a vast number of small points to be covered under the general topic of working arrangements and it is only too easy for the supervisor to overlook a few. Keeping a complete check-list of all the points to tell the new employee can save embarrassment later. The list would include the following points where appropriate:

1   danger areas
2   special regulations concerning smoking

3 departmental and sectional boundaries
4 allowances for washing
5 locker and cloakroom facilities
6 maintenance rules
.7 fire hazards and procedure
8 special routines concerning tools, oils, equipment
9 use and issuing of safety devices
10 first aid
11 emergency arrangements

Work assignment

Check that the employee already understands the assignment. If the job involves working a particular machine or being at a control point, make sure that the employee realises the importance of being on the spot and knows the procedure to follow if he or she leaves the workplace for some reason. The procedure for tool and materials requisitions should be clearly outlined.

The chargehand, leading hand or a responsible employee should act as a guide during the initial period, helping as much as possible to develop the right attitudes in the newcomer. The importance of the work and its place in the general pattern of production should be stressed.

Follow-up

The object of induction is to make newcomers feel part of the organisation which enables them to contribute their capabilities to the full. This sense of belonging is not achieved in a few days; it takes weeks and often months before a new employee really settles in.

Induction must be treated as a lengthy process of indoctrination and the supervisor should check periodically to note progress, see if he or she can assist and help out with any problems. There will be at least one problem which is bothering a newcomer, and the supervisor should try to gain the individual's confidence by asking how he or she is progressing and noting general reactions.

Performance appraisal

As newcomers develop they will probably need further training followed by performance appraisal. Good results should not be expected immediately. Individuals learn at different rates and improvements depend partly on the patience and understanding of the supervisor and colleagues.

Appraisal is essential for a number of reasons: to give the employee a clear indication of progress and performance, to encourage, to assess the results of training, to obtain useful feedback information for the supervisor, and to provide an accurate measure of progress for assessing merit rating relating to remuneration, transfers, promotion and manpower planning.

For both the newcomer and seasoned employees the appraisal must be conducted along sound and comprehensive lines. Various methods and interview techniques are available and the personnel department should be consulted. A sound scheme will include an interview by a trained assessor, opinions sought from the manager, supervisor and other contacts associated with the individual's work. The assessment takes into account the job specification and personal attributes.

1 *Employees' viewpoint.* Feelings of frustration and uncertainty are experienced at work when no indication is given of progress. Such discourtesy and insensitivity on the superior's part is unforgivable. People want to know to whom they are responsible, what is expected from them, the boundaries of their job and the rules and standards involved. Indeed, in many cases they need a clear idea of their promotion prospects and the essential promotion requirements: further study, transfers, mobility and scope.

Favouritism and any indications of unfair treatment in appraisals naturally cause unrest and discontent. This applies also to groups and certain individuals who feel they are always being picked on.

2 *Management's viewpoint.* To achieve the over-all aim of higher productivity there must be adequate information on performance so that appropriate steps may be taken, especially with those who fall below certain standards. Often the unions in Britain are unco-operative in this matter as their traditional aims do not coincide.

The appraisal scheme is seen by management as promoting two-way communication which helps to evaluate managerial potential – vital for manpower planning, management development programmes and further training.

Appraisal methods

Basic requirements include the involvement of all managers and supervisors who should feel totally committed and know how to appraise. Employees must be fully informed, any queries should be settled and their personal views sought. They should know that not only current performance is considered but also latent talents, personality traits and manpower requirements.

Below are the main methods involved.

Grading

A number of factors is assessed by awarding a figure or a letter relating to performance on a set scale. The factors could be accuracy, creativeness, co-operativeness, sensitivity towards people, resourcefulness, productiveness, judgment, dependability and loyalty. A typical scale is:

1 – excellent 2 – very good
3 – good 4 – satisfactory
5 – poor 6 – very poor

Letters may be substituted if desired. Figure 17.6 illustrates the type of form in use.

The disadvantages are subjective judgment, inaccurate measurement, a tendency to use the middle grade and being too vague for many appraisal aims.

Personal characteristics

Assessing these characteristics could be based upon the following example of ratings:

A: exceptional – displays unusual qualities
B: high standard – exceeds usual standards
C: standard – meets accepted standards
D: below average – improvements needed to meet accepted standards
E: well below average – needs major improvements in many areas to meet accepted standards

The written assessment

The superior is expected to write a comprehensive report often within some guidelines. This method suffers from the writer's literary limitations and subjectiveness, is time consuming, and may be biased between departments.

Target setting

This approach is often used for managers. The technique is known as MBO (Management By Objectives) and is dealt with in Chapter 12. Setting targets and assessing the results equally applies to manual and clerical jobs. However, setting a target and acceptance of the target may cause problems. Certainly a sound scheme can be devised but it must be sold to employees and applied objectively. Figure 17.7 shows an example of a target setting/appraisal form.

Typical statements (under comments) alongside each task number for 'above standard' would be: personal achievement, standard needs revising, enforced supervisory support or result affected by external influence. For 'below standard': lack of control information, external influence, standard needs revising, training needed or change in priorities.

Performance Appraisal												
Superior: Position Title: Department:		Age: Time in present job:					Name: Date: District:					

Present job							Personal characteristics					
	1	2	3	4	5	6		A	B	C	D	E
Knowledge							Initiative					
Skills							Cooperation					
Problem solving							Relations — peers					
Decision making							Relations — sections					
Delegation							Relations — customers					
Output							Adaptability					
Quality							Persuasiveness					
Administration							Leadership/power					
Communication — oral							Confidence					
— written							Judgment					
Creativity							Personality					

Total performance rating [   ]
Prepared by:

Review Panel — comments:

Signature: Date:

Supervisor's Notes:

Signature: Date:

Employee — response/comments:

Signature: Date:

Fig. 17.6 *Performance appraisal form*

PERFORMANCE REVIEW					
Superior: Department:				Name: Period: Title:	
Task No.	Performance				Comments
	Target	Actual	Variance		
			+	−	
1					
2					
3					
4					
5					
etc.					

Fig. 17.7 *Outline framework of a target setting/appraisal form*

Ranking

This crude method is to list employees from the highest performance level to the lowest. It suffers from obvious disadvantages: all may be below average, and subjectiveness and juggling between two or more similar levels are typical difficulties.

Rating

A merit rating scheme has already been covered. More sophisticated techniques may be used by listing appropriate factors in the job and applying similar measures. Useful for training purposes as well as remuneration, it highlights the weaknesses and strengths which may be used to advantage in the job.

Self-appraisal

A more active and responsible role by the employee is achieved with this technique. The form layout varies considerably depending upon the approach. A more personal style might be to divide the form into sections with headings such as 'How I have progressed', 'My breadth of knowledge', 'What I hope to accomplish in the next period', 'How I plan to go about it', 'How management could help'.

The supervisor may go through the same process, using a more formal form before arranging for a discussion with the employee to agree on the various factors. Generally the question of remuneration is omitted from these talks.

Transfers and promotion

The personnel department acts as a centre for dealing with transfers and promotions. By keeping records and checking on all employee movements, it can ensure that the most suitable members are given the opportunity for promotion.

The problem of balancing the labour force in time of expansion or contraction becomes easier when controlled from a central point. Supervisors, however, have considerable responsibility in deciding upon transfers which they cannot offset as the personnel department's responsibility. Supervisors must be very careful not to make mistakes on transfers, promotions and terminations as the responsibility for such action rests squarely on them and mistakes may be disastrous.

Supervisors should be constantly on the look-out for changes which occur in individuals and in jobs which are the main reason for transfers. An employee may be unsuitable for a particular job because his or her capabilities are not up to standard or the person's health may be suffering because of the strain involved. The job may have gradually or drastically changed but the employee may not be able to adjust or may have new interests.

Reorganisation within the company often provides a surplus in some sections and a shortage in others which can be solved by a careful selection of transfers.

As an employee develops capabilities through experience in the job and through education and training schemes, the possibilities of a suitable transfer or promotion should always be considered, otherwise he or she may become frustrated and possibly leave. Schemes for improving employees' performance and capabilities must be related to a policy of up-grading employees.

Interdepartmental transfers

The usefulness of the personnel department is well illustrated when the problems of transferring employees between departments is considered. Successful placing of individuals in the departments depends upon adequate information on vacancies or likely transfers and on assessments of employees. The personnel department can co-ordinate this activity smoothly with the help and co-operation of supervisors.

The responsibility for such transfers lies naturally with the personnel department, and all supervisors should realise how they can assist and also avoid any friction with fellow supervisors. A supervisor should never try to entice an employee away from another department. Providing sufficient information and referring all cases of transfers to the personnel department ensures a smooth running scheme.

Promotion

The importance of finding the right person for the right job is recognised by most employers. The principle applies at all levels. Employees, however, become more critical of appointments as the levels of supervision are ascended. The responsibility involved in making a promotion, therefore, is always highlighted. Any mistakes made by the personnel department or by supervisors who make recommendations receive considerable attention from most members of the concern. Promotion generally includes a pay increase, additional privileges, a rise in status and more authority and responsibility.

The main points for consideration are whether the scheme of promotion is fair and whether the concern as a whole will benefit. For the concern and all employees to benefit it is essential that the best person is found for the particular job. A fair scheme with this view in mind is to assess all possible internal applicants and if a suitable person is found he or she should be appointed, provided a more suitable person is not available outside the company. Such a policy of promotion from within whenever possible is sound and is seen to be fair by existing employees. Fair operation of the scheme depends upon the supervisor who must continually assess subordinates and recommend on a strictly objective basis those he or she considers are suitable for promotion.

Some of the problems which arise concern those who have given long, loyal service but are unsuitable material for promotion, and those who may be excellent workers but lack other essential qualities. Favourites or friends of the supervisor also pose a problem as possibly they may be suitable, but the opinions of colleagues are often against such people and ill-feeling may develop.

Terminations

If an employee wishes to terminate his or her employment with the company the personnel officer should conduct a termination interview to find out the true reason for leaving. This form of personnel counselling may prevent a good person from leaving the concern because a particular grievance has not been aired. Of course, the supervisor will have interviewed the employee earlier, but the truth might not have appeared at that stage.

The reasons for leaving are important, as personnel policy – and the success of management and supervision – is difficult to assess unless actual accounts of employees' opinions are sought and classified.

The trend of labour turnover indicates the level of morale and the effectiveness of selection, induction and training among new employees. Comparison may be based upon the following formula:

$$\frac{\text{Number of terminations a month}}{\text{Average number of employees}} \times 12 \times 100 = \text{Monthly labour turnover expressed as an annual percentage}$$

The reasons for leaving may be categorised as follows:

1 Dismissal – poor performance, violation of rules or poor code of conduct.
2 Redundancy – market depression, seasonal business or organisational change.
3 Resignation – promotional gain, better company located, domestic problems, dissatisfied or personal circumstances.
4 Retirement – reaching retiring age, physical ill-health, mental ill-health or company succession plans.

Dismissals

The authority to dismiss an employee is a serious and very responsible duty which demands the application of absolute fairness. Where a personnel manager is not employed the right to dismiss may rest with the supervisor at departmental level generally. Higher management would normally sanction such an action first.

The introduction of a personnel manager normally changes the system and final responsibility for dismissal is taken by that person. The supervisor recommends the action to the personnel manager who is in the position of being able to consider the case objectively and without bias. In the eyes of the employee an appeal to an individual outside the immediate jurisdiction of his or her superiors is much fairer.

Supervisors in these circumstances often feel that their status is lowered, some power is lost or their authority is reduced. If supervisors are relying upon such forms of authority and power they are obviously out of date and do not appreciate the value and effect of modern democratic supervision which allows appeal to an outside authority.

Reasons for dismissals

The real blame for the dismissal may lie with management when employees are placed in unsuitable jobs or when no attempt is made to help the employee to adjust to new surroundings, changes or incapacity.

The dismissal should be avoided if possible, especially where the fault is two-sided. Much can be done to help employees to adjust and on grounds of economy and morale alone the effort is worth while.

Disregarding the problem employee, some of the reasons leading up to a dismissal involve personality clashes which make adjustment to the job very difficult. Lack of co-operation, absenteeism, lateness, laziness, rudeness, dishonesty and carelessness all seem to point to a supervisory problem. Help at the time when the employee becomes disgruntled may prevent an untenable situation developing.

Further reasons concern the individual and his or her ability to carry out the allocated tasks. In the case of the trainee, if he or she is unable to do the job after training, the reasons are either that the person is lacking in the necessary ability or has not been taught properly. Basically this means that selection procedures are faulty or that the training scheme needs revising. The employee is not to blame in either case.

Another reason connected with work is where the person actually loses the ability and finds that he or she can no longer cope with the job. This state may be due to the development of mental trouble or physical incapacity. Some large companies provide rehabilitation centres to assist the employee with a physical or mental handicap. New jobs are located which often mean a demotion, but provided the approach is made in such a way that the employee feels it is worth while and is not down-graded in front of colleagues, the demotion is generally acceptable.

Employees' legal rights

Under the Employment Protection (Consolidation) Act 1978, an employee (subject to certain exceptions) has the right not to be dismissed unfairly and may seek a remedy by complaining to an industrial tribunal.

The Employment Acts 1980/82/88 also protect non-unionists. These Acts should be consulted before taking any action (*see* Chapter 19).

MEANING OF DISMISSAL

Dismissal may be defined as employment termination by the employer with or without notice, employee's resignation with or without notice where the employer implies that he or she is not to be bound by the contract of employment, the expiry of a fixed-term contract without renewal, or the employer's refusal to allow an employee to exercise her legal right to return to employment after the birth of her baby.

FAIR DISMISSAL

Dismissal can only be fair if the employer can show that the reason for it was one of those listed below and that he or she acted reasonably in the circumstances in treating that reason as sufficient to justify dismissing the employee.

The reasons are as follows:

1   A reason related to the employee's capability or qualifications for the job.
2   A reason related to the employee's conduct.
3   Redundancy.
4   A legal duty or restriction on either the employer or the employee which prevents the employment being continued.
5   Some other substantial reason which could justify the dismissal.

UNFAIR SELECTION FOR REDUNDANCY

Dismissal on grounds of redundancy will be unfair if:

1   the employee was selected for dismissal on account of trade union membership or activities
2   the employer unreasonably disregarded the customary arrangements or the agreed procedure relating to selection of employees for redundancy
3   the selection was unfair for some other reason. For example, the employer failed to give adequate warning of redundancy or failed to consider alternative employment for the employee.

DISMISSAL ON GROUNDS OF PREGNANCY

It is unfair to dismiss an employee because she is pregnant or for any other reason connected with her pregnancy unless at the effective date of termination she will, because of her pregnancy, be incapable of doing her work adequately or her continued employment would be against the law. For dismissal to be fair the employer must have no suitable alternative vacancy. If there is a suitable alternative with not less favourable terms and conditions of employment then the employer must offer the employee a new contract.

DISMISSAL DURING A DISPUTE

Where, at the date of dismissal, there is a lock-out by the employer or a strike or other industrial action by the employees, an industrial tribunal will not determine whether the employee was fairly or unfairly dismissed unless it is shown that not all the relevant employees have been treated equally.

SPECIAL CASES

For those employees who consider they may have been dismissed for a special reason, for example, trade union membership, or in special circumstances such as arise from a woman's right to return to work after pregnancy, the Department of Employment guide, *Dismissal – Employees' Rights*, will be of particular use.

Application to an industrial tribunal

An application to an industrial tribunal claiming unfair dismissal may be made as soon as the employer has given notice of dismissal and it must normally be received within the period of three months beginning with the employee's effective date of termination. If the application is received any later than that date the tribunal will consider the complaint only if they believe it was not reasonably practicable for the employee to have made the complaint earlier.

The remedies for unfair dismissal are:

1 reinstatement (the employee is to be treated in all respects as though the dismissal had not occurred)
2 re-engagement (the employee is to be re-employed but not necessarily in the same job or on the same terms and conditions of employment)
3 compensation

CONCILIATION

ACAS (Advisory, Conciliation and Arbitration Service) receives a copy of the employee's application to the tribunal and a conciliation officer will contact one or both of the parties involved. The officer then considers whether or not the parties can be helped to reach a settlement without the need for a tribunal hearing. Conciliation can take place at the request of both parties (or their representatives), or, if there is no such request, if the officer thinks there is a reasonable chance of success. If a settlement seems possible the parties may apply for a postponement of the tribunal hearing but the time-limit for applying to an industrial tribunal is not extended because of any such discussions.

Where a complaint of unfair dismissal could be made to an industrial tribunal but this has not yet been done, conciliation may take place at the request of either or both of the parties or their representatives.

Conciliation officers encourage employees to use any procedures that exist within their employer's organisation for appeal against their dismissal. While these procedures are running their course the employee should ask both the conciliation officer and the tribunal not to take any further action on the complaint to the tribunal. (*See* also Chapter 19.)

Supplementary provisions

Supplementary provisions include interim relief, recoupment of unemployment and supplementary benefit, provisions relating to the death of employer or employee, and the right of employees to receive on request a written statement of the reasons why they have been dismissed.

Redundancy

An unhappy fact of business is that often companies are forced into declaring some of their employees redundant through such circumstances as a market depression, a seasonal variation in business or essential organisational changes. To remain competitive at home and abroad a company may need to increase mechanisation or automation programmes which also could result in redundancies.

The social responsibilities of management in these situations are complex. For example, a decision not to automate may throw the *whole* labour force into unemployment if the company becomes insolvent.

In addition to the company's social problems there are a number of legal requirements under Part IV of the Employment Protection Act 1975 (now incorporated in the Employment Protection (Consolidation) Act 1978). Where redundancies are planned, independent trade unions and employees are given certain rights. The Act and any special orders should be studied before taking any action.

Rights of trade unions

An employer has a duty to consult with appropriate trade unions about proposed redundancies to see whether there are ways of reducing the numbers involved or of mitigating the effects of redundancy. This consultation must be conducted before redundancies are announced. An employer who wishes to dismiss an employee as redundant and who recognises an independent trade union to which the employee belongs must consult the TU representative about the dismissal before it occurs. If the employee is not a member the employer must still consult the trade union.

Minimum periods for consultation are given in the Act, depending upon the number of employees involved. An employer must provide reasonably full information in writing and include the reasons, the numbers and descriptions of employees involved, the total number of employees of any such description, the proposed method of selecting the employees, and the proposed method of conducting the dismissals, taking into account any agreed procedure including the period over which the dismissals will occur.

If the trade union replies, the employer must consider the points raised and reply to them giving reasons if he or she rejects any of them. If the trade union does not reply the employer need take no further action.

The trade union may complain to an industrial tribunal if it feels that an employer has not met the consultative requirements. Before the hearing, an ACAS conciliation officer must have the opportunity to consider whether he or she is able to help the parties settle the dispute. The officer may be asked for help by either party or may proceed independently.

The tribunal, after hearing the complaint, may make a declaration if the union's complaint is justified. This declaration may tell the employer to postpone dismissal notices if there was failure to consult so that consultation may proceed.

The tribunal may also make a protective award which safeguards the employees' remuneration. It requires the employer to pay a normal week's wages for a specified period, regardless of whether or not the employees are still employed.

Rights of employer

In certain circumstances it may not be reasonably practicable for an employer to meet fully the requirements for minimum consultation periods, disclosure of information or the manner of dealing with the union's representations.

In these special circumstances the employer must do all that he or she can reasonably be expected to do to meet the requirements. In defence, an employer must show that he or she *did* fully comply, or state the special circumstances, or show that all possible steps were taken to comply.

Rights of employees

If an employee is covered by a protective award he or she has a right to be paid a normal week's pay for the protected period whether that person is still working for the employer or not. However, there are certain conditions for claiming these rights.

An employee who is still employed will be paid under a protective award only when entitled to payment under the contract of employment or under statutory rights during a period of notice. For this purpose the whole remaining part of the employment is treated as if it were a statutory period of notice. Thus an employee who goes on strike, or is absent from work without leave and without good reason, or is granted leave at his or her own request, or has time off from work under certain other provisions of the Employment Protection (Consolidation) Act, will not be entitled to payment.

An employee who is absent under contractual holiday arrangements, or who is ill, or during any period where the employer has no work available for that person, will be paid.

An employee who is fairly dismissed for a reason other than redundancy or who gives up the job during the protected period without good reason will, however, lose the right to payment for the rest of the protected period.

OFFER OF RENEWED OR NEW EMPLOYMENT

An employer may offer to re-engage an employee in his or her old job or in a different but apparently suitable job before the end of the protected period. If the employee refuses the offer without good reason he or she loses the right to payment for the rest of the protected period.

RIGHT TO A TRIAL PERIOD

An employee who accepts an offer of a different type of job is allowed a trial period to see if the job is suitable. For calculating continuity of employment this trial period will be regarded as starting from when the employee's old job ends even where there is in fact a gap between·the two jobs. The trial period will normally continue for four weeks after the employee starts work in the new job but may, however, be extended by agreement between employer and employee in order to retrain the employee for the new job.

An employee who leaves the job for any adequate reason or who is dismissed for a reason connected with the new job during the trial period keeps the right to payment under the protective award. If, however, he or she gives up the job or the training without adequate reason or the employer dismisses that person fairly for reasons not connected with the changed terms of employment, he or she will lose the right to payment for the rest of the protected period.

EXTENSION OF TRIAL PERIOD

The trial period may be extended to retrain the employee for the new job by agreement between the employer and the employee. The agreement must be made before the employee starts work in the new job, it must be in writing, and must specify the date that the trial period ends and the terms and conditions of employment which will apply after the trial period ends.

The period allowed for trying out the new job is the same length as under the redundancy payments provisions. However, the employee has a right to a trial period if he or she starts a different job with the same employer at any time during the protected period. Nor does it matter whether the employer offers the new job before the end of the old job or after.

COMPLAINTS

If an employer does not pay the money under a protective award the employee has a right to complain to an industrial tribunal. Where a number of·employees is concerned in a single protective award a test case could be arranged by agreement between the parties, including the union concerned.

A complaint can be made within three months from the last day for which there has been failure to pay but if tribunals consider that it was not reasonably practicable for the employee to make the complaint in time they can allow longer. Application forms can be obtained from local offices of the Department of Employment and the Employment Service Division. A copy of the completed form will be sent to a conciliation officer of ACAS who will at the request of the parties, or on the officer's own initiative in appropriate cases, consider whether he or she can help settle the complaint without the need for a tribunal hearing.

A conciliation officer will also act at the request of the employee or the employer who can get in touch with a conciliation officer through the nearest ACAS regional office.

Where conciliation is not possible or fails, the tribunal will hear the complaint. If justified it will order the employer to pay the employee or employees concerned the money due to them under the award.

The Department of Employment

An employer must also notify the Secretary of State for Employment if there is a proposal to make ten or more employees redundant at one establishment within a relatively short period. This action allows the Training Commission to take any necessary measures to redeploy or retrain redundant employees and government departments and agencies to consider any further steps to avoid or minimise the redundancies.

Similar enforcements apply in terms of disclosure of information. Moreover, the employer's defence of 'reasonable practicability' also applies. There are penalties for non-compliance.

Lateness and absenteeism

The adverse effects of lateness and absenteeism on output and morale are well known. Poor supervision is commonly revealed as the underlying cause although there are some genuine direct causes for bad time-keeping.

The importance of the problem is demonstrated when the effects are shown to permeate the whole concern. The burden of covering for latecomers and absentees often falls on the rest of the employees who must apply extra effort and suffer the additional strain of trying to do more than one operation at once. Such unnecessary strain on supervision and employees is unfair. Continually trying to rearrange operations and machine loading inevitably causes some hold-ups and idle time which is reflected in lower output and possibly poor work quality.

The personnel department through personnel counselling attempts to improve those employees who are constantly causing this trouble. The true causes should be sought and the supervisor should note such cases for reference when up-gradings and pay increases are considered.

Some of the reasons put forward for lateness are domestic problems, transport difficulties, ill-health, fatigue and over-sleeping. In cases of continued employee negligence, the supervisor ought to investigate and pass the case to personnel if the situation does not improve.

Similar treatment is needed for absentees. Some of the reasons are domestic difficulties, sickness, accidents, fatigue and the weather. Some employees fail to give reasonable excuses after a while and develop into chronic cases who need firm treatment to protect the conscientious employees.

The drag on operational effectiveness results in higher costs and increasing discontent if bonus schemes are affected. Those employees who have avoidable reasons for lateness or absenteeism should be interviewed and given a clear understanding of the effects of such irresponsible actions. Some companies apply pressures by cutting pay, stopping bonuses, suspension, discharge after a number of warnings, loss of seniority and loss of holiday rights.

Although there are many external influences which cause employees to act in certain ways, the supervisor who practises good human relations and takes a genuine interest in each employee will have less difficulty with lateness and absenteeism.

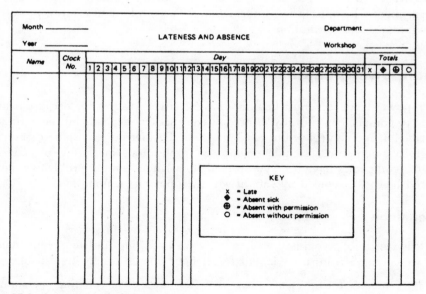

Fig. 17.8 *Lateness and absence chart*

This is a typical control chart for a department, recording any lateness and absence among the operators for each day of the month

A typical control chart for lateness and absence is given in Fig. 17.8. Comparisons may be made for each period such as a month or a year by using the following formulae:

(a) $$\frac{\text{Total number of days lost through absence}}{\text{Average number of employees for period}} = \text{Average number of days lost per employee for period}$$

(b) $$\frac{\text{Total number of days lost}}{\text{Total planned days}} \times 100 = \text{Days lost expressed as a percentage of planned working time}$$

This second formula may be applied on a basis of hours, shifts or days.

Remuneration

The question of financial incentives has been covered in Chapter 12. The other major aspect of remuneration is achieving a fair system.

Responsibility for recommending wages policy and negotiating wage rates comes under the personnel department which operates the wages scheme as fairly as possible. Within such a scheme the maintenance of correct differentials – through the operation of a merit rating scheme – is of particular importance to the supervisor. His recommendations provide the personnel department with appropriate information for establishing new rates, potential up-gradings and promotions.

Manpower planning

Manpower resources must be utilised as effectively as possible because being able to compete successfully in present day markets depends on the accurate prediction and control of future labour costs. Furthermore, corporate or strategic planning must include manpower implications in setting objectives. Often companies have been confronted with labour supply problems which could be easily avoided by careful MP (Manpower Planning).

Definition

MP is generally recognised as a strategy for acquiring, utilising, improving and retaining a company's labour force. Four phases are distinguishable.

1 Evaluate the present manpower resource by collating personnel records.

2 Set a forecast period and calculate the manpower losses by estimating

the effects of wastage – terminations, retirements, etc. – changes in labour productivity – alterations to hours and conditions – and external labour market demands.

3   Assess the manpower requirements for the end of the forecast period. This will involve output per employee and manpower utilisation required to achieve objectives.

4   Draw up a manpower plan to cope with the difference between existing resources and forecast resources for the end of the period, taking into consideration the estimated losses.

Objectives

- To avoid any shortage or surplus of labour over a significant period.
- To discover at an early stage any critical aspects of labour which demand attention.
- To control accurately the costs of labour and any associated ancillary costs.
- To anticipate redundancies and early retirements.
- To determine the optimum cost balance between plant and manpower utilisation.
- To forecast the cost and types of training schemes for managers and employees.

Essential requirements

The consultation and participation of employees and unions should be conducted by manpower planners who must have the backing of senior management. Adequate communication with employees helps considerably in explaining the importance of MP and the part it plays in achieving company objectives. The personnel department has a critical role in ensuring that records are immediately available, up-to-date and accurate. Other aspects, apart from those above, that may affect the supervisor are associated with the operation of MP. They include the centralisation of MP responsibilities, the length of the forecast period, the forecasting technique to be used and the degree of accuracy recommended.

The supervisor's part

The degree of involvement depends partly upon the size of the organisation and personnel policy. In general, the supervisor will be associated with the co-ordinating mechanism of informing, consulting and fostering support from employees. This aspect has deeper implications than first suspected. A good supervisor will possess considerable useful information on each employee's personal circumstances and opinions which might affect the employee's stay with the company or his or her possible transfer or promotion. Thus an efficient manpower planner will endeavour to utilise the supervisor and always include him or her in relevant discussions with management. The supervisor, in turn, will be seeking such information and, with management's help, achieve genuine exchanges of views.

In the smaller firm the supervisor may be confronted with more complex MP tasks, although the problem is often easier to solve and less demanding on the use of advanced statistical techniques which are outside the scope of this book.

Questions

1　Outline a method of conducting a job grading scheme and illustrate your answer with suitable diagrams.
2　How would you assess a candidate's suitability from the technical aspect?
3　Discuss the question of induction.
4　Outline a list of information that you think a new employee should receive before he or she commences employment.
5　What arrangements should be made to receive the new employee on the first morning at work?
6　Discuss the problem of transfers and promotion in connection with fairness and justice.
7　How would you conduct a termination interview?
8　What action would you take if labour turnover began to increase in your department?
9　Explain the implication of the statement 'Employees are often discharged through no fault of their own.'
10　How would you deal with an employee who is continually late? Include in your answer the reasons for your actions.
11　As a new supervisor, outline a plan to improve lateness and absenteeism which is particularly bad in your section.
12　State how you would conduct a fair programme of assessment for each subordinate under your control.
13　What advantages are likely to accrue from the establishment of an efficient selection procedure in a company?
14　Discuss the problem of labour turnover and the importance of keeping records on this factor.
15　If the company were forced to contract, discuss the various ways of deciding which people's employment should be terminated. Give your personal choice of the method to be used and explain the reason for your choice.
16　List the records you would expect to find in a personnel department and explain their uses.

Case study 1

John Lawton Limited was a small engineering company. At a recent works council meeting the urgent need to improve design was expressed by the production superintendent.

Everyone agreed as it was well-known that the market was toughening up. One employee suggested that each job description should include a duty to look for better design features. Most members thought this was a good idea.

The personnel officer, however, thought she would like time to consider the proposal first.

What aspects of the proposal would probably need further consideration by the personnel officer?

Case study 2

Within a department in a very large company there was James, the head; his deputy, Sue; four section supervisors and thirty-two female staff. James was invited to a retirement party which started at 12.30 pm. These parties were notorious for heavy drinking sessions funded by the company.

At about 3.30 pm James telephoned his secretary and told her to fetch Robert, a section supervisor. He was told to seal an empty envelope and write the retiring manager's name on it; give the envelope to Pauline, a young attractive temporary clerk; and direct her to the senior executives' dining room, implying it was the manager's office.

Entering the room Pauline was taken aback when greeted by twenty men seated round a table. Before she could withdraw, her boss beckoned her in and told her to deliver the envelope to the retiring manager.

At 5.10 pm an inebriated senior executive entered the deputy's office and asked for Pauline. He was told she had gone home. Whereupon he asked Sue if she knew what happened. She had no idea what he meant. He said he had come down to apologise for their behaviour, explaining that Pauline had been ordered to sit on the manager's lap and he had behaved rather like an octopus.

Sue was furious and even more incensed when he told her to apologise to Pauline for him. James returned to the office at 5.30 pm, inebriated.

Senior personnel executives and departmental heads were present at the party. When Sue asked Robert, the section supervisor, why he had not objected he said, 'What can you do? He's the boss!'

1 If you were Sue what would you do?
2 Consider Robert's conduct.
3 What action would you expect the managing director to take if he is notified?

18 Training

Importance of training

Any country possessing a highly-trained industrial labour force has a distinct advantage over others that may have neglected this vital factor in economic development and increasing productivity. In Britain there has been a shortage of skilled labour since World War II and many companies have shirked their responsibilities for training employees. This situation has contributed towards the slow rate of economic expansion.

All supervisors have a responsibility to improve the level of skill of their staff so that there is more readiness to cope with changes in work and organisation. The personnel officer also has a responsibility for assessing education and training requirements of the company as well as advising on the methods and suitability of training courses.

Manpower development

The government's attempt to deal with the problem of skill shortages was to introduce the Industrial Training Act in 1964 to supplement the good work of the Industrial Training Federation which had been established in 1958 by the Trades Union Congress, the British Employers Confederation (now the CBI) and the nationalised industries.

The Act gave the Secretary of State for Employment the power to establish training boards for each industry. Out of twenty-five Boards established covering 15 million employees only seven Boards remain. The Employment and Training Act 1974 set up the Manpower Services Commission (MSC) which, among other activities, controlled the Boards through the Training Services Division. The Boards impose levies and give grants to companies who send employees on approved courses.

In 1987 the Government announced new proposals and decisions affecting the role and composition of the MSC. Renamed the Training Commission in 1988, the Commission's role is to improve competitiveness and support employment growth and job creation by fostering the development of a better trained, more adaptable workforce. Programmes will be set up for assessment, rehabilitation, education, training and work experience. The Commission will promote initiatives to improve operation of the training market and the effectiveness of the training infrastructure. It will also continue to help back into the labour market those people who have been unemployed for a long time.

Certain activities have been transferred to a new comprehensive employment service established within the Department of Employment. The Commission's planned expenditure for 1987/88 on the services retained is £2.9 billion.

The scope of training

Training is a natural part of the sequence of selection and induction of employees. If this important stage does not receive sufficient attention from supervisors or managers, the possibility of using each individual's full capabilities becomes very remote. In this sense training becomes a continuous programme of employee development achieved by formal education and training schemes run or arranged by the personnel department and by localised training which is mostly given by immediate superiors.

Certain fundamentals of good supervision cannot operate effectively unless training is recognised as an integral part of supervisory policy. For example, increased proficiency, delegation of responsibility and safety all depend upon proper training.

Increased proficiency

Newly-trained employees and raw recruits naturally need special attention until they are fully proficient and capable of working entirely on their own. Even new employees who are already skilled expect and should receive training in their particular job which invariably differs in some respects from similar jobs they may have done previously.

An essential part of issuing instructions on work, rules and regulations and procedures is to provide training on any aspects which are new or unusual. New methods are introduced periodically on the recommendation of work study engineers or as a result of the supervisor's study of existing methods, and such changes obviously make additional training necessary.

Where employees are below standard and lack the essential knowledge or dexterity to improve quality and output, additional training will help to improve performance.

Delegation of responsibility

Successful delegation depends upon the recognition of employees' potential and their effective training for the tasks to be delegated. Further training of employees to expand their abilities and prepare them for promotion is essential, both for morale and improved efficiency. Often the supervisor must rely on deputy supervisors to assist and take over part of the supervisory planning and organising activities as well as more straightforward tasks. The supervisor's responsibility then is to ensure that subordinates are adequately trained to cope with these tasks. The supervisor has frequent opportunities during the daily routine to demonstrate methods and reasons for his or her actions to the deputies, thus giving them an invaluable insight into the job.

Safety

Proper training as well as sufficient close supervision is needed if the accident rate is to be kept down. An assessment of accidents over a period will indicate particular areas where more training is required to cut down dangerous practices. Extra instruction will help to convince employees of the full danger of various bad habits such as not using protective clothing or goggles, operating machines without using appropriate guards and safety devices, abusing machines by working above specified speed limits, standing in dangerous positions near equipment, ignoring precautions for conveyors and transport systems, interfering with other employees and distracting their attention from their work, ignoring fire regulations, etc.

The legal requirements for safety which affect both employer and employee are discussed fully in Chapter 20. The supervisor should remind staff of their duties under ss. 7 and 8 of the Health and Safety at Work Act, and of the powers of inspectors under s. 20.

Training methods

Trial and error

In a company adopting this method employees are either placed on their own and learn the job by performing operations, making mistakes and correcting them or they watch another employee, ask questions and copy the operations. Such unsound methods are still very common.

In this way the trainee picks up bad habits which are very difficult to break, so that he or she is unlikely to become proficient. If an employee is asked to help a trainee there is no incentive to assist, as invariably time is wasted which affects the employee's wages in the case of piece work and bonus schemes. These forms of training are slow, disrupt organisation, are relatively expensive and generally ineffective.

Planned programme

This scheme is based upon scientific principles of learning and psychology. A set pattern of procedure is followed on a step-by-step basis, which allows the trainee to develop rapidly towards using the most effective and economic methods of performing the job.

One of the main problems in training schemes is how to overcome the *learning plateau* which generally appears when the trainee is about half-way towards the speed of a proficient employee.

Figure 18.1 illustrates the learning plateau which generally occurs when the traditional method of training is used. The analytical method of training shows considerable saving by dispensing with the plateau. While conducting the basic exercises at the beginning a short time lag occurs before production commences. Both methods are described below.

The psychological effect on the trainee under the standard method may be severe, as frustration sets in through lack of further advancement at the plateau stage.

Many reasons have been suggested to explain the cause of the learning plateau. One reason is that the skills which are acquired in the early stages of training are not capable of development to the advanced stages of full speed operation without being modified. This suggests a strong case for learning each small part of the job separately, using the advanced skills from the beginning, until full speed is attained. The trainee can then concentrate on increasing speed by intensive repetition without being concerned with the over-all job until he or she is proficient at all the required skills.

On assembly-line type jobs where the operator controls the speed of work, the feasibility of the scheme (the analytical method) should be carefully examined. There may be snags such as increased training time, breaking down the job into skills, and the problem of slowing down advanced skills to speeds that can be readily assimilated, but these should be weighed against the savings through dispensing with the learning plateau.

A summary of the two schemes is given below.

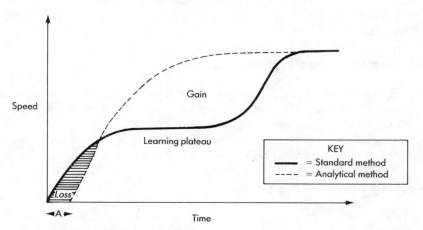

Fig. 18.1 *Overcoming the learning plateau*

This diagram shows how the analytical method of training overcomes the 'learning plateau' normally met with the standard training method. The analytical method employs initial exercises with no productive work involved, therefore a time lag occurs (A) before production begins

Traditional method of training

1 Explain the whole job.
2 Demonstrate the operations.
3 Practise the operations slowly and carefully.
4 Increase speed until the learning plateau is reached.
5 Place trainee on the job under some form of supervision.
6 Eventually increase speed to that of a proficient employee.

Analytical method of training

1 Conduct basic exercises.
2 Break down job into individual skills.
3 Demonstrate each skill separately.
4 Practise each skill until full speed is reached.
5 Gradually combine the skills and parts of the job, maintaining full speed until the whole job is performed.
6 Place trainee on the job and allocate periods of practice at full speed under supervision.
7 Gradually increase the practice periods until the whole day is spent at full speed.

The training environment

Training may be carried out at the workplace or at a separate training centre. The correct attitude and approach to learning is also a factor to be considered.

Learning at the workplace

The supervisor is generally responsible for training at the workplace acting as instructor. This is an additional burden; nevertheless, it is an important aspect of his job. Allocation of his time becomes more difficult as less time will be spent on actually supervising; the success of this scheme depends upon his ability to instruct and to spend sufficient time with the trainee.

Learning at a training centre

There are certain advantages if a training centre is utilised. Less distraction provides the trainee with suitable conditions for concentrating and learning although reality is probably missing. The use of a specialist instructor is an obvious advantage, provided suitable discipline makes up for loss of workshop atmosphere. The trainee receives more attention and guidance on his or her weaknesses and, therefore, should progress more rapidly.

The background to learning

A number of useful guides have been discovered through research into the learning process.

Planning

Although it is essential to draw up a careful plan of training, such aspects as current alterations, difficulty with a particular topic and coping with particularly slow learners must be allowed for in the schedule. A degree of flexibility is required, otherwise adherence to a rigid programme becomes the objective whereas the aim must be to produce trained employees.

Trainee ability

The instructor should assume that effective selection of trainees has provided individuals who are capable of learning and have sufficient ability to perform the tasks involved. Lack of confidence in the trainees is immediately apparent to them and has an adverse effect on the learning process. Displaying confidence in trainees builds up enthusiasm and spurs individuals on to greater efforts.

Motivation

Creating the desire to learn, i.e. being able to motivate trainees, is part of the instructor's job. The reasons and advantages of learning a job should be given to make the trainee feel he or she is doing something of importance with definite objectives in mind such as financial gain, regrading or increased status.

The learning rate

Although people learn at different rates there is a certain amount of uniformity in learning progress: it starts from a low position, rises rapidly and levels out to a plateau, already mentioned under Training Methods. The position of the plateau varies with individuals and the type of job.

Generally the quick learner progresses more rapidly in the long run as against the slow learner, but invariably any individual learns some processes quickly and others more slowly. The main factors are intelligence and a flair for the particular task. Further factors affecting learning speed are lack of interest, physical weaknesses, resistance to change, established working habits, lack of incentive, and sometimes deeper psychological reluctance. Age itself is of less importance as a single factor except that it has some bearing on strength and experience. Very old employees, however, are frequently incapable of being retrained as their mental and physical powers are failing.

Correct sequence of learning

Whenever possible the operation should be taught in correct sequence, that is, in a logical pattern from the beginning to the end of each operation. Although this procedure may not be economic in some circumstances through excessive waste, the fact remains that skill is acquired by performing movements in correct sequence. Skill is largely developed through muscle sense which feels the movement of a lever for example, and automatically decides by the degree of sensation the next movement to be carried out. Familiar examples of this effect are handling the steering wheel in a car and changing gear.

Depth of understanding

Creating a deeper understanding of the job and the process is better than imparting a superficial knowledge of the job. The success of this more sophisticated training scheme largely rests with the intelligence of the trainees and their keenness to possess a deeper understanding of principles and their wider application.

Those with considerable insight into their work as well as ability are more versatile and become valuable assets to a concern.

Instruction

The process of instruction, i.e. passing on information, may be carried out in a variety of ways, including explanation by direct speech or written notes and practical demonstration and examples illustrated by a range of visual aids such as the blackboard, models, diagrams and sketches.

The process of passing knowledge must, however, be distinguished from the process of learning. Learning is an active process in which the trainee must be physically and mentally involved.

Simplification

Some instructors fall into the trap of making things more difficult for trainees in order to stress their own importance because they know the answers. Such feelings must be replaced by aims to make training schemes as simple and easy as possible to assimilate. It is psychologically bad to impress trainees with continual propaganda on the difficulties and complexities of the job. The instructor must make the operations look easy, show that they can be performed easily and not allow trainees to form the impression that even the expert finds the job difficult.

Encouragement and confidence are important to the trainee, and it therefore helps considerably to arrange the programme so that teaching the easy tasks comes first followed by the more difficult ones later.

Ability to discriminate effectively

Many jobs involve processes or operations which demand a particular type of response to certain situations. The response may be to push a button, pull a lever, stop a machine or to process a piece of material in many different ways, depending upon requirements. The situation which demands attention may be made evident by lights, sound, touch, visual appearance and measurement.

The training process should develop the correct response to situations; associations should be built up so that the trainee learns to use the most suitable sense organs to provide an adequate response to the situation as it arises. A simple example would be to check the smoothness of a surface by touch rather than by sight.

Another example would be the operation of a transfer machine where the operator is expected to press a button when twenty-four red lights are all glowing. The response to a number of lights may be much slower to learn than reaction to more familiar signs like a bell or a buzzer sounding. The operator must learn to judge when the critical moment is coming.

Practice

Continued practice or participation forms an essential part of the learning process. The trainee must be given the opportunity to ask questions, examine the machine or tools or the work in hand, try out the process, show the results of his or her efforts, discuss the queries or problems and so become absorbed in the process of learning. A genuine interest in the job should develop as the trainee notices improvements and is appropriately encouraged when he or she performs the operations correctly.

The instructor should point out any errors or bad practices and demonstrate the differences to show the advantage of performing the process correctly.

Use of analogies

When trainees are confronted with strange or complex assemblies or operations it can be helpful to explain the assembly, for example, by showing a similar device which is more familiar to them and then pointing out its likenesses to the unfamiliar assembly.

The importance of repetition

As already stated, the trainee develops skills through continual practice. The instructor should apply the same principle: learning is easier and lasting impressions are achieved by repeating the information or demonstrating the technique many times.

Most individuals' powers of absorption are limited, so repetition is essential. If difficulty is experienced, repetition should also be supplemented by varying the approach, giving different forms of examples.

Spaced repetitions for learning skills

Skills are acquired more easily in a carefully planned number of regular learning periods over a length of time than in the same number of lessons grouped closely together over a short period. Although this scheme is often difficult to arrange in many industrial conditions, wherever possible the principle should be used.

Continuity

Through the nature of change in processes, design and machines, training is essentially a continuous activity. Newcomers, transferees and existing employees all require training as changes occur. Follow-up become very important also to ensure that the correct methods of performing operations are being practised.

Progress reports

All trainees should have immediate and regular reports on their progress so that they can correct and practise to a scientific programme.

Unless criticism or praise is given quickly, valuable time is wasted by all concerned. Emphasis during the early stages of training should be placed on the correct method. The incorrect ways will continually appear, but they should not be highlighted by drawing attention to them unduly. Repetition of the correct method at these times is more positive and directs the efforts of the trainee in the right direction.

Asking questions regularly helps to keep trainees alert and fosters the feeling of actively taking part in the learning process. The question should be phrased so that an explanation is required which will immediately show whether there is a true understanding of the subject rather than a simple yes or no which tells the instructor nothing. If any particular difficulty is highlighted the instructor should deal with the problem immediately. Regular reviews of progress also provide an excellent opportunity to summarise the important aspects.

The training programme

A planned programme of training is discussed in three stages:

Stage 1: Available facilities
Stage 2: Choice of methods
Stage 3: The plan

Under Stage 1 an investigation of available facilities will provide sufficient information to prepare the plan. Information on accommodation, visual aids and learning material will also assist in the choice of methods discussed in Stage 2. Methods include lecturing, hand–outs, discussion, practical demonstration, examples, practice and improvisation.

Finally, Stage 3 outlines the important aspects of the plan, such as objectives, the budget, organisation, the programme, allocation of trainees, methods of instruction, training environment, progress reports and follow-up.

Stage 1: available facilities

Accommodation

The supervisor has to cope with the accommodation which management is prepared to offer. Often this is inadequate and simply amounts to a re-arrangement of existing space at the workplace. In some establishments, however, a separate training centre is available to supplement training at the workplace and allowances are made to accommodate trainees on the shop floor so that they can practise, listen to lectures and watch demonstrations all in the most suitable surroundings.

Visual aids

The object of using visual aids is to assist the instructor, supplementing verbal explanation. Many very useful aids are cheap and require a small amount of preparation. Such items as blackboards and white chart pads allow the instructor to develop ideas visually stage by stage. Diagrams and models can also be made up cheaply and are most effective in demonstrating practical work. There are many more expensive aids such as overhead projectors, slide and cine projectors and television, but it should be borne in mind that they are aids and not ends in themselves.

Only one aid should be used at a time and without any fuss, otherwise the trainees give more attention to the aid than to the subject matter. To avoid any delays the aid should be checked beforehand so that the operation runs smoothly.

Learning occurs when the trainee becomes mentally involved in the process by seeking out knowledge, asking questions and visualising the operation. Actual practice is the natural complementary process, so that the trainee learns from relating physical experience and visualisation of the operation.

Lecturing material: the job breakdown

Adequate preparation of lecturing material is an essential part of the instructor's job. Besides the obvious advantage of presentation of the procedure to be learnt in correct sequence without hesitancy, it provides an excellent opportunity to check the method currently used. The critical points in the operation should be given particular emphasis, with additional explanation and practice to overcome the crucial stages.

A job breakdown should contain an up-to-date, step-by-step account of the operation. The usual method is to watch the operation, build up the steps by asking questions and ensuring that the steps are in the correct sequence. If a work study department exists then probably records may be obtained from there.

Make sure that the most effective method or standard method is being used by the operator. If there is time, another opinion is a good way of assessing the job breakdown.

The amount of work involved is worth while; the instructor will be fully prepared and the actual teaching will be in correct sequence. Any questions should be answered with confidence and understanding of the difficulties which trainees are likely to experience.

Stage 2: choice of methods

The various methods of instructing are detailed below. Instructors use all these methods as part of a full training programme where courses are included for acquiring both knowledge and skill.

Lecturing

In its narrowest sense the lecturing method is used to give information to trainees; their approach to the topic is strictly limited to playing a passive role of listening.

As their knowledge of the topic increases the one-way process of lecturing is gradually replaced by a two-way process of participation with the questioning technique, i.e. teaching rather than lecturing. The instructor continually checks by asking questions to see whether the knowledge has been absorbed accurately and trainees are encouraged to ask questions to supplement the lecture.

Lecturing is a fundamental method of imparting information, concepts and explanations, but although the theory and a guide to the practice of a skill can be imparted, the reality of performance is still something remote.

Hand-outs

A useful supplement to lecturing is to distribute duplicated copies of notes on the subject matter and any additional information. The dictation of notes is avoided which saves considerable time and energy. Suitable reading matter such as textbooks and periodicals may be recommended for further reading.

Part of a training programme may be conducted by basing the training periods upon previous preparation by the student. The particular topics to be dealt with are outlined in a programme so that the student can read in advance of the lecture. The scheme encourages discussion and permits questions to be asked by the instructor to assess the degree of absorption. He or she may then supplement the trainees' reading by elaborating on particular topics.

Discussion

The essential requirements for successful discussion are a group of individuals who possess similar basic knowledge of the topic for discussion, but preferably with varying backgrounds and experience to provide a balance of opinions. The size of the group will also affect the discussion. Such stringent requirements may limit the use of this method for training.

The discussion technique is becoming increasingly popular as a method of airing problems in order to stimulate individuals into thinking up new ideas. The use of discussion groups in supervisory and management training schemes is commonplace.

Such schemes include seminars, case studies, role playing and business games. Seminars are conducted either by asking a member to give a lecture on a given topic or by holding a discussion on a topic to stimulate an exchange of ideas under a chairperson from the group. The use of case studies is another method where information on a problem is given and the group attempts to find a satisfactory answer by discussing and analysing the case. Role playing involves members in actually taking part in controlled situations by assuming the identity of a supervisor, for example, and dealing with a complaint. The business game is similar to role playing, but more involved. A number of members may participate on similar lines and, when properly conducted, they soon tend to 'live the part'.

Gathering a group of employees from the workplace often causes a certain amount of disruption to which management may object. The gains may be considerable, however, not only from the training viewpoint, but also because of the excellent suggestions that can emerge from such discussions.

Examples

Some topics are difficult to explain adequately by speech alone. This predicament can often be solved easily by using suitable examples to illustrate the situation or point. Some of these aids are sketches, diagrams, models, pictures and analogies.

Practical demonstration

Skills are mainly acquired by imitation and practice. Naturally the only way a trainee can imitate an operation is to watch a practical demonstration and be provided with facilities to copy and practise what he or she has seen.

The demonstration must be clear, in strict logical sequence and according to the standards given in any hand-outs. The complete operation should be demonstrated and any particular problems pointed out and accompanied by illustrations of special techniques and critical points.

Practice

As already stressed, the vital stage of acquiring skill is reached when practice begins. Continual practice is essential, together with assistance from the instructor who should regularly check and correct when necessary. He or she must encourage the trainee if progress is poor as it is easy to be disheartened as this time. Criticism should be positive in nature by showing the correct method and techniques. Quick learners must be watched to see that speed is not leading them into bad habits. Slow learners need plenty of encouragement and sympathy.

Improvisation

All instructors should practise the art of improvisation because the moment straight lecturing ceases and the opportunity is given for trainees to ask questions it will be necessary to some degree.

If a topic is difficult to understand, invariably the instructor will have to think up examples and illustrations on the spur of the moment which are in tune with the atmosphere at the time and meaningful to that particular group.

Successful improvisation demands a broad and deep knowledge of the subject matter, plus the ability to expand a point and to construct suitable teaching material at a moment's notice.

Programmed learning

This method uses a technique of learning by breaking down the subject into simple stages which are presented to trainees in sequence; they learn, test themselves, move to the next stage, and so on. The sequence should be designed to motivate trainees to learn quickly.

Stage 3: the plan

The main aspects of the training plan to be considered are given below.

Objectives

A good plan is based upon clear objectives which should be stated and understood by everyone who is concerned with the training scheme. Some of the aims of training are to improve quality of work, increase output and to increase productivity by reducing errors, reducing the accident rate and creating positive attitudes.

The budget

Management must agree a budget to cover all possible expenditure such as for equipment, teaching materials, training centre and instructors.

Organisation

The appointment of individuals who are responsible for training generally and for particular training schemes is essential. They must have sufficient authority to act within the over-all framework of training programmes so that arrangements may be put into practice and controlled effectively.

The programme

An assessment should be made of all the training schemes which can be accommodated. Each scheme should be titled and timetabled with sufficient detail and suitable progress points to form a logical sequence of training at different levels. An over-all schedule may now be drawn up to accommodate the schemes, e.g. on a half-yearly or yearly basis.

The programme should be as simple and flexible as possible to cope with probable alterations later on.

Allocation of trainees

Allocation should be made on a fair and logical basis in accordance with personnel policy. Selection of suitable trainees and choice of training are additional factors which will depend upon circumstances. To avoid any misapprehension the method and results of allocations should be publicised.

Methods of instruction

Deciding upon the methods of instruction will depend upon a number of factors including training environment, the budget, the standard of trainees and existing facilities. The initial decision on methods depends upon whether the aim is to acquire knowledge on a particular subject or to acquire a skill.

Training environment

Where a choice of facilities is available, full use should be made of the advantages of each training environment. As a general guide the quiet atmosphere of a classroom is ideal for lecturing and discussions; the training centre may accommodate lectures, demonstrations and practice, while the workplace provides the atmosphere of reality and is, therefore, useful for advanced practice.

Progress reports

Adequate control depends upon conscientious recording of progress and results. Measuring performance and improvements at appropriate stages in training ensures that corrective measures will be taken such as additional tuition or, in extreme cases, removal of a trainee from the course.

The reports are normally recorded on personnel records and statistics are prepared for management appraisal. The trainee should also see the reports as part of the normal practice of informing the individual of his or her progress.

Follow-up

A good training scheme is essentially a continuous process. Genuine interest in the progress of trainees after the course is essential for successful follow-up. Further training or retraining may be necessary in some cases whereas in others rapid progress may result in promotion. Recording such information is vital for statistical purposes when coupled with progress reports. Assessment of long-term results may indicate changes in the training programme. Individuals might develop particularly bad habits after certain periods on machines or practice in the job and these may be corrected in subsequent training schemes by additional emphasis at the appropriate stage of the operation. Long-term effective control of training relies upon conscientious follow-up.

Sequence of instruction

The main steps in an instruction plan are as follows:

1 Prepare the trainee.
2 Explain the job.
3 Demonstrate the operations.
4 Practise.
5 Check performance.
6 Follow-up.

The plan follows a logical sequence of training which is fundamental to all schemes for acquiring skill. The basis of most of the schemes is taken from the work of Charles R. Allen (1919) and the main points connected with each step are given below.

Prepare the trainee

Reduce nervousness and concern by attempting to establish a friendly relationship with the trainee. Take the person's mind off the subject of training for a while.

Useful information can be gained by getting him or her to chat about previous jobs and this provides a lead to give general information on the product, the processes involved, where this particular job fits in, and its importance.

The trainee's interest should be further aroused by giving more details of the objectives of the company and his or her particular part in achieving them.

Explain the job

The job should be explained in outline but with sufficient detail for the trainee to appreciate its significance. At this stage explanations should be given on special tools or equipment, standard layouts, measuring devices, specifications, drawings, job language and materials. The trainee should also be told the value of the equipment, tools, materials and assemblies, and be instructed on safety precautions, cost of waste and the importance of quality standards to encourage conscientiousness.

Demonstrate the operation

Each important step should be adequately explained, shown and illustrated. Each key point must be stressed. The trainee should be as near as possible to the operation position. The instructor should be certain that all stages are clearly understood, which means that he or she must be painstaking and check the effectiveness of the teaching by constantly asking questions.

A run-through at normal operating speed is followed by a slowed-down version to a point where each movement may be clearly seen and connected with preceding and subsequent movements.

Practise the operation

When the trainee feels sufficiently confident to attempt the operation, he or she should be allowed to have a trial run under close supervision. A complete run of the whole operation at normal speed is recommended but, as mentioned previously, it is not always possible owing to economic considerations such as high cost of materials.

Mistakes should be corrected immediately by showing the correct way with more detailed explanations. Often the cause of error is forgetfulness and a quick reminder is sufficient. If the trainee explains the tasks as he or she performs them it helps in memorising the key points and hastens the learning process. Practice continues until the instructor is satisfied with the performance.

Check performance

At this stage the trainee is put to work alone. A nearby colleague or supervisor should take over to offer immediate assistance when needed while the instructor should check frequently for any deviation from the correct method.

Continued personal contact is required to boost the trainee's spirits at this time. Questions should be asked on any work problems. Extra coaching should be gradually diminished as performance improves.

Follow-up

The final stage of follow-up ought to be considered as a process which continues indefinitely. If good relationships have been established the instructor will be able to encourage and make employees feel more important by taking an interest in their progress on a long-term basis. Any bad working habits that may appear later must be checked and any advice which is desirable should be given freely.

This broad interpretation of follow-up should be encouraged as such a scheme provides a close-knit system of communication for promotion and other purposes. Sufficient information should flow between the Personnel Department, the supervisor, the instructor and post-trainees to provide more reliable indications of the true working situation.

Training existing employees

A supervisor is often faced with the difficult tasks of persuading existing employees to change their present jobs, stimulating them to learn new jobs and actually training them.

The main reasons for job changes are as follows.

Incapacity

Employees' physical or mental health may deteriorate and so prevent them from performing the job successfully. They may have suffered an illness, had an accident, or be under emotional stress.

This condition may be difficult to deal with. Sometimes employees persuade themselves that the blame for their shortcomings lies with the supervisor who continually gives them the 'hard jobs' to perform.

Production method

Most employees will appreciate the economic necessity of keeping up to date with production processes in the face of competition. Obsolescent machines must be replaced, new and more suitable materials must replace the old and the introduction of better methods is essential. Unfortunately, these changes often cause human upheavals which include retraining and regrouping employees. Adequate explanations are essential otherwise there is less chance of achieving cooperation.

Fluctuations in output

Seasonal lines and changes in demand through competition cause output fluctuations which often result in temporary redundancy. The introduction of patterned seasonal lines (such as ice-cream in summer and hot dogs in winter) solves the problem of output, but probably demands a more versatile labour force with many employees capable of performing more than one job.

It is essential to encourage and persuade existing employees so that they want to learn new jobs. Important factors such as losing face in front of colleagues, breaking up working groups, separation from a particular colleague and resistance to changing a long-established routine should all be considered. Reasonable solutions to such problems must be established before interviewing the employee.

Adequate information on the background to these changes helps considerably. If the employee can see and accept the reasons for any changes, the possibility of agreement and co-operation is much greater.

The results

The aim of a training programme is to produce a highly trained versatile labour force.

Some top managers strongly contest the installation of a training programme on the grounds that it is costly and time-consuming. They claim that many other pressing jobs should receive priority and that training is uneconomic became the trained employees leave and other firms receive the benefit.

More enlightened managers refuse to shirk their social and professional responsibilities and gain the following advantages.

- Higher productivity
- Increased output
- Improved quality
- Less waste

- Less machine maintenance
- Fewer accidents
- Shorter learning periods
- Less labour turnover
- Higher morale
- More confidence in management

Training is an essential part of the supervisor's job. If this activity is neglected the time spent on other aspects of supervision increases sharply. The vital point is that neglect of this aspect to spend more time on other matters is false economy. Other matters demand far more time, cost and effort than training without showing such effective results.

Questions

1   Why is training considered to be so important today?
2   Discuss the supervisor's fundamental task of training.
3   Discuss the question of training schemes, mentioning their effectiveness and any limitations.
4   What is meant by the 'learning plateau' and how can it be overcome?
5   Discuss the analytical method of training mentioning the advantages.
6   Suggest some useful guides to training which would assist the supervisor in improving his or her capability as an instructor.
7   Discuss the problem of acquiring a skill.
8   Outline a planned programme of training.
9   Draw up an instruction plan for acquiring a skill.
10   What difficulties should a supervisor be prepared to overcome when retraining existing employees?
11   What are the aims and advantages of an organised training programme in a company?
12   Discuss the problem of skill shortages in the UK.

Case study

Chris Tanger was being groomed for promotion. She had been a supervisor on the clerical side of the business for five years and her superior was pleased with her performance. The personnel manager arranged for her to work closely with one of the middle managers on the maintenance service side of the business.

As Chris had expected from her studies the approach by this manager towards staff did not coincide with her own ideas. Although she thought the treatment was insensitive it seemed to work very well. Everyone seemed to respect Mr Winston and the department worked smoothly.

When Chris was being interviewed by the personnel manager six weeks later one of the questions that came up caught her unprepared. 'Did you know that Mr Winston was disliked by most of his staff *and* he knows it?'

Chris replied, 'I must admit I didn't realise that. I thought he was a bit hard on them but they didn't react openly towards him.'

For what reasons would the personnel manager have chosen Mr Winston for Chris?

19   Industrial relations

Introduction

The term 'industrial relations' covers all the complicated bargaining and discussion between management and trade unions, and management and employees. These activities may be formal or informal, involve certain legal machinery, and use accepted negotiation procedures.

Unfortunately, attitudes, rather than adherence to facts, tend to dominate negotiations. Managers seem to rely on generalised assertions and personal judgments. Trade unions face many accusations such as being out-of-date, too militant, too powerful, too political, and sometimes of holding the country to ransom to win a dispute.

Collective bargaining

This is a process where trade unions representing their members negotiate with employers. Successive governments have strongly supported sensible collective bargaining by making recommendations and legislating.

Bargaining for manual workers may be conducted at an industry level – especially in manufacturing industries – and at local levels. At national levels minimum wage rates are often agreed for skilled and unskilled groups; then at local levels negotiations are conducted for each job classification. Similarly hours of work are set but the number and length of shifts is decided locally.

Bargaining units

To gain strength trade unions tend to group up and form bargaining units. These may cover an established group of employees such as all operators. Salaried staff and perhaps skilled workers would form separate units. These units might cover an industry, a company, or a department in a concern, and all or some of the employees generally below first-line management.

This scheme sometimes suits employers: fewer negotiating bodies may emerge, leap-frogging claims are avoided, and negotiating time is probably reduced. However some employers resist this move by (a) refusing to recognise the union's case to negotiate for a group, or (b) trying to exclude certain groups.

The changing scene

Up to about 1960 bargaining units concentrated on traditional approaches relating to pay, working hours and holidays. In the 1960s bargaining extended to include fringe benefits. This change occurred through a continuation of full employment and nationalisation programmes, governmental incomes policies and weak Sterling. About thirty-five years of full employment caused both negotiating parties to concentrate on other features such as pensions, lay-off pay, pay structure changes and productivity bargaining.

In the 1980s a drastic change in the economy and unemployment caused an increased awareness of fundamental faults in the British economy and an increased resolve to take more positive action to rectify them. Typically, the media focused on poor industrial performance, inflation, standards of living and overseas competitors. The government adopted polices to reduce inflation, reduce trade union power, and encourage enterprise.

Main features of change

Six main features are clearly seen.

1 Trade unions can no longer strongly influence government ministers; they are not treated by the government as partners in a so-called social contract; they are practically ignored by the government; and they have been powerless to resist legislation to regulate their activities.

2 Many managers have established new channels that by-pass trade union representatives and now communicate directly with employees.

3 More harmony has developed between managers and trade union representatives. The trend is a more favourable response towards problems presented by managers and suggesting ways of solving them.

4 Reducing the monopoly power of trade unions through legislation has (it seems) created an improved climate. For example the number of recorded disputes in 1985 was the lowest for fifty years.

5 Trade unions are now trying new tactics to tempt employees to join them.

6 More comprehensive consultation is being conducted on many economic and non-economic issues between various parties at many different levels.

Aims of the parties

Although the aims of the two parties obviously differ there could be some common ground: for example, to prevent high-calibre employees leaving and taking up jobs abroad, to make the company more productive to avoid competitive pressures, and to avoid damaging disputes which affect the community. Ideally both parties should recognise the importance of profit, productivity, investment and the community.

The union's aims should bear in mind employees as well as its members since a bargaining unit may also include non-members. Their commitment and aspirations may differ from the union's ideas. Consequently there could be conflicting views, therefore balance has to be found.

Generally union aims are in priority order:

1   pay increases
2   improving working conditions
3   reduced working hours
4   non-economic features such as representation on boards, and
5   being included in decision-making activities.

Employers' aims are straightforward:

1   to reduce or maintain labour costs, or to allow for reasonable increases to keep high-calibre employees
2   to avoid damaging disputes and poor publicity
3   and to keep in line with general conditions in other companies or industries.

Government influence

Various governments have attempted to influence wage settlements either through a planned economy or non-interventionist policies. Evidence from econometric studies and economic models supports the claim made by many business people that a slower growth of wages would mean more jobs. A recent Treasury review suggests that if real pay were to rise to a level 1 per cent lower than otherwise, that would lead in time to between 0.5 per cent and 1 per cent more jobs, that is 110 000 to 222 000.

As the UK's largest employer the government can strongly influence pay settlements and the type of settlement, by setting norms related to productivity. Nevertheless the shortage of labour from 1945 to about 1979 obviously had some influence on wage levels as market forces operated. Also it is arguable that trade unions exercised monopoly power that prevented market forces deciding. Furthermore companies – it should be remembered – are concerned with labour costs which are determined by not only pay but also fringe benefits, administration costs for each employee, and productivity levels of the labour force.

The process

The supervisor should find the process a useful indication of how negotiations successfully escape from entrenched positions, how different behaviour patterns are used to cope with situations, and the part communication plays. Also he or she should recognise the negotiation stages when discussing the situation with employees.

An indication is now given of the usual process.

1 *Planning stage* The situation and environment are considered here. The employer will assess the financial state of the business, sales orders and competition. Also the claim is subjected to a detailed analysis, the union's policy and strength is examined, and employees' feelings canvassed. The cost of various increases is calculated, and plans to off-set through, say, a productivity deal are completed.

2 *Presentation* A claim is presented and assessments by both sides determine priorities and possible outcomes. Parties will be seeking opinion on possible objectives, degree of co-operation and general responses to negotiations.

3 *Integrative bargaining* To avoid deadlocks the negotiators must show a willingness to abandon their entrenched positions to some degree. They may use various cross-cultural skills to demonstrate some flexibility. Gradually by taking various stands and altering stances a more personal approach develops and person-to-person skills become demanding. Thus proposals and counter-proposals ensue until common ground is reached.

4 *The decision* Persuasive skills gradually erode the unacceptable features until a satisfactory agreed compromise is reached. Each party must judge what is acceptable, followed by one party adopting a closing technique such as attempting to summarise and stating the decision. After clarifying minor points the issue is resolved.

5 *Commitment* Enforcement of the deal depends on moral obligation since negotiated agreements are not usually legally binding. The union's representative must sell the deal to the members and receive a majority support. Communication is important since misunderstandings later become embarrassing for both sides.

When it is ratified the union's representative reports to the employer to record the agreement and arrange for implementation. The employer in turn should ensure that the agreement is understood by managers and supervisors and that the reasons for the agreement are clear. This essential communication link provides a firm basis for discussion with employees so that criticisms may be countered with direct knowledge not hearsay.

Legislation

Sensible collective bargaining has always been stressed. The Royal Commission on Labour in 1891 supported the use of negotiations through representative machinery, as did the Royal Commission on Trade Unions and Employers Associations in 1968 (The Donovan Report).

The Whitley Committee (1917) even established 200 Joint Industrial Councils to fill the need for negotiating machinery at national level. These are non-standardised structures but the majority of national agreements on wages and conditions of employment have been negotiated through these councils.

When the Donovan Report was published, about 500 negotiating arrangements for manual workers were known to exist between employers (or employers' associations) and trade unions, and about two-thirds of the working population had their terms and conditions of employment regulated by collective bargaining.

In 1971 the Industrial Relations Act was passed in an attempt to create a legislative framework acceptable to all parties. The enactment caused considerable controversy mainly on the grounds that legislation is not the proper vehicle to carry the many facets of relationship between employer and employee.

A change of government occurred in 1974. The new government prepared a threefold labour legislative plan:

1 to repeal the 1971 Industrial Relations Act
2 to legislate afresh on collective and individual employment rights.
3 to launch 'industrial democracy'. (Research for this part of the plan was conducted by the Bullock Committee.)

Many of the issues were studied in depth in the UK and in overseas countries. Each phase of the threefold plan is now discussed.

Repeal of the Industrial Relations Act 1971

The statutory replacement of the Industrial Relations Act was the Trade Union and Labour Relations Act passed in 1974. TULRA, as it is often called, repealed the 1971 Act but re-enacted with some changes the provisions of the older Act regarding unfair dismissal along with certain supplementary provisions.

The 1974 Act provided a new fuller portrait of the trade union, its immunities and the legal position of the collective agreement. Schedule I of the Act received much publicity; this covered the basic rules regarding unfair dismissal as well as the jurisdiction and procedure of industrial tribunals. In 1976, for example, over 31 000 applications were received by the industrial tribunals on unfair dismissals alone, thus illustrating the importance of this single region of employment law. (It should be noted that these provisions are now contained in the Employment Protection (Consolidation) Act 1978.)

New legislation

The Employment Protection Act 1975

This comprehensive statute, containing 129 sections and 18 schedules, made many inroads into labour law. Many quarters have heavily criticised the Act but the general aim was to establish statutory minimum requirements of employment for those who did not happen to work for 'enlightened' companies.

Undoubtedly the Act forcibly squashed the old 'hire and fire' philosophy.

Moreover, it has been generally recognised that Britain compares unfavourably with its EEC partners in the area of indirect labour costs which is money expended on the general well-being of a company's labour force. The EPA went some way towards bringing Britain in line with its Common Market partners in this field of 'benefits'.

Two areas of major significance were Part I, which dealt with the machinery for promoting the improvement of industrial relations, and Part II, which covered the individual rights of employees. Basic coverage was also given to such items as the procedure for handling redundancies and the law dealing with terms and conditions of employment. (The provisions of the Act relating to individual employee rights are now contained in the Employment Protection (Consolidation) Act 1978.)

Apart from establishing the well-known ACAS, the Act also set up the Employment Appeal Tribunal to hear appeals from industrial tribunals and the office of the Certification Officer who is appointed by the Secretary of State after consultation with ACAS. He or she is responsible for functions which were formerly performed by the Chief Registrar of Friendly Societies and for certifying that a trade union is 'independent', which means that it is free of such control by employers which may inhibit the union from acting in its own best, independent interests.

The Employment Act 1980

This significant change in legislative policy was designed to restore balance in employment legislation. The Act is involved and needs careful study on the many facets covered which include trade union ballots, codes of practice, exclusion from trade union membership, unfair dismissal, maternity rights, protection for non-unionists, picketing and industrial action.

The Employment Act 1982

The main provisions relate to dismissals in connection with strikes and other industrial action, the prohibition of union membership requirements, restricting closed shop agreements and immunity of trade unions from civil liability for industrial action.

The Employment Act 1988

This Act is a further stage in trade union reform. Four new rights are given to union members:

1 The right not to heed a strike call from a union without a secret ballot producing a majority in favour of industrial action.
2 The right not to be disciplined by a union if a member decides to go to work regardless of whether or not a pre-strike ballot has resulted in a pro-strike majority.

3   The right to a postal vote in (a) elections for a president, general secretary or governing bodies and (b) ballots on political funds.
4   The right to scrutinise a union's financial affairs.

CLOSED SHOPS

All legal immunity is removed for industrial action taken by a union to create or maintain a closed shop. Furthermore an employee may claim unfair dismissal if he or she is dismissed for not belonging to a union.

PROTECTION OF RIGHTS

A Commissioner for the Rights of Trade Union Members is established. The Commissioner is appointed to help union members who wish to take legal action against a union. He or she has the power to pay for legal advice and to provide representation. Unions are forbidden to discipline a member who takes action against them.

The Trade Union Act 1984

This Act covers the election of trade union leaders, secret ballots, and trade union expenditure on party political activities.

Part I   There must be a secret ballot every five years to elect each voting member of the trade union governing body. A register must be kept of members' names and addresses. Minimum requirements for the conduct of elections include frequency and balloting arrangements, voting entitlement and conditions for a candidate to stand for election. Complaints by a member may be made to the Certification Officer or to the courts.

Part II   Before organising an industrial action a trade union must first hold a secret ballot among all those due to take part, and the resulting majority vote must be to take part in the action. Minimum requirements include who can vote, voting arrangements, the ballot question, counting, and announcing results of the ballot.

Part III   Trade unions with political funds must regularly ballot their members to seek agreement on continuing expenditure for party political activities. Furthermore any trade union possessing a political fund must pass a new resolution by secret ballot, at no more than every ten years, seeking agreement to continue expenditure on political objects.

Also employers who deduct trade union subscriptions by 'check-off' arrangements must not continue deducting political contributions if an employee certifies exemption from, or is contracted out of, paying these contributions.

State intervention

Although all political parties admit that pay is a significant feature in economic control their approaches differ. The Conservative Party aims to reduce trade union power and its influence on pay and productivity. The Labour Party tries to gain trade union co-operation by legislating and adopting policies that please the unions.

Unlike some European countries where industrial relations law is based on positive rights for unions, UK laws are based upon immunities. Thus trade union power is used to gain improvements or to defend its position.

Industrial democracy

There has been wide debate for many years on the role of industrial democracy or employee participation. Since the publication in 1977 of the Report of the Committee of Inquiry on Industrial Democracy (the Bullock Report), immense controversy has developed but as yet no legislation is in force.

Probably the British business interests' hostile comments could be summarised as implying that the Bullock proposals, regardless of whether they were right or wrong, were too radical for employers. Indeed, this 120,000 word report was not without its own division of opinion. A minority report of employers' representatives published by three of the Committee's members broadly alleged that industry in Britain was not yet ready for such fundamental changes as were envisaged in the majority report.

In the body of the report the Committee envisaged its creed as follows: 'We believe that there must be a joint approach to decision-making in companies, based on equal representation of employees and shareholders on the board. In our view it is no longer acceptable for companies to be run on the basis that in the last resort the shareholders' view must by right always prevail.'

The Committee envisaged that a basic legal framework – 'of necessity, complex' – should be laid down but that within this sphere great freedom should be allowed for each individual company to create its own board of directors. This device clearly indicates that the success or failure of industrial democracy depends on co-operation between management and trade unions.

Also, an independent Industrial Democracy Commission was advocated to provide 'advice, conciliation, and ultimate decision for those within a company whose task it is to devise an agreed system of employee representation on boards.'

The German model of a two-tier board was considered unsuitable, although the minority group favoured it. The unitary board was favoured with an 'ultimate responsibility for decisions'.

The philosophy of industrial democracy

The disastrous consequences of poor relationships between employers and employees in Britain are well known. Equally obvious is the need for

Britain's managers and trade unionists to revise their ideas on industrial democracy, individually and collectively.

Many reasons are often given for lack of industrial harmony. Some of the glaring examples are: failure by employers to recognise the strength of trade unions, the continual use of outdated methods of treating employees, reliance on obsolescent managers who are out of touch with reality, failure in appreciating the educational level of employees who understand far more about industrial and commercial operations than is generally imagined, and finally completely underestimating the ingenuity and capability of employees.

Employees must also take some of the blame. Often there is a tendency to take advantage of management and the company if the opportunity arises such as improving on their share of 'perks', slacking whenever possible, bargaining for excessive wage claims if they think they hold the company or an industry to ransom, and in general not co-operating. This selfish approach, often at the expense of fellow workers in other industries, is indicative of one of the basic problems that prevails in industry and commerce.

Finally the trade unions also must take their share of the blame for lack of industrial harmony. Some trade union leaders openly declare their political beliefs and even go so far as to admit that their aim is to overthrow the government in office at the time. Others develop a minority interest through improving earnings and conditions for a particular group of trade union members, despite the discontent created in other groups. Certain unions have held the public to ransom at times and also issued grave warnings such as anticipating industrial chaos under particular conditions. Excessive militancy by some shop stewards, outdated policies and general misuse of trade union power have also been levelled against trade unions in recent years.

Problem areas

Such a philosophy outlined above raises many fundamental issues. Some examples are given below but there are many others.

1 Does a particular formal approach to industrial democracy seen operating well in a foreign country mean that a similar approach would be successful in Britain?
2 How can a trade union equate nominating some of its members to a board of directors with its freedom of action?
3 How would collective bargaining be affected considering (2) above?
4 Would employee nominees to a board of directors have sufficient expertise to contribute at this level in the organisation?
5 How can enthusiasm be generated among employees to participate effectively in management decision-making?

6 If one of the declared objectives of a trade union is to develop a minority interest through improving earnings and conditions for its members despite the discontent of other groups, how does it reconcile this aim with the national interest?

The consultative bodies

The main consultative bodies are the employers' associations and the trade unions. At this level negotiations for wages are usually handled directly without referring for active assistance to the two central federations, the Confederation of British Industry and the Trades Union Congress.

The federations advise, provide information and statistics to their members, and give their views to the government, the national press and international organisations. Their officials sit on a number of councils and committees which advise the government and statutory bodies.

Employers' associations

Employers have grouped together generally within the particular industry but not to any set pattern. Their associations vary in size from small local groups to sections of an industry to a whole industry on a national level. Some of these associations were formed to cope with industrial relations problems while others were organised to deal with trading problems in addition. In some cases an association deals only with trading questions.

The role played by employers' associations varies, depending upon overall policy. Some have an enlightened policy and actively promote good relations between employers and employees, offering such facilities as practical advice and information on wages standards and conditions of employment, training programmes and specialised services. Others are rather negative in their approach. They will examine proposals and advise revisions based upon the protection of members' interests, but seldom initiate action themselves.

A typical organisation consists of a small number of full-time staff, controlled by a director who is responsible for the daily activities of the association, plus representatives from member firms and officials who form a central committee. This committee meets about four times a year to formulate policy and to elect such committees as are considered necessary. The chairpersons of these committees usually meet regularly with the association's officials to co-ordinate activities.

There are approximately 1400 employers' organisations and most of these are federated to about eighty-five national organisations. Most of the national organisations are members of the Confederation of British Industry and they negotiate with trade unions to reach national collective agreements.

The Confederation of British Industry

This confederation represents the employers' associations at national level and internationally. The nationalised industries and many individual companies are affiliated to the CBI which puts forward the views of all these groups to the government. CBI representatives are members of a number of government advisory committees and voluntary bodies who deal with labour problems.

Trade unions

Employees have organised themselves into trade unions in most industries today. The process has been long, involved and often haphazard in growth, resulting in a complex structure of many different types of union. Gradually the movement is becoming more organised and uniform as amalgamations and mergers of the smaller unions into larger ones continue.

Membership reached 10.3 million in 1969 (about 40 per cent of all employees) and by 1976 had increased to 12.3 million (about 48 per cent) in 462 unions. By 1987 membership had dropped to around 9 million.

The last available information on *registered* unions was in 1972. In that year there were 229 on the register as a result of the Industrial Relations Act 1971. Income was £4.8 million from members and £2.4 million from other sources. Funds at the end of that year were £14.2 million.

Objects

The main object of a trade union is to protect and help its members. So far this object has been partially achieved by negotiating for higher wages and better conditions of employment. The trend now is towards more joint consultation to be distinguished from joint negotiation which is limited to questions of wages and conditions of employment.

Forms of organisation

In general there are four main forms of organisation: the professional workers' union for clerical, administrative or executive workers; the craft-type union for skilled trades; the industrial union for all workers in an industry such as mining; and the general labour union for workers below the skilled level. The first-mentioned is expanding rapidly while the others tend to be static now.

The structure

There are many different types of internal organisation. A typical example of a structure has four levels. First, shop steward (delegate or collector); he or she collects dues, handles complaints and grievances, and operates from the workplace. Second, branch secretary; he or she is elected, deals with matters within the branch area, and is an important liaison link. Third, district controller (or regional controller); salaried and full-time he or she heads powerful committees and links with central organisation through coupling committees. Fourth, general secretary; he or she heads the central organisation, is responsible to a national executive committee, is salaried, full-time, and may be elected in various ways.

The Trades Union Congress

The trade union movement is represented as a whole by the TUC to which most large unions belong. About 180 unions are affiliated. The remaining unaffiliated unions account for about a million members, who are mainly government servants and teachers.

   The objects of the TUC are 'to promote the interests of all its affiliated organisations and generally to improve the social and economic conditions of the workers.' In practice, the objects are extended to include consideration of the broad issues of national policy where they affect trade unions.

Registration

Any organisation of workers (such as staff associations) or employers may apply for registration to the Certification Officer who is appointed by the Secretary of State after consultation with ACAS. Certain provisions are necessary, including having the power to alter its own rules, being independent, and controlling the application of its own property and funds.

   The advantages of being registered and granted a certificate of independence are many and real and include the right to demand information from an employer for collective bargaining purposes, the right of employees who are members of an independent trade union to have time off work – with pay – to engage in union duties, the right to refer a 'recognition' issue to ACAS and the right to tax exemptions in respect of investment income and in capital gains devoted to the payment of provident benefits.

Disputes

Failure to settle a dispute by collective bargaining generally leads to a stoppage of work through either a strike or a lock-out. Such cessations of work not only affect the interests of the parties concerned but also have serious repercussions on the national economy.

   For many years successive governments have attempted to introduce effective machinery to promote settlements. This machinery has taken the form of advice, conciliation and arbitration. Conciliation means introducing a third party who attempts to help the parties in dispute by suggesting possible solutions which may be acceptable to both. There is no question of compulsion.

Similarly, arbitration is a voluntary process where both parties agree to submit the dispute to a person (or persons) who will give a valued opinion. The parties also agree to accept this opinion or award beforehand.

Figure 19.1 gives a simplified indication of the negotiating machinery which is available in the settlement of disputes.

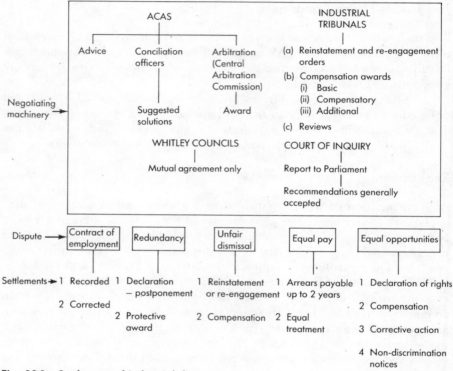

Fig. 19.1 *Settlement of industrial disputes*

The Advisory, Conciliation and Arbitration Service

The aim of ACAS is to promote the improvement of industrial relations by strengthening collective bargaining and by assisting in various ways when a dispute arises. It is independent of government control – this is its distinguishing feature.

Employers are offered advice on a wide range of industrial relations and employment matters. They may ask for assistance from its officers in helping to settle disputes and arbitration can also be arranged. In addition, employers may, in most cases, seek the assistance of an ACAS conciliation officer when a trade union or employee complains to an industrial tribunal. The officer will try to settle the dispute by agreement between the parties rather than resorting to a tribunal hearing. Indeed, a copy of the complaint submitted to an industrial tribunal is sent, as a matter of course, to a conciliation officer.

ACAS may conduct inquiries into industrial matters and publish its findings. A Code of Practice has been produced called *Disciplinary Practice and Procedures in Employment* which provides guidance on how to draw up disciplinary rules and procedures and how to operate them effectively. This is discussed in detail below.

ACAS may refer disputes to the Central Arbitration Committee (CAC) for arbitration provided the parties concerned agree. The CAC has powers in connection with trade union recognition and disclosure of information, and it took over the functions of the Industrial Arbitration Board which included cases involving fair wages.

The Employment Protection Act 1975 established a new Employment Appeal Tribunal which hears appeals from the decisions of industrial tribunals on points of law and appeals from the decisions of the Certification Officer on points of law and fact when the dispute concerns either an entry on the list of trade unions or applications for certificates of independence. *The Industrial Relations Handbook* (HMSO) is an appropriate guide.

The Code of Practice on disciplinary procedures

The aim of the Code is to help employers, trade unions and individual employees by providing practical guidance for promoting good industrial relations to encourage improvements in individual conduct. Failure to observe any provision does not render a person liable to proceedings. However, in the event of a dispute being taken to arbitration or being put before the Central Arbitration Committee, the Code shall be admissible in evidence and if any provision in the Code appears to be relevant to the case it will be taken into account.

The essential features of disciplinary procedures are that they should:

1 be in writing
2 state to whom they apply
3 provide for matters to be dealt with quickly
4 indicate the disciplinary action which may be taken
5 state the levels of management which have the authority to take various forms of disciplinary action, ensuring that immediate superiors do not normally have the power to discuss without reference to senior management
6 arrange for individuals to be informed of the complaints against them and to be given the opportunity to state their case before decisions are taken

7   give individuals the right to be accompanied by a trade union repre-
    sentative or by a colleague of their choice
8   ensure that no employees are dismissed for a first offence except in the
    case of gross misconduct
9   ensure that no disciplinary action is taken until the case has been care-
    fully investigated
10 ensure that individuals are given a proper explanation for any penalty
    imposed
11 provide a right for the individual to appeal
12 specify the procedure to be followed in the event of an appeal.

The supervisor and the code

The initiative for establishing adequate disciplinary rules and procedures lies
with management, but for them to be fully effective they need to be accepted
as reasonable by both supervisors and employees. Thus all levels within the
organisation should be involved when new or revised rules and procedures
are being formulated.

Some degree of interpretation of rules is inevitable and the supervisor
should ensure that employees know and understand them. Verbal explanations are needed as well as written copies; these should form part of an
induction programme for new employees.

To avoid misunderstandings the supervisor should make known the likely
consequence of breaking rules and indicate clearly the type of conduct which
could lead to summary dismissal.

The following items could well constitute an acceptable disciplinary
procedure.

1   Establish the facts immediately including statements from witnesses.
2   Consider a brief period of suspension with pay while the case is
investigated.
3   Interview the individual before any decision or penalty is imposed.
Give him or her ample opportunity to state the case.
4   Advise the individual of his/her rights under the procedure including
the right to be accompanied.
5   Decide whether to give a formal oral warning in the case of a minor
offence or a written warning if it is more serious. Set out the nature of the
offence and the possible consequences of further offences. The individual
should be told that the warning, oral or written, constitutes the first formal
stage of the procedure. If, however, the supervisor decides to give only an
informal oral warning for the purpose of improving conduct, then naturally
this does not apply. Remember to satisfy the test of reasonableness of action
in all circumstances, not forgetting also the employee's record and any other
relevant factors.
6   A further breach of discipline could warrant a final written warning.

This should include a statement that any recurrence would lead to suspension or dismissal or some other penalty as the case may be.

7 The final stage could be disciplinary transfer or disciplinary suspension without pay provided these are allowed for by an express or implied condition of the contract of employment, or dismissal, according to the nature of the misconduct. Disciplinary suspension without pay should not normally be for a prolonged period and it demands special consideration before proceeding with such a course of action.

8 Details of the disciplinary action should be given in writing to the employee or employee's representative. This does not apply to an oral warning.

9 Notify the employee of any right of appeal and how to conduct such an appeal in terms of procedure and the people involved.

Exceptional cases

Occasionally special consideration must be given in circumstances where the use of the standard disciplinary procedure may be too rigid or difficult to comply with. Three typical examples are the following.

1 If the full disciplinary procedure is not immediately available for some reason then special provisions are essential. Nightshift workers may not be able to consult a trade union representative, there may be no one in authority to take appropriate action, or there could be problems associated with remote working sites.

2 There may be an apparent attack on a union's functions if a union official has committed an offence. This could lead to a serious dispute and, therefore, it may be more diplomatic to give an oral warning until the circumstances of the case have been discussed with a senior union official.

3 A criminal offence outside employment may not be sufficient to dismiss an employee. Consideration should be given as to whether the offence makes the employee unsuitable for his or her type of employment or whether he or she would become unacceptable to colleagues.

Industrial tribunals

Although these tribunals have already been explained in Chapter 17 on Employment, they feature generally in disputes. Complaints are heard in the main from individual employees on a range of jurisdictions given to the tribunals under employment laws passed since 1964.

Courts of Inquiry

Under Part II of the Industrial Courts Act 1919 the Minister may appoint a Court of Inquiry to investigate the causes and circumstances of a trade dispute and submit a report. Such a dispute would naturally be of high importance where an impartial opinion is considered necessary in the public interest and when other methods of negotiation have broken down.

The Court has the power to call witnesses who give evidence under oath, to ask for any relevant documents and to sit in private or public as it so desires. Its findings or recommendations carry no legal weight but because of its impartiality the decision is invariably either accepted outright or as a firm foundation for further negotiation between the parties leading to an agreement. Any report (and any minority report) must be laid before both Houses of Parliament 'as soon as may be'.

Individual rights of employees

These rights were established through many Acts which are mentioned in Chapter 21 on Welfare. A summary of the main rights is given below.

1   To take a complaint to an industrial tribunal on a wide range of juris-dictions under the various employment laws passed since 1964.

2   To receive a written statement of the terms and conditions of his/her contract of employment after thirteen weeks of continuous employment with an employer.

3   To a certain minimum period of notice after four weeks' continuous employment. Duration is dependent upon length of service and the employee will usually be entitled to pay during notice. After four weeks' continuous employment the employee is required to give a minimum of one week's notice.

4   To qualify as a person entitled to a full range of legal protection provided continuity of employment of sixteen hours a week or more can be shown. A person also qualifies if he/she had worked for the same employer for eight or more hours a week (but less than sixteen) for five years or more.

5   To receive itemised pay statements showing gross pay, take-home pay and the amounts and reasons for all variable and fixed deductions. As an alternative fixed deductions may be shown as a total with the amounts and reasons supplied in a separate annual statement which must be amended during the year when the occasion arises.

6   To receive guarantee payments for a limited period during short-time working or lay-offs. The employer must make this payment only if a full day's work is lost. The limit is £9.50 a day and guaranteed for five days in any calendar quarter. Payment is excluded if there is no work due to action involving other employees of the same or an associated employer.

7   To receive normal pay (up to a maximum of twenty-six weeks) during medical suspension covered by special health and safety regulations following examination by an employment medical advisor or an appointed doctor.

8   To be a member of, or take part at an appropriate time in the activities of, an independent trade union.

9   To refuse to join a non-independent trade union or to object to joining on religious grounds any trade union whatsoever.

10   To be allowed reasonable time off with pay during working hours to carry out trade union duties if the employee is an official of an independent trade union. Furthermore, this applies to receiving training in trade union duties provided it is concerned with industrial relations.

11   To take reasonable time off without pay for the performance of certain public duties such as the holding of offices as Justices of the Peace, members of a local authority, members of any statutory tribunal and members of certain health, education, water and river authorities.

12   To take reasonable time off with pay while under notice of redundancy to seek new employment or to make arrangements for retraining. Entitlement is also based upon the employee being continuously employed for at least two years by his/her present employer.

13   If a woman is expecting a baby she has a right not to be dismissed because of pregnancy or for a reason connected with her pregnancy. If her condition does not allow her to do her job adequately or her continued employment while pregnant is against the law she must be offered a suitable alternative job if one is available. Furthermore, she is entitled to maternity leave, time-off for ante natal care, and statutory maternity pay.

14   To complain to the Certification Officer or industrial tribunal against unfair or unreasonable disciplinary action. This aspect is discussed in detail in Chapter 17 on Employment, along with rights on redundancy pay.

15   To claim from the Department of Employment any pay outstanding as a result of an employer becoming insolvent.

16   To reject any attempt to deduct money from pay unless there is an agreement in writing, and to refuse paying back any money from the pay packet to the employer. Exceptions: statutory deductions and lawful payments to third parties.

17   To be informed by all data users whether they hold relevant records on the employee; to have right of access; and to demand corrections or deletions if appropriate.

The supervisor and the shop steward

Although the supervisor needs a sound knowledge of the procedures and regulations controlling industrial relations, the day-to-day contact with these problems will be through the shop steward.

A sound and friendly relationship between supervisor and shop steward is essential to keep industrial friction to a minimum. The problem of establishing and maintaining such a relationship is complex and demanding on a number of individuals, for the supervisor and shop steward not only have to consider the other's viewpoint but are also under pressure from employees and management in various ways. When a difficult situation is aggravated by temperamental employees and outdated management, disputes can scarcely be avoided.

The problem is therefore examined from the viewpoints of the employee, the shop steward, the supervisor and management.

The employee

The employee is continually reminded, through daily occurrences at work and a steady stream of publicised cases, of injustice and victimisation of various descriptions and intensity. It is difficult to resist the influence of this constant external pressure, therefore he or she feels insecure and sensitive to any suggestion of injustice or harshness.

Employees obviously feel the need to belong to an association which will support them and fight for their rights. Even those who are not members of any employees' association are mindful of the role it plays and would probably join very quickly if their continued non-membership meant disbanding the association.

Whether employees are misguided, have incorrect attitudes or wrong impressions is beside the point. They distrust management, strongly feel the need for protection, and are prepared to stand by the association which will support them.

The shop steward

Most shop stewards are very conscious of their responsibilities to the union and its members. They are voluntary representatives of the union and recognised as officials in negotiating procedure.

Many are untrained in a role which is practically impossible to fulfil adequately without a true understanding of industrial relations and all the other matters connected with it. Both trade unions and educationists are aware of this lack and are actively engaged in improving the situation.

The shop steward's job is time-consuming and such qualities as leadership, patience and the ability to sift fact from opinion are essential. He or she has the power to improve the atmosphere within an establishment with due co-operation from supervisors and management, or can destroy relationships, often with disastrous consequences for all concerned including employees.

Although shop stewards are appointed to represent the will of their colleagues and the policy of the union, they also have a social responsibility to act in an impartial and fair manner. In circumstances where they sincerely feel that colleagues are biased to a point beyond a reasonable limit, they must have sufficient courage to disagree with demands and stand by their word.

The supervisor

Any attempt – whether real or only apparent – by a shop steward to undermine the supervisor's authority will naturally get a hostile reception. Unfortunately, shop stewards often create this impression in performing their duties and the supervisor feels he or she is losing prestige in the face of criticism and interference.

The soundness of the supervisor's position depends to a large extent on management's policy towards supervision and the degree of active participation in negotiations which is allowed at supervisory levels. If queries, complaints and grievances are to be settled quickly, the closest point to the trouble is on the shop floor which gives the supervisor a distinct advantage. The supervisor is more familiar with the situation than is management and, provided that he or she is adequately informed of all communications and agreements with the union by management, should be able to deal effectively with the problem with a minimum of disruption.

Management

Management's attitude and relationships with shop stewards vary with general policy which is largely governed by procedure agreements and awareness of the need to work together.

Individual managers may find themselves working strictly to set terms that tend to cause unnecessary rigidity and narrowness of outlook; this is not conducive to friendly working relationships with employees.

A progressive management recognises the importance of supporting the supervisor and developing friendly relationships among the parties concerned. The vital need to work together must be recognised, and active steps to encourage co-operation must come from management otherwise the efforts of supervisors and shop stewards will be wasted.

Working together

Good relationships between supervisor and shop steward depend on each party appreciating and recognising the other's position and the role each plays. This foundation of understanding and the good sense of both parties will provide the opportunity to improve industrial relations considerably.

The supervisor should appreciate the need to keep the shop steward fully informed of any problems, plans, grievances, complaints and possible changes so that the steward is not surprised by any action and likely to lose prestige in front of colleagues. Similarly, the supervisor looks for an adequate return of information from the shop steward; this exchange of information is vital if the improvement of communication and confidence is to be maintained. Furthermore, the information should include adequate explanations of changes and all the known facts whenever possible. Any reasonable person will respond to this straightforward approach and try to co-operate.

Naturally, there is always the possibility of being faced with an antagonistic shop steward who is suffering from some emotional problem. The importance is stressed of standing firm in these circumstances and being scrupulously fair. Most employees recognise fair play when they see it, but the provision of full information is essential otherwise the employees are not made aware that the supervisor is acting fairly.

The supervisor reserves the right to discuss any problems that subordinates put forward, but if they involve a union agreement he or she should recognise the need for the shop steward to be present. Similarly the supervisor should try to settle all problems at this level with the co-operation of the steward, who should ensure that colleagues abide by the set procedure. Each case should be judged on its merits and sufficient facts – as opposed to mere opinion – are essential in order to reach a solution that satisfies both parties.

Working together in the way described produces mutual respect and a marked improvement in atmosphere in the workplace.

Questions

1 Discuss the function of the Industrial Relations Officer.
2 Why should the supervisor need a reasonable knowledge of industrial relations?
3 What is meant by the term 'collective bargaining'?
4 Explain the role played by employers' associations and the Confederation of British Industry.
5 Describe the growth and organisation of trade unions. Comment on the organisation and effectiveness of their activities.
6 Discuss the part played by the Trades Union Congress in industrial relations.
7 What is meant by the terms 'conciliation' and 'arbitration'?
8 Explain the purpose and effectiveness of arbitration.
9 What is a Court of Inquiry?
10 Give your personal advice to a new supervisor in dealing with the shop steward.
11 Discuss the functions of shops stewards.
12 What are the main difficulties that the supervisor and shop steward have to face when trying to work together?
13 Outline the use of joint consultation in industry.
14 Discuss the changing role of the shop steward.
15 State the main tasks of the Certification Officer.
16 What is meant by the term 'industrial democracy'?
17 Outline the general aims of the Employment Protection Act 1975.

Case study

Tom Johnson's promotion to supervisor was greeted calmly by Charlie, the shop steward who had worked with him on the shop floor for three years. They had got on well together. Charlie always gave Tom the latest information before the previous supervisor received it from management. It was a standing joke and Tom always took full advantage of his advance knowledge.

Now the 'tables were turned'; he soon learned how irritating it was being the last to find out what was going on. Eventually he complained to his superior. To his amazement he was told that his promotion was mainly due to his strong relationship with Charlie. He was expected to keep up the good work and not to 'rock the boat'.

Unfortunately Charlie had other ideas and did not confide in Tom.

1 What should Tom do now?
2 Outline the communication and industrial relations problems that are likely to exist in this organisation.

20 Health and safety

The background

The need for more effective programmes to improve occupational health and safety has been recognised for many years. The enormous cost of industrial accidents and the distress and anxiety of employees and families justify more expenditure on research.

Although many studies have been conducted, the resulting evidence is conflicting and incomplete. Certainly research suggests that personality, emotional problems, age, and poor group relations contribute to higher accident rates. Furthermore research indicates that theories do not explain adequately the causes of all the varied accidents, but it does show that accidents are generally caused by a number of interrelated factors, some of which are often hidden.

Accident theories

Attempts to classify so-called *accident activators* have produced many theories. Positive correlations with accident rates exist in three main features. First, age – young workers through inexperience and irresponsibility, and older workers through a reduction in physical and mental capabilities. Second, health and physical characteristics related to a particular job. Third, inexperience during the first five months in a job.

Typical complex theories include accident-proneness, maladjustment to stress, lack of job involvement, withdrawal – trying to avoid work, industrial conflict, anxiety, pure chance, biased liability, and unconscious motivation – self-destructive tendency.

Main features

These are divided into:

- sources of law which attempt to protect the employee
- major aspects for management
- calculation of injury rates for control purposes
- the supervisor's role
- a short survey of ergonomics.

They are discussed more fully later.

Safety legislation

In addition to the social obligations of health and safety there are two main sources of law which protect the employee. The first is 'common law' which is *unwritten*, established by custom and is supported by precedents (created by judges) which are referred to as *case law*. The second source is 'statute law', i.e. Acts passed by Parliament, and these over-ride 'common law' in the event of conflict.

Common law

Under common law there is a liability for safety of employees. Employers may be sued for damages if they do not provide reasonably safe systems of work. If employers ignore this obligation to take reasonable care and avoid unnecessary risks, a civil wrong or tort of negligence is committed. The injured person may sue for damages and, in serious cases, the State may consider the offence a crime and prosecute.

Another legal aspect of safety arises when an employee commits a civil wrong or tort during the course of his or her employment such as injuring another person. This means that if an employee carried out an improper action while working which causes injury to a colleague, although he or she may have been expressly forbidden to do so, the employer is liable for the civil wrong and damages provided the employee was told what to do and how to do it. This is known as *vicarious liability*. If a person is told what to do but has complete freedom as to how the work is done, the relationship changes to one of employer and independent contractor in which case the employer is not liable.

Statute law

The various Acts are involved and in complex legal language. Courts are considered competent to interpret and apply the Acts within which certain words and phrases raise problems as to their exact meaning.

Factories Act 1961

There are a number of provisions laid down in Part II, ss. 12–56, Part IV, ss. 63–79, and Part V, ss. 80–5. These cover precautions concerning machines, fire risks, lifts, cranes, boilers, floors, tanks, masks and goggles, removal of offensive fumes and dust, some health and welfare requirements, and regulations in dangerous trades. Accidents which result in death or affect pay for more than three days, and specified fires or explosions must be notified to the factory inspector.

Under Part X a general register is required to record accidents and other aspects of safety. An example of a typical accident report for internal use

---

ACCIDENT REPORT

Name..............................   Date..............................
Staff/works.........................   Time..............................
Clock number.......................   Place..............................
Department.........................   Supervisor........................
Section ....

Description of injury:

Cause of accident

Treatment

Hospital: Rehabilitation course:

Doctor: Date:

Date: Results:

Action to avoid recurrence
Directive issued:
Date:
Circulation:
Authority:

Remuneration

Absence: From   Time...................   Date..................
         To   Time...................   Date ....

Reductions:
Compensation:

Records
Entry general register:
Factory inspector notified:
Employee's record card:
Circulation: Wages supervisor ....
             Safety officer ....
             Works manager...
             Personnel manager.......................................

Date ....   Signature of supervisor: ....

Fig. 20.1 *Accident report form*

An accident report form using this layout provides sufficient details for the regulation general register and also for safety control purposes

which would provide sufficient detail for the register and for control purposes is given in Fig. 20.1.

Factories, construction and demolition sites, civil engineering sites, docks, shipyards and electrical stations are covered by the Act.

Offices, Shops and Railway Premises Act 1963

Apart from railway workshops, the title of the Act indicates the sites that are covered.

Some of the standards laid down for the working environment do not necessarily agree with those in the Factories Act. A typical example is lighting regulations which conform to modern practice whereas in the Factories Act they are out-of-date.

Alkali Works Regulations Act 1906

This Act outlines the measures to be taken in the control of emissions into the atmosphere of certain chemicals from specified classes of factories.

Agriculture (Poisonous Substances) Act 1952

The use of certain specific dangerous substances in agriculture may be regulated by the Minister under this Act.

Agriculture (Safety, Health and Welfare Provisions) Act 1956

Standards for washing, lavatory facilities and first aid are laid down.

Explosives Acts 1875 and 1923, Petroleum (Consolidation) Act 1928, and Radioactive Substances Act 1960

These Acts cover similar broad requirements for use, storage, manufacture, and labelling of the products, and the licensing of premises within which they are contained.

Mineral Workings (Offshore Installations) Act 1971

Installations associated with underwater exploitation and exploration of minerals in waters in and around Britain are covered in this Act which enables regulations to be drawn up for health, safety and welfare.

Mines and Quarries Act 1954

In addition to the areas in the title the Act includes buildings on the surface associated with the mine. Certain processes are covered by the Factories Act provided they are not for the purpose of working the mine or for preparation of minerals extracted.

Nuclear Installations Acts 1965 and 1969

Precise standards are applied to all nuclear reactor sites.

Railway Employment (Prevention of Accidents) Act 1900

Rules may be made to cover a number of specific hazards. In addition there are rules produced in 1902 and 1911 which cover shunting arrangements, wagon brakes, lookouts and wagon labelling.

Road Traffic Acts and Transport Act 1968

Extensive regulations are applied for road transport and railways. Included are vehicle construction, licensing, hours of work and movement of dangerous goods.

Shops Act 1950

This Act includes shops and similar premises for the purpose of limiting hours of work.

The Health and Safety at Work etc. Act 1974

This legislation is known as an 'enabling' Act because it is broad and generalised in nature rather than going into a great deal of detail. Thus powers are given to the Secretary of State for Employment to introduce regulations and codes of practice on specific health and safety matters. The Secretary, in turn, acts through the new Health and Safety Commission.

In other words, the Act is a broad framework from which future legislation will be introduced to make up a comprehensive body of legislation (including existing Acts) on health and safety.

Although the Act imposes many extra general duties on employers, it does not cut out, cancel or affect any existing legislation which will continue until new legislation replaces it. Naturally this does not apply to the 8 million employees who are now covered for the first time by the Act.

Aims of the Act

1 To secure the health, safety and welfare of people at work by involving everybody at the workplace including workers, supervisors and managers in taking responsibility for this task.
2 To protect people other than those at work against any risks to health or safety arising out of or in connection with the activities of people at work.
3 To control the storage and use of explosive or highly flammable or otherwise dangerous substances, and generally preventing the unlawful acquisition, possession and use of such substances.

4   To control the emission into the atmosphere of noxious or offensive substances from prescribed premises.

The Act's approach

To achieve the above-mentioned aims the Act is designed to provide for one, comprehensive, integrated system of law on health, safety and welfare. The main approaches are as follows.

1   To overhaul completely and modernise the existing law covering health, safety and welfare at work.
2   To create a new Health and Safety Commission.
3   To provide a range of new general duties for employers.
4   To reorganise and unify the various government inspectorates.
5   To impose new powers and penalties for the enforcement of safety laws.
6   To establish new methods of accident prevention and new ways of operating future safety regulations.
7   To establish Codes of Practice instead of regulations whenever possible.

The establishment of Codes of Practice was an interesting innovation recommended by the Report of the Committee on Safety and Health at Work in July 1972 (the *Robens Report*). The advantages are that Codes may be formulated by people in industry with practical knowledge, they may be written in non-legal language which should be more easily understood, and they are easily revised to keep up with changing technology.

The Codes will not be statutory requirements but they may be used as evidence in courts of law. Anyone charged with a contravention of a statutory provision will have to prove that the practices used were better than or at least as good as the relevant approved code. Contrary to traditional legal practice, the person will be guilty until proved innocent.

General duties of the Act

Within the provisions of the Act there are a number of general duties mentioned which apply to employers, employees and people other than employees. An outline is given below.

Duties to employees

The general duties of employers to their employees are given in s. 2 of the Act.

Section 2(1): 'It shall be the duty of every employer to ensure, so far as is reasonably practicable, the health, safety and welfare at work of all his employees.'

Section 2(2): further provides that 'without prejudice to the generality of the preceding subsection, the matters to which that duty extends include in particular . . .'

Section 2(2)(a): '. . . the provision and maintenance of plant and systems of work that are, so far as is reasonably practicable, safe and without risks to health.' This is a general requirement covering all plant which the Act defines as including machinery, equipment and appliances used at work. It does not supersede the more detailed and specific provisions covering certain equipment contained in existing legislation, but it goes beyond such provisions in requiring a more wide-ranging assessment of risk.

Section 2(2)(b): '. . . arrangements for ensuring, so far as is reasonably practicable, safety and absence of risks to health in connection with the use, handling, storage and transport of articles and substances.' This subsection is concerned with the materials and articles used at work. 'Substance' is defined (in s. 53) as 'any natural or artificial substance, whether in solid or liquid form or in the form of a gas or vapour', so that the subsection covers everything used at work and all work activities.

Section 2(2)(c): '. . . the provision of such information, instruction, training and supervision as is necessary to ensure, so far as is reasonably practicable, the health and safety at work of his employees.'

Section 2(2)(d): '. . . so far as is reasonably practicable as regards any place of work under the employer's control, the maintenance of it in a condition that is safe and without risks to health and the provision and maintenance of means of access to and egress from it that are safe and without such risks.'

Section 2(2)(e): '. . . the provision and maintenance of a working environment for his employees that is, so far as is reasonably practicable, safe, without risks to health and adequate as regards facilities and arrangements for their welfare at work.'

Section 2(3): 'Except in such cases as may be prescribed, it shall be the duty of every employer to prepare and as often as may be appropriate revise a written statement of his general policy with respect to the health and safety at work of his employees and the organisation and arrangements for the time being in force for carrying out that policy, and to bring the statement and any revision of it to the notice of all his employees.' Regulations have since prescribed that all employers with five or more employees must have a written safety policy.

Duties to people other than employees

An employer also has responsibility for protecting other people such as the public. Duties in this respect are shown in s. 3.

Section 3(1): 'It shall be the duty of every employer to conduct his undertakings in such a way as to ensure, so far as is reasonably practicable, that persons not in his employment who may be affected thereby are not thereby exposed to risks to their health or safety.'

Section 3(3): places a duty on employers in circumstances which will be prescribed to give to persons who are not their employees information about such aspects of the way in which they conduct their undertakings as might affect the health or safety of these persons.

Duties relating to premises

Any person who is in control of non-domestic premises where people work who are not their own employees or where these people use plant or substances provided there for their use has duties to follow under s. 4.

Section 4(2):'It shall be the duty of each person who has, to any extent, control of premises to which this section applies or of the means of access thereto or egress therefrom or of any plant or substance in such premises to take such measures as it is reasonable for a person in his position to take to ensure, so far as is reasonably practicable, that the premises, all means of access thereto or egress therefrom available for use by persons using the premises, and any plant or substance in the premises or, as the case may be, provided for use there, is or are safe and without risks to health.'

The term 'premises' is defined by s. 53 and 'includes any place and, in particular, includes any vehicle, vessel, aircraft or hovercraft; any installation on land (including the foreshore and other land intermittently covered by water), any offshore installation and any other installation (whether floating, or resting on the seabed or the subsoil thereof, or resting on other land covered with water or the subsoil thereof); and any tent or movable structure.'

This is a general provision and the person in control of premises may also have other duties under other enactments, for example with respect to means of escape in case of fire, and general fire precautions, and also with respect to public health.

Duties relating to harmful emissions in the atmosphere

Any person controlling premises which may emit into the atmosphere noxious or offensive substances has certain duties under s. 5.

Briefly, the best practical means for preventing such emissions should be used. This applies also to rendering such emissions harmless and inoffensive.

Duties of employers etc. concerning articles and substances at work

Section 6 applies to all persons who design, manufacture, import, supply, erect or install any article, plant, machinery, equipment or appliances for use at work, or manufacture, import or supply any substance for use at work. It also applies where research is conducted by designers and manufacturers. The provisions are given below.

Every employer is likely to be affected by these provisions as a purchaser and user of articles or substances and, in addition, many will have duties as a member of one of the classes of persons named in the section.

An 'article for use at work' is defined as:

1 any plant, machinery, equipment or appliance designed for use or operation (whether exclusively or not) by persons at work, and
2 any article designed for use as a component in any such plant.

A 'substance for use at work' is any natural or artificial substance whether in solid or liquid form or in the form of a gas or vapour intended for use (whether exclusively or not) by persons at work.

Section 6(1): 'It shall be the duty of any person who designs, manufactures, imports or supplies any article for use at work,

(a) to ensure, so far as is reasonably practicable, that the article is so designed and constructed as to be safe and without risks to health when properly used;
(b) to carry out or arrange for the carrying out of such testing and examination as may be necessary for the performance of the duty imposed on him by the preceding paragraph;
(c) to take such steps as are necessary to secure that there will be available in connection with the use of the article at work adequate information about the use for which it is designed and has been tested, and about any conditions necessary to ensure that, when put to that use, it will be safe and without risks to health.'

Section 6(2): 'It shall be the duty of any person who undertakes the design or manufacture of any article for use at work to carry out or arrange for the carrying out of any necessary research with a view to the discovery and, so far as is reasonably practicable, the elimination or minimisation of any risks to health or safety to which the design or article may give rise.'

Section 6(3): 'It shall be the duty of any person who erects or installs any article for use at work in any premises where that article is to be used by persons at work to ensure, so far as is reasonably practicable, that nothing about the way in which it is erected or installed makes it unsafe or a risk to health when properly used.'

Section 6(4): 'It shall be the duty of any person who manufactures, imports or supplies any substance for use at work,

(a) to ensure, so far as is reasonably practicable, that the substance is safe and without risks to health when properly used;
(b) to carry out or arrange for the carrying out of such testing and examination as may be necessary for the performance of the duty imposed on him by the preceding paragraph;
(c) to take such steps as are necessary to secure that there will be available in connection with the use of the substance at work adequate information about the results of any relevant tests which have been carried out on or

in connection with the substance and about any conditions necessary to ensure that it will be safe and without risks to health when properly used.'

Section 6(5): 'It shall be the duty of any person who undertakes the manufacture of any substance for use at work to carry out or arrange for the carrying out of any necessary research with a view to the discovery and, so far as is reasonably practicable, the elimination or minimisation of any risks to health or safety to which the substance may give rise.'

Section 6(6): 'Nothing in the preceding provisions of this section shall be taken to require a person to repeat any testing, examination or research which has been carried out otherwise than by him or at his instance, in so far as it is reasonable for him to rely on the results thereof for the purposes of those provisions.'

Section 6(7): 'Any duty imposed on any person by any of the preceding provisions of this section shall extend only to things done in the course of a trade, business or other undertaking carried on by him (whether for profit or not) and to matters within his control.'

Section 6(8): 'Where a person designs, manufactures, imports or supplies an article for or to another on the basis of a written undertaking by that other to take specified steps sufficient to ensure, so far as is reasonably practicable, that the article will be safe and without risks to health when properly used, the undertaking shall have the effect of relieving the first-mentioned person from the duty imposed by sub-section *(1)(a)* above to such an extent as is reasonable having regard to the terms of the undertaking.'

Section 6(9): 'Where a person ("the ostensible supplier") supplies any article for use at work or substance for use at work to another ("the customer") under a hire-purchase agreement, conditional sale agreement or credit-sale agreement, and the ostensible supplier:

(a) carries on the business of financing the acquisition of goods by others by means of such agreements; and

(b) in the course of that business acquired his interest in the article or substance supplied to the customer as a means of financing its acquisition by the customer from a third person ("the effective supplier"), the effective supplier and not the ostensible supplier shall be treated for the purposes of this section as supplying the article or substance to the customer, and any duty imposed by the preceding provisions of this section on suppliers shall accordingly fall on the effective supplier and not on the ostensible supplier.'

Section 6(10): 'For the purposes of this section an article or substance is not to be regarded as properly used where it is used without regard to any relevant information or advice relating to its use which has been made available by a person by whom it was designed, manufactured, imported or supplied.'

Duties of employees

Sections 7 and 8 cover the duties of *all* employees, which implies that managers also come under this heading. These duties are quoted below.

Section 7: 'It shall be the duty of every employee while at work:

(a) to take reasonable care for the health and safety of himself and of other persons who may be affected by his acts or omissions at work; and

(b) as regards any duty or requirement imposed on his employer or any other person by or under any of the relevant statutory provisions, to co-operate with him so far as is necessary to enable that duty or requirement to be performed or complied with.'

Section 8: 'No person shall intentionally or recklessly interfere with or misuse anything provided in the interests of health, safety or welfare in pursuance of any of the relevant statutory provisions.'

Charge to employees

Section 9 of the Act states that no employer shall levy or permit to be levied on any employee any charge in respect of anything done or provided in pursuance of any specific requirement of the relevant statutory provisions.

Enforcement of the Act

Section 10 establishes two bodies, the Health and Safety Commission and the Health and Safety Executive. The Commission is responsible to the Secretary of State.

Health and safety commission

The Commission was established in 1974 and consists of a full-time independent chairperson and nine part-time commissioners. The commissioners are made up of three TUC members, three CBI members, two from local authorities and one independent member.

This body has taken over responsibility formerly held by various government departments and is responsible through the Executive for the new, unified inspectorate.

The Commission is empowered to make agreements with government departments, or others, for them to perform functions on their behalf. It is also responsible for maintaining the Employment Medical Advisory Service which forms the medical arm of the Executive.

The fire authorities and the Home Office are responsible for general fire precautions at places of work under an amendment of the Fire Precautions Act 1971. However, the Commission remains responsible for control over 'process' risks which covers those incidents where there is a risk of outbreak of fire associated with particular processes or particular substances.

The executive

This operational arm of the Commission is responsible for implementing the Commission's advisory functions and for enforcing the relevant statutory provisions. These include the existing legislation, the provisions of this Act and the regulations made under it unless other bodies are specifically made responsible by the legislation for enforcement in certain circumstances.

The Act covers the appointment of inspectors to carry out its enforcement functions through the Executive. Local authorities are also given powers to enforce the legislation in some areas of employment including many covered by health and safety legislation for the first time. These relate broadly to non-industrial activities. Allocation of responsibilities has been made in regulations after consultation.

Although the Executive possesses the main responsibility for enforcement except where local authorities have powers, other organisations may also be given responsibility under the guidance of the Commission. This allows for those particular organisations to continue with their related responsibilities or where expert knowledge is available.

The unified inspectorate

Inspectorates that were previously scattered throughout several government departments are now all under the control of the Health and Safety Executive. They have powers to enforce the Act which may be grouped into three categories: 1 improvement notices, 2 prohibition notices, and 3 increased fines and the threat of imprisonment.

1 *Improvement notices.* An inspector may serve an improvement notice if he or she is of the opinion that:

(a) there is a contravention of one or more of the relevant statutory provisions; or
(b) there has been a contravention in circumstances that make it likely that the contravention will be repeated.

The notice states that the inspector is of that opinion and specifies the provision or provisions contravened. It gives details of the reasons for the inspector's opinion and asks the employer to remedy the situation within a specified time.

2 *Prohibition notices.* An inspector may issue an immediate prohibition notice if he or she considers there is an imminent risk of serious personal injury. Such a notice requires the work concerned to be stopped immediately. If the inspector does not think the risk of serious personal injury is

imminent he or she may issue a deferred prohibition notice which requires the work to be stopped unless the matters are put right within a specified time.

Appeals against both improvement and prohibition notices may be made to an industrial tribunal. An improvement notice is automatically suspended during an appeal. A prohibition notice is only suspended if the appellant applies to the tribunal for suspension and if the tribunal agrees.

3   *Penalties.* An offence is committed if there is non–compliance with these notices. The penalties are·a maximum fine of £1,000 on conviction in a magistrates' court or an unlimited fine in the case of a trial by indictment (in a court higher than a magistrates' court). A person convicted in a higher court of failure to comply with a prohibition notice may also be liable to up to two years' imprisonment either in addition to or instead of a fine. There could also be a continuing fine of £100 a day for every day of non-compliance with a notice after conviction.

Powers of inspectors

Under s. 20 power is given to inspectors to enter at any reasonable time any premises which may be suspect for the purpose of carrying into effect any of the legal provisions within the field of the inspector's enforcing authority.

Inspectors may take with them any duly authorised person and any equipment required. They may take measurements, photographs, recordings and samples, and can require people to provide information and to answer questions and ask them to sign a declaration of the truth of their answers.

Inspectors may require any person to afford them such facilities and assistance within the person's control or responsibilities as are necessary to enable the inspectors to exercise any of the powers conferred on them.

The power of inspectors is given in writing by their enforcing authority and they must when invited produce a copy of their instrument of appointment.

Offences

Under s. 33 of the Act fifteen provisions as to offences are listed:

1   to fail to comply with the general duties under ss. 2 to 7
2   to contravene ss. 8 or 9
3   to contravene any health and safety regulations
4   to contravene any requirement relating to the power of the Commission under the Act to direct investigations and inquiries
5   to fail to comply with any requirement imposed by an inspector in the exercise of his or her powers
6   to prevent or attempt to prevent any other person from appearing before an inspector or from answering any question to which an inspector may require an answer

7   to fail to comply with an improvement or prohibition notice
8   intentionally to obstruct an inspector in the exercise of his or her power
9   to fail to comply with a notice issued by the Commission under the Act
    and requiring information to be supplied
10 wrongly to disclose information obtained by the Commission under the
    Act
11 to make a statement which is known to be false or recklessly to make
    a statement which is false when the statement is made in order to show
    compliance with a requirement or to obtain a document
12 intentionally to make a false entry in a register or document required
    by the statutory provisions and to make use of such an entry
13 with intent to deceive, to forge or use a document issued under the
    statutory provisions
14 to pretend to be an inspector
15 to fail to comply with a court order made under the Act.

Major aspects for management

Some of the main measures for management to consider under the Act are
as follows

1   To issue a written statement of safety policy.
2   To establish an organisation and allocate responsibilities for health and
safety matters.
3   To train members of the company in health and safety matters as
considered appropriate.
4   To ensure that adequate first-aid facilities exist.
5   To provide appropriate fire-fighting equipment and ensure that
everyone is familiar with fire drill.
6   To establish a safety committee.
7   To provide appropriate procedures and documents to minimise
accidents.
8   To consult with safety representatives appointed under the Safety
Representatives Regulations with a view to making and maintaining arrangements which will promote and develop measures to ensure the health and
safety at work of the employees, and checking the effectiveness of such
measures.

Accident reports

Accidents must be notified to the relevant enforcement authority. Under the
Notification of Accidents and Dangerous Occurrences Regulations 1980
(NADO) any fatality, major injury, or any prescribed dangerous occurrence
should be reported immediately by telephone and confirmed in writing
within seven working days. Furthermore all accidents resulting in incapacity

for more than three days should be recorded and forms completed for industrial disablement or sickness payment if the Department of Social Security so desires.

In 1985 updated regulations were introduced. The Reporting of Injuries, Diseases and Dangerous Occurrences Regulations (RIDDO) unified all previous reporting procedures for injuries causing more than three days absence, certain industrial diseases, and immediate reporting of fatalities, etc., as previously applied through NADO. The regulations should be consulted since the revised list of accidents is extensive. Examples are fatalities; certain fractures, amputations and eye injuries; injuries including burns requiring immediate medical treatment or loss of consciousness; decompression sickness; and acute illness relating from exposure to infected material.

Injury rates

A considerable amount of information is available on accidents in industry. Various theories on the causes of accidents have been propounded over the years. An interesting theory concerning the importance of minor injuries states that for every one injury causing loss of time from work there are 29 minor injuries and 300 accidents which do not cause personal injury. This theory is based upon the study of many thousands of cases and it follows that by reducing the number of minor injuries a proportionate number of serious and major injuries will be avoided.

Statistical analysis of the immediate cause of injury in a company can indicate the avenues to follow in accident prevention. For example, one industry analysis may show that only one injury in every hundred arises from accidents involving hand- or power-driven machinery, but forty out of every hundred injuries arise from handling materials, and so on.

For control purposes the following two formulae are often used to indicate trends in accidents and to form a standard basis for comparison in industry.

Frequency rate:

$$\frac{\text{Number of lost time accidents} \times 100{,}000}{\text{Total man hours lost}} = \text{Frequency rate}$$

The term 'lost time accident' refers to one which stops the employee from working at his or her normal job beyond the day or shift during which the accident occurred. A reduction in the frequency rate indicates less frequency of accidents. A satisfactory figure should be lower than 1.

Duration rate:

$$\frac{\text{Total man hours lost}}{\text{Total number of lost time accidents}} = \text{Duration rate}$$

The term duration rate is the average number of hours spent away from the job by an injured person. Naturally, to avoid distortion, fatalities are not included in the calculation.

Another formula often used is given below. Note that all the formulae use 100,000 hours in the calculation as this is thought to be about the average number of hours worked by an employee during his or her working life.

Severity rate:

$$\frac{\text{Number of man hours lost} \times 100,000}{\text{Number of man hours worked}} = \text{Severity rate}$$

If the injured employee is away for more than three days the absence should be reported to the Factory Inspector. The injury is then termed 'reportable'.

The supervisor's role

Although management may ensure that all possible electrical and mechanical precautions are taken, the personal aspect of safety precaution rests with the supervisor, whose task is to convince employees that safety is mainly a question of attitude and that safety awareness must constantly be kept in mind during working hours.

Occasionally a serious accident occurs; it is then too late to think about the precautions that should have been taken. For peace of mind alone supervisors cannot afford to ignore their role in improving safety.

The main aspects of the supervisor's role in promoting safety are described below.

Electronic safety precautions

The supervisor should liaise with the safety representative and the representative responsible for new technology· installations. He or she should check the devices in operation – preferably before their introduction – to assess any health or safety hazards. The workplace should be examined to ensure that all ergonomic aspects have been properly considered.

Should complaints such as eye strain and headaches be received it is essential to investigate the possible causes and treat them as a health hazard. Institutions recommend regular eye tests and keeping records of tests and complaints.

Employees should be informed of any particular dangers associated with high voltage equipment and instructed not to tamper with devices. The BSI Publication *Electrical systems in office furniture and office screens* is a useful guide. New hazards are emerging as information technology develops. Typical examples are given below.

Visual display units

Many VDU operators and other users have to spend many hours a day peering at a screen. Some installation and design features that avoid excessive fatigue are:

1 Large screen with easily readable characters.
2 Stable images – flicker-free.
3 Sharp images that are easy to read.
4 Adjustable brightness and contrast controls.
5 Information presentation not too cluttered.
6 Glare problems eliminated.
7 Adjustable horizontal and vertical axes of machine.
8 Well-designed keyboard.
9 Reduction of harmful or distracting noise levels from equipment.

System design

Poor design may induce monotony, boredom and fatigue. If the operator is expected to perform short cycle operations for long periods he may feel overcontrolled and denied any job satisfaction.

Building into a program more flexibility and the opportunity for the operator to use his initiative, are fundamental requirements of good system design.

Stress

Long periods of high concentration may cause a variety of ailments. Typical possibilities are eye soreness, headaches and backaches. The operator may feel he or she will suffer with eye strain and induce concentration lapses.

Mechanical safety devices

Supervisors should check that safety devices are functioning properly and that employees have not interfered with them in any way. They should encourage employees to suggest improvements and should point out the dangers which are avoided by the use of the devices. They must convince workers that the best way of doing a job is the safest way for all concerned and ensure that the use of devices becomes a regular part of the routine. On those occasions when supervisors demonstrate or use a machine it is essential that they should conform with the precautions regardless of high skill or any other excuse.

Work rate and fatigue

As the rate of working increases, the risk of an accident rises in proportion.

Similarly, fatigue also contributes towards higher accident probability. The problem, therefore, is to find a safe working rate, using the best method and the optimum working period to keep fatigue and the accident rate to a minimum.

In order to maintain and improve productivity in these circumstances it is necessary to apply work study techniques. This subject is discussed in Part 3, Chapters 23 and 24.

Protective clothing

The effectiveness of such devices as goggles, gloves, boots and protective clothing depends upon the employee's good sense and the supervisor's watchfulness. The tendency to discard the protection often occurs if it hampers the work or if the employee considers its use an additional burden rather than a safety precaution. There is always, in addition, the individual who has a false idea of courage and discards the device to show off prowess. In some instances people simply forget and, inevitably, the lapse coincides with the accident.

The supervisor must try to discipline employees into observing safety routines always as a personal protection. Periodical campaigns are unsuccessful as the accidents nearly always occur between the periods of enforcement. Continuous checks and appropriate reprimands are essential, although demanding on the supervisor who is inclined to allow safety to be overshadowed by production problems through pressure of work.

Safety attitude

Most accidents are caused by various forms of neglect such as careless use of machines or tools, failure to wear protective clothing, taking risks (including horseplay), inconsideration for nearby colleagues, lack of concentration and failure to use safety devices. All these faults amount to a poor attitude towards safety.

Improving poor safety attitudes hinges upon human relations and the supervisor's ability to create a team spirit that encourages employees to work safely. The supervisor must set the tone of safety consciousness by insisting on thorough checks for possible hazards on new and existing machinery and by insisting on correct methods of working all the time. This attitude towards accident prevention must be clearly demonstrated to subordinates whom the supervisor must train and discipline to observe all precautions.

Working safely is habit forming, and rapidly develops into group pride in maintaining accident-free workplaces when employees appreciate the dangers and stupidity of taking risks. Surveys indicate that most accidents could have been avoided by more personal care; therefore, fostering the correct attitudes in employees can reduce the accident rate to a very low figure.

Accident proneness

The problem employee is invariably accident prone, probably because he or she has great difficulty in concentrating for any length of time. Those unfortunate people who are suffering with some nervous disorder which manifests itself in periods of moodiness, temperamental outbursts, unco-operativeness and general anti-social conduct are often unsuitable for operating machines. They are a menace to nearby colleagues who may be injured by their sudden lapse of concentration.

Some individuals who suffer with hypochondria are frequent visitors to the sick bay and through their low vitality and general concern over their health they become accident prone. Whether their complaint is real or imagined is beyond the scope of the supervisor to determine, but he or she must take action to place such employees in work of a low hazard nature.

The importance of maintaining a regular careful watch on subordinates is highlighted when considering safety. Naturally the emotionally unstable employee is recognisable in chronic cases through personal contact over a period, but normal people will suddenly change under the stress of a domestic or social problem. A sudden development of emotional instability makes the person very susceptible to accident proneness and should be removed from a hazardous job until he or she recovers.

Training

Lack of experience and poor training also cause many accidents. The question of safety and the correct method of performing a task are an essential part of any training scheme. The importance of correcting bad habits as they appear is emphasised from the safety aspect and the supervisor must constantly check new and existing employees. Allowing a newcomer to work alone before he or she has reached a suitable level of competence is inviting an accident to happen.

Supervisor's safety summary

1   Ensure that all health and safety measures are implemented within the area of the supervisor's responsibility.
2   Ensure that safe working methods are always used.
3   Insist on the maintenance of good housekeeping.
4   Conduct a daily inspection of the area, machines, tools, ancillary equipment and so on.
5   Issue safety equipment and protective clothing as laid down by management and ensure that they are used at all times.
6   Report all accidents, near misses and hazards.
7   Train subordinates and induct newcomers.
8   Communicate developments and changes in procedures.

9   Liaise with superior on all aspects of safety, health and welfare.

10   Remind employees that they have a duty to take reasonable care to ensure that they do not endanger themselves or anyone else, to co-operate with management and others in meeting statutory requirements and to avoid misusing anything provided in the interests of health or safety at work.

11   Provide any information requested by the safety representative on such things as a substance, process or piece of equipment. If there is any doubt as to the accuracy of the information, make this point clear.

12   Ensure that all staff are aware of all possible fire hazards and are familiar with fire drill and related procedures.

Ergonomics

The study of human capabilities and performance in relation to the demands of the job is known as ergonomics. The knowledge accumulated by biological scientists in their study of operators and their working environment is now – after many years of neglect – being applied considerably more in industry.

For many years designers in industry have concentrated on machine design because it was the limiting factor, but in recent years the operator has been overtaken by the machine. The operator in turn has now become the limiting factor. The result is the study of the anatomical, physiological and psychological aspects of the operator who must now be viewed as an integral part of the machine, i.e. as part of one working unit.

Operators are subjected to new stresses and strains of a mental as well as a physical nature as they become machine minders. The various aspects of ergonomics dealt with below are becoming very important in reducing mental and physical fatigue.

Anthropometry

Anthropometry is the measurement of the physical dimensions of the human body. The findings of anthropometric study are essential for the correct design of seats, benches, machines and other equipment used by people. The British Standards Institution Advisory Committee on Anthropometrics has recommended dimensions which are published in a booklet called *Anthropometric recommendations for dimensions of office machines, operators' chairs, and desks*, No. BS 3404.

Conventional seating is a typical example of incorrect practice which results in unnecessary fatigue and, therefore, must affect operator performance. The so-called conventional height for seats is 18 in (457 mm) which – according to specialists – is too high for about 50 per cent of the working population. The mean lower leg length for the male is 17 in (432 mm) and for the female 15 in (381 mm); therefore, the maximum suitable height should be no more than 17 in.

Applied human physiology

The study of applied human physiology reveals that considerable improvements are possible in the general working environment. This science studies the function of the body in relation to applied forces and the tolerances it can stand in various surrounding environments. Such factors as noise, heat, light, vibration and heavy physical effort are measured and the effects recorded.

Numerous booklets are available which give adequate information on maximum and minimum levels for each factor. In addition, the use of kinetics in handling and lifting activities is essential to avoid strain and injury. The Royal Society for the Prevention of Accidents (RoSPA) conducts courses and issues leaflets and posters illustrating the essential points for smooth and easy handling of all kinds. The main aspects are: the correct methods for drum and cylinder handling, pushing and pulling, and stowing and stacking.

Applied psychology

A study of the operator's ability to receive information in various forms through the different senses, to process the information and to take appropriate action is termed 'applied psychology'.

The importance of this science and its application is illustrated by an experiment conducted during World War II on the ability of a radar operator to concentrate on the radar screen for long periods. Tests proved that concentration was lost after thirty minutes: clear signals were not seen after that time lapse because of monotony and mental fatigue. Similar dangers exist today where critical processes and procedures demand long periods of concentration.

The design of dials provides a further example. Visual displays of information can confuse and easily be misinterpreted unless careful attention is given to these problems. Control movements connected with visual displays can cause a serious error if they do not conform to expected standards, e.g. turning a wheel in a clockwise direction, resulting in the movement of a pointer to the right, or pushing a lever forward, resulting in a pointer moving forward or upward. (A clockwise turn is also anatomically more natural for a right-handed person.)

Some confusion occurs when movements are learned or made through experience, e.g. in Britain a downward movement switches *on* the light whereas in the USA a downward movement switches *off* the light. An imported American machine can confuse and irritate a British worker unless the switch system is adjusted.

Applied biology

The scientific design of visual displays, the established optimum rate at which an operator can receive information and the planning of suitable surrounding conditions are partly based upon a knowledge of applied biology.

The study of human beings in terms of physical structure and capacity includes the following topics: an understanding of the bone structure, the physical effects when work is performed, the production of energy and the disposal of resultant waste, the receptors (nerves) which feed in information to a central control mechanism that processes and takes decisions which are transmitted through the motor system (nerves and muscles) to appropriate points of action, the self-governing system that automatically controls the heart, glands and other parts of the body which function without conscious effort.

Typical applications

Some important features in the working situation are to avoid confined spaces for working; to arrange for a natural working position with facilities to change position periodically and the opportunity to sit whenever possible; to arrange for flexible seating and working heights to suit individuals, along with feet and arm supports; and to use devices to hold or support work so allowing hands free.

Questions

1   Give a brief account of the supervisor's responsibility in connection with the safety of subordinates.
2   How can the supervisor establish a safety-conscious group under his or her control?
3   You are asked to attend the first meeting of a newly formed safety committee. What topics would you expect to be raised and what suggestions would you put forward?
4   Discuss safety in connection with maintenance of machinery and equipment.
5   What precautions could a supervisor take to minimise the risk of accidents?
6   How would you deal with an employee who refuses to wear goggles when operating a machine which has a high eyesight hazard?
7   An employee suddenly has two accidents within a few days. What action would you take?
8   Describe the formulae used for control purposes to provide information on the frequency rate and duration rate of accidents.

9 Discuss the employer's liability for safety under common law.
10 Draw up a suitable framework for an accident report form.
11 Why is the Health and Safety at Work etc. Act 1974 known as an enabling Act?
12 Briefly outline the general duties of employers under the Health and Safety at Work etc. Act 1974.
13 What is the Health and Safety Commission?
14 What are the powers of health and safety inspectors?

Case study

For the second year running Mike Robins received a certificate for his department's safety record. He put a congratulatory memo on the notice board along with the award.

Later on he was chatting with one of the charge hands who criticised the memo. 'It seems to me that people are getting pretty fed up with all this pressure on safety. They know their stuff and they resent all these safety checks you keep giving them.'

Another chargehand joined them. 'I've had similar moans. Why don't we give it up for a while and see how it goes? They think you're after promotion and driving them too hard.'

1 How should the supervisor respond to this question?
2 Consider the chargehands' role in this case.

21 Welfare

The employee's position has improved beyond recognition over the past century and workers' welfare is now safeguarded in numerous ways by legislation. The supervisor, however, still plays an important part in ensuring that employees have adequate and comfortable surroundings at their work conducive to higher productivity. In addition many concerns offer employees extra benefits, and these are discussed in conclusion.

Legal requirements

As already mentioned in Chapter 20, there are two main sources of law which protect the employee: common law and statute law.

English law may also be considered from another aspect: *civil law* and *criminal law*.

A civil offence does not concern the community; it deals with the relationships between private individuals when redress for grievances is sought legally. The remedies are damages (payment of money) or an injunction (either forbidding or commanding some course of action).

A criminal offence is against the community and the police may take action even if the victim involved declines. The offender is punished by either imprisonment or fine.

Some offences are both criminal and civil wrongs. For example, an industrial injury may involve a breach of the Health and Safety at Work Act and also provide grounds for damages at *common law*. Under *common law* the employer has an obligation to provide safe working conditions which include the place of work, machinery and equipment. This obligation is also reinforced by the Health and Safety at Work Act.

Outline of legislation

Considerable legislation has been introduced in recent years to safeguard employees' interests and improve their general position. An outline of the main acts is given below, including those treated more fully in other chapters.

Contracts of employment: Employment Protection (Consolidation) Act 1978

This Act lays down provisions relating to contracts of employment previously contained in the Contracts of Employment Act 1972. The following requirements are placed on employers.

1 Give a written statement of the specified terms of employment including commencing date, rate of pay, intervals at which pay is given, hours of work, holiday entitlement and holiday pay, calculation of accrued holiday pay payable on the termination of employment, provisions for sick pay, period of notice, rights to belong or not to belong to a trade union, and rights where an agency shop or approved closed shop is applicable. The statement must also include the name of the person whom the employee may contact to seek redress of any grievance, the method of making such an application, and the sequence of steps he or she should consequently take.

2 Communicate to the employee within one month any alterations in the terms of employment.

3 Give an employee who has been employed for more than four weeks but less than two years at least one week's notice. If employment is over two years one additional week's notice must be given for each additional year of service up to a maximum of twelve weeks' notice for twelve years' service or more.

Wages Councils Act 1959

In a small and decreasing number of industries no adequate machinery exists to regulate wages; therefore the trend is for remuneration to fall below a reasonable level. In these circumstances the above Act empowers the Secretary of State to establish and operate Wages Councils for fixing the minimum remuneration in such industries where the Secretary considers that rates are below standard. A Council is composed of equal numbers of employers and employees in the appropriate industry.

A Council is restricted to regulating pay for adults over twenty-one years, and it may only lay down a single minimum hourly rate for all workers in an industry plus overtime rates, rates of permitted reductions for accommodation and special rules for pieceworkers.

The Department of Employment's Wages Inspectorate assists in interpreting the wages regulation orders for employers and employees and ensures that the employers comply with the orders.

Truck Acts 1831, 1837, 1896 and 1940

These Acts protect employees against bad practices connected with the payment of wages such as paying in kind instead of in cash and forcing employees to spend their money in a particular shop owned by the employer. The Act states the following:

'(*a*)   A contract is void if it states that a manual worker is to be paid in any form other than cash (but *see* Payment of Wages Act below).

(*b*)   Manual workers must be free to spend their money where and how they choose.

(*c*)   No deductions are allowed to be made from wages except those legally enforceable.

(*d*) An employer must not withhold an advance, or charge for granting it, in those circumstances where it is customary for workers to receive a "sub" before the wages are actually due.'

The Payment of Wages Act 1960 was introduced to bring the Truck Acts in line with modern practice. Employers are permitted to pay wages in the following ways, provided written agreement is obtained from employees.

1   Payment into a bank account.
2   Payment by postal order or money order.
3   Payment by cheque.

National Insurance Act 1965 and Social Security Pensions Act 1975

Payment of regular weekly contributions to the national insurance scheme provides a comprehensive insurance against sickness, unemployment, old age, maternity, widowhood, orphanhood and death. The insurance benefits are comparatively small (insurance companies still have adequate opportunities to supplement the payments through private schemes). A married man's contribution includes coverage for his wife and children for certain benefits.

Under the Social Security Pensions Act 1975, retirement, widows' and invalidity pensions will be made up of two parts: basic pension and an additional pension. Both parts are paid for by national insurance contributions. Employees who are covered by an occupational pension scheme may be contracted out of the additional part of the retirement and widows' pension. In this case insurance contributions will be reduced for both employers and employees.

The Employment Acts 1980, 1982 and 1988

These Acts were designed to restore balance in employment legislation. They are involved and need careful study. The many facets covered include trade union ballots, codes of practice, exclusion from trade union membership, unfair dismissal, maternity rights, protection for non-unionists, picketing and industrial action, and union members' rights.

National Insurance (Industrial Injuries) Act 1965

An employee who is injured at work may claim damages from the employer if the employer is negligent, that is according to the interpretation of the word under the tort of negligence and provided negligence was the cause of the accident.

Often the employer is not to blame for the accident, therefore the employee cannot make a claim and possible hardship may result through loss of wages. These cases were covered under the Workmen's Compensation Acts 1890, but they were inadequate and were eventually replaced by the Industrial Injuries Scheme in 1946 which operated from 1948 and was consolidated in 1965. The scheme provides cash benefits for those who are injured at work or suffering with one of the prescribed industrial diseases and are unable to work or are disabled. Benefits also are paid to widows and certain other dependants of the casualty. In general it is a compulsory scheme for all employees except for self-employed and non-employed people.

The rates of contribution and benefits are constantly changing. Current figures are obtainable from the local offices of the Ministries concerned and any queries can be settled at the same source.

Law Reform (Personal Injuries) Act 1948

At one time employers could avoid the general rule that they were liable for any tort (civil wrong) committed by an employee if the injuries to an employee were caused by a fellow employee. This was known as the 'rule of common employment'.

Eventually the Employers' Liability Act was passed in 1880 which limited this right in particular circumstances. In 1948 the right was completely abolished by the Law Reform (Personal Injuries) Act. An employer can no longer use 'common employment' as a defence if sued by an employee for personal injuries caused by a fellow employee. Moreover, the Act makes void any provision in a contract of service or apprenticeship which excludes or limits an employer's liability in respect of personal injuries caused by another employee.

In certain circumstances an injured person may claim damages from the employer and from the Industrial Injuries Scheme. To prevent this form of double compensation the Law Reform (Personal Injuries) Act states that one half of any industrial injury benefits received for five years from date of injury must be taken into account against any earnings loss or profits arising from the injuries if actions for damages for personal injuries are undertaken.

Redundancy payments: Employment Protection (Consolidation) Act 1978

Those employees who are dismissed because of redundancy may claim a lump sum compensation called a redundancy payment. In certain circumstances employees who are laid off or are placed on short-time for a substantial period may also claim. The lump sum is related to pay, length of service and age of employee.

A Redundancy Fund was established by the original Redundancy Payments Act 1965. Contributions collected with the employer's National Insurance contribution are paid into the Fund which provides a refund to employers who may claim a rebate of part of the cost. The rebate varies from two-thirds to a little over three-quarters. The industrial tribunals established under the Industrial Training Act 1964 hear any dispute about entitlement to redundancy payments or rebates from the Fund.

Certain employees are not eligible. Those who are must have at least 104 weeks' continuous employment with their employer after the age of eighteen years. Any service before the employee's eighteenth birthday cannot be included. The term redundancy under the Act is interpreted to mean where the whole or main reason for the employee's dismissal is because the employer's labour requirements have diminished or ceased. An employee who either does not receive a payment or believes he or she has received an insufficient amount should approach the employer – through the union representative if appropriate. In the event of a disagreement the employee should ask for the necessary application form at the nearest employment office or jobcentre. If the employer is insolvent and cannot pay, the employee should approach the Department of Employment. Arrangements for payment are then made through the Fund and the Ministry claims from the employer as a non-preferential unsecured creditor.

Industrial Training Act 1964

The Act established Training Boards for each industry to plan, supervise and advise on training schemes and control standards (*see* Chapter 18). Only seven Boards now remain.

Factories Act 1961

This Act covers a wide range of general working conditions. The main sections are as follows.

1 *Health* Regulations are laid down concerning cleanliness, overcrowding, ventilation, temperature, lighting, drainage of floors, sanitary accommodation, meals in certain dangerous trades, underground rooms, lifting excessive weights and lead processes.

2 *Safety* Regulations include such topics as fencing, transmission machinery, new machines, hoists or lifts, chains, ropes, lifting tackle and cranes, construction of floors, safe means of access and place of work, cleaning machinery, precautions against gassing, explosions of flammable

dust or gas, steam boilers, air receivers, fire, protection of eyes, training of young persons and notification of accidents and dangerous occurrences.

3 *Welfare* This covers such topics as drinking water, washing facilities, accommodation for clothing, facilities for sitting and first aid.

There are a number of welfare orders which require special facilities for workers in particular jobs where there is a hazard to the skin or where the process is known to be dirty. These orders generally enforce the provision of protective clothing, first-aid facilities, washing facilities to a higher standard than normal, dining rooms, special accommodation for clothing, baths and drinking water.

4 *Employment of women and young persons* Topics included are normal hours of work, overtime, employment outside the factory, prohibition of sundry employment, holidays, two-shift system, van boys and errand boys, exceptions and certificates of fitness.

Offices, Shops, and Railway Premises Act 1963

This extensive Act applies to all offices and shops and to most railway buildings near the permanent way. General requirements include registration of premises and a number of regulations for such aspects as cleanliness, overcrowding, temperature, ventilation, lighting, sanitary conveniences, washing facilities, drinking water, accommodation for clothing, seating arrangements, seats for sedentary workers, eating facilities, floors, passages, stairs, fencing of exposed parts of machinery, cleaning of machinery, training and supervision of persons working at dangerous machines, prohibition of heavy work and first aid.

The Act also ensures that reasonable fire precautions are taken in premises. Buildings that possess a greater potential fire hazard must be inspected by an expert who advises on the precautions to be adopted and issues a fire certificate which states certain restrictions depending on the fire hazard.

Enforcement of the Act is now carried out under the provisions of the Health and Safety at Work etc. Act 1974 (*see* below and Chapter 20).

Equal Pay Act 1970

This Act provides that a woman doing the same or broadly similar work to a man in the same employment qualifies for equal pay and conditions of employment. A similar provision applies if she is in a job which may differ from those of men but is considered to be of equal value through the findings of job evaluation. Any disagreements may be referred to an industrial tribunal for a decision.

Race Relations Act 1976

This Act replaced the 1965 and 1968 Acts and makes unlawful any discrimination on the grounds of colour, race, or ethnic or national origin. It applies to employment and the provision of goods, facilities and services. Individuals who feel they have been discriminated against in employment may complain to an industrial tribunal.

The Act established the Commission for Racial Equality which replaced the Race Relations Board. The Commission is responsible for promoting the objectives of the Act, for investigating discriminatory practices and for advising the government on measures to improve the legislation. It also has the power to assist individual complainants.

Health and Safety at Work etc. Act 1974

All people at work except domestic servants in private households are covered in this Act. It is an enabling Act imposing a general duty of care on most people associated with work activities. The Act is capable of being changed, expanded and adapted to cope with risks and problems which may arise in the future. The Act's aims, approach and general provisions are dealt with in Chapter 20.

Employment Protection Act 1975

This Act promotes the improvement of industrial relations through the Advisory, Conciliation and Arbitration Service and encourages the extension of collective bargaining. New rights and greater job security which were given to employees are now contained in the Employment Protection (Consolidation) Act 1978 (*see* Chapter 19 and below).

Trade Union and Labour Relations Act 1974

This Act established for employees (with certain exceptions) the right not to be dismissed unfairly. These provisions are now contained in the Employment Protection (Consolidation) Act 1978. If employees think they have been unfairly dismissed they may seek a remedy by applying to an industrial tribunal (*see* Chapter 17).

Employment Protection (Consolidation) Act 1978

This Act brings together under one enactment the provisions on individual employment rights previously covered in other Acts: Trade Union and Labour Relations Act 1974, Contracts of Employment Act 1972, Redundancy Payments Act 1965 and the Employment Protection Act 1975. The rights conferred in those Acts are in no way altered, nor are the corresponding obligations on employers.

The vast majority of sections and schedules which have been consolidated from the earlier Acts mentioned are repealed with some exceptions. Careful inspection of the various Acts is essential to ensure where each provision is now located.

Sex Discrimination Act 1975

Discrimination in employment on the grounds of sex or marriage is prohibited under this Act. Any discrimination regarding training, promotion, short-time working or dismissal is also unlawful. More details are given in Chapter 17.

Employers' Liability (Compulsory Insurance) Act 1969

Section 1 of the Act states that all employers shall insure, and maintain insurance, under one or more approved policies with an authorised insurer or insurers against bodily injury or disease sustained by their employees arising out of and in the course of their employment in Great Britain.

A copy of the certificate of insurance should be displayed at all places of business and in a prominent position where it can easily be seen and read.

Data Protection Act 1984

This complex Act protects the individual whose personal data is held in a computer or on microfiche where electronic means are used for retrieval. Traditional files are excluded.

An employer is termed a 'data user' if he or she holds data which is part of an accumulation of data for processing or intended for processing. Processing is described as amending, augmenting, erasing, rearranging or extracting information.

Data users must conform to the basic data protection principles outlined in the first schedule of the Act. Briefly these state that data must be obtained and processed fairly and lawfully; held for only one or more specified and lawful purposes, not used or disclosed in any way other than for the purpose intended; must be adequate, relevant and not excessive, considering the purpose; must be accurate and up-dated; erased when it is no longer necessary for the purpose intended; and held under appropriate security measures.

An individual is entitled to know if personal data is held; to have access; and to have such data corrected or erased where appropriate.

Wages Act 1986

Deductions from pay are clarified in the Act which applies to employers and self-employed contractors engaged by an employer.

The fundamental rules are:

1 money must not be deducted from pay due to an employee
2 the employee cannot be forced to pay back any money from his or her pay.

There are exceptions:

1 Statutory deductions such as income tax and national insurance.
2 Payments to third parties, for example a court order to pay off a fine.
3 Employee requests such as union subscriptions, sports club fees, or an external pension fund. The request must be in writing before deductions.
4 Agreed deductions for, say, spoilt work, absenteeism or lateness. The agreement must be in writing (before deductions) or stated in the contract of employment. A written note must be handed to the employee who should sign a receipt.
5 Accidental over-payment of wages or expenses may be deducted from later pay.

Additional rules protect employees in retailing. Included are a variety of occupations such as bank tellers, petrol station attendants, cashiers, milkmen, and bus conductors.

Employment Liability (Defective Equipment) Act 1969

An employer is considered (deemed) to be negligent if an employee dies or is physically injured due to a defect in plant or equipment supplied at work.

Should employers pass responsibility back to a manufacturer or supplier of the defective product that is a matter for them. This strict liability for death or physical injury is extended to the community in the Consumer Protection Act 1987.

Social responsibilities of management

Working conditions

In addition to the legal requirements under the various Acts mentioned above the supervisor has a social obligation to insist on adequate working conditions and to maintain a satisfactory standard. The main aspects which require special attention are now discussed.

Cleanliness

The workplace should be kept clean by arranging for daily removal of all rubbish and dirt and regular floor cleaning at least every week. Constant checks are needed to maintain a reasonably clean establishment. A programme for redecoration and general cleaning of walls and ceilings should be drawn up.

Overcrowding and ventilation

There must be at least 11.3 cu m of space for each employee in the workshop. The calculation should be based upon the capacity of the factory between the floor and a height of 3 m.

Adequate ventilation is also very important to ensure the circulation of fresh air. Tests have shown that high temperature and polluted air have an adverse effect on physical work. The harmful effects on health when no attempt is made to remove dust, fumes and other impurities from the air are well known. The installation of air conditioning is often worth while because clean air of the correct temperature and humidity encourages better work and improved output.

Layout is also important: subjecting an employee to a draught or allowing an operator to work in surroundings where rapid temperature changes are occurring is inviting lower effectiveness. The risk of accidents and sickness is also increased. Many other factors have to be considered depending upon the work situation. For example, in a foundary some employees will perspire excessively and require salt tablets to replace the loss.

Temperature and humidity

The human body is influenced by the surrounding temperature and the humidity of the atmosphere. These two interacting factors must be considered together because the heat conductivity of air rises as the moisture content increases. In cold humid conditions, therefore, the body may lose heat rapidly and the air would feel colder than its actual temperature. A further factor in these conditions is that high humidity will retard the evaporation of perspiration in which case the cooling process of the body is upset. Thus, warm humid air may feel warmer than the actual temperature.

These facts will explain why the temperature in the workplace may be adequate but employees may still complain of discomfort. A reasonable temperature for the workplace should be not less than 15°C (60°F). Particular temperatures are recommended for some occupations and where a major part of the work is carried out in the sitting position this temperature should be reached by the end of the first hour. Many wet processes must be taken into consideration as these naturally increase the humidity of the atmosphere. Adequate drainage is necessary to minimise this effect.

Lighting

The problem of lighting is particularly involved and is often neglected in industry. A thorough knowledge of the behaviour of the human eye and the psychological problems connected with vision is needed before adequate lighting conditions can be determined. Such factors as intensity, wave length and distribution of light are very important and to some extent they interact with each other. The services of a lighting specialist are essential, considering the effects on morale and production when poor illumination of the work-place is endured. The employee suffers eye fatigue and discomfort which in turn induces irritability. These tensions may cause accidents and errors and output will be affected. On the other hand, good lighting has a stimulating effect on individuals. This effect is similar to the change in feeling experienced on a sunny day compared with a dull rainy day.

Some of the common faults in lighting are:

1 flickering light
2 intensity too low
3 uneven distribution over the whole visual field
4 poor reflecting qualities of walls
5 bright spots outside the working area which tend to attract the eyes away from the working area
6 glare and intermittent glare from various highly reflective surfaces.

An indication of lighting intensity for various parts of the factory as recommended by the Illuminating Engineering Society is given below.

200.2 lx: for corridors, gangways, loading bays, general stores and warehouses.
430.6 lx: for general assembly work and reading large print.
861.1 lx: for close assembly work, reading small print, and drawings.
1076.4 lx: for very fine work.

These rough guides form only part of the over-all lighting conditions as already stressed. Maintenance of lighting is essential because the light intensity of lamps is considerably reduced after being in operation for some time and coatings of dirt also impair the efficiency of lighting units.

Seating requirements

Although there is a legal obligation to provide seating facilities where a reasonable opportunity to be seated exists and where a large portion of the work can be done sitting down, the importance of seating requirements is often overlooked.

According to the medical profession standing for long periods is tiring and induces tension. Standing causes the muscles of the thighs and calves to contract to keep the body upright, thus energy is used for this purpose. Specialists also are of the opinion that frequent position changes such as alternate sitting and standing are beneficial as excessive tiredness is avoided.

Another important factor is the design of the seat. The purpose of the seat is to support the body in such a way that a stable posture is maintained while relaxing muscles which are not used at work. An ergonomically designed seat eliminates discomfort due to unnecessary pressure on the underside of the thighs which is recognised often by 'pins and needles'. Efficient design also allows for varying the position so that the body weight may be shifted during a work period without losing support.

Lavatories and washrooms

The bare minimum requirements are laid down in s. 7 of the Factories Act and s. 9 of the Offices, Shops, and Railway Premises Act. To provide pleasant and agreeable amenities, however, modern practice is more demanding. For example, two wash-basins instead of one are recommended for every 20 employees, and three instead of two for 21–40 employees. The ratio may be applied to other areas such as cloakroom and toilet facilities.

Cloakrooms, etc.

Although provisions for cloakrooms, changing rooms and showers are mentioned in various Acts, there is an element of interpretation involved because such terms as 'suitable' and 'adequate' are quoted. Some companies, for example, provide baths where people are engaged in hot or dirty work although they are not legally required to.

Another example of interpretation concerns the term 'adequate' for clothing accommodation. A High Court decision stated that although there was no absolute obligation to keep clothing safe, the risk of theft had to be considered when deciding whether accommodation was adequate. The Factory Inspectorate gives the following six points as being essential for satisfactory clothing accommodation.

- Adequate precautions against theft
- Adequate space for changing clothes and footwear
- Adequate ventilation and lighting
- A separate peg or locker displaying the name or works number for each operator
- Facilities for drying outdoor clothing and overalls worn in wet processes
- A high standard of cleanliness

Noise

Although many employees regard noise only as a nuisance, in fact it is now recognised as a major health hazard. Excessive noise can cause long-term damage to health and it accelerates the normal loss of hearing process through age.

Research findings indicate that prolonged exposure to noise of more than 90 decibels is harmful and when levels above 100 decibels are reached, extensive and permanent damage to hearing can occur. Inexpensive instruments are available to measure the noise level.

The two main ways of reducing noise levels are to deal with it at source or to wear ear defenders. Modifications to equipment such as machine tools, generators and compressors are possible by fitting sound proof shields, baffles or absorbent-lined compartments. The main types of ear defenders are ear plugs, ear valves and the ear muff. They can reduce the level by as much as 50 decibels.

The Inspectorate's code of practice gives a limit of 90 decibels. Where machines exceed this level they should be masked, prominent warning notices should be displayed and entrance to such areas controlled, and ear defenders must be worn. The code proposes a number of general methods of control and measures for reducing exposure duration are suggested. These include: rearranging work so that part is done in a quiet place, there is job rotation, and the use of quiet restrooms.

Benefits

Most concerns offer benefits which vary considerably from company to company. In addition, unofficial benefits or 'perks' are often received. Employees tend to take these for granted with or without the knowledge of management. Some examples are petrol from the company's pump, raw materials, components, stationery and the use of machines and equipment for private purposes. Sometimes the traffic in these 'perks' is unbelievably high and loss to the company amounts to very large sums of money.

Official fringe benefits may be divided into the following groups.

1 *Social facilities* A wide range of social and recreational facilities is offered in the form of dining rooms, sports clubs, social clubs, outings and entertainments.

2 *Financial assistance* Various forms of assistance are available, covering items such as further education, loans for house purchase, discount on purchases of certain products and reduced prices for company products.

3 *Insurance schemes* Various insurance schemes to cover retirement, sickness and injury are still operated by concerns, but some schemes have been superseded by the National Insurance Scheme described above.

4 *Payment for non-working time* Within this category there are various national agreements and legislation which cover holiday pay including bank holidays. Allowances for part-time day further education, various concessions for visiting sick relatives, funerals, visits to arrange house purchase and for other legal problems are often given.

5 *General benefits* General awards include gifts for long service, bonuses, free luncheon vouchers and anniversary payments which are not directly connected with employee output.

Questions

1 Discuss the question of 'perks' or unofficial benefits.
2 Outline some of the benefits offered to employees under various schemes of welfare.
3 Explain how the law protects the employee.
4 Give a general outline of the Factories Act 1961.
5 What statutory regulations exist concerning wages and conditions of service?
6 Explain the legislation on national insurance.
7 To what extent would you consider that working conditions affect the attitude of employees towards management?
8 Do you think there is any connection between the quality of working conditions and the quality of work in a factory?
9 Is it possible for the supervisor to promote the health of subordinates?
10 If the social and recreational facilities are poorly supported in a concern, what do you think are the likely causes?
11 Outline the legislation which provides for compensation of operators in the event of industrial injury.

Case study 1

Amy Thomas, in the Accounts office, was very agitated when she approached her supervisor, Andrew Ralton. 'I have just seen Michael, the new computer operator, going through my coat pockets. When he saw me he left hurriedly. What are you going to do about it?'

Andrew calmed her down and suggested they should check to see if anything was missing. They walked over to the coat rack at the end of the office. Amy examined her pockets and pulled out a lighter. 'This isn't mine!' she declared. 'That's Ron's, I'd recognise it anywhere!'

They checked and Ron remembered it was in his raincoat pocket. Going through his raincoat pockets he pulled out a bunch of keys. 'These aren't mine but my cigarette case is missing.'

It took about fifteen minutes to sort out the contents of the coat pockets as others were also involved. Andrew tackled Michael who strongly denied going through Amy's pockets. 'Amy's got it in for me because I'm a faster worker than she is. She doesn't like it because I won't take breaks. She won't talk to me in the office now, not even to say good morning. She probably did it herself to get me the sack,' Michael declared.

How should the supervisor proceed now?

Case study 2

It was one month before the Christmas party and Terry remembered clearly last year's fiasco when he had agreed to a disco. The older employees had complained they could not hear themselves talk because of the noise. The volume was turned up and down repeatedly.

At the meeting the older members asserted they would not support another disco party. The younger members insisted on a disco. There were insufficient numbers for two parties which would defeat the object anyway.

How could this problem be resolved to satisfy both groups?

Part II: suggested projects

1 Attempt an assessment of morale in your concern.
(a) List all the possible factors which affect morale and investigate each one.
(b) Draw up a summary of your findings and suggest constructive methods for improving the situation.
2 Write an account of five human problems on the shop floor from your own experience.
Each account should include your personal observations, the opinions of other colleagues wherever possible, the causes of the problem, the actual situation as it arises, the way it is solved, and any after-effects.
Attempt to summarise your work and furnish suitable conclusions.
3 Investigate the operation of the grape-vine in your concern. Classify the rumours, sources and accuracy, and estimate the effects.
Do *not* attempt to trace the *human chain* back to the original source of information.
After an adequate number of cases has been established, attempt to draw conclusions from your work.
4 Carry out a continuous survey for about four months to ascertain the number of occasions when problems or trouble-spots arise through a break-down in communication.
Classify the causes (such as lack of information, misunderstandings) and summarise the findings, making suitable recommendations.
5 If the concern's personnel policy is publicised, investigate the effectiveness of its operation in practice.
Choose a group and study each individual's reactions and problems within the province of personnel policy.
Tabulate and explain your findings with a view to constructively criticising the policy, its interpretation by management and the reactions of employees.
6 Prepare and maintain a record of negotiations between management and the trade union in your concern. Include such aspects as date, subject, negotiations, results and follow up.

Attempt to assess the effectiveness of the talks and the possible causes of disagreements when they arise.

7   Maintain a record of negotiations between yourself and the shop steward. The report should include all relevant details of the talks and each disagreement or problem should be amplified to show the possible causes and the opinions of both sides.

Prepare a summary of your conclusions, indicating some of the basic problems or difficulties encountered and how you would overcome them if given the opportunity.

8   Attempt to assess the importance of welfare in your company. Make notes on individuals' reactions to welfare facilities, their complaints concerning welfare, whether schemes are supported and the general attitude towards welfare.

Write a comprehensive report and include your recommendations.

9   Examine the jobs of five employees who have the reputation of being lazy. Consider whether or not they would benefit if the jobs were enriched.

10   Study the job structures in your section and attempt to enrich them.

Part Three   Controlling the Work

22   The nature of control

Importance of control

The term 'control' has many meanings: power of directing, ability to restrain, means of restraint, standard of comparison for checking inferences deduced from experiment, or as a verb to dominate and to regulate. Any term which has a variety of meanings leads to confusion in practice unless the meaning intended is carefully detailed. Control as applied to business may be defined as the direction of activities to achieve an objective according to predetermined plans and standards.

A basic control procedure

The ability to control effectively requires a sound understanding of certain logical steps which form a basic procedure. Three steps are essential to ensure that everything has occurred in accordance with the plan. The basic procedure is to:

1   set standards
2   check performance
3   correct deviations.

This simplification of procedure does not indicate the logical sequence involved in a control cycle for Step 2, 'check performance', covers the whole process of feedback of information and comparison of the actual with the standard. The procedure for starting a machine forms a simple example below and is called a closed-loop system. Omitting feedback in any system is called an open-loop system.

Cycle	Observation
Instruction and action:	Press starter button
Feedback of effect:	Machine refuses to start

Information: Electric power switch is off
Adjustment: Switch on power
Instruction: Press starter button

This concept of a control cycle as applied to starting a machine is illustrated in Fig. 22.1 which should be studied carefully. Cycles of action are represented as loops. A fault is corrected by means of the *transient loop*, and the *terminal loop* is only completed when the action taken to start the machine is successful, i.e. only one terminal loop can be made for each event. This means that after one loop is completed to start the machine the next terminal loop may be to feed the machine and the next to switch it off. The transient loop, however, must be repeated in the same sequence until the action is successful, that is until the machine is finally started.

Under normal conditions a transient loop must be followed by a terminal loop before a stimulus (instruction) is satisfied. If an action fails to achieve its purpose, a sequence of five steps is necessary. First, the transient loop operates through three stages:

1   feedback, which notifies the controller of the failure
2   information, which provides a reason for the failure
3   adjustment, which should rectify the fault

Second, the terminal loop must follow by:

4   repeating the original instruction
5   feedback, which notifies the controller that the desired effect is achieved.

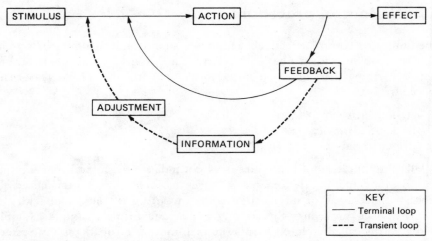

Fig. 22.1 *Terminal and transient loops in control*

An effective control cycle must contain a *transient* loop to provide: 1 feedback (notify failure to achieve desired result); 2 information (cause of failure); 3 adjustment (rectify fault). This is repeated until the *terminal* loop is successful, providing: (*a*) action (repeat instruction); (*b*) feedback (notify success)

If the transient loop is unsuccessful, the five steps are repeated until the terminal loop is completed.

The waste of time and frustration may be considerable when transient loops continually occur through lack of adequate control such as faulty feedback of information and ill-considered adjustments.

It must be appreciated that control is essentially a *continuous process of adjustment* to situations like steering a vehicle which is constantly deviating from a straight course.

This aspect of control is illustrated diagrammatically in Fig. 22.2. The input factors are those variables which may be altered by the controller when corrections are necessary. These factors – when properly manipulated – can alter the output variables according to need in the particular circumstances. Take a simple example such as riding a bicycle. The input variables such as steering, rate of pedalling and use of brakes, are manipulated by the rider to adjust the output variables – direction and speed – according to desire and conditions.

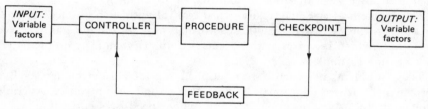

Fig. 22.2 *Basic control procedure*

Control is a continuous process of adjusting input variables in order to produce the desired output effects. These variable factors, or variables, are also termed 'parameters'

Control appraisal

From the three basic steps of control (set standards, check performance, correct deviations) a more elaborate appraisal of the organisation of production can be built up which is essential before any effective system of control can be applied. This appraisal may take the form of a number of control questions and these are listed below, together with the various functions which provide a means of answering them.

Control questions

1 Who is responsible for each section of the work and for doing the work? *Organisation plan-division of responsibility and delegation.*
2 What is the work content? *Job description.*
3 How is the work to be performed? *Method study.*

4   How long should the work take to perform? *Work measurement.*
5   Where should the work be performed? *Method study and layout.*
6   When should the work be performed? *Planning and scheduling.*
7   What is the cost of performing the work? *Accounts and costing.*
8   How is work performance regulated? *Human relations, motivation, cost reduction, progress.*
9   How is quality of work checked? *Quality control.*

These questions indicate the complexities of control as an aspect of production, its difficulties and the demands it makes on supervision and management.

Problems of control

Many problems arise in the final stage of correcting deviations. The ability to correct effectively depends upon knowledge, experience, imagination and judgment, all of which can be overshadowed by an unexpected occurrence such as a power cut, machine breakdown or an accident.

The problem of size may easily defeat control with such obstacles as feedback delay, the excessive growth of information flow, the general haze over operations which increases with size and complexity, human problems and lack of time to think.

These problems of control are multiplied considerably at higher levels of management where additional external factors and uncontrollable variables impede decision-making often at a time when speed is essential.

Criticism of any person who is controlling is exceptionally easy because immediately some form of action is taken the situation is changed, requiring further adjustments which may appear illogical or contradictory to someone not knowing all the facts. Constructive criticism is far more difficult.

Computerised control

In situations where imagination and judgment are not needed control may be programmed in a *computer system*. Properly adjusted this automatic control process is more efficient than human operation, but the risk of breakdown is evident.

An example is a machine that administers drugs to patients automatically. This computerised infusion pump controls blood pressure by monitoring and administering a drug through a drip in the blood stream. Results show that it consistently controls blood pressure better than a nurse operating a drip manually.

Realtime information

One advantage of computerised control is the use of realtime information:

data made available on the outcome of events as they occur. Many operations may be captured for realtime control. Examples are booking seats on aircraft, transmitting sales data in supermarkets to a central storage point to update stocks, and holiday reservations.

The benefits depend upon whether such information is of direct and crucial use. In some situations the correction procedure is long, therefore the expense is not worth while. In most business situations day-to-day controls are helped by realtime.

Prediction control

Feed-back control is fundamentally historical: indications of what *has* happened and correction required. Ideally more effective control is achieved if a 'feedforward system' explains what *will* happen if action is not taken. Understandably, accurate forecasting or prediction is difficult. A more accurate prediction is possible, however, by conducting forecasts repeatedly, updating each time and comparing results. Such future-directed control is much easier on a computer. Also PERT networks (explained later) use this concept.

Applications

Extreme cases such as weather forecasting for farmers (and alerting safety measures) highlight the hazardous nature of some events. More predictable situations are in daily use everywhere.

Examples fall mainly into two groups: effective and ineffective action. If a car driver ascends a hill he or she may consciously press the accelerator further to maintain a set speed. But a heavy lorry driver will be forced to change gear to climb the hill and lose speed. If the aim is to reach B from A with no imposed time limit then both actions are successful.

The concept

The idea is to analyse inputs (feedforward) – not outputs (feedback) – noting the interaction, and adjusting inputs before outputs occur. In some manufacturing processes prediction control is essential when any surges or changes occur within the process and are noticeable at the input stage. Thus adjustments to compensate can be made.

Although arguably feedback is involved in prediction systems there is a distinct difference. Information feedback occurs on the input side to make possible adjustments to input before output occurs. Feedback from output is still essential to verify results since there is no guarantee of complete success.

Briefly to operate prediction control the supervisor should:

1   identify the important input variables
2   construct a model to illustrate their interrelationships
3   collect data regularly on input and inject into the system
4   note the differences between planned and changed inputs
5   assess results and conduct further alteration to achieve success.

Quantitative control techniques

The term *management science* also covers these techniques. Their purpose is to aid planning, controlling and decision making by using complex formulae which provide appropriate data and models quickly in a suitable form. Among many the techniques examined here are:

- cybernetics
- operational research
- network analysis
- simulation.

Cybernetics

The study of communication and control mechanisms in machines and living creatures is known as cybernetics. The subject harbours a field of research with an enormous potential for improving the effectiveness of industry.

The science of cybernetics is complex and extensive. Briefly, the cybernetic attitude adopted towards industry accepts it as actually living or working as if it were living.

Considerable progress has been made since a group headed by Norbert Weiner, the American mathematician, called this science 'cybernetics' in 1947. This group of scientists had been working together for about five years on the problems of control. They realised that common ground existed between control systems in a number of different sciences. Thus, a number of eminent statisticians, mathematicians, biologists, sociologists, logicians, psychiatrists, engineers and other specialists commenced research with a common aim.

The engineers were particularly interested in applying this new science to automation and computer sciences and considerable progress has been made in this direction. The basic notions of cybernetics are outside the scope of this work, but additional reading on this subject – which will probably influence the future of industry – may be found in the book *Cybernetics and Management* by Stafford Beer.

The basic cybernetic model is similar to the open-system approach already described. The interrelationships in an organisation operate through communication networks which are self-regulating and cope with environmental changes. Thus homeostasis (or a stable condition) is achieved by reliable information feedback to control points that adjust automatically to changes.

If the system is deterministic – meaning changes in behaviour are completely predictable – there is no problem; typically temperature change and sales order movements. If behaviour is probabalistic – meaning involving estimates or possible changes – only trial and error will determine correct input/output in the system. An example is advertising a product and attempting to assess sales orders, or throwing dice once and attempting to determine the result.

Sometimes bionics is thought to be synonymous with cybernetics; together they have been compared with two sides of a coin. Bionics attempts to develop machines through biological design principles whereas cybernetics attempts to understand organisation through making analogies to machines.

Operational research

Although operational research is difficult to define accurately in the space allowed, it may be briefly termed the application of scientific analysis and careful reasoning to provide a quantitative basis for measuring possible courses of action, thus assisting management in decision making. There is no limit to its breadth of application in industry and as a general aid to decision making.

The term operational research (OR) was coined at about the beginning of World War II, when various specialists were grouped to study wartime operations such as setting up radar systems and fuse setting for depth charges. Since then a number of large concerns have introduced OR teams to study such problems as the optimum loading of machines, efficient use of staff, economic methods of transportation, stores congestion, effective maintenance schemes and optimum stock levels.

Today OR is applied throughout industry and other fields in many countries. OR societies are established and international conferences are held regularly. The approach is to use a basic planning procedure and apply sophisticated mathematical concepts and models which determine optimum courses of action. Such techniques as linear programming, queueing theory, critical path scheduling, replacement theory, and stock control theory demand specialists who usually are advisors. Also existing staff are often trained to operate certain OR techniques.

The main difficulties are finding (a) suitable staff with mathematical backgrounds and managerial experience to approach problems, and (b) high computer time. An inevitable problem is the X factor. This applies when some activities defy measurement through intangible or probabalistic situations and guesswork takes over.

Applications

OR may be applied in any complex situation such as involved sequential activities, bottle-necks, probability difficulties, choice of action, location queries, scheduling, optimum level requirements, economic quantities, determining priorities, and improving systems and procedures.

Many books are available which describe techniques and applications in detail.

Network analysis

This term covers a number of techniques to plan and control complex projects. Two typical forms are critical path method (CPM) and programme evaluation and review technique (PERT). In many ways they are similar and represent sequential relationships between activities by a network of lines and circles. These activities are coupled to show how the total time may be reduced to a minimum. Such optimum coupling is called the critical path.

CPM assumes an accurate time for an activity while PERT estimates the time. The former is used typically for large construction jobs; the latter applies to highly complex projects such as a space shuttle.

A basic network

Figure 22.3 is a simple illustration. Circles represent an event which is a significant point of time and marks the start and finish of an activity. Lines

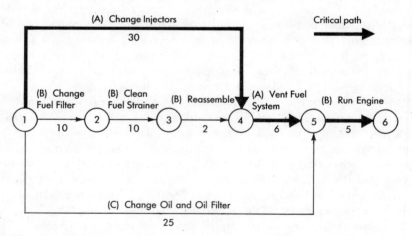

Fig. 22.3   *A simple network*

This part of a diesel engine service illustrates the critical path. (B) for example has 8 minutes spare time (float) which could be used to clean the air intake, plus extra time (6 mins) between events 4/5. The team (A, B and C) could obviously cope with more ancillary tasks

indicate activities which take time to complete, such as level site, mix concrete, pour, and level concrete.

In the diagram the minimum project time follows the critical path: 30 + 6 + 5 = 41 minutes (events 1–4–5–6). All these events are critical and to avoid delay must be completed on time. Spare time is called float; for example operator B uses 22 minutes (10 + 10 + 2) with 8 minutes to spare before event 4. Float values indicate where improvements lie.

Even drawing this simple arrangement immediately raises queries which may not have been obvious before: Is the team a good idea? How critical is the time to complete the whole service? How many other ancillary activities are involved? How many engines are being serviced?

Computerised networks

In practice many thousands of events and enormous amounts of data become difficult to handle. The use of computer graphics and appropriate programmes helps to solve the problems which may include rearranging sequences successfully in parallel and utilising float times.

In this way all the advantages of network analysis are covered. They include rapid presentation of data and graphics for immediate control and co-ordination; assisting in planning; identifying critical data immediately; and presenting data for calculating costs, times and resources required – further summarised as appropriate.

Simulation

This branch of OR has been used for many years. A model of a process or system is developed to predict reaction to input changes. The model is an attempt to resemble reality by using a quantitative or a mechanical approach to illustrate how the situation will be affected when inputs vary. Such predictions use probability theory to supply answers to the variables, therefore they are not precise, are incomplete and tend to be over-simplified.

A typical problem for simulation would be to predict the effects on sales volume of certain variables such as competition from Japan in the next two years, changes in world trade, and effects of new technologies. This complex model would be computerised as many runs are essential under different economic conditions. The basic procedure is:

1 define carefully the problem
2 assemble the data
3 develop a model
4 test in various ways
5 gather more appropriate data for experiments
6 run simulations
7 analyse output

8   re-run with appropriate changes
9   repeat testing and simulations as considered necessary.

Other applications are computer games, various training simulations for car driving, piloting aircraft and operating machines.

Statistical method

This may be defined as various ways of abstracting, classifying and comparing information for control purposes. The stages in a statistical investigation follow a set pattern:

1   define the reasons for the investigation
2   collect the information required
3   collate the data
4   analyse the data
5   interpret the results
6   use the information.

The use of statistics is essential for effective control. In such fields as stock control, production control, quality control, market research, sales, finance and most other functions a high degree of control is not possible without full use of statistical method.

Two sets of figures can only be accurately compared when they are measured in the same units (pounds sterling, kilograms, percentages, etc.) and are expressed in similar terms (fractions, decimals, etc.).

Analysis of information

The main aspects of interest may be obtained from any textbook on statistics. These include:

1   *graphical representation* – bar charts, pie charts, pictograms, graphs, trend charts, frequency distributions, histograms and frequency polygons;
2   *tabulation* – simple, complex and frequency tables; and
3   *numerical methods* – averages, dispersion and measures of skewness.

The use of modern calculators and computers simplifies analysis of data and interpretation of results, and to some extent dispenses with the need to study statistics in depth.

Establishing standards

Scientific control is not possible unless most of the variable factors involved in a process are measured and standards are established. Standards may be set for factors such as methods, performance, quality, forms, equipment, working conditions, grading individuals, work batches, layout, materials and tools.

Some supervisors are very reluctant to set standards, possibly because they fear that their estimate will be very inaccurate. This possible error is of no importance. The vital point is to provide some basis against which the actual figure may be measured so that the reason for the deviation may be ascertained and corrective action taken if necessary. If the actual figure is justified after investigation, the standard is revised and no harm is done – in fact the process of scientific control has commenced.

Naturally the burden on the supervisor of setting standards largely disappears where a work study specialist is available.

Questions

1 What is 'feedback' and why is it so important in connection with management control?
2 Define control and give an example of its meaning as applied to a machine.
3 What is meant by a terminal loop and a transient loop in control theory?
4 Outline a simple basic control procedure.
5 Discuss the basic steps which are necessary to set up control of a plan.
6 What is meant by control appraisal?
7 State the main aspects of control in a business and give a brief account of each one.
8 'Control may be said to be a continuous process of adjustment.' Discuss this statement.
9 'Control is an essential part of supervision.' Give a reasoned account of this statement.
10 Give a brief description of OR, mentioning the main techniques included in this term.
11 How can network analysis help the supervisor?
12 Outline the main applications of cybernetics.
13 Explain the term 'model' in simulation.
14 Describe some typical applications for OR.

Case study

Stephen Braddock was employed in a large departmental shop as the store detective. While in the cosmetics section he overheard two women talking about a lipstick one had just bought. '. . . and what do you think? She gave me change for a ten pound note instead of a fiver!'

He contacted the supervisor, Jill, and explained. At the end of the day Jill checked the till. The takings agreed with the tally roll.

1   What would you do about this situation?
2   Consider Jill's action related to the possible explanations.

23 Introduction to work study

The function of work study

Britain has suffered severe economic setbacks during the last half century partly because of the inability of large groups of employers and employees to recognise the importance of work study in productivity drives. The reasons and excuses for this oversight, such as complacency, lack of information, resistance from trade unions, suspicion of managements' intentions, are incidental.

Work study now is generally recognised as an essential specialised function to increase productivity and maintain an effective business. No company can afford to ignore work study today in the face of swiftly increasing competition from other countries, some of whom are already far advanced in this field.

Admittedly management must bear the responsibility of appreciating the situation and taking appropriate steps such as setting up a work study department, using an industrial consultant or training employees in work study according to the size of the company and circumstances. The supervisor, however, still remains at the critical position between employees and management. Unless he or she is genuinely convinced of the vital need for work study and is prepared to support the specialist, most of the improvements suggested will be neutralised through lack of support from employees.

Once employees can be persuaded to change their routine and try out new proposals, the advantages are soon appreciated and accepted. The barriers of suspicion and resistance to change can be removed by the supervisor who is convinced of the need for work study and imparts enthusiasm to the employees. The supervisor must also possess sufficient knowledge of the subject to apply it and explain the purposes of each technique adequately.

Definition of work study

Work study may be broadly described as a scientific study of any form of work. It involves the study of such factors as people, machines, equipment, tools, materials and layout with a view to increasing productivity by improving the effectiveness of each factor involved.

Cruder forms of work study naturally commenced at a time when human beings first used their brain to reason out a better way of performing a task such as trapping an animal for food. Today work study is highly sophisticated and continually expanding into a number of techniques which involve complex scientific calculations and the use of an electronic computer. All these modern techniques are not concerned with increasing the speed of processes. They are aimed at locating the optimum utilisation of individuals, machines, processes, materials, equipment, space and any other factors which are involved in the particular work under investigation.

The usual interpretation of the phrase 'optimum utilisation of individuals' is that people must work harder to increase productivity. This must be expected not only because people confuse the word *optimum*, the best, with *maximum*, the greatest, but also because it is not unusual to see numbers of employees idle – often through no fault of their own – while others are working well beyond a normal rate. The fact remains that forcing people beyond a natural or normal rate of working under supervision does not largely increase output. The aim – as the word *optimum* implies – is to create the most favourable utilisation of individuals which includes minimising fatigue and ensuring that all concerned perform a normal day's work.

Far greater savings are possible by improvement of methods, more detailed planning and control of work and effective utilisation of machines and other facilities than by driving employees at too high a rate.

The definition of work study by the British Standards Institution is:

A generic term for those techniques, particularly method study and work measurement, which are used in the examination of human work in all its contexts and which lead systematically to the investigation of all the factors which affect the efficiency and economy of the situation being reviewed in order to effect improvement.

The aims of work study

1 The most effective use of economic resources available to the concern, i.e. people, machines, space, equipment and capital.
2 A more even spread of work among employees.
3 Improved standard procedure for more effective control.
4 Improved planning by the provision of standard times and procedures.
5 Fairer wages schemes through the careful assessment of job values.
6 A more contented work force. The streamlining of production should eliminate many sources of frustration and tension, provided that management does not neglect the human element when introducing changes.
7 Increased productivity. This should help to bring economic benefits both to the concern and to the community as a whole.

The scope of work study

For the purpose of explanation only work study is divided into two main categories:

1   *Method study*   To find better ways of performing jobs with available facilities.

2   *Work measurement*   To determine the time a proficient operator takes to perform a specified job, based upon a given level of performance.

In practice the two categories are closely integrated but generally method study comes first, followed by work measurement which is based upon the revised method. Often the practice of measuring the work reveals further improvements which are incorporated in the standard method originally devised.

The field of work study is expanding continually and is resulting in some degree of overlap in new terms and techniques as they emerge from the study of various aspects of the function. For example, there are many terms meaning more or less the same as work study, such as production engineering, organisation and methods, methods engineering and operational research.

The function of work study as a service department has broadened from the study of work on the shop floor to include the study of a vast range of managerial activities. This critical, analytical and scientific approach to problems is now applied to: new projects, all main and sub-functions within the organisation, the organisation itself, and all managerial activities with particular emphasis on planning, control and general and operational policies.

The diagram in Fig. 23.1 attempts to show the modern extent of work study and to indicate its complex developments with overlapping of techniques and terms.

Attitudes to work study

The work study practitioner

The supervisor should possess some knowledge of the qualities of a good work study practitioner and what he or she hopes to achieve. The object is not to be critical of the practitioner's shortcomings but to assist in achieving the purpose which, like all specialists, is to help the supervisor and the employees.

The work study practitioner's reputation rests entirely with the supervisor and subordinates – they can make the proposals work well or ruin them – and most practitioners are aware of this fact.

Inevitably he or she needs the supervisor's help and the assistance and suggestions of employees. Any supervisor who deliberately forestalls and attempts to create the wrong atmosphere between the practitioner and employees is hindering both parties and openly displaying ignorance and conceit.

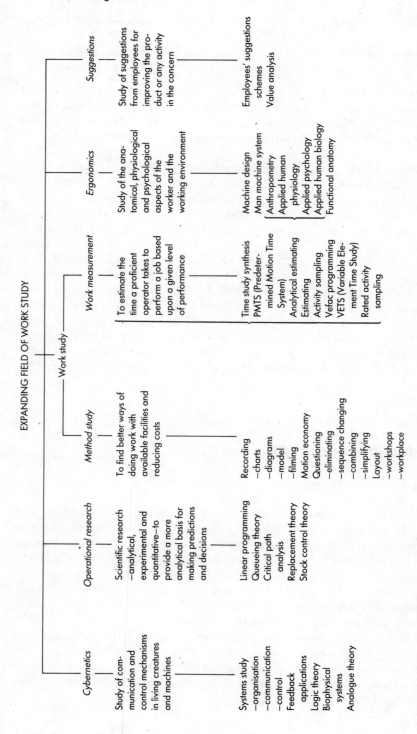

EXPANDING FIELD OF WORK STUDY

Work study

Cybernetics

Study of communication and control mechanisms in living creatures and machines

Systems study
 —organisation
 —communication
 —control
Feedback applications
Logic theory
Biophysical systems
Analogue theory

Operational research

Scientific research —analytical, experimental and quantitative—to provide a more analytical basis for making predictions and decisions

Linear programming
Queueing theory
Critical path analysis
Replacement theory
Stock control theory

Method study

To find better ways of doing work with available facilities and reducing costs

Recording
 —charts
 —diagrams
 —model
 —filming
Motion economy
Questioning
 —eliminating
 —sequence changing
 —combining
 —simplifying
Layout
 —workshops
 —workplace

Work measurement

To estimate the time a proficient operator takes to perform a job based upon a given level of performance

Time study synthesis
PMTS (Predetermined Motion Time System)
Analytical estimating
Estimating
Activity sampling
Vefac programming
VETS (Variable Element Time Study)
Rated activity sampling

Ergonomics

Study of the anatomical, physiological and psychological aspects of the worker and the working environment

Machine design
Man machine system
Anthropometry
Applied human physiology
Applied psychology
Applied human biology
Functional anatomy

Suggestions

Study of suggestions from employees for improving the product or any activity in the concern

Employees' suggestions schemes
Value analysis

Fig. 23.1 *Expanding field of work study*

This chart indicates not only the modern extent of work study, but also the complexity of its development in various directions

The individual and work study

Unfortunately there is an inherent belief, whether people are managers, supervisors or employees, that any suggested change in the way they (or even their subordinates) perform their work is a direct reflection on their own ability. This natural resistance can be overcome by sound explanations of the need for improvements so that people realise that work study is only an extension of the specialist function, is very time-consuming and is not a personal criticism of their methods.

Redundancy and wages are two problems which management must be prepared to face squarely if the recommended changes are to be successful. Guarantees that employees will be absorbed into other jobs and retrained or planned reduction of numbers through normal labour turnover are essential if employee co-operation is to be achieved. The wages system also needs reconsideration on matters such as incentives and – if productivity is improved – the employees' share of savings. Solutions must be acceptable otherwise fresh problems will emerge and more than offset the improvements.

The full support of employees is essential in work study. Management must provide information and guarantees while supervision must create the desirable atmosphere and achieve co-operation from operators.

The supervisor and work study

The results of work study provide the supervisor with improved standard procedures, standard methods of performing jobs and established performance times for operations. All this is vital information for purposes of planning and control which, with intelligent application by supervisors and managers, should improve productivity.

Whether the improvement in productivity will reach the targets set by management and the work study specialists depends largely upon the supervisor. He or she may not have sufficient faith in the effectiveness of the new methods to take full advantage of them. On the other hand, the supervisor may become so engrossed in procedure and methods, in timing, recording and controlling work flow – all elements of production – that he or she neglects the operators who must put the new methods into practice.

The full implications of motivation and human relations have been stressed in previous chapters. The supervisor, therefore, has to achieve a balance: he or she must pay sufficient attention to production details to gain the benefits of work study findings, at the same time providing subordinates with guidance and encouragement to maintain their morale and to achieve maximum results from the new methods.

To summarise, an effective supervisor does not allow production tasks to over-ride the human element.

Usually employees are inclined to wait for the supervisor to propose better ways of doing the work, although some take the initiative and develop their own short cuts. Probably they think it is the responsibility of supervision or perhaps suggestions have been ignored in the past and as a result a general apathy has developed.

There is also the attitude that new methods mean more work, and job changes may mean redundancy. People are not inclined to take the risk of bringing about changes, especially if they are already happy and secure in their jobs. This natural resistance to change is understandable. The supervisor must accept the problem as a challenge to convince employees of the necessity for progressive thinking and the dangers of lagging behind in productivity.

The case for work study is strengthened if the supervisor remembers that usually individuals are disinclined to ask for more work. Generally people do the work allocated to them and they manage to spread it very accurately over the time available.

The ability to assess a reasonable time for a given work-load is a distinct advantage to the supervisor, who will became more aware of those who are slacking and can apply appropriate pressure. He or she can also avoid putting unnecessary pressure on those who are working at a reasonable speed. The latter point is very important: the conscientious employees are fully aware of the slackers and grow resentful if they seem to be treated no better. In addition, timing the work-load to keep people fully occupied has a stimulating effect on output as there is less tendency to slacken off when the end of a load is in sight.

Finally, when jobs are measured the standards set provide a good indication of quality and output requirements to employees who appear to prefer working with clearer objectives in mind. This allows the supervisor to relax very close control over employees who then have, where practicable, the opportunity to work at their own variations of speed to suit their personality therefore enjoy more freedom in their work generally.

The application of work study for the supervisor

In many concerns supervisors will be without the services of a work study specialist and will have to rely upon their own resourcefulness and energy to attempt improvements. The main fields of improvement which do not involve capital expenditure and, therefore, come within the scope of the supervisor are as follows:

- Workplace layout
- Work flow
- Individual workplace layout
- Use of machines and equipment
- Method of work
- Measuring the work

Each aspect should be examined critically and in accordance with method study procedure which is explained in the next chapter. Some degree of improvement is always possible if time is spent examining the situation and possible rearrangements are carefully considered. Employees always have ideas for improvements as they are most closely concerned. The problem is persuading them to give their opinions and to co-operate during and after the changes.

Workplace layout

Gradual and subtle changes occur in many workplaces all the time; a cabinet may be moved to accommodate a supply of materials, a bench moved nearer to an electrical point and so on. As processes and output change, some re-arrangement occurs and unless the supervisor maintains a constant check and plans ahead even the best layout gradually deteriorates into a muddle, especially if individuals are allowed to move equipment without permission.

It pays to carry out periodical surveys of the workplace layout. The problems of storage, clear gangways, maximum use of overhead space, locker location, siting of benches, desks, machines and equipment should be listed and possible solutions noted. The question of safety and the existing locations of supply lines such as air, electricity, water and gas must be considered. Workplace layout is naturally closely allied with work flow which must be considered at the same time.

One useful method of trying out ideas is to make scale models of all the workplace furniture in the form of cardboard cut-outs and locate them on a scale plan of the workplace. All the essential supplies should be marked in. Various layouts can be arranged quickly and the snags noted until the most suitable layout is found.

Work flow

The main principles to apply are: no crossing flow lines, no backtracking, clear points for materials feeding in to the line at appropriate places to avoid congestion, due allowance for testing and inspection points and correct sequence of operations arranged to minimise movements of materials and assemblies through each process.

Transporting is expensive; therefore, each unnecessary movement of materials or assemblies must be eliminated. Carefully-planned work flow can avoid bottlenecks at the junctions of gangways, the loss of time and temper which such delays cause and the danger of accidents.

Individual workplace layout

Some of the reasons for poor workplace layout for individuals are: lack of forethought, overcrowding, changes in job content, untrained employees and disregard for new work study techniques.

A number of advantages may be gained by attending to this problem. Employee fatigue and accident risk should be reduced and work quality and output should improve.

Like the general workplace layout, the layout of the individual workplace must be considered in relation to the work flow and many of the same principles apply. Such fundamental items as the points of arrival and departure of materials and assemblies on the bench, the positioning of jigs and fixtures and the siting and use of the most appropriate tools for the job are too easily accepted without question. Other techniques applied in the improvement of workplace layout are ergonomics (study of a person's physical abilities in relation to working environment) and motion economy (eliminating unnecessary, awkward and fatiguing movements). The importance of general working conditions such as lighting and ventilation was discussed earlier (Chapter 20).

Use of machines and equipment

The inadequacies of existing machinery which may be obsolete or to some extent unsuitable are frustrating but the importance of making full use of machines and equipment must not be ignored. Precious capital has been spent on these items and unless they are fully utilised the concern will suffer a loss. Idle time on machines is an irrecoverable loss and therefore it must be kept to a minimum by careful planning. It is the supervisor's responsibility to make the best possible use of existing facilities and he or she cannot be excused on the grounds that predecessors or management have purchased unwisely.

The supervisor may make recommendations for replacements and additional mechanisation, but these must be justified in terms of savings in time and labour and improved quality. Capital expenditure is a complex and risky part of management's job. One major error of expenditure in a small concern may result in the eventual liquidation of the company. A certain amount of sympathy and understanding is essential in such cases where the need for expenditure seems obvious but management is inclined to be cautious for no apparent reason.

Method of work

A critical study of the operations performed in a job is an essential part of the technique of method study. The supervisor must adopt a questioning attitude towards each activity in the work with a view to either eliminating, combining, changing the sequence of or simplifying various activities. Most jobs can be streamlined in this way and, coupled with the application of the principles of motion economy, productivity should improve through quicker and less fatiguing methods.

Measuring the work

Unless the supervisor has a fairly accurate assessment of the time jobs take to perform, the effectiveness of planning and control is considerably reduced.

The supervisor does not have to be an expert to time a job within reason. Experience of the work and knowledge of subordinates who are performing the operations should enable him or her to make a fair assessment in the absence of a specialist.

Sound planning and control is now possible but naturally the set times must be acceptable to employees before they can be utilised for incentive schemes.

Organisation and methods

The application of work study in the clerical field is called O & M, in full – Organisation and Methods.

Problems of supervision encountered in offices are very similar to those on the shop floor. Managers and supervisors are forced to spend most of their time running the departments while the question of improvements tends to fall into the background. The employment of an O & M officer provides the concern with a specialist who concentrates on this activity, keeps up to date and advises and helps to introduce more effective clerical systems based on work study techniques.

Questions

1 Discuss the importance of work study in connection with higher productivity.
2 How would you convince an employee of the necessity for work study?
3 Define work study and give a brief outline of its scope.
4 Explain the terms *method study* and *work measurement* and show their interrelationship.
5 What are the main problems which confront the work study practitioner during the normal course of duties?
6 How can the supervisor assist the work study practitioner?
7 What part must management play if the suggestions for improving work are to be successfully employed?
8 Discuss the reactions from employees that should be expected by the supervisor when they are informed of the proposed visit of a work study practitioner.
9 How can the supervisor ensure that the proposed improvements made by the work study practitioner are successfully installed?

10 What should the supervisor do if an employee strongly objects to the presence of a work study practitioner at the workplace?

Case study

'Roger keeps giving me the rotten jobs and I'm fed up with it!' declared Ron Evans, an old hand who was quite capable and could easily tackle the more difficult tasks successfully. 'Why not give these youngsters a go? I want some straightforward work for a change.'

'I know, Ron, but the trouble is they can't cope, as you well know,' sympathised the supervisor.

1 What work study techniques could be used in these circumstances?
2 Comment on the supervisor's role in this case.

24 Techniques of work study

Introduction

The supervisor should at least have an appreciation of the most common techniques of work study. He or she will then be able to speak intelligently with work study specialists when the occasion arises and understand their reports and diagrams. The supervisor will also be able to participate more effectively during investigations and meetings when opinions and ideas are required.

Whenever possible the terms used in describing the various techniques conform to the definitions in the *Glossary of Terms in Work Study*, issued by the British Standards Institution (BSI) and are reproduced with their kind permission.

Method study

The BSI's definition of method study is: The systematic recording and critical examination of existing and proposed ways of doing work, as a means of developing and applying easier and more effective methods and reducing costs.

Method study procedure

A logical sequence for applying method study is in five steps.

Stage I: Select the job to be studied.
Stage II: Record all the appropriate facts.
Stage III: Critically examine the facts.
Stage IV: Develop a new method.
Stage V: Install and maintain the new method.

Each step is now dealt with in turn, illustrating the main techniques where necessary.

Stage I: select the job to be studied

Generally selection is based upon economic considerations. Where costs are abnormally high there is a good opportunity to make considerable savings.

The signs which reveal likely areas for investigation are trouble-spots, bottlenecks, low and erratic output, poor quality work, excessive scrap, high accident rate, excessive overtime, high fatigue, high labour turnover and a high number of complaints and grievances.

Stage II: record the facts

A clear picture of all the existing operations and flow of work provides a sound basis for examining the system followed and stimulates ideas for improvement often not apparent until the over-all scene is portrayed. Faults become more obvious when operations are recorded.

The recording techniques may be grouped into four categories:

- charts
- diagrams
- models
- filming

CHARTS

1. *Process charts*   A sequence of events is portrayed diagrammatically by means of a set of process chart symbols. There are various types of process chart. The main ones in use are: the *outline process chart* which gives an over-all picture of one job by recording in sequence the main operations and inspections, the *flow process chart* which sets out the sequence of the flow of a product or a procedure by recording all the events under review and the *two-handed process chart* which records the activities of an operator's hands or limbs in relationship to one another.

The flow process chart may be drawn up to record what the operator does (operator type), or what happens to material (material type), or how the equipment is used (equipment type).

There are two sets of process chart symbols in common use, but the trend is to use the symbols developed by the ASME (American Society of Mechanical Engineers) in preference to Gilbreth's, (which are given on the right in Fig. 24.1 as alternatives).

Examples of an outline process chart and a flow process chart, material type, are given in Figs. 24.1 and 24.2.

2   *Time scale charts*   There are three time scale charts used for recording the activities of more than one subject at once and for recording all the movements taking place in an operation. These are as follows.

(*a*) *Multiple activity chart:* this chart records the activities of two or more subjects which may be operators, machines or equipment on a common time scale to show their interrelationship.

(*b*) *Simo chart:* this abbreviated name for a *simultaneous motion cycle chart* is often based upon film analysis. The chart records simultaneously on a common time scale the *therbligs* or groups of therbligs performed by various

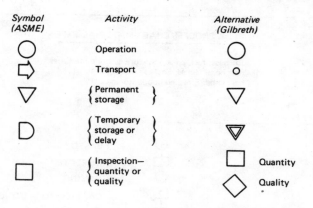

Symbol (ASME)	Activity	Alternative (Gilbreth)	
○	Operation	○	
⇨	Transport	○	
▽	{ Permanent storage }	▽	
D	{ Temporary storage or delay }	▼	
□	{ Inspection— quantity or quality }	□	Quantity
		◇	Quality

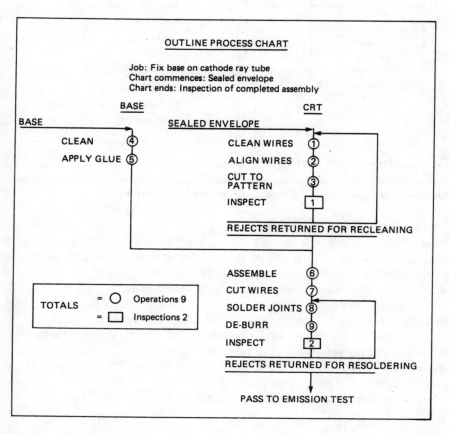

OUTLINE PROCESS CHART

Job: Fix base on cathode ray tube
Chart commences: Sealed envelope
Chart ends: Inspection of completed assembly

BASE   CRT

BASE   SEALED ENVELOPE

CLEAN   ④   CLEAN WIRES   ①
APPLY GLUE   ⑤   ALIGN WIRES   ②
                      CUT TO PATTERN   ③
                      INSPECT   □1

REJECTS RETURNED FOR RECLEANING

                      ASSEMBLE   ⑥
                      CUT WIRES   ⑦
TOTALS = ○ Operations 9   SOLDER JOINTS ⑧
        = □ Inspections 2   DE-BURR   ⑨
                      INSPECT   □2

REJECTS RETURNED FOR RESOLDERING

PASS TO EMISSION TEST

Fig. 24.1 *Outline process chart*
This gives an over-all picture of a job – to fix the base on a cathode ray tube –
recording in sequence the main operations and inspections. Various symbols are used
for different operations (*see above* and Fig. 24.2)

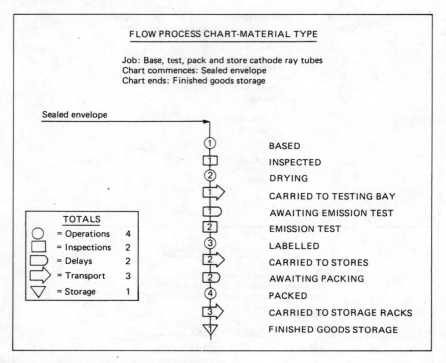

Fig. 24.2 *Flow process chart, material type*

This chart shows the sequence of flow of a simple product, recording each step in the procedure. The symbols used are those developed by the ASME

parts of the body of one or more workers. The name 'therblig' was given by Frank Gilbreth to each of the specific divisions of movement according to the purpose for which it is made. (The name was coined by the reversal of his surname.) They cover movements, states of being and pauses, e.g. select, grasp, assemble, inspect, transport loaded, rest, plan, delay. Each therblig has a specific colour symbol and letter for recording purposes.

(*c*) *PMTS chart:* the *predetermined motion time system chart* is used to record all the movements taking place in any operation by means of one of the predetermined motion time system codes. These codes represent through combinations of figures and letters basic human motions and qualifying conditions with corresponding time values.

DIAGRAMS

Effective indication of movement is achieved by using diagrams of various types. A *flow diagram* shows the location of specific activities carried out and the routes followed by operations, materials or equipment in their execution. A *string diagram* is a scale plan or model on which thread is used to trace and measure the path of operators, materials or equipment during a specific sequence of events.

In addition, there are various photographic means of recording movement by attaching a light source to the moving object and recording the path taken. These devices are called *cyclegraphs* or when timed *chronocyclegraphs*.

MODELS

A more expensive method of recording is the preparation of three-dimensional models. They have the advantage of being easily understood, and proposed changes may be visualised more accurately.

A more popular method is the two-dimensional model which is drawn to scale: cut-outs or loose templates are used to indicate the positions of machines, benches and equipment.

FILMING

Recording operations by ciné film or still film provide a permanent record and is unobtrusive in operation. The main techniques are as follows.

1   *Micromotion analysis:* a frame-by-frame analysis of a ciné film prepared in the form of a simo chart.

2   *Film analysis:* a frame-by-frame examination on a ciné film of an operation to determine the state of activity of the subject during each exposure.

3   *Memomotion photography:* a form of time lapse photography which records activity by a ciné camera adapted to take pictures at longer intervals than normal. This method makes it possible to record activities continuously over a long period.

Stage III: critically examine the facts

An objective attitude is essential for the examination of any work if a new method is to be satisfactorily evolved. Any personal bias towards people or the work must be forgotten in favour of a broad outlook free of narrow viewpoints; painstaking attention to detail and an analytical and logical approach to the problem are also vital.

The critical examination of the recorded operations is conducted by means of the questioning technique. Each activity in turn is subjected to a systematic and progressive series of questions.

There are two stages in this technique.

PRIMARY QUESTIONS

The primary stage queries the fundamental need for the performance, place, person, sequence and means of every activity recorded. The main headings for the primary questions, therefore, would be as follows.

1   *Purpose*: Is the work needed? What is achieved? Why is it needed?

2   *Place*: Where is the work done? Why is it done there?
3   *Person*: Who does the work? Why does that particular individual do it?
4   *Sequence*: When is the work done? Why is it done then?
5   *Means*: How is the work done? Why is it done in that way?

If all these questions are answered correctly a thorough understanding of the existing method should result and at this stage clear indications of improvements in various sectors should be seen.

SECONDARY QUESTIONS
The second stage subjects the answers to the primary questions to further inquiry. The secondary questions determine whether possible alternatives of place, people, sequence and means are practicable and preferable as a means of improving the existing method. Some typical questions would be the following.

1   *Purpose*: Could the work be altered or eliminated in any part? Is the whole operation needed?
2   *Place*: Are there other places available? Is there a more convenient place?
3   *Person*: Who else could do the work? Could a person with lower skill do the work with some alterations?
4   *Sequence*: When else could it be performed? Would it be cheaper if performed earlier or later?
5   *Means*: How else could the work be done? Are the principles of motion economy used? Are the most suitable machines and tools used? Could the working environment be improved?

Stage IV: developing the new method

Developing the new method from the answers hinges on four factors for improving an operation. These are:

- elimination
- change of sequence
- combination
- simplification

ELIMINATION
The first consideration should be whether or not the operation can be dispensed with entirely. The operation may appear necessary until a more searching investigation reveals that it no longer serves any purpose in the end product.

CHANGE OF SEQUENCE
When satisfactory proof of the need for the operation has been found the merits of the existing sequence can be considered. A change of sequence may

be justified by an improvement of work flow and the removal of unnecessary or duplicated work. For example, an assembly may be carefully cleaned at one stage, receive dirty treatment at the next and then be cleaned again. A more glaring type of sequence fault occurs when an assembly must be partly dismantled to fit a component and then re-assembled.

COMBINATION

The possibility of combining operations is the third consideration. Can any time be saved by eliminating unnecessary movements between operating points or by cutting down operation time? For example, sometimes work is performed in two places when one place would be sufficient; perhaps operations can be combined by slight modification; perhaps tools and machines can be more fully utilised through combination. The gains may be considerable and time is well spent in exploring these possibilities.

SIMPLIFICATION

The fourth consideration is probably the most important way of improving the essential operation. Invariably there are easier ways of performing an operation. The problem can be approached from a number of aspects. Some are described below and include motion economy, materials, the operator, design, power, handling, tools, machines and equipment.

1 *Motion economy* The principles of motion economy should be used to save time and reduce fatigue. They are described later in the chapter.

2 *Materials* Often a different material which is easier to work with can save time. Perhaps a cheaper material is available which will not affect the quality of the finished product, or a lighter or heavier gauge could be used to advantage. The possibility of using waste or rejects should be examined. Another factor is whether the most economical lengths or sizes are being purchased; cutting can often be avoided by wiser purchasing, thus reducing scrap costs.

3 *The operator* The suitability of a particular operator is often over-looked. Details such as height and weight may interfere with the work. For example, a tall operator may be at a disadvantage and suffer from fatigue quickly if he or she is working in a confined space inside an aircraft. The principles of ergonomics or 'fitting the job to the worker' (*see* Chapter 20) should be applied to avoid unnecessary fatigue.

4 *Design* Unfortunately designers do not always manage to create the simplest designs. Various short cuts are possible and these small rearrangements result in large savings. Tolerances can often be opened without loss of quality and standardisation of parts simplifies assembly. Methods of reducing the number of parts in an assembly through redesign are often obvious to the operator.

5 *Power and handling* Greater use of power for assembly and materials handling is recognised as making work easier, but not always applied for

reasons such as lack of capital, lack of interest or dislike of changes and inconvenience. A careful choice of equipment is essential to achieve substantial economies, otherwise the expenditure will cancel out the saving.

6 *Tools, machines and equipment* Although these aspects overlap with power and handling they are treated separately from the operating viewpoint. A vast number of questions could be raised about these items such as: positioning? running speeds? location of controls? sequence of use? loose or fixed tools? combination tools? use of jigs and templates? could automatic feed be used? Imagination and the questioning technique can produce large savings.

Stage V: install and maintain the new method

Studying the system and evolving a new method is only half the work. Installing the new method requires great care, detailed planning and the co-operation of everyone concerned with the change.

Naturally the magnitude of the change must be a major consideration. A small rearrangement is comparatively easy, but when transfers of operators, retraining and rearranged layouts of workplaces and workshops are involved, the disruption of production is obviously considerable and timing becomes important. Detailed planning must include giving adequate information to all concerned who must support the change wholeheartedly if the scheme is to be successful.

Periodic review of the new method is needed to check on and correct any deviations from the procedure. During these reviews the effects of the change should be noted for future improvements, and resistance points examined more closely to find the cause.

The supervisor has a heavy responsibility during the period of installation and in maintaining the new method. Acceptance of change and ability to arouse enthusiasm and confidence in subordinates are the key factors for successful operation of the revised scheme.

Motion economy

The principles of motion economy are a fundamental part of method study. Any movements in an operation which can be eliminated, reduced or made easier will reduce fatigue and wasted time. Motion economy makes some contribution, therefore, towards increasing the effectiveness of the operator.

Economy in human movement was studied by Gilbreth who classified the principles of motion analysis to form a foundation for constructing layout of workplaces and patterns of movement. Observation of working movements quickly highlights those principles which are being abused and in many instances improvements can be made by minor rearrangements.

The seven principles of motion economy

The seven principles of motion economy are only indications or guides and, as stressed in other chapters, much depends upon particular circumstances in deciding upon courses of action.

- Minimum movements
- Simultaneous movements
- Symmetrical movements
- Natural movements
- Rhythmical movements
- Habitual movements
- Continuous movements

These principles are described as follows:

Minimum movements

All materials, tools and equipment should be arranged so that the minimum amount of movement is necessary for their use. The degree of movement necessary to carry out an operation was classified by Gilbreth into five groups:

1 finger motions only
2 fingers and wrist movements
3 fingers, wrist and forearm
4 fingers, wrist, forearm and upper arm
5 fingers, wrist, forearm, upper arm and shoulder

The use of the first three classifications constitutes the *normal working area*. The inclusion of the last two classifications provides the boundary for the *maximum working area* which will have to be used if all the tools, materials and equipment cannot be accommodated within the normal working area.

The aim is to reduce the movements of the upper arm and shoulder (classifications (4) and (5)) to a minimum. The natural sweep of the arms at each side of the body produces areas in the shape of arcs in the horizontal and vertical planes. These are illustrated in Fig. 24.3 and form the working areas described.

Items used more frequently should be placed as close to the assembly area as possible and workplaces should be planned in accordance with the natural arc of working area.

Simultaneous movements

When different limbs are working at the same time they should be balanced by synchronising the movements, e.g. stretching out both hands at once to pick up a bolt and a nut. This principle is very important because balance

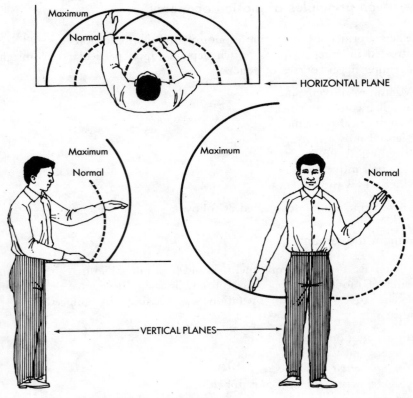

Fig. 24.3 *Normal and maximum working areas*

The normal working area is covered by movements of the fingers, wrist and forearm, in both horizontal and vertical planes. The natural sweep of the arms forms arcs around the body. The maximum area is covered by bringing in areas of the upper arm and shoulder as well

is achieved, less effort is required as concentration is reduced and learning is easier. Fatigue is reduced because the natural reaction of a body is to divide exertion evenly between the left and right sides. Thus, when the left hand is moved the right hand tends to move in a similar fashion.

Symmetrical movements

A further refinement – closely associated with simultaneous movements – states that movements should be balanced by performing them on the left and right-hand sides of the body about an imaginary line through the centre of the body. A common example of the combination of simultaneous and symmetrical movements is the range of physical exercises which involve both arms and a swinging motion.

Natural movements

Natural movements are those which make the best use of the shape and design of the body. The use of the feet, for instance, is often overlooked. They can be used either to perform an operation if they are more suitable than hands or as an additional function when the hands are occupied. For example, if an assembly is held in a particular position for drilling by the hands, a foot may be used to operate the machine.

Rhythmical movements

Movements should be so ordered as to induce a natural rhythm in the cycle of operations. Regular repetition of movement develops speed and reduces mental and physical fatigue.

Habitual movements

This principle is closely associated with rhythmical movements. Precise repetition is habit forming and as mental effort is reduced the movement nears that of a reflex action.

Habitual movements are not possible unless conditions such as layout, supply of materials and placing of tools are standardised. Any slight alteration will defeat the object because extra mental effort is introduced to locate the item and the automatic movement is wasted.

Continuous movements

Any acute change in direction of a limb causes it to slow down, stop and have to accelerate back to the original speed. Such action involves extra muscle movement and tension; therefore, it is more fatiguing compared with movements which are smooth and curved. Layout should be planned with this principle in mind.

The supervisor and motion economy

Although a detailed study of an operation may require the services of a specialist, there are often many obvious faults which the supervisor can easily improve.

Some of the glaring faults are as follows:

1 Cramped and dangerous positions of working.
2 Poor siting of tools, materials, machines and equipment which require extra and awkward movements to use them.
3 Long stretching movements.
4 Using unnecessary force such as pulling excessively, levering, hammering and ramming.

5 Eye-strain and groping movements.
6 Loss of control of the operation.
7 Unnecessary movements such as changing the position of tools and materials and walking round to various positions.
8 Lengthy adjustments.
9 Long pauses where fatigue is indicated as the cause.
10 Inadequate tools.

With a little ingenuity the supervisor can eliminate many of these faults. The use of the principles of motion economy described above and small mechanical aids (e.g. simple transportation devices such as gravity feed containers and rollers, drop deliveries into bins, and quick release clamps) are a few of the methods of improvement.

Work measurement

The BSI definition of work measurement is:

the application of techniques designed to establish the time for a *qualified worker* to carry out a specified *job* at a defined level of performance.

Application of work measurement

Sensible application of work measurement provides essential information for effective planning and control of production and other main functions. It is also used for improving systems of wage payments, more accurate costing, improving work-loads through more accurate budgeting and more accurate estimates.

Standard time

Human work can be divided into physical work which is measurable and mental work which can only be estimated. Machine work must also be considered in work measurement, but in this case the work can be calculated easily and presents no problems of developing techniques.

People vary considerably in their rate of working; therefore, the time determined by work measurement is the average time a number of operators would take to perform the operation without feeling more than healthily tired at the end of each day. This value is known as the *standard time* for a job.

Procedure

A typical procedure for applying work measurement is described below.

1   *Select the work to be measured*   A similar investigation for selection should be carried out as in method study to ensure that work is studied on a priority basis.

2   *Record all the relevant information*   All available data on the job should be collected and recorded. Such sources as production schedules, inspection records and drawings provide useful information.

3   *Define the job in detail*   A job analysis should be carefully carried out, breaking the work down into elements or distinct parts, convenient for observation, measurement and analysis.

4   *Measure the work*   Measurement of the work is conducted by using one of the techniques described below.

Techniques of work measurement

The main techniques of work measurement are as follows.

- Time study
- Synthesis
- PMTS (predetermined motion time systems)
- Varifactor sampling
- Activity sampling
- Rated activity sampling

Time study

The basic technique is time study, a direct observation of the job while it is being performed by the employee. The observer must possess an adequate job breakdown, the ability to estimate the rate of working and a stop-watch to measure the elements accurately.

1   *The rating*   The employee's rate of working is given a numerical value. The observer must judge the rate relative to a standard rating scale which runs from zero to 100, based upon the BSI recommendation.

Standard performance is represented by 100 and is defined as: 'the rate of output which *qualified workers* will naturally achieve without over-exertion, as an average over the working day, provided they know and adhere to the specific method, and provided they are motivated to apply themselves to their work' (BSI). Other rating scales use 80 and 133 in place of 100.

2   *The basic time*   Given the rating and the actual time taken to perform an element of the job, the basic time for that element can be calculated.

For example, if the observed rating is 90, the observed time is 0.10 minutes, and the standard rating is 100, this would appear as:

$$\text{Basic time} = \frac{90 \times 0.10}{100} = 0.09 \text{ minutes}$$

3   *Relaxation allowance*   An addition to the basic time is provided to allow for the general physiological and psychological effects of performing the work and to allow for attention to personal needs. The time allowed varies depending on the nature of the job.

Synthesis

Many jobs contain some elements which are common to all of them. Therefore a saving in time study is possible by building up a range of element times which can be referred to when required in a particular job. Ultimately a sufficient range of element times may be accumulated to provide the correct time for the whole job even before the job is performed.

The process of building up a stock of synthetic data may be accelerated by planning a series of studies to cover a wide range of elements. This is a long-term scheme and the question of whether it is economic must be considered.

Predetermined motion time systems (PMTS)

Whereas the synthetic data in synthesis are established by observation of the separate elements of a job, the data obtained by predetermined motion time systems are calculated from standard times for basic human motions. These times are classified according to the nature of the motion and the conditions under which it is made.

The purpose is to remove the factor of human judgment and briefly the basis of the technique is that all work in an industrial environment consists of various combinations of a relatively small number of basic human motions. Times for these are measured from high-speed films and scaled to allow for circumstances, e.g. a heavy weight takes longer to lift than a light weight. The specialist analyses the job into its basic movements in detail and then computes the times required from special tables to find the total for the job plus any allowances to be made.

The two main systems are known as 'Work-Factor' and 'MTM' or Methods-Time Measurement. The 'Work-Factor' system originated in the USA in 1934; later a similar system was introduced by the Methods-Time Measurement Association.

Varifactor synthesis

This heading may be subdivided into four specific techniques.

1   *Estimating*   The BSI defines estimating as: a means for assessing the time required to carry out work, based on knowledge and experience of similar types of work, without a detailed breakdown of the work into *elements* and their corresponding times at a defined level of performance.

2   *Analytical estimating*   Some types of non-repetitive work such as maintenance jobs do not lend themselves to complete synthesis of all the elements involved by observation alone. This problem is overcome by analytical estimating which is a development of estimating. In analytical estimating the time required to perform elements is estimated from knowledge and experience of the elements concerned. The degree of accuracy depends largely upon the ability of the estimator.

3   *VeFAC programming*   VeFAC programming (formerly known as variable factor programming) is a technique developed by WOFAC Corporation of America for reducing and controlling payroll costs in such areas as clerical work, data processing, drafting, inspection, maintenance, packaging, sales and design. The scope is virtually unlimited. Briefly the steps are: collection of the facts, preliminary reporting, developing target times (from WOFAC prime work time data), establishing work schedules and periodic reporting.

VeFAC programming is not a speed-up, but a way of encouraging workers to use their time more productively.

4   *Variable element time study (VETS)*   This procedure was introduced by Dr Whitmore. It is a method of setting time standards for non-repetitive jobs and is based on calculating *average* times for complete jobs. Rating is employed using four multipliers corresponding to slow (0.5), average (0.8), fast (1.0) and very fast (1.2) rather than on the detailed rating scales used in time study.

A maintenance engineer, for example, may spend time on cleaning machines, repairing them, replacing assemblies, building special equipment, writing reports, visiting dispersed areas and installing new machines. He or she may be observed cleaning machines, the average time to clean (per machine) being determined by timing with a watch. The rating multiplier is applied (say, 0.8 if engineer is working at an average rate). If the average time is eighteen minutes for cleaning each machine the time allowed would be:

$$18 \times 0.8 = 14.4 \text{ minutes for each machine.}$$

Although it may be argued that the time to clean individual machines will vary according to size, if the average time determined is a good average for all machines, the time lost while cleaning complex machines will be regained when dealing with simple ones. This system does not give precise measurement but the times will be sufficiently accurate to provide reasonable control of indirect labour (*see* Chapter 28).

Activity sampling

The work content of some jobs is so varied that normal techniques of work measurement cannot be effectively applied.

When a reasonable assessment is required for these jobs a form of statistical sampling is used which assesses the results of a few samples of work content or individual movements. The samples are selected at random intervals from an appropriate period. Each observation records the work occurring at that instant and is expressed as a percentage of all the observations which record that particular activity. This provides an indication of the percentage of time spent on that particular activity.

Rated activity sampling

This technique is an advanced form of activity sampling where each work element is rated to determine the work content in addition to the percentage of time spent on the activity.

Questions

1   For what purpose should a supervisor have a reasonable knowledge of work study techniques?
2   Outline a logical sequence for applying method study.
3   Illustrate by examples the main recording techniques in method study.
4   What is meant by the 'questioning technique' in method study?
5   Explain and give examples of four main factors for improving an operation.
6   How can the supervisor ensure that a new method is installed and maintained with the minimum of disruption?
7   Discuss methods of reducing operator fatigue.
8   State and explain the seven principles of motion economy.
9   Describe some of the glaring common faults that the supervisor can eliminate easily.
10   Discuss the uses of three time scale charts including a brief description of each chart.
11   What are the objects of work measurement?
12   Explain the term 'standard time' in connection with work measurement.
13   Outline a typical procedure for applying work measurement.
14   Briefly describe the main techniques of work measurement.
15   Give an account of time study including the rating and calculation of the basic time.

Case study 1

Dennis had not thought seriously about using work study in his section until the works manager sent for him and said quite bluntly that he was not satisfied with the section's performance levels. 'We have to improve our productivity, Dennis, otherwise we shall all be out of a job now that we're without that cosy contract with Eclipse Engineering.'

On the way back to his section Dennis called on Mary, one of his fellow supervisors. 'Just been told in no uncertain terms by the "old man" about productivity and all that.' Mary looked up in surprise, 'Me too! I was going to come along and see you.'

At that point another supervisor arrived with the same story.

1 Consider the courses of action open to the supervisors.
2 What other approaches could have been used by the works manager?

Case study 2

Regina Tool Company was in financial difficulties. A lucrative long-standing order had been cancelled. Reliance on other erratic orders has meant that either the work force rapidly becomes more flexible and efficient or the plant will be forced to close down.

Andy, the shop steward, had little trust in management and over the years many employees had experienced unfair treatment. The company's poor industrial relations reputation was not helping to solve the problem at the general meeting of employees being held by the managing director who was attempting to convince them of the urgent need for drastic changes.

Andy spoke up. 'We've heard all this before – many times in fact – but we're still here. Why don't you give us some facts and figures? We also hear that you've just given yourselves handsome increases and yet *you* are expecting *us* to take cuts.'

1 Consider the managerial philosophy in this company and discuss the alternative that might have paid off now.
2 What could be done to rectify the immediate situation?

25 Production control

Types of production

The three types of production are job, batch and flow. These were mentioned in Chapter 3. The main factors affecting type of production are the length of runs, variety of goods produced, spreading fixed costs (those that tend not to change with the length of production runs), and preparation costs.

Job production

All products of the 'one-off' type such as a bridge, an office block, an ocean liner, a special purpose machine or a very large transformer come under this heading, often known as 'jobbing'. A large proportion of small concerns and some very large companies are engaged upon this type of production, mainly by contract.

The usual procedure is for prospective buyers to advertise or to approach companies for a tender or quotation which is an estimate of the cost, quality and delivery date of the job. Drawing up the estimate can be costly for large products. The design and pre-planning may take considerable time and effort to compile and must be reasonably accurate considering the large sums of money often involved and the profit margins. The element of competition is always present. Invariably at least three tenders are required by the prospective buyer to assess the value of each one and to make a choice.

When the contract is received it is usual to place an engineer in charge who schedules the work. Special requirements for this type of work depend upon whether the product can be manufactured in the factory, on the site or a combination of the two. Site engineers must be of high calibre and the supervisory staff under them play an important part in controlling the job. The operators must be highly skilled with a wide range of experience in many cases; often specialised operators are needed for short periods. Machinery must be versatile, therefore general-purpose machines are used in conjunction with equipment of a similar nature.

Materials can be a problem unless they are ordered to a set schedule which allows for delays in delivery and the time required for usage. A missing piece of material or component can cause an expensive hold up. Storing materials must be considered. For example, a large storage site near to the work would be necessary to house the many assemblies for constructing a suspension bridge. Site workshops would also be required on many projects.

Products which can be manufactured in the factory include a variety of equipment and assemblies for industry. Examples are special-purpose machines, castings and tools.

Batch production

When a range of products is manufactured in quantities that do not justify the continuous flow line method, batch production is adopted. General-purpose machines can be used and scheduled to ensure that the maximum possible machine utilisation is achieved. This principle of machine utilisation, meaning that each machine may be performing operations on a number of different components, illustrates the main distinguishing feature between batch and flow production. The diagram in Fig. 25.1 shows the difference

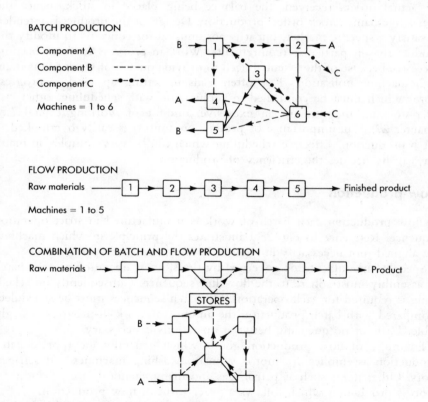

Fig. 25.1 *Machine layout, batch and flow production*

In flow production the machines are laid out in strict operational *sequence* whereas in batch production the machines are grouped according to *function*. Each machine may perform its particular operation on a number of different components

between the two types. It should be noted that in batch production the machines are grouped in types to suit the particular function which involves specialist supervision, tooling and inspection, whereas in flow production the machines are laid out in strict operation sequence, each machine performing a particular job at maximum efficiency while the flow line is in operation. A combination of the two types may be seen in many large concerns. The majority of products which are manufactured in quantity come under this heading: for example, ready-made suits, paint brushes, watches, books, lamp-shades, mirrors, furniture and plain bearings.

The batch production of components feeding a flow line within the same factory is often seen. For example, in motor car manufacture the flow line will be fed with batch-produced engines, wheels complete with tyres and back axle assemblies. This combination of types is known as *batch/flow production*.

To produce an economic batch size, the amount is often increased above the actual orders received, the balance being placed in stock, hence the alternative name 'stock order' production. Design of the product is intended to satisfy a specific market, but it is not unusual for concerns to modify the product to suit particular requirements. Work-in-progress tends to become excessive because of the essential need to provide queues of work to maintain high machine utilisation. This often leads to setting up work-in-progress stores which must be controlled in conjunction with scheduling, otherwise over-stocking may tie up an excessive amount of working capital (see Chapter 27). The importance of production control is easily overlooked in batch production. Effective scheduling which can be very complex in many ways really decides the efficiency of production.

Flow production

In flow production each batch of work is manufactured in strict operation sequence. Reference to Fig. 25.1 illustrates the principle in which machines are aligned (not necessarily in straight lines) in order of operation.

Speed of manufacture is governed by the slowest operation as each batch or assembly must adhere to the flow-line sequence. Consequently no scheduling is required for each operation, but batch sequences must be scheduled. Compared with batch production the amount of work-in-progress is negligible. Little or no queueing between operations is necessary.

Examples of flow production goods which generally incorporate batch production assemblies are motor vehicles, washing machines and refrigerators. Other items such as petrol, gas and many chemicals are produced by process production which follows a purer form of flow production.

Some of the advantages of flow production are that when careful planning is completed the problem of production control is not so complex, breakdowns and faulty work are immediately apparent, and corrective action can be concentrated on the fault. Full utilisation of special-purpose machines produces large savings. Floor space is used more economically mainly through the reduction of work-in-progress.

Effective planning in minute detail before production commences is essential. The market must be carefully analysed and sounded periodically to ensure adequate sales of the large output levels.

Heavy losses occur when the plant is shut down through labour troubles or lack of materials. Similarly, when a new line is introduced, change-over time is costly and must be reduced to a minimum.

Two techniques within flow production are group technology and flexible manufacturing systems which are discussed now.

Group technology

Bearing in mind the advantages of flow production it seems worth while to convert production stages into a flow-line wherever possible. This conversion is called group technology (GT) or cell machining. A simplified diagram of GT is shown in Fig. 25.2.

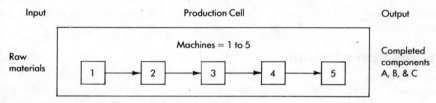

Fig. 25.2 *Simplified diagram of group technology*

A cell consists of machines set up to produce in strict flow-line sequence a family of completed components

A typical definition is grouping machines on flow production lines to produce complete components previously manufactured in batch production. Such components are grouped into families, meaning they are either recognised as similar physically or through complex analysis.

GT has developed in various ways over the past twenty years. Originally the technique grouped together similar components to improve standardisation and achieve rationalisation. This led to grouping machines into production cells on flow-line principles to avoid batch production problems. Finally adaptations were made to accommodate modern work group concepts.

ADVANTAGES AND DISADVANTAGES

The advantages of GT are similar to flow-line benefits. These include reduced costs in manufacturing, tooling, process planning, total setting-up time, and manufacturing lead times; lower investment in work-in-progress, working stocks, and buffer stocks; and simplified production control.

Additional benefits could be more effective supervision, increased job satisfaction, and more humanised work groups. Disadvantages might be reduced machine utilisation, higher change-over time, and initial installation problems.

Flexible manufacturing systems (FMS).

Many companies manufacture goods for mature markets that constantly demand product diversification and new products. This pressure causes intense competition and the urgent need to automate. Within manufacturing technology are many techniques, the ultimate goal being computer-integrated manufacturing (CIM).

FMS is a computerised manufacturing cell that caters for such flexibility. Automated with flexible machining centres and automatic vehicles or transporters between operations, the system copes rapidly with design changes and component mix. FMS is controlled by a computer that makes decisions for moving parts and components from machine to machine. The machine centres have 'intelligence' that checks parts, the operational state of machines, tool wear and tool capability. Quality may be monitored automatically by statistical process control (SPC) equipment.

Production planning

A detailed programme of all the operations necessary to complete the product is essential before production and effective control can commence.

The first stage of planning involves gathering information on the product in the form of drawings, specifications from the designers and drawing office records. When a clear picture is drawn up of all the processes involved, further investigation of work content and reference to past production records provide information for deciding whether to purchase components or assemblies from outside or to produce them internally.

The next stage involves more detailed problems of setting up stock lists and parts lists, determining the availability of jigs and tools, preparing supplies of drawings and specifications together with many other general jobs to ensure that a complete planned programme is presented to production control.

It is now possible with the aid of information on existing machines and equipment available for production to produce *process layout instruction sheets*. An example of one is shown in Fig. 25.3. A *detailed process operation sheet* given in Fig. 25.4 illustrates how the time allowed is calculated by setting out all the elements in an operation.

A master plan may be drawn up for a new product to show the dates when each production stage must be ready and each phase completed so that the delivery date agrees with the estimate. The type of chart which is most suitable for this control function was developed by Henry L. Gantt and is known

PROCESS LAYOUT INSTRUCTION							
Part name: Part No.: Date: Material unit: Time/100 parts: Weight/100 parts:				No. of sheets: Sheet No.: Drawn by: Checked by: Standard order quantity:			
Dept.	Operation	Op. No.	Time allowed	Set up time	Machine	Tools	Special equip't

Fig. 25.3 *Process layout instruction sheet*

This is used to record in sequence each operation needed to produce a part

DETAILED PROCESS OPERATION SHEET					
Part name: Part No.: Time allowed:			Operation: Material/unit: Date:		
No.	Element	Time allowed	No.	Element	Time allowed

Fig. 25.4 *Detailed process operation sheet*

as the *Gantt chart*. Each part of the plan is subjected to an estimated time which is plotted. The actual time taken is also plotted underneath the estimated or standard time, thus clearly indicating the true position in relation to time and subject.

The Gantt chart is versatile as it can be adapted to any control system where a number of functions are allied to the time factor. Fig 25.5 illustrates a simple target date chart using the Gantt chart principle. There are certain disadvantages, however, particularly in showing interrelationships between activities. More advanced systems involve the use of critical path or network analysis (*see* Chapter 22).

Plant and equipment

When process planning is complete the selection of, or changes in, plant and

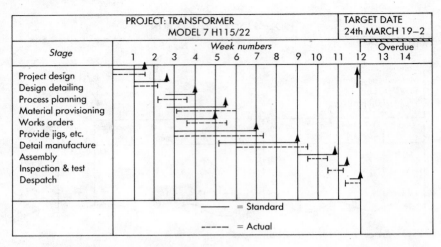

Fig. 25.5   *Gantt chart, production sheet*

This is a simple target date chart using the Gantt chart principle. As a master schedule it controls the production of a new transformer from initial design through to delivery. Actual production progress is measured against estimated "standard" times for achieving delivery by the target date

equipment is undertaken. Many factors influence selection: type of production, technological developments, availability and training of operatives, physical and environmental constraints, reputation of suppliers, compatability with existing facilities, maintenance aspects, and safety.

The trend towards integrated manufacturing systems involves careful consideration of current rates of change in technologies, the use of computer-aided design (CAD) and computer-aided manufacture (CAM), and market forecasts on which to base capacity requirements, bearing in mind economic aspects. Of increasing importance is effective maintenance to avoid costly breakdowns.

Production control

The purpose of production control is to ensure that the correct quantity of a product is manufactured at the right time at the required quality by the most economic method.

Production control may be defined as the direction of all production activities according to the planned programme fully utilising available facilities in the most economic way.

Planning and controlling production depend upon many factors peculiar to the particular industry and the products being manufactured. Basic principles apply and can be discussed and borne in mind when building up a practical system within the particular concern.

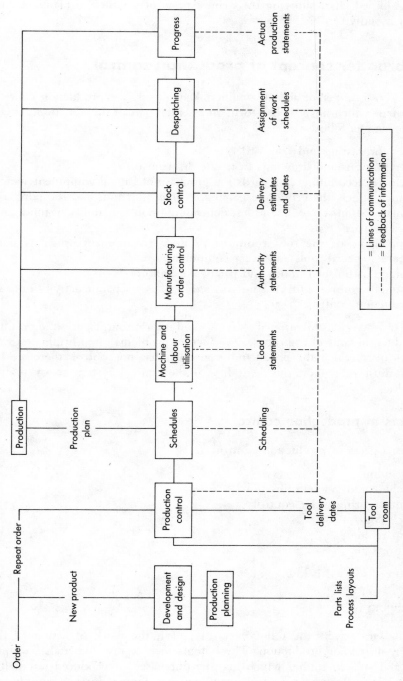

Fig. 25.6 Simplified diagram of production planning and control

A simplified chart showing the main aspects of production planning and control is shown in Fig. 25.6.

The broader concept of production control

There are a number of activities undertaken outside the production control department which nevertheless form an essential part of this function. These activities are as follows:

1   Sales forecasting and sales orders.
2   Specifications and drawings from the drawing office.
3   Financial accounting as regards the purchase of capital equipment which in turn affects the economic batch size of production, and the purchase of materials in certain quantities, depending upon availability of funds and storage space.
4   Capabilities of the tool room to produce requirements such as jigs, fixtures, special tools and other equipment.
5   Storage of finished goods and partly finished goods.
6   Materials control – this is sometimes treated as a separate activity outside production control.

The few activities mentioned above should indicate sufficiently the breadth of production control in practice. Production problems often originate from services over which the production controller has no control; therefore he or she must rely upon the flexibility of the control system to overcome difficulties.

Aspects of production control

The six aspects of production control are:

- Scheduling
- Machine and labour utilisation
- Manufacturing order control
- Stock control
- Despatching
- Progressing

They are discussed below.

Scheduling

This activity covers the following areas. *First*, the work of listing all the items required for production. These items include raw materials, components and sub-assemblies which may be purchased or produced internally. *Second*, placing them in a convenient sequence for production considering such problems as time taken to produce, time taken to deliver from supplier, time required on the production line, the production cycle and allowance for scrap and waste. *Third*, routeing the materials and assemblies from section to section so that the plan of production illustrates to everyone concerned the whole sequence of operations from commencement to completion of the programme.

Scheduling presents a workable programme of production in workshop language. The sequence of manufacturing and the quantities will depend upon sales orders, economic batch size, manufacturing time and delivery dates.

On this basis the information required for effective scheduling includes the following:

1 Sales orders.
2 Promised delivery dates.
3 Planning layout.
4 Parts lists.
5 Machine load statements.
6 Labour utilisation estimates.
7 Supply details for tools, equipment, materials, items from subcontractors, components from suppliers and jigs and fixtures.
8 Scrap and waste statements.
9 Information from progress section as work proceeds. Schedules are revised as feedback from progress is compared with estimates.
10 Information on finished goods, storage facilities and despatch.

The main types of schedule are the master schedule, the production schedule and the workshop schedule.

The *master schedule* generally provides a weekly or monthly indication of requirements over a period of, say, a quarter, half year or year. The schedule

Master schedule														
Component: Helical spring Component No: 6:8940						Maximum Run: 7000 Minimum Run: 2000								
Production	Quarter (in week Nos.)													
	1	2	3	4	5	6	7	8	9	10	11	12	13	
Scheduled Below schedule Above schedule Total														

Fig. 25.7 *Master schedule*

indicates plant capacity; as orders are received they are entered and the resultant capacity calculated for the period. When capacity is filled, orders are either carried forward to the next period or arrangements made to increase capacity for that period. This scheme shows immediately the current position to be noted, the basis for increasing output to accommodate delivery dates and the over-all loading of plant in the factory.

An outline of the main requirements of a master schedule is given in Fig. 25.7. Production schedules (Fig. 25.16) and workshop schedules (Fig. 25.17) are discussed later in this chapter.

Machine and labour utilisation

The purpose of this aspect of control is to organise the loading of machines and labour so that idle time is reduced to a minimum and co-ordination is achieved. The activities within this function include maintenance of accurate records of plant capacity, preparation of statements which compare the current loading with the maximum capacity available and compilation of machine and labour records indicating the actual and possible utilisation.

Information for preparation of these records may be obtained from plant records, planning sheets, operation layouts, work study department records and previous records of machine and labour utilisation. The uses of this information are to provide management with efficiency ratios and production shops with schedules, and to feed back information to scheduling for revision purposes. Examples of a labour utilisation chart, a labour utilisation summary sheet and a machine loading chart are shown in Figs. 25.8, 25.9 and 25.10.

Many different types of production control board, using discs, pegs or rotary devices to display information, are also available. Set-up time for these control boards is much quicker and the current situation is more easily seen than from a chart which needs to be read.

NOTE: Some ratios of efficiency are:

Labour utilisation:

$$\frac{\text{Net machine running time}}{\text{No. of operators} \times \text{average hrs. worked per wk.}} \times 100$$

Machine effectiveness:

$$\frac{\text{Net machine running time}}{\text{Net machine running time} + \text{stoppages}} \times 100$$

Machine utilisation:

$$\frac{\text{Net machine running time} + \text{set-up time}}{\text{Total working hours of machine section}} \times 100$$

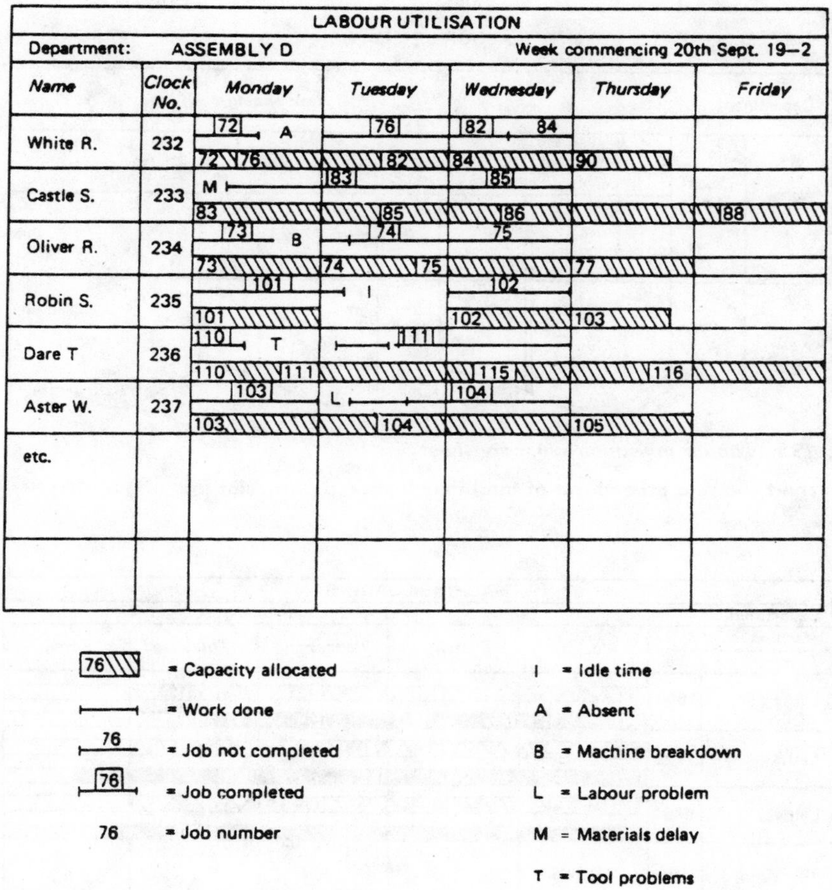

LABOUR UTILISATION						
Department:	ASSEMBLY D				Week commencing 20th Sept. 19—2	
Name	Clock No.	Monday	Tuesday	Wednesday	Thursday	Friday
White R.	232	[72] A / 72 \76\\\\\	[76] / \\\\\82\\\\\	[82] 84 / 84\\\\\\\\\\	90 \\\\\\\ ∇	
Castle S.	233	M ⊢ / 83\\\\\\\	[83] / \\\\\85\\\\\	[85] / \\\\\86 \\\\\\\\\\\		[88 \\\\\\\
Oliver R.	234	[73] B / 73\\\\\\\	[74] / \74 \\\\\\\75\\	75 / \\\\\\\\\\\	77 \\\\\\\	
Robin S.	235	[101] ⊣ I / 101\\\\\\\		102 / 102\\\\\\\	103 \\\\\	
Dare T	236	110⌐ T / 110\\\\\\\111	⊢—⌐[111 / \\\\\\\\\\	\\\\115\\\\\	\\\\\116 \	\\\\\\\\\\\
Aster W.	237	[103] L / 103\\\\\\\	⊢—⌐ / \\\\\\\104\\\	[104] / \\\\\\\\\\\	105\\\\\\\	
etc.						

76\\\ = Capacity allocated   I = Idle time

⊢———⊣ = Work done   A = Absent

⊢—76— = Job not completed   B = Machine breakdown

⊢—[76]—⊣ = Job completed   L = Labour problem

76 = Job number   M = Materials delay

                                        T = Tool problems

Fig. 25.8 *Gantt labour utilisation chart*
The chart shows the current job labour ratio at any given time

Manufacturing order control

The provision of documents which give authority to the production shops
to produce (according to the schedule and the plan) is known as manufacturing order control. This clerical function controls all activities requiring the
issue of paperwork such as the movement of materials from stores to the first
operation point and from operation to operation until the product is
completed. Similar controls are applied to the preparation of tooling, jigs and
fixtures and their movement from process to process, commencement of
work on each operation, and recording progress of the job through the
production shops.

LABOUR UTILISATION									
Department...........................					Week ending...........................				
Name	*Clock No.*	*Hours*							
		Work completed	*Idle time*	*B*	*L*	*M*	*A*	*T*	*Total time lost*

Fig. 25.9 ***Labour utilisation summary sheet***

This chart shows a breakdown of total time lost on a particular job

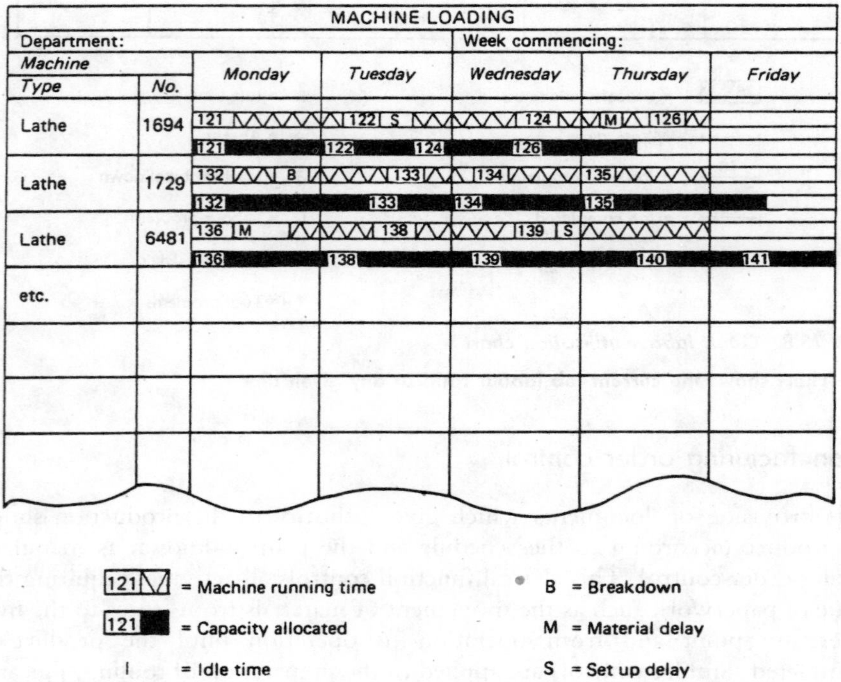

Fig. 25.10 ***Gantt machine loading chart***

This chart shows allocated work, running time and lost time for each machine

The system varies widely depending upon the size of the organisation and the type of product. The information normally required to operate the procedure is obtained from process layout sheets, schedules and details of scrap and shortages. Documents are prepared to cover all the activities connected with manufacturing the product. A typical list of these documents and schedules – in sequence of use – is given below:

	Production Factor	Paperwork	Operation
1	Operator	Labour loading schedule	Operator allocated
2	Machine	Machine loading schedule	Machine allocated
3	Materials and drawings	Material requisition	Issued
4	Tools	Tools requisition	Issued
5	Authority to produce	Works order	Carry out operation
6	Identity	Identity label	Affix to assembly
7	Inspection	Inspection order	Inspection – passed/ rejected
8	(a) Move to next operation	Authority to move	Transport
	(b) Move to scrap	Reject order	Transport
9	Control	All copies of documents	Complete and despatch to control
10	Costing	All copies of documents	Complete and despatch to costing dept.
11	Wages and bonus	Works order copy	Complete and despatch to wages section

The main types of manufacturing order are first single cards which have all the information on the front and act as identity labels, second multi-copy orders which reduce writing to a minimum, third single copy tear-off orders which have perforations dividing each section. Fig. 25.11 shows an example of the single card type.

If the product is manufactured in one department a job card is generally raised with works orders attached for each operation. When more than one department is involved a route card travels with the assembly from department to department.

Stock control (or inventory control)

The two main aspects of stock control are materials control and stock control proper. *Materials* control covers the purchasing and cost of materials and the organisation of material flow within the company.

Manufacturing Order				
Order No.	Batch No.	Quantity	Part name	Part No.

Materials	Quantity	Date required

Tools	Quantity	Date required

Operator	Clock No.	Machine	No.	Part No.	Quantity		Standard time	Actual time
					Passed	Rejected		

Signature inspection:....................................

Signature foreman: ....

Date ....

Fig. 25.11 *Manufacturing order*

This single card type of manufacturing order provides a record of the progress of a production job from the initial order to the final inspection

Stock control is the means of controlling the quantity and quality of materials and components in accordance with the production plan.

The purposes of stock control are to ensure by using clerical procedures that:

1 material required for production or other uses is available on time in the right quantity and quality
2 information is provided for financial control
3 stock is safeguarded
4 accurate stock records are maintained.

The clerical nature of stock control allows the function to be carried out in a section other than the stores where the physical movement of stock actually occurs. The various records include job analysis sheets, purchase requisitions, manufacturing orders, goods received notes and material requisitions. A record card for each type of material may contain details such as description of material, part number, location in stores, reordering level, maximum and minimum quantity levels, quantities on order, receipts, issues, balance, any quantity appropriated and the price.

Usually stock levels are reviewed regularly to dispense with obsolescent and obsolete materials. Physical stock checking is essential to prove the accuracy of the stock records.

There are two main ways of stock checking:

1 By *annual stocktaking*, which involves suspending the movement of all materials during the count.

2 By *perpetual inventory* along with continuous stocktaking which avoids the suspension of all material movement. This method operates through a reliable individual who is fully employed checking physical stocks against stock records throughout the year. He or she maintains a register of all the counts and variances. This record is acceptable by the auditors who must certify its accuracy for entry in the balance sheet under the Companies Act.

Despatching

This activity may be defined as the act of authorising the operator to carry out work allocated in accordance with the standard method by using the allocated tools, drawings and scheduled information. The despatching section is responsible for:

1 assigning the work to the workplace or machine
2 preparing, assembling and issuing the materials, tools, fixtures and gauges for production
3 releasing works orders and production sheets
4 co-ordinating the movement of work in progress by using a recording procedure.

Despatching may be decentralised or centralised. A description of each system is given below together with its advantages and disadvantages.

DECENTRALISED DESPATCHING
The orders are issued in a batch to the despatcher or to the supervisor in each department. His responsibility is to decide upon the most suitable sequence for issuing the orders and to ensure that materials, tools and the manufacturing orders arrive on time to each operator or machine. The advantages of this scheme are that the supervisor has more control of production activities within his section. There should be more flexibility of operation, and paperwork is reduced considerably. The capabilities of the supervisor or despatcher decide the success of this arrangement and probably maximum machine utilisation is more difficult to achieve.

CENTRALISED DESPATCHING
Orders are despatched directly to operators or machines from a centralised office where records and charts are kept of capacities, any backlog and loadings of operators and machines. Greater control of production is claimed for this method which gives more over-all flexibility when operating near the optimum level of production.

Unfortunately it is said that the foreman or supervisor merely runs the machines to produce in the sequence outlined, and therefore is not responsible for all the production aspects of the section. Further disadvantages are that there is more red tape, a duplication of effort and that quick action is difficult, although the supervisor can object to an order if he or she feels justified.

Progressing

The progress section provides the means for co-ordinating the production programme by revealing and if possible eliminating or correcting any deviations from the schedule.

Regulating the progress of materials and parts through the various production processes is known as *expediting*. Other names given to this task are progress chasing, stock chasing and follow-up. This difficult task is carried out by the following procedure.

1   Taking responsibility for all production orders after they have been issued.
2   Co-ordinating the production activities to produce work in progress at the correct time at the right place in the right quantity and quality.
3   Investigating and reporting variances from the schedules.
4   Providing alternative routes for production processes when breakdowns or bottlenecks occur.

5 Recording and analysing progress records of production for comparison between planned and actual output at each stage.

There are two methods of expediting which are explained below.

UNIT EXPEDITING

This method gives the expeditor responsibility for progressing a unit or contract from the commencement to the final stage of production. Slow moving and complex products and long runs are suitable for this method as all the problems connected with the unit are centralised through one person who is fully aware of the whole situation. Unfortunately this often results in a number of expeditors who are all dealing with one foreman in each department which adds to the problem of over-all control.

DEPARTMENTAL EXPEDITING

When the expeditor is responsible for all work passing through a department the method is called departmental expediting. This scheme is suitable for fast moving products but it can cause control problems. The supervisor must be prepared to pass to the expeditor the responsibility for production progressing otherwise a conflict will result.

Some typical causes of production delays

Innumerable factors can cause considerable delays in production, although many of these delays could be avoided with a little more care and forethought.

1 *Personnel problems* Absenteeism, labour turnover, disputes, poor selection, lack of training.

2 *Machines* Breakdowns, poor maintenance, bottlenecks (through lack of duplication of vital pieces of equipment), inefficient operation, loading errors or oversights, unsuitable machines.

3 *Materials* Overdue deliveries, inefficient ordering, poor quality materials, poor stores handling and transportation.

4 *Design* Poor design creating production difficulties, unsuitable materials recommended, accuracy required is too high for equipment available, tolerances and allowances too tight without good reason.

5 *Equipment* Lack of correct tools, jigs and fixtures, delay in delivering equipment.

6 *Planning* Excessive set-up times due to uneconomical batch sizes, poor estimates of work content.

7 *Inspection* Inadequate causing excessive scrap at later stages.

The supervisor and production control

Supervisors must avoid looking upon production control as another attempt to reduce their status and responsibility. Production control assists supervisors by relieving them of the numerous routine activities necessary to control production. These may be successfully carried out by individuals who can devote all their energies to ensuring that the various factors of production such as loading, materials and tools movement, authority to proceed, inspection, costing and wages control, drawings and chasing are dealt with effectively. Thus supervisors are able to devote more time to their true role of supervising their department.

In the small concern this concept of relieving the supervisor of routine is not possible. As the concern grows, however, the opportunity is open to relieve the supervisor gradually of these tasks and allow him or her to develop into a specialist who concentrates on directing, ensuring that individuals become fully productive. The supervisor's influence should be increased rather than lessened as he or she becomes the link between subordinates and management. In addition, this person has the important task of co-ordinating the many separate activities which will develop as the company grows. These activities include production planning and control, costing, inspection, materials control and preparation of wages and bonuses. Successful co-ordination depends upon the supervisor's knowledge of the systems. To be able to appreciate fully the other person's point of view, the supervisor must clearly understand the person's exact job, responsibility and the environment under which he or she operates. This concept elevates the supervisor's job to one of higher responsibility and importance.

Production control in the small concern

Organised production control is often non-existent in the small company. The works foreman controls by keeping most of the relevant activities in his head and making arbitrary decisions as the problems arise. This lack of method is usually demonstrated by impracticable estimates (e.g. of delivery dates) and general inefficiency. If the works foreman is sick, chaos quickly develops.

A guide is given now illustrating a simple production control system which can be elaborated or rearranged to suit the particular workshop. This scheme is divided into the following aspects.

- Information from the office
- Information from the workshop
- The estimate
- The production schedule
- The workshop schedule
- Additional records

Information from the office

The supervisor or works foreman should receive the following information:

1 orders received
2 promised delivery dates
3 any special information on orders
4 revised delivery dates
5 urgent orders – delivery required as soon as possible
6 materials and equipment received
7 promised delivery dates for materials and equipment.

Information from the workshop

The supervisor should keep a check on the following matters and also report them promptly to the controlling office.

1 progress of work through each stage of manufacture
2 any breakdown of plant
3 shortages of materials, components and assemblies
4 any other reasons for stoppages.

The transmission of this information may be conducted in many ways. Written forms of feedback to various control points (e.g. the cost office, wages section, progress section and the supervisor) are often essential, but in the very small concern they may be dispensed with entirely. The three main records in use are the *operator's work ticket*, the *job card* and the *detachable ticket*. A brief description of each one is given below.

1 *Operator's work ticket* Generally this ticket is a simple document used by the operator to record output. When completed the form is passed to various sections for calculating wages or for costing purposes. An example is given in Fig. 25.12.

2 *The job card* This document states the work to be performed by the operator. Generally the cards are completed and collected on a daily basis and the information is used for making entries in the workshop schedule. Figure 25.13 illustrates the type of card which can be used for this purpose. The card may be designed to include details of bonus schemes and any other information required.

3 *The detachable ticket* A ticket may be designed with a number of perforated sections containing information on each operation. As each operation is completed in sequence a section is torn off and signed by the operator who places it in a box which is emptied daily. Generally the ticket is tied to the assembly and each section bears the job number, the operation and any other relevant information. Fig. 25.14 gives an example.

The estimate

The estimate must be based upon the production schedule and the capacity

	WORK TICKET		

Operator's name ....   Week commencing ....

Clock No. ....

Section ....

Operation	Quantity produced	Total	Checked

Operator's signature ....

Supervisor's signature ....   Date ....

Fig. 25.12 *Operator's work ticket*

This record of the operator's output is used for calculating wages or costs

	JOB CARD		

Job No. ....   Date job required ....

Operation ....   Operation No. ....

Section ....

Date	Operator's name	Clock No.	Time			Passed	Rejected
			Commenced	Finished	Total		

Fig. 25.13 *Job card*

This states the work to be performed by the operator. A card like this one can be completed daily and used to make up the workshop schedule

JOB NO.	Operation 5	Operation 3	Operation 1
Operation 1 = : Hrs Mins 2 = : 3 = : 4 = : 5 = : 6 = :	Op. Clock No...... Job No............. Time............. Date..............	Op. Clock No...... Job No............. Time............. Date..............	Op. Clock No..... Job No............ Time............ Date.............
Total time = :	Operation 6	Operation 4	Operation 2
Passed/Rejected Inspector................	Op. Clock No...... Job No............. Time	Op. Clock No...... Job No............. Time.............	Op. Clock No..... Job No............ Time.............
Storekeeper................ Date......................	Date............	Date..............	Date.............

Fig. 25.14 *Job ticket*

The perforated sections are torn off as each operation is completed

of the workshop to provide an adequate delivery date. The question of costing is covered in Chapter 28. Although the estimate is closely related to the order which is dealt with in the office, the foreman may have to prepare the estimate. The type of form which would be circulated internally is shown in Fig. 25.15.

The production schedule

This schedule records the progress of each manufacturing order which is raised when the estimate is accepted. The schedule should be located in a convenient place for easy access. The example of a production schedule in Fig. 25.16 shows the information generally recorded.

The workshop schedule

This schedule indicates the jobs to be undertaken by the workshop and provides information for the supervisor or progress chaser to expedite the work. A refinement of this system would include a weekly summary or an arrears schedule to facilitate the preparation of the revised workshop schedule. A diagram of a typical workshop schedule is given in Fig. 25.17. The information in this diagram is only intended to indicate the standard framework which may be varied to suit particular requirements.

Additional records

In some establishments further records may be necessary owing to such factors as the complexity of the operations and the size of the stores. For

ESTIMATE

Internal Use Only

Customer **Est. No.** ....

Name .... **Date** ....

Address ....

....

Job ....

....

....

Price ....

Date estimate despatched ....

Closing date for acceptance ....

Accepted/Rejected .... **Date** ....

Job No. ....

Drawings ....

Tools ....

Manufacturing order No. ....

Signature ....

Fig. 25.15 ***An estimate***

This is the type of form used for internal circulation

example, if a large number of operations and machining is necessary, the use of loading charts and additional progress sheets would be worth while. The size of the stores is another example. In some concerns the range of materials is small, therefore visual inspection may be sufficient for reordering purposes, especially if the materials are commonplace and present no problem of delivery delays. The other extreme may warrant the use of stock records, material requisitions and a strictly regulated reordering system. In conclusion, it must be stressed that good sense and a thorough grasp of the particular requirements of the work situation must over-ride stereo-typed systems. They are intended to act as guides and provide basic principles upon which a sound production control system should be based.

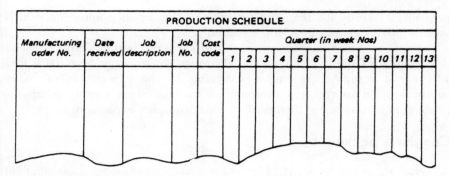

Fig. 25.16 *Production schedule*
It records the progress of each manufacturing order raised when the estimate is accepted

Fig. 25.17 *Workshop schedule*
This standard framework can be varied to suit the particular conditions. The schedule should indicate the jobs to be done by the workshop and provides information for expediting

The tendency is to create unnecessary paperwork and controls. Each proposed document and each existing document should be subjected to a stringent test for its usefulness before it is printed. Such answers as 'It may be useful' or 'We should really keep a record' do not justify its existence. Paperwork is very expensive and a definite reason for raising a document is essential.

Computer systems

The effectiveness of manual systems tends to rely upon supervisors and employees who develop experience and use it, often without creating any permanent records for reference by others. This reliance upon individuals understandably creates problems eventually.

Properly managed manual systems are efficient but limited compared with the benefits offered by a computer. However, great care is essential before adopting a computer system – according to the experiences of many companies. To appreciate a computer system one short visit to an appropriate company is better than reading long, complex explanations.

Computer packages

A wide range of proprietary packages (each containing a number of programs) is available. These packages vary in cost, comprehensiveness and suitability. Provided the appropriate packages are discovered and properly installed an indispensable, powerful resource is made available to management. Being available is insufficient, however, without effective managers to exploit the resource.

Packages cover all the previously mentioned production control activities. Documentation is different to accommodate computer printers; sophisticated analysis is easy but must be appropriate to needs; and large amounts of data can be rapidly processed.

Benefits

Many questions can be answered which are essential for formulating long-term strategies and for day-to-day running of the business. Accuracy, however, does rely upon correct information being fed into the computer. Typical advantages are more accurate data on bills of material, engineering alterations, inventories, goods received and materials movements; reduced work-in-progress; and improved control of many activities.

Computer knowledge

Certainly users need to know the capability of packages, how to use the programs to suit their requirements, and how to operate a display terminal. Why and how the computer works is relatively unimportant since programs are designed to be 'user-friendly', meaning that clear hints and advice on how to proceed are displayed for the user.

Probably three basic concepts are helpful: online processing, data base, and batch processing.

Online processing

The user of a terminal may enter information which is used immediately by the computer. Rapid response with appropriate data is displayed and the information is fed into various programs automatically. Thus the user interacts directly with the system and is capable of updating and retrieving information.

Data base

Information stored in the computer is called a data base. Such information may be added, deleted or modified (updated) by input from a terminal, provided the user is authorised. Other users may view data without changing it.

The information is stored in electronic files and records similar to physical information stored in cabinets. Access is rapid by pressing appropriate keys on the keyboard of the terminal. The information is stored only once to serve many different purposes.

Batch processing

Processing operations together as a group is called operating in batch mode. This is a method of running jobs not needing continuous operator attention, as for example printing reports.

Main aspects

An example of a computerised system is shown in Fig. 25.18 illustrating the main application programs or modules, and the information flow between them. This system is called the Communications Oriented Production Information and Control System (COPICS) offered by IBM.

Modules in Fig. 25.18 are briefly described now.

Customer order servicing

Orders are entered in central control where the status of orders is checked and any changes are entered. Users may retrieve and display up-to-date information. All data for invoicing is in the data base along with sales statistics as required.

Engineering and production data control

Three programs cover bill of material, online routing and facilities data management. A production definition data base provides bills of material or parts lists and any changes in the product through engineering alteration. Comprehensive data on each item allows design engineers to retrieve and view, determine usage, and change as required.

Online routing describes an item's manufacturing process or routing which may be used for costing, production planning, shop order release, and progressing. The facilities management program is used to capture and main-

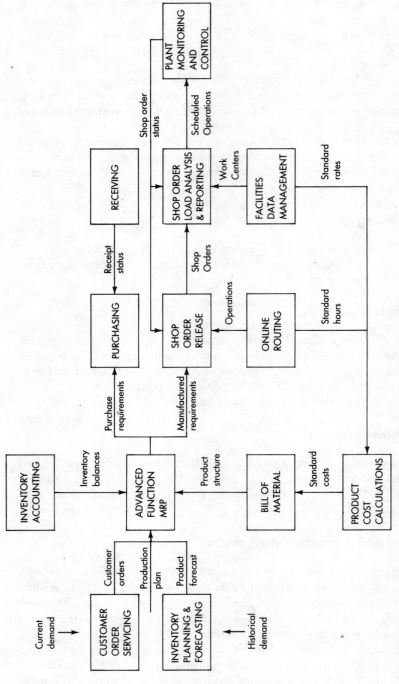

Fig. 25.18 *Production information and control system*

This IBM system (COPICS) provides management and operating personnel with the architecture and tools needed to develop individual, functional systems that are elements of a dynamic, integrated, online planning and control system for a manufacturing company

tain plant resource data and plan utilisation of plant resources. Engineers use a terminal to create, maintain and retrieve work centre machines and tool data; designate alternative centres; and identify machines and centres by cost centre or department.

Cost planning and control

Cost accountants may create, maintain and retrieve cost data. The program allows analysis and simulations. Online the user can change cost factors, simulate cost changes and review the impact.

Inventory management

Three programs are used. The first – inventory accounting – gives a basic inventory status of all items; thus supervisors and inventory controllers can enter and record material movements and physical counts. Users can receive immediate responses to enquiries on material availability.

The second – inventory planning and forecasting – helps planners to analyse demand, forecast sales, establish order quantities, set re-order points, and calculate safety stock.

The third – material requirement planning (MRP) – allows planners to view the material plan and respond to exceptions, thus keeping the plan valid at all times.

Shop floor management

- shop order release
- shop order load analysis and reporting
- plant monitoring and control

These three programs provide a complete scheduling, release, execution, and feedback reporting system which is of particular importance to supervision.

The first assists in preparing shop documentation, shop order release, and issue of materials. The second schedule starts and finishes dates of operations, calculates loads for machines and times, and maintains plans of work-load input and output for work centres. The third is of special interest and is detailed below.

PLANT MONITORING AND CONTROL
A set of data bases is maintained in the following areas.

1   *Employee data base*   Employee administrative data, work schedules, labour activities, and attendance including overtime, leave, and holidays.

2   *Shop order data base*   Released shop order information with routings, schedules, standards, and status.

3 *Department data base* Valid department numbers with corresponding work schedules and supervisors.

4 *Work centre data base* All valid work centres used by regular and rework operations.

5 *Transaction data base* All transactions entered during the shift as feed-back data to appropriate programs.

The program provides online functions for department supervision; production control, department employees, and administration. It captures in realtime the shop floor activity information needed to meet due dates and to reduce the cost of unnecessary chasing and expediting of parts.

The department supervisor, by using the operation start and finish dates, has the information to work on the right jobs while continuing to supervise the department efficiently. He or she can display the current status of employees and jobs currently in process or due to arrive, and manage the assignment of these jobs to utilise fully the resources available.

The production control supervisor, when expediting, may locate the in-process orders for the required part, review the status of a particular shop order, change the priority, change to alternative operations, and perhaps split the shop order to relieve a critical situation.

Purchasing and receiving

These programs help to ensure that the right quantity and quality of material is available when needed. Purchasing data is maintained in supplier and purchase order data bases.

Buyers are provided with production requirements, comprehensive information on suppliers including quotation data, previous orders and delivery dates. Requisitions and official orders may be created, and follow-up is easier.

The receiving program assists in reception and inspection control.

Questions

1 Explain the importance of production planning to the supervisor.
2 Describe the Gantt chart and draw up a simple example of one.
3 Give an account of the various stages of planning production.
4 What is the purpose of production control and how is it achieved?
5 Outline the main aspects of production control and illustrate the purpose of each aspect.
6 Describe the activity of scheduling.
7 Discuss machine and labour utilisation illustrating some efficiency ratios which may be used to control these activities.
8 Outline the purpose of manufacturing order control in a production control system.

9 Discuss the two main aspects of stock control.
10 What are the purposes of stock control and how are they achieved?
11 Give a detailed account of the purposes of despatching and expediting in a system of production control.
12 Give an account of the typical causes of production delays. Illustrate wherever possible with examples from your own experience of this problem.
13 'The supervisor must adopt the right attitude towards the production control department.' Explain this statement thoroughly.
14 Explain the three main types of production and give examples of products manufactured under each type.
15 Explain group technology and list its advantages.
16 Discuss the possible limitations of manual production control systems compared with the probable benefits of computer systems.

Case study

Bill Pritchard, the recently appointed works manager, had heard rumours that some departments were overloaded with work compared with others. Every time he aired this subject at his weekly meetings he was assured by the supervisors that there were no unfair work loads.

Bill decided to introduce a work distribution chart and instructed the supervisors to complete daily logs as a check on the production control reports.

After four weeks to Bill's surprise there were no discrepancies. Expecting at least some mismatch between records he conducted some spot checks. The first check in one of the suspect sections revealed that a fitter was not performing the task written up in the log. On querying it with him the fitter replied: 'I was told to build up hours on this one. We do it all the time. It's the system.'

Similar cases were found in other sections.

1 Consider carefully the choices of action that Bill could take.
2 What are the deeper implications of this discovery?

26 Quality assurance

Introduction

The modern concept of 'quality' is a philosophy which aims continually to satisfy customer requirements. The term 'requirements' covers all aspects of customer relationships – not the product alone. Acceptance of this philosophy is long overdue in the UK. An obvious truth is that if a customer perceives a product or service as being of high quality it becomes more attractive.

Traditional views on quality were generally restricted to the product being manufactured to a specification which was monitored by 'quality control' techniques. Modern approaches absorb the whole organisation in a *quality culture* which aims to provide the customer with a product and service of highest quality consistent with price.

Dr Juran's contribution

The modern approach was adopted in Japan in about 1954 when Dr J. M. Juran's ideas on quality management (which included quality circles) were discussed and accepted. Elsewhere they were discussed and, in general, dismissed although Juran is an American.

Japan's previous reputation for shoddy goods was quickly transformed. Juran's approach is essentially a top-down process which aims to prevent rather than cure faults.

General influences

Control of quality is essential in any concern for three major reasons:

- Influence of competition
- Technical necessity
- Legal liability for defective products

Influence of competition

Japan's lead and continued successful development in many activities and markets is serious for the West. Indeed a company's reputation for quality products and service is now vital for survival.

Research has shown that managers rather than employees are to blame for quality failures. Managers often seem to adopt a complacent attitude. They accept defects as inevitable and make little attempt to improve quality. A negative outlook is also prevalent: wait and see if the customer complains; inspect quality rather than prevent faults; and ignore or fail to seek employees' comments.

Zero defects concept

'Zero defects' (ZD) philosophy is commonplace in Japan. It means aiming for a 100 per cent quality target and ensuring that each job is done correctly first time.

Arguably this is humanly not possible since people are fallible. The philosophy, however, is sound and generates enthusiasm and co-operation. Without such high aims a company will have difficulties in competing against one obsessed with ZD.

Technical necessity

Often manufacturing processes are made less costly by using interchangeable parts; these may be selected at random and when assembled conform to the standards laid down. This practice allows designers to maximise tolerances without interfering with set quality standards. Inspection is adjusted to allow permissible variations from the standard to pass within set limits.

Legal liability for defective products.

The influence of recent legislation is given below.

The Consumer Protection Act 1987

Part I of the Act provides effective remedies to consumers who have suffered loss from defective products, thus implementing the 1985 EEC Council Directive on Product Liability. A producer of a defective product is strictly liable for the damage caused unless the person or company can rely on one or more defences listed in the Act.

A product is *defective* if it fails to provide appropriate safety to be expected in the circumstances. *Safety* includes components; a product is 'unsafe' if it is a danger to other property apart from risk of death or injury.

Damage refers to death, personal injury, or loss or damage to any property, including land. Claims related to property, however, are excluded since financial or pure economic loss (for the purposes of CPA) may be recovered under Contract or Negligence in appropriate cases.

Under Part II it is a criminal offence to supply consumer goods which do not comply with general safety requirements. Part III replaces existing law on misleading price indications; commencement date not yet announced.

THE IMPLICATIONS

The need to improve quality assurance procedures is obvious. Also more care and caution are essential when drafting advertisements, sales promotion projects, instruction booklets, and any particular safety precautions.

Customer satisfaction

The importance of market orientation has already been stressed in Chapter 4. To achieve maximum customer satisfaction market research should provide an accurate forecast of all customer wants. The total organisation must be geared whole-heartedly to planned quality improvement programmes. Everyone should feel totally committed if market dominance is to be achieved.

Many employees contact the customer either directly or indirectly through correspondence. All such contacts affect customer satisfaction.

Senior management's roles

Poor quality often originates before reaching the shop floor through defective raw materials and components, poor design and incorrect scheduling. Furthermore machine maintenance and working conditions cannot be ignored, which of course are also outside the operator's control.

If accepted, typical new roles are:

1   Supporting an aggressive strategy to overcome quality problems.
2   Putting the customer first.
3   Finding out exactly what the customer wants.
4   Ensuring that all services are treated as important activities which affect the customer's opinion of the company.
5   Setting standards with continual updating in mind – aiming high.
6   Continually establishing projects to improve gradually. All employees should be involved; a quality assurance manager may be appointed for this purpose.

Total quality management

Adopting a quality culture is often termed TQM. The ultimate responsibility for TQM is at board level, but in many concerns which use this strategy both managers and supervisors are appraised on their capability and performance in quality improvement.

Successful quality improvement

Success is generally measured by growth and changes in share price, market share, return on investment, and workforce stability.

Successful competitive strategy naturally embraces other activities such as choice of products, production strategy and tactics, selection of particular market segments, and investment policy.

Cost of poor quality

Apart from consumer dissatisfaction the financial cost of mistakes, corrections, waste and unproductive work is enormous. Often hidden by costing systems or by inefficient managers, such costs increase the danger of insolvency.

The cost in terms of frustration and stress is difficult to estimate. Certainly wasting time and energy in rectifying faults and working with poor materials, or whatever, is soul-destroying. Employees' opinions of management in this poor situation can be imagined especially when blame for poor quality is attributed to them.

Quality culture

So far supervisors may feel that there is little they can do to improve quality, with their limited influence on senior managers. Although quality culture often demands a change in management style and to be effective must come from the top, supervisors can help by practising various basic concepts.

1 Each employee will admit that he or she is also a customer. Relating this idea to the next employee (another customer) who receives the former person's work, should foster more responsibility. The situation is clearer compared with relating to a remote customer outside.

2 Allow as much freedom as possible in working arrangements; consequently the employee will feel more commitment.

3 Ensure that adequate feedback on quality is received by all employees and discuss the causes of faults with them.

4 Tell superiors why faults are occurring – do not assume they know.

5 Whenever the opportunity occurs transmit information on quality well up the line.

Quality techniques

Understandably any quality technique must follow a lead from top management with its committed quality assurance programmes and indoctrination of a quality culture. The techniques are introduced when the climate is right. To help attitude change an employee must be appropriately trained.

Typical techniques are quality control including statistical quality control, quality circles and value analysis; these are discussed soon. Other schemes are process analysis techniques, departmental activity analysis and Juran project training.

Quality control

The three main activities are:

- Establishing standards and specifications
- Inspection
- Statistical quality control

Establishing standards and specifications

The establishment of standards and specifications makes it possible to ensure that the product conforms to the requirements. The standard is set by top management in conjunction with production engineering which assesses the feasibility of the proposed standard. The sales department assesses the market requirements. The purchasing department provides information on standards of material available and the production department then gives an indication of the feasibility of manufacturing at the proposed standard within a proposed cost.

Perfect standards in production are both costly and difficult to achieve. The basic standard for a product to sell effectively must conform to the consumers' minimum standards at a selling price which is acceptable for that level of quality. Naturally there is an area of acceptability which allows for slight variations that do not drastically change the performance of the product. These variations are caused by chance variables and assignable variables.

1   *Chance variables*   These are inherent in the production processes, e.g. machine limitations, material imperfections, limitations of inspection equipment and human error.

2   *Assignable variables*   These are external influences such as incorrect operation of machines, misuse of equipment, incorrect sequence of operations, worn and faulty machines, worn inspection equipment and variations in working conditions, including humidity, temperature and vibration.

Inspection

The purpose of inspection is to separate defective goods from those conforming to the standard of accuracy laid down by management. This important aspect of quality control attempts to ensure that only goods of adequate quality pass to the consumer, and that faults are located in materials, components, work in progress and finished goods. The inspection department often supervises the task of salvaging rejected work or the disposal of scrap to reduce the possibility of defects returning accidentally (or sometimes intentionally) to the production line. The department is also responsible for the general control of all inspection devices.

Inspection also provides information for statistical quality control but setting quality standards is outside its function. Quality standards must be measurable, reasonable and understandable, therefore they must be in writing. Rigid inspection is uneconomic since it tends to increase scrap by rejecting anything that does not conform exactly to the drawing, whereas reasonable inspection is flexible and allows a degree of departure from the drawing provided that adequate operation of the product is not impaired and quality standards are maintained. Quality control provides these limits within which inspection can operate effectively.

Inspection methods

There are two methods of inspection: 100 per cent inspection method and the sampling method.

1 *100 per cent inspection* This method entails the inspection of every single item in a batch or process which is costly, difficult to carry out satisfactorily because of human error and, in general, is avoided whenever possible. This method is justified for large and complex products with critical stages of production which would involve heavy losses if faults were not discovered in the early stages.

2 *Sampling method* The sampling technique involves selecting at random a given number of pieces for inspection. Statistical tables provide the appropriate sample size for the total number involved at a set level of quality. The number of rejects gives a fair indication of the quality level for the whole batch.

Statistical quality control

This approach to quality control uses statistical method to provide information for supervisors and operators to maintain control of the actual processes.

This method (using the theory of probability) establishes a set of control limits for each process by determining the range within which the chance variables are likely to occur. When these limits are exceeded an immediate indication is given that some action must be taken to correct an assignable variable which has forced the process over the specified limits. The physical

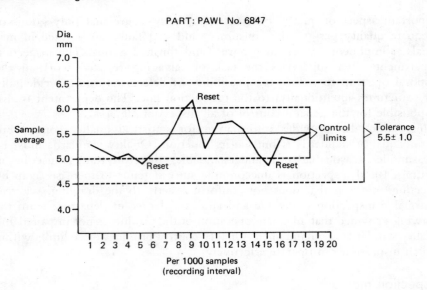

PART: PAWL No. 6847

Fig. 26.1 *Statistical quality control chart*

Control limits are set for each process. Results of sampling are plotted on a graph to show trends. Corrective action can then be taken at an early stage, wherever trends indicate that the control limits are in danger of being exceeded

side of process control involves sampling at regular intervals and the plotting of results on the chart as quickly as possible to show the current trend. Figure 26.1 shows such a chart.

Control charts of this nature are provided for each process and a running record is maintained. When the plot falls outside the limits the incident is reported and an immediate investigation follows to find out why the deviation has occurred. Remedial action must be taken to steer the process back to within the limits specified. After some experience it becomes more obvious when the process is veering away towards the limits and corrective action may be taken earlier. Thus a greater percentage of the product is manufactured within the specified limits.

This emphasis on controlling the process which ensures increased quality in the early stages of production also results in higher machine utilisation in later stages, less possibility of damage to machines and a reduction in further processing of faulty work.

The concept of statistical quality control has been over-simplified here for the purpose of explanation. The method can be very successful when correctly applied in suitable circumstances. The need for consistently good quality is vital in a competitive market.

Quality circles

The Japanese were the first to exploit quality circles (QC) in the early 1960s, although the concept originated in the USA some years earlier. Development elsewhere has been very slow until recently when more attention has been paid to the successful application of the technique in Japan.

QC is based on 'motivation by participation': a small group (usually from five to ten people) who are engaged in *similar* activities meet regularly under the leadership of the supervisor to discuss work problems. Topics may include quality, materials, machines, equipment and safety. The meetings are voluntary and in company time, although once established there is a tendency to meet at other times. The group identifies the problem, analyses and solves it, and makes recommendations to management. On receiving agreement the group implements the solution whenever it is feasible.

Initial considerations

If the decision to install QC comes from top management the first stage may be to establish a steering committee. Its functions will include financial allocation and cost considerations, responsibility for training, launching the scheme, the appointment of leaders and a facilitator, and co-ordination of the project.

Objectives

The main aims are to improve productivity by participation, to improve quality at less cost, to reduce frustration and grievances, to reduce labour turnover and to push real power down to lower levels in the organisation.

Membership

There are various forms of group composition. The simple one is where a supervisor decides that the idea is worth trying, receives permission from management, and asks for volunteers to make up a group. A more structured group may include an inspector and a quality engineer. A full-scale launch will include a training seminar on QC, a collective decision to attempt the technique, establishing a steering committee to guide and advise, training sessions for circle members and chairmanship training for the leader.

Training requirements

Considerable improvements are possible even when utilising simple approaches. Many brilliant ideas are locked up in employees' heads and remain there for various reasons. No training is necessary – the solutions often already exist.

In highly complex situations, however, it is argued that training in some areas is particularly important: problem solving techniques, use of initiative, brain storming, pareto analysis, data gathering and cause-effect diagrams are often mentioned.

General approaches

Obtaining the backing of management is absolutely vital otherwise the outcome may be a lowering of morale and a demotivating effect may be experienced. Also the union should be consulted and direct involvement encouraged. During discussions within the group, all members are encouraged to contribute, the subject matter is thoroughly aired, all possible solutions are considered and a written report is submitted to management. After agreement, implementation by the group must be handled with extreme care, remembering all the human problems that may be involved.

The initial reaction from other employees may cause concern, therefore it is worth taking a low-key approach until the outcomes are appreciated. Considerable work is necessary and the meetings are time-consuming. Anything worthwhile, however, takes courage and perseverance before successful results are seen. Previous experiences have shown the need for a trained facilitator, general training for circle members and the usefulness of speaking directly with other companies who have adopted the technique.

Below is a typical structured approach which a QC group could apply.

1 Allow members to select the problem. Brain storming or individual proposals may be employed.
2 Draw up a list and vote on the selection of a problem.
3 Gather data and analyse.
4 Establish solutions and determine the most suitable one. Possibly set a target and a time-scale.
5 Obtain agreement from management.
6 Implement the proposal.
7 Check periodically and revise as considered necessary.

Appropriate organisation levels

The orthodox sites for QC are on the shop-floor, in the office or, for instance, on the retail stores-floor. Within these sites are found the majority of employees – using similar skills and experience – who easily identify with each other in the work situation. They can distinguish similar problems and both individually and collectively determine ways of overcoming them and of implementing their ideas.

This distinction avoids confusing QC with other forms of group activity such as works committees, project teams, value analysis groups and joint consultative committees. These groups are composed of employees who do different work and who generally deal with tabled problems or plans.

Remembering the definition, however, it may be argued that groups of supervisors could also form a QC. Indeed, in France there is at least one known group of this nature.

Some essential points

- Group formation – *all* volunteers performing similar work except leader.
- Selection of the 'right' circle leader.
- Careful preparation at all stages of implementation.
- Management commitment.
- Union support and involvement.
- Adequate training programmes for QC members.
- Receptive co-workers.
- Implementation by members unless there are exceptional circumstances.

The supervisor's part

The main features are that if a simple approach is used the supervisor must approach management and receive full backing first. He or she should remember the background to constitutional management and participative supervision with emphasis on the analytical aspect of the radical framework explained in Chapter 2.

If management takes the initiative the supervisor should insist on adequate training as a leader and for the members of the group. He or she should do everything possible to win the support of employees and the union. The supervisor's reports to management should be in line with all the requirements outlined in Chapter 16 and if there is any debate he or she should insist on implementation by the members unless there is a very good reason for denying them the opportunity.

The supervisor should be convinced that the concept is sound and that in the event of failure the cause should be looked for elsewhere.

Value analysis

This technique aims to improve the reliability and reduce the cost of an existing product by studying critically the product and its components to assess their function and cost. At the design stage the technique is called value engineering.

A psychological questioning attitude is essential in attempting to improve design at lower cost. Success depends upon allocating sufficient time, using imagination, and creating an atmosphere where people feel free to come up with new ideas or suggestions regardless of how absurd they may seem. Invariably savings occur, either by changing the method of producing a component, redesigning it, or dispensing with it entirely by redesigning other components.

Method

A typical procedure follows six phases.

1 Select the product for study.
2 Define the function of each part; note its cost and design.
3 Determine the various ways of performing the function and how they could be incorporated in a design, or designs.
4 Cost each design idea and compare with previous costs. If one is cheaper continue with the study; if more expensive abandon and try again.
5 Select the optimum design considering cost and reliability.
6 Implement design and review periodically.

The value analyst

Generally this person is an engineer, trained in value engineering, enthusiastic, and creative. Ideally a multi-disciplinary team is chosen to conduct the study. However the supervisor may also conduct similar studies with a group of operatives. Many improvements in quality and reliability have been recorded.

The supervisor and quality control

Although the supervisor is assisted by the quality controller, inspector and other specialists who perform functional duties within the department, he or she is still responsible for the quality of the work. The supervisor's responsibility may be considered from three aspects – operators, materials and machines – which are now discussed.

Operators

The supervisor should encourage operators to be quality-minded and conscientious. They ought to be proud of the product and the company and their enthusiasm must be aroused by dynamic leadership. Most employees are basically conscientious and take pride in their work, therefore the supervisor should constantly counteract any undesirable pressures that tend to change this outlook.

Other important factors affect quality. If operators are not fully aware of the standards set for each process they can hardly be expected to aim for high quality. Similarly, if operators are not fully trained or familiarised with better methods of performing operations, quality will suffer. Careful selection also is important otherwise employees will be misplaced and those who lack the necessary ability to work without set standards will naturally produce inferior parts. Finally, there is the problem of dealing with careless operators who for various reasons have difficulty in concentrating. Scrap is very costly so it is essential to deal firmly with these careless employees.

Materials

If materials are reported to be faulty or the wrong type, the supervisor should report the fact together with recommendations to his or her superior. The cost of production rises as more time is spent on unsuitable materials and every effort must be made to rectify this situation.

Machines

If a machine develops a fault the supervisor must either order the machine to be stopped to avoid excessive scrap or report the defect immediately to his or her superior according to circumstances. The servicing of the machine and the rearrangement of the production programme should follow as a natural sequence of control.

Service industries

In this sector the term *reliability* is often used instead of quality. Reliance means trust, confidence, dependence upon, and feeling safe. Relating these definitions to transport services, energy supplies, communication (telephones etc.), health facilities, education, the legal system, repair and delivery services, and financial services, clearly emphasises their importance to consumers.

Reputation

The need for improved reliability is illustrated daily in press reports. Typical causes of low reliability are poor ethical standards, human fallibility, insufficient funds, poor management, environmental and economic conditions, and governmental policies. Causes mentioned vary, depending on the particular service. Increased pressure on the government to improve reliability through legislation has been partially successful.

Measurement of reliability

Reliability is of a conceptual or abstract nature in some service industries. Consequently there are application difficulties in the technical and human fields. Intangible outcomes are sometimes inescapable: the performance of many professional service occupations is difficult to measure, considering probability and depth of existing knowledge (typical examples are surgeons, doctors and research scientists); some service activities do not necessarily respond to quantitative techniques; expertise and ethical standards may not respond to testing techniques; and revising or setting standards is not a straightforward process.

Despite these inherent difficulties certain aspects can be improved. Examples are injecting more funds; legislating against unethical behaviour and unfair charges; improving management by training, and relieving human fallibility by installing electronic equipment.

Financial Services Act 1986

This Act is an important addition and a good example of the urgent need to protect the customer. It is so complex that implementation has been undertaken in stages over two years. Practically all types of investment business are affected. Investors are more protected through a framework of organisations which establish and enforce rules of good practice.

Heading the framework is the Securities and Investments Board under which a number of Self-Regulatory Organisations (SROs) operate. Each SRO sets its own rules based on general principles which amount to: anyone who advises on or sells investments must observe high standards of integrity; act with due skill, care and diligence; and deal fairly with customers. In brief, an adviser must extract as much information as possible on the client's personal financial situation, identify the person's needs, and give the best possible advice.

'Best advice' naturally depends on the uniqueness of each case, therefore only guidelines are suggested. Clearly proof of best advice demands careful record keeping of information from clients and advice offered.

Questions

1   What is meant by the term 'quality assurance'?
2   Outline the long-term effects of Dr Juran's ideas on quality management.
3   What are the likely long-term effects of the Consumer Protection Act 1987?
4   Explain the Zero Defects concept.
5   Discuss the modern concept of consumer satisfaction.
6   'A quality culture is essential for company survival.' Discuss this statement.
7   Describe the three main activities of quality control.

8   How can the supervisor develop a quality-conscious attitude in operators?
9   Discuss the various factors that help to achieve high quality.
10 Explain the difference between chance variables and assignable variables in quality control. Give examples of each.
11 What is the purpose of inspection?
12 Discuss the nature and uses of statistical quality control.

Case study 1

A sales representative was paying her usual three-monthly visit to a long-established client who was obviously upset. 'I've had enough of your firm. You cause me more and more paperwork. The time I spend on 'phone calls and correspondence is now beyond a joke.'

The representative attempted to placate him. 'I do understand, but it's the computer. They're trying hard to sort things out but it takes time.'

'Look, Linda, I'm not interested in your problems. I've got enough of my own. Your invoices are never right, orders get mixed up and it takes ages for them to deliver the right items.'

'But we're the best in the field – there's no-one to touch us.'

'You may think so, but I don't. I'm adding up all the costs now and your company isn't top of the hit parade, I can tell you!'

'I'm sorry, Peter. You're a valued customer and I'll have a go at them when I get back next week.'

When the representative returned to the office she was told that the client had cancelled his standing order.

1   Was it the computer's fault?
2   Outline the main causes of the problem.
3   Comment on the representative's approach.

Case study 2

'I can see that we're never going to solve the quality problem until you both appreciate the other's point of view.' The managing director looked wearily at the managers of the sales and production departments and continued, 'We know the sales representatives have to take the blame and we risk losing repeat orders *and* we know the production people have to maintain the performance criteria. You're dependent upon each other and somehow we must figure out a way.'

The production manager was quick to reply: 'In production we are subjected to continual pressure from sales to get the orders out on time, but we have to consider the cost factors as well.'

The sales manager reacted, 'What you do not understand is we're only a small firm. If my reps promise a delivery date for something, customers expect it to be there on time and in top condition. They're not bothered about our problems!'

What could be done in this situation?

27 Financial control

Introduction

Financial control of a concern is obviously a critical activity. Serious errors may lead to bankruptcy or liquidation of the business. Careful recording of all financial transactions is necessary as a measure of control and to satisfy certain legal requirements.

Actual control is achieved by measuring expenditure and income, ensuring that a reasonable balance is kept in hand and sufficient cash flow is maintained. The business must be able to pay its debts, allow for replacement of its fixed assets such as machines, equipment and vans and build adequate reserves for expansion programmes.

Important decisions have to be taken on the capital structure of the business, the acquisition of funds, the determination of dividends, the degree of liquidity, short-, medium- and long-term investments and in areas associated with mergers and take-overs.

In view of these aspects the financial function will vary in operation, depending upon the circumstances and size of the company. In a small company it may be possible to calculate the profit or loss on each transaction. As a company grows the recording of all financial activities increases. Difficulties arise unless sound basic principles are established and followed by all employees. Essential guidelines ensure realistic recording and valuation of activities and assets to arrive at a reasonably accurate profit or loss. Problems of controlling expenditure also increase with growth.

Often personnel do not appreciate the importance of adhering to financial procedures. As a result the quality of accounting data is reduced and management's decisions based upon such data are impaired. Financial accountancy is essentially a *tool* for use by managers, employees and shareholders.

Roles

Clearly the roles of financial controllers are to provide financial information to management which will help in deciding on the best courses of action; financial forecasts and plans; and in deviations from the plan, to undertake corrective action, and to make adjustments if required.

These roles apply to short- and long-term plans.

Short-term plans

These are formulated by interpreting in detail long-term plans for control on, say, a daily or weekly basis. Such calculations indicate shifts in profit, income or expense when deviations are likely. Typical shifts would be raw materials prices, wage changes and output variations. This aspect, known as budgetary control, is covered in the next chapter.

Long-term plans

Based on policy decided by senior management, forecasts are prepared for, say, the next five years. These cover sales, market growth prospects, and new and existing products. Their critical nature should be understood since expansion or contraction programmes hinge on these plans.

The chief accountant forecasts profit, capital employed and cash needs for each year. Management assesses their significance and may adjust selling prices, sales volume, quality, and advertising and sales promotion plans. Management will also consider various financial programmes involving research and development, cost-cutting, concentrating on more profitable lines, diversification, disposing of surplus assets, marketing strategy, overdrafts, and loans.

Dynamic effects

The dynamic nature of business demands a continuous updating and revision of financial plans. Forecasts and plans will be inaccurate and must be viewed as flexible estimates with built-in controls to revise as circumstances change.

To work effectively this mechanism contains arrangements for continuous monitoring and immediate action when deviations occur, careful and precise allocation of responsibilities for each financial sector, and provision for major adjustments when daily monitoring fails, due to unforeseen changes.

Computerised financial control

With a complete suite of programs it is possible to manage all financial accounting activities through the computer. Reports may be printed giving the financial position when required to control progress and profitability. Display terminals in appropriate locations provide immediate updates and online processing.

Packages are available to:

1 analyse current financial situations with previous periods and with budgets
2 maintain accounting controls and satisfy auditing needs

3   control strictly cash flow
4   prepare the payroll, sales invoices and accounts payable.

Appropriate control programs can provide valuable marketing statistics, market research data, sales performance of representatives, customers' buying trends, and many other sales reports in financial or quantity terms.

Problems of financial accounting

The purpose of both financial and cost accounting is to record all transactions and analyse them so that information is presented in the most suitable form for various purposes. The four main problem areas which usually arise are associated with debts, legal requirements, managerial requirements and social obligations.

Debts

The launching of a product from the idea stage to the sale is generally a slow process. This time-lag often causes problems as expenditure may commence with the purchase of various assets such as buildings, plant and materials and continue with the payment of wages and a variety of other expenses as plans are developed.

A considerable period of time may elapse before any income is received, but during this time funds must be found to pay all the debts.

The degree of indebtedness of a company is important and it is the responsibility of the accountant to provide accurate evidence on this item. In addition banks and other financial institutions will require such evidence along with other information to calculate the risk involved in granting a loan. Thus creditworthiness may be established considering the orders in hand, profits over the years, the value of fixed assets and other liabilities outstanding.

Legal requirements

The accounting requirements of the Companies Acts 1948/1985 are intended to protect and safeguard the investor. Every company must keep proper books of account as laid down in a comprehensive schedule of detailed requirements covering all the important items in the balance sheet and profit and loss account. A copy of these statements is sent annually to the Registrar of Joint Stock Companies. They may be seen by any individual on payment of a small fee.

The Acts also increased the rights and duties of auditors to include a report on the profit and loss account as well as the balance sheet and any group accounts. The report must conform to a stringent list of requirements in the schedule. Furthermore, only those who possess the qualifications stated in the Acts may be appointed as auditors.

The accounts must give a true and fair view of the company's activities and state of affairs. They must also be acceptable to the Commissioners of Inland Revenue who require a copy for taxation calculations.

Managerial requirements

Unfortunately conventional accounting procedures for the preparation of final accounts and records do not provide information in its most suitable form for managers to become more effective. The exercise of managerial skills demands complex analysis of external economic affairs and internal business activities. The use of cost accountancy, budgetary control and other forms of management accountancy is essential for this purpose.

The management accountant needs considerable expertise to provide all relevant information to managers who may then use their skills with a thorough knowledge of possible consequences.

Social obligations

The modern approach is for a company to recognise that there are obligations to its employees, shareholders, the community and trade unions. Today these social obligations tend to be based on the concept of adequate reward for all social groups rather than the maximisation of profits alone. Probably this change was caused by the reduced influence of shareholders, the increased power of trade unions and the strengthening of the bond between the company and employees/consumers.

Another trend is the increased emphasis on long-term stability and growth in view of the risk undertaken by the shareholder and the over-all effect on the community. Naturally a person who invests in a company expects an adequate return on the capital invested. How much dividend should be expected is another question. Certainly the investor does not expect management to take extreme risks unless that person is a gambler who chooses to invest in a concern where the dangers of collapse are recognised.

To satisfy these obligations companies generally produce interim and final accounts which give considerable detail. The annual report is usually particularly informative; explanations on financial matters are included along with photographs of the products and factories. Most companies allow visitors to tour the premises and talks are often arranged on specific financial topics.

Employment of capital

A company seldom stagnates – it is either expanding or contracting. Healthy expansion demands adequate supplies of cash and careful planning of expenditure. The amount of cash required is very difficult to assess, considering the large range of expenditure involved. The financial requirements of a business may be divided into two main groups: *fixed* or permanent capital, and *circulating* or working capital.

Fixed capital

All fixed assets such as land, factory and office buildings, plant and machinery, furniture and fittings, vans and cars come under this heading. They contribute to profit by their use in the business, therefore a charge for depreciation is included as an expense in the annual accounts. Many fixed assets depreciate in value through use, age and obsolescence. Eventually they must be replaced and, in the case of machines, it may be more economic to scrap and sell a model which has been superseded by a more efficient type. Some fixed assets such as vans and tools have a very limited life and provision is needed for replacements. Inevitably the prices of new fixed assets tend to rise so replacement plans must include this factor.

The prudent company also keeps reserves for unexpected occurrences such as legal costs, accidents and damage. Some fixed assets actually appreciate in value, land being a typical example. Intangible assets such as goodwill, patents and trade marks may be of considerable value within a prosperous company. These also are regarded as fixed or permanent capital.

Circulating capital

Current assets continually change their form and are not retained in the company for any long period of time unlike fixed assets which remain for a number of years. The money used to acquire current assets is known as circulating capital. Such items as raw materials are purchased, salaries, wages and expenses are paid, and the finished goods are sold. Although salaries and wages are paid in cash or by cheque, the other items may involve credit transactions. The length of the credit period also affects the amount of cash required at any time. Briefly, cash changes its form into goods through various processes and returns to its original form when products are sold, hence the name circulating capital.

All current assets are sometimes called working capital, but it is more realistic to deduct current liabilities from the current assets to arrive at a figure which represents the actual cash available as working capital.

The term current liabilities refers to all current debts owed by the concern which would include creditors, a bank overdraft and short-term loans. These debts are current in the sense that they must be paid in the near future, that is within one year.

Balance of capital

Establishing and maintaining a correct balance between fixed and working capital is an important factor in financial control. If too much cash is spent on fixed assets, the situation will develop where insufficient working capital is available to utilise fully the plant and machines which have been purchased. On the other hand, insufficient allocation of cash to fixed assets indicates either surplus cash lying idle in the bank or inefficient use of working capital. Effective use of working capital is vital for growth.

Forecasting and budgeting

Forecasting the financial activities of a company is based upon previous financial records of income and expenditure and on predictions of the trends in sales, production costs and general expenses. The difficulties of forecasting are aggravated when markets are unstable or when there are no previous records to indicate trends as in the case of a new business.

Forecasting the future is naturally guesswork and the correct attitude towards the forecast is to be ready for the unexpected. Precautions and a degree of flexibility in plans based on forecasts are essential.

The forecast or estimate is used to plan the financial budget which is adjusted to make the best use of available cash. Such adjustments include decisions on cash requirements or cash investments if there is a surplus and consideration of the choices of expenditure. Budgeting for cash flow in the form of income and expenditure is essential as an indication of events, but financial controls must check continually and promptly on the *actual* cash flow to make corrections and revisions of the budget as the situation changes.

Sources of capital

The ways of raising capital depend upon the type of business and its reputation. The 'one-man' business or sole proprietor is very restricted; when the person wishes to start the business no reputation exists in most cases, therefore the sole proprietor must depend upon personal resources and loans from friends and relatives.

A similar situation exists with partnerships. As the business develops and appears to be stable and thriving, the opportunity to increase its credit will be established. If the creditworthiness of the business is acceptable, suppliers will deliver more goods at longer credit terms. Banks will also allow overdrafts and loans on this basis. Other ways of raising money are to sell property already owned and lease it back, or to raise a mortgage on property owned. Indirect methods are to buy assets on hire-purchase or hire on a rental scheme.

Continued expansion of the concern often demands large sums of cash, more easily raised by forming a private limited liability company.

Further expansion may mean inviting the public to invest which involves conversion to a public limited company. Conversion is conducted by an issuing house or, if the company is very secure and of high reputation, it may make a direct issue to the public. The issuing house will handle all the requirements including capital gearing (proportion of ordinary and preference shares and loans), advertising and legal aspects.

Shares and debentures

Certain responsibilities rest with the concern when capital is raised and these cannot be shrugged off as unimportant; investment must be paid for in various ways such as interest and dividends.

There are two main types of shares offered by a public limited company to the general public. These are ordinary and preference shares. They should not be confused with debentures which are loans. All three, however, form the permanent capital of a concern.

The ordinary share or 'equity share' normally carries voting rights, therefore the holders have a degree of control over the running of the business. There is more risk attached to this type of share because the amount of dividend depends upon the prosperity of the business. Before any dividend is payable, both preference shareholders and debenture holders must receive their fixed rate of dividend or interest respectively. A share of the surplus profit, if any, is then divided among the ordinary shareholders.

The preference shareholders are entitled to a fixed rate of dividend, as the name implies, in preference to ordinary shareholders. With cumulative preference shares, the amount of dividend due may accumulate annually if no dividend is declared in one year or in a number of years.

Debentures are loans and they do not form part of share capital. The holders are creditors of the concern, therefore the fixed interest rate is payable regardless of profit or loss. Debentures are safer than shares and – in some cases – mortgage debentures are issued which means that the loan is secured by a fixed charge on the concern's assets.

The Stock Exchange

The raising of permanent capital through the issue of shares is safe-guarded by the Council of the Stock Exchange. The Council is aware that any investor who is prepared to subscribe to a new issue may not wish to leave the money indefinitely in the company, therefore the person needs an assurance that the shares will be negotiable through the Stock Exchange. This does not mean that when the shareholder sells the shares the cash is withdrawn from the company and then replaced. Only the shares change hands and often the shares are bought and sold several times over a short period before the share certificate is issued by the company to the eventual new holder.

Permission to deal in a company's shares or a quotation must be obtained from the Council which insists on very stringent requirements before agreeing. Unless the Council is satisfied with its investigations it will not grant a quotation or permission to deal in the particular shares and, in these circumstances, it is doubtful whether many prospective subscribers would be interested in buying them.

A further legal precaution is embodied in the Companies Acts 1948/1985 which states that if a company implies that an application has been made to the Council for a quotation and the application is refused, all application cash must be returned to the investor and all allotments of shares are void.

The main function of the Stock Exchange is to provide a market for stocks and shares which can be bought and sold in a fair and straightforward manner.

The prices of shares are controlled by supply and demand, *not* by the Stock Exchange. If there are more buyers than sellers for shares in a particular company, the price rises; if sellers predominate then the price falls.

Some idea of the importance of the market may be imagined when it is estimated that around four-fifths of industry and commerce in Britain is conducted by companies with capital owned by the public. The total value of securities officially listed is about £400 000 000 000.

Although people are inclined to speak of the Stock Exchange located in London, there are twenty-two stock exchanges throughout the country which collectively form the Stock Exchange. They are strongly bound together by common regulations and connected with each other by private telephone lines or teleprinters so that information is immediately available at all centres.

Share ownership

About 20.5 percent of the UK adult population (nine million people in 1988) now own shares compared with 7.5 percent in 1979. This change is due to government initiatives: the privatisation programme (the major factor), favourable tax treatment of employee share schemes, and the introduction of personal equity plans (PEP's). This compares with about 25 percent in USA, 14 percent in France, 9 percent in Japan, and 9 percent in West Germany.

Profit and accounts

Although the object of a business may be to provide goods or services for the community, the achievements of a concern are based upon its ability to run the establishment at a profit.

Owing to sociological change the amount of profit has become an important factor in managerial policy. The surplus must be sufficient to pay shareholders and to provide adequate sums for replacement of capital equipment and expansion programmes. Excessive profits, however, should be avoided because of the social obligations towards the community to provide quality products at a fair price. Management must also consider the question of high productivity and its part in the national economy (e.g. the need for competitive prices in the export market).

In general terms it may be said that the consumer will only buy within a price range that is considered adequate for the quality of the goods; this fixes the upper limit of the price range. The supplier will attempt to market a product of his or her choice which provides sufficient return to pay for all expenses and provide a suitable amount of profit.

Accounting for profit

At this point two terms should be considered: 'trading profit' and 'net profit'. *Trading profit* is calculated by deducting all the costs directly connected with production from the total sales. *Net profit* is arrived at by deducting all the indirect expenses from the trading profit. In other words, net profit is the amount remaining after all expenses for a period have been deducted as indicated in the accounts in Fig. 27.1.

In financial accounts trading profit and the direct expenses involved in production appear in the manufacturing and trading account, while the net profit and indirect expenses appear in the profit and loss account.

Finally, the net profit is appropriated or divided into three main groups: income tax, dividend and general reserve. The general reserve or undistributed profit is the amount previously mentioned which is retained by the company for replacement of capital equipment or fixed assets and for expansion programmes. The appropriation of profit to reserves is known as 'ploughing back the profits'. How the profit is divided depends upon such factors as the total amount of surplus, commitments towards shareholders and the prudence of the concern in establishing adequate reserves for future plans.

An example of each account is given in Fig. 27.1, outlining the main items of expense likely to be seen.

The profit and loss account produced for public companies may be a summary of the complete account. There is no need to disclose all the information so long as the provisions of the Companies Acts are met. Many companies, however, issue full accounts to satisfy their obligation to shareholders. A pro-forma example is given in Fig. 27.2. To avoid excessive length a number of notes are usually given at the end of the report which give greater detail and explanations where considered necessary.

PWB COMPANY LIMITED

Manufacturing and Trading Account
for year ended 31st December 19—9

Items directly connected with production		£	Income		£
Wages & Salaries		10,500	Sales		40,000
Raw materials		7,000			
Expenses		2,500			
Trading profit	c/d	20,000			
		£40,000			£40,000

Profit and Loss Account

Items not directly connected with production		£			£
Rent		800	Trading profit	b/d	20,000
Rates		300			
Depreciation		700			
Insurance		130			
Salaries		6,400			
Directors' fees		500			
Stationery		520			
Interest on loan		80			
Telephone		170			
Lighting & heating		400			
Net profit	c/d	10,000			
		£20,000			£20,000

Appropriation Account

	£			£
Income tax	4,500	Net profit	b/d	10,000
Dividend	2,500			
General reserve	3,000			
	£10,000			£10,000

Fig. 27.1 *Layout of the annual accounts*
Trading and net profit are clearly shown in these accounts

The balance sheet

The balance sheet is a statement of all the assets and liabilities at a certain date which is normally the last day of the financial year. The liabilities are located on the left-hand side and are divided into two main groups called fixed and current liabilities. Fixed liabilities include capital, reserves and any debentures or long-term loans. The capital is generally shown as the amount authorised and the amount issued, authorised capital being the amount that the company has power to issue, stamp duty being already paid on the sum

Profit and Loss Account for the Year Ended 31st December 19–8

	19–8 £	19–7 £
1. *Turnover* Deduct: Trading and manufacturing expenses Wages and salaries Materials consumed Overhead costs		
2. Total expenditure	£	£
3. Gross profit (1–2) 4. *Deduct:* Depreciation on cost		
5. *Trading profit (3–4)*	£	£
6. Income from investments 7. *Profit after taxation (5 + 6)* 8. Taxation 9. *Profit after taxation (7 – 8)* 10. Minority interests 11. Extraordinary items		
12. *Net profit (9 – 10 – 11)*	£	£

Appropriation Account

1. *Net profit* Deduct: Dividends Transfer to fixed assets replacements fund Transfer to debenture redemption reserve Transfer to preferred share redemption fund		
2. *Total appropriations*	£	£
3. Profit and Loss Balance (1 – 2) Add: P & L Balance from previous year		
Balance of profit carried forward	£	£

Fig. 27.2 *Pro-forma profit and loss account*

quoted, whereas issued capital is the sum offered by the company and subscribed by shareholders.

The assets are shown on the right-hand side and are divided into two main groups called fixed and current assets. The fixed assets are listed first followed by current assets. Intangible assets such as goodwill and patents may be shown separately. The traditional form of balance sheet is shown in Fig. 27.3 but several variations are common. For example, the capital employed may be shown on the left-hand side (which amounts to all the

PWB COMPANY LIMITED

Balance Sheet as at 31st December 19—9

Fixed liabilities	£	Fixed assets	£
Capital	45,000	Land & building	18,000
General reserve	5,000	Plant & machinery	12,000
Loan	5,000	Vans	4,000
		Furniture & fittings	3,000
Current liabilities		Current assets	
Creditors	11,700	Stock	11,500
		Debtors	14,500
		Cash in hand	3,700
	66,700		66,700

Fig. 27.3 *Layout of a balance sheet*

This is the traditional form of balance sheet showing liabilities on the left-hand side and assets on the right

fixed liabilities) and on the right-hand side, the fixed assets are followed by current assets *less* current liabilities which gives the working capital. Thus, the capital employed on one side equals the employment of capital on the other side consisting of fixed capital (or fixed assets plus working capital).

Many companies now issue a vertical balance sheet, an example of which is given in Fig. 27.4. In practice a number of notes would be appended, explaining each main item in more detail. In this example ordinary shares and cumulative preference shares have been included to show a typical layout. For detailed information and in order to comply with the strict legal requirements it is essential to study the complex Acts within which various formats are given for the balance sheet and profit and loss account.

Interpretation of accounts and statements

From management's viewpoint the ability to interpret the accounts and statements greatly assists control and co-ordination and provides trends for forecasting and planning. Unfortunately incorrect impressions are easily created by studying the figures. To aid management 'accounting ratios' are available which provide a guide. The British Institute of Management and the British Productivity Council established the Centre for Inter-firm Comparisons in 1959. This Centre is an independent body that acts as a data collection point, compares the results of a number of firms which contribute and indicates achievements and weaknesses.

The investor is interested in the true financial position of a concern and its prospects. These are often very difficult to assess. For example, the current value of fixed assets may not be indicated and the progress of

Balance Sheet at 31st December 19—8
CAPITAL EMPLOYED (*sources of funds*)

				19—8	19—7
				£	£
1.	*Ordinary share capital*	Authorised			
		19—8	19—7		
		£	£		
	Ordinary shares of 50p each				
	'A' Ordinary shares of 50p each				
2.	*Capital reserves*				
	Share premium account				
	Debenture redemption reserve				
	Capital redemption reserve fund				
	Fixed assets replacement reserve				
	Preference share redemption fund				
3.	*Revenue reserves*				
	Profit and loss account balance				
	General reserve				
4.	*Deferred taxation*			£	£
	TOTAL EQUITY CAPITAL				
	Asset value of ordinary share				
5.	*Preference share capital*	Authorised			
		£	£		
		19—8	19—7		
	7½% Cumulative preference shares				
	8¼% Cumulative preference shares				
6.	*Preference capital*				
	Interest of minority shareholders				
7.	*Minority interest*				
8.	*Loans*				
	TOTAL CAPITAL EMPLOYED (1 to 8 added)			£	£

EMPLOYMENT OF CAPITAL (Employment of funds)

				NET	
				19—8	19—7
	Fixed assets	Cost	Aggregate depreciation	£	£
	Freehold property				
	Leasehold property				
	Plant, machinery, furniture				
1.	Total fixed assets			£	£
	Investments				
	Trade investments				
	Associated companies				
	Interests in subsidiaries				
2.	Total investments			£	£
	Current assets				
	Stocks				
	Debtors				
	Bank balances and cash				
	Marketable short-term securities				
3.	Total current assets			£	£
	Deduct: Current liabilities and provisions				
	Bank overdrafts				
	Creditors and provisions				
	Taxation				
	Fixed dividends				
4.	Total current liabilities			£	£
5.	Net current assets (3 — 4)			£	£
	TOTAL CAPITAL EMPLOYED (1 + 2 + 5)			£	£

Fig. 27.4 *Pro-forma vertical balance sheet*

research and development schemes is naturally not revealed. Predicting the future of a company is as hazardous as picking the winner of the Derby with just as many variables involved which affect the result. Reasonable guesses can be made on the possible progress of a concern by studying the reputation of the managing director, the trend of the particular market and the efficiency of the organisation, though hidden factors can still influence appearances. If the market trend is sufficiently favourable and there is a strong demand for its product, a concern may prosper in spite of inefficiency and mismanagement. It is easy to be misled in such ways, even with inside knowledge of a business.

The over-all trend in a group of companies can be very misleading when a variety of products is manufactured; an individual may be employed in a division where prosperity is high, but another division may fare so badly that it is necessary to reduce over-all profit to a level which immediately affects the share value when the results are disclosed.

These examples should give an indication of the complex problem concerned with assessing the prospects of companies. There is always some contributory factor which is unknown, whether to management or to prospective investors.

Questions

1　Discuss profit and loss and how they affect the business.
2　Outline some of the common risks that a concern will have to face.
3　Give your opinion of a sound financial policy for a company.
4　What are the objects of an accounting system?
5　Why is financial control so important?
6　How may capital be raised in a concern?
7　What is the purpose of the balance sheet and profit and loss account?
8　State how you would explain to an employee the problems involved in dividing up profit among shareholders and for other purposes.
9　How would you explain to an employee the need to make a profit?
10　What forms of protection are afforded to shareholders in a public limited company and what facilities are available if an investor wishes to sell shares?
11　What is meant by the terms *fixed* and *circulating capital*?
12　Give a brief account of forecasting and budgeting.

Case study

'The trouble with these budgets is that the finance department sees us as just a mass of figures and nobody up there seems to appreciate the problems *we* have to face. They think that all they've got to do is pull the budget strings and we'll dance the tune!' Ted Noake spoke harshly and meant every word.

The works manager agreed. 'I know what you mean, Ted. Your section is a difficult one to handle with so many different runs every week. But you know they have to get the figures right otherwise we would have cash flow problems.'

'They'll have bigger cash flow problems if they don't put a little common sense into their planning. All they think about is the past and the future. It's about time we had some plain talking about the present between finance and production!'

Consider how this barrier between the two departments could be overcome.

28 Cost control

Introduction

Although financial control discussed in the previous chapter provides control statements on the general financial position, these statements do not give detailed information on processes and operations. Control at these activity levels relies on cost accounting.

The costing function provides a means of scientific control over all expenditure in the concern which is vital for directing its activities, for estimating accurately and for assisting in establishing the selling price. Neglect of costing and its uses places a concern in a vulnerable position. Although a company may escape repercussions for a number of years, eventually keener competition from home or abroad will force the issue.

Costing may be regarded as a service or maintenance programme of expenditure, e.g. it is wiser with machine maintenance to plan a programme of careful assessment and preventive maintenance than to wait until machines break down thus causing upheavals, delays and heavy losses. The same applies with control of expenditure.

The expense of effectively running a costing system which checks and provides information for control purposes is negligible compared with the savings and lessened risks which otherwise remain hidden and are difficult to assess. One fact should be sufficient to indicate the strong need for costing: many firms fail to estimate accurately the cost of a job and therefore suffer a considerable loss.

The clerical aspect of costing can be time-consuming for supervisors who may feel that the burden is not worth while. Clerical assistance is necessary to relieve them of this problem, thus allowing more time for controlling the variances (which are explained later). Although supervisors are mainly concerned with the control aspects of costing they should understand the *costing environment* within which they operate. Unless they appreciate the type of system or techniques in operation, they may fail to grasp the significance of procedures and activities which seem totally unnecessary.

Definition of costing

Costing may be defined as collecting, recording, classifying and allocating expenditure to ascertain the cost of products or services for planning and control purposes by indicating points where corrective action is required.

Main objects of costing

- To provide promptly the cost of each item of expense.
- To summarise and apportion costs thus giving the total cost of each product or service.
- To provide budgets and standards for control.
- To advise management on costing aspects which affect the selling price and economic production.

Costing systems

The main systems (or techniques) for recording costs and dealing with costing problems are described below, followed by a survey of the methods of costing (finding actual costs based upon the type of production) which may be grafted upon any of the main costing systems.

Historical costing

This system records actual costs when or after the expense occurs. The basic costing methods associated with historical costing are *job costing* and *process costing* (*see below*); both methods provide essential information but fail to give economic indications of the expected performance level of each cost. In other words, a yardstick is not provided to measure efficiency.

Standard costing

The definition of standard costing is a method of cost accounting which estimates or predetermines the costs of each element, compares them with the actual costs, calculates the variances and presents management with reports on those items requiring some action to stop the trend away from the standard.

The sphere of standard costing

Standard costing can be used in most concerns regardless of size or type, although it is easier to apply in some industries where the product is standardised and long production runs are used.

Standards are based upon prevailing conditions and a particular output level; if these factors change then the standard costs are distorted and must be revised.

Establishing standard costs

The most usual methods of establishing standard costs are described below.

DIRECT LABOUR

Setting reasonable standards for labour costs demands the services of work study engineers who can assess the work content and establish suitable times for each operation. Wage rates can now be applied and standard costs calculated. These costs should remain stable until there are alterations in the operation content or changes in rates of pay.

DIRECT MATERIALS

The quantity of material required for an operation is found by compiling a standard material specification. This is based upon drawings and on experience of the particular operation, and may include average scrap and waste through cutting. The standard quantity can now be priced by reference to the purchasing officer or a price manual, and an allowance should be made for forecasted changes in price for the period in mind.

OVERHEADS

Normally the overhead expenses for each department are found by reference to a budget, calculated on such factors as machine hours, direct labour hours or on prime cost. These factors are based upon the capacity of the particular department, the costs being divided into fixed and variable. Fixed costs tend not to fluctuate with the rate of production whereas variable costs tend to alter in sympathy.

The capacity of a department is open to a number of interpretations and a choice must be made to ensure standard treatment of all overheads allocated to departments. Supervisors should understand clearly which definition of capacity is used otherwise they will not be able to assess the variances accurately and take appropriate action.

If an assumption is made that the department runs without any loss of time, this is known as the *maximum theoretical capacity*. When normal time losses such as setting up times, idle time and breakdowns are deducted from the maximum theoretical capacity, the capacity is called *normal capacity to manufacture*. A further reduction for recessions in trade, especially seasonal sales, reduces the capacity to the definition of *normal capacity to manufacture and sell*. Finally, when each year's sales capacity is used as a guide, it is known as *short period capacity to sell*.

Some aspects of standard costing

1   The essence of standard costing is to provide management with vital information for effective control. Whether effective control is achieved depends upon two main factors; *first* the ability of management to take the correct actions and *second* the ability of the cost accountant to provide the information on time. Time is most important, and delays are expensive when costs are moving sharply away from standards. The supervisor must

appreciate the importance of time and ensure that cost returns are made promptly.

2   The use of standards provides a measurement for comparison with actual costs which is superior to any other form of comparison. For instance, comparing the actual costs of one period with those of another period can be misleading. It gives no positive indication which is the more efficient cost or, if the costs are similar, no indication is given that they are at an effective level.

3   Variances from the standard are easily seen by using the *principle of exceptions*, i.e. presenting management with those costs which are deviating from the standard and omitting or excepting those that are conforming to the plan. Much time is saved in the avoidance of sorting through pages of costs and more time can be spent on thinking out the correct action to be taken.

4   Clerical operation of this system is more economic because only information which is actually used is recorded as against other systems where masses of data are produced with no specific purpose in mind.

5   The effects of changes, e.g. different types of material, revised wage rates, bonus schemes, varying output and new tools or machines, can be easily seen by 'before and after' comparison.

6   The inherent process of maintaining a constant watch on standards and revising where necessary encourages management and supervision to become cost conscious and aware of those costs which tend to deviate continually.

7   A reliable indication of the effectiveness of managers and supervisors is provided for top management. Reports on variances, the action taken and the results in the next period clearly show the weak spots in the organisation. These in turn demand action from top management and the results of such action provide a guide to the effectiveness of this level also.

8   The system should not always be condemned if it does not work properly. The supervisor must appreciate that 'standard costing' is sound. It should be clear from preceding paragraphs that much of its effectiveness depends upon individuals. Operators must record details accurately, and appropriate decisions are necessary throughout the various levels up to the board of directors.

Budgetary control

Budgetary control is a system which establishes departmental budgets by pre-planning all the activities within the concern to form an over-all budget, through which co-ordination and control may be achieved.

Each budget is determined by the policy planned for the forthcoming period and the expectations of expense based upon previous experience and estimated changes.

Co-ordinating all the budgets to maximise profit and maintain a stable business is one of the main problems of budgetary control. The system has the advantage, however, of setting clear targets for each department, all aligned in the same direction.

Similarity between budgetary control and standard costing

Certain fundamentals are common to budgetary control and standard costing. These are:

1 a pre-planned standard for each item of expense
2 measurement of actual costs
3 comparison of actual with standard costs
4 discovery of reasons for the variances
5 recommended courses of action to correct the variances.

The practice had developed of relating standard costing to production activities alone, whereas budgetary control is a system applied to all activities in the concern including sales, production, stock, plant and buildings and finance. Although budgetary control and standard costing are interrelated, some industries may have difficulty in introducing standard costing but would be able to operate budgetary control effectively.

Control

Effective control depends upon allocating responsibility to competent managers and supervisors for each activity or function, providing them with operating statements on time, with details of the standard, actual expense and the variances, together with recommendations for action.

The time factor is important. Although the budget may be drawn up for a year, control is too remote over such a long period. Short periods of, say, four weeks allow frequent comparisons, thus providing a firmer basis for control if reports are made promptly.

Advantages of budgetary control

1   All the functions of the concern are co-ordinated and controlled, indicating clearly to supervisors in the organisation their responsibility for a particular section of the over-all budget and the importance of achieving the objective stated.

2   The continuing process of budgetary control gives more accurate indications of trends and eases the problems of forecasting. Signs of change become evident much earlier and management has the opportunity to take full advantage of the situation in its planning.

3   The risks connected with operating and financing the concern are reduced as close control of working capital including cash in hand is assured

through the budget statements. Similarly, all income and expenditure is both forecast and checked as results become available, thus enabling any deviation to be brought under control quickly.

4   An effective system of budgetary control is a means of convincing prospective investors of the concern's stability when more capital is required for expansion programmes.

Budgetary control procedure

Co-ordination and control of the budgets may be carried out by a budget controller or budget committee. When studying operating results the controller would meet with the managing director and senior executives to discuss the circumstances, the current position and possible courses of action. Changes in policy may then be decided upon at such meetings.

Actual forecasting of budgets follows the policy which governs sales targets, production of new lines and financial activities. Subsidiary budgets are forecast at this stage and they would include the following:

Sales budget   Research & development budget
Production budget   Capital expenditure budget
Plant utilisation budget   Personnel budget
Stock budget   Purchasing budget
Production cost budget   Cash budget
Selling cost budget   Profit & loss forecast
Distribution cost budget   Balance sheet forecast
Administration cost budget

After the completion of forecasts, meetings are held to finalise the budgets by considering various plans submitted. The over-all budget is drawn up and issued. When period statements are circulated, the executives – who are responsible for the budgets – take appropriate action. The statements and reports from executives are fed back to the controller for discussion under the three aspects of policy-making, forecasting and budget preparation, thus completing the control cycle.

The budgetary process

The over-all budget and the budgetary process are equally important since the latter forces managers and supervisors to prepare for changes as they think ahead, interpret and anticipate. Co-ordination is possible as each department attempts to integrate operational plans with other departments. Thus supervisors visualise operating relationships with each other and aim to improve them.

A comprehensive understanding of the process is essential to avoid misconceptions. Managerial and supervisory performance is judged by capability to adhere to the budget. Supervisors should understand the process, its importance, and co-operate. Unfortunately many view a budget as another administrative or bureaucratic hindrance.

Responsibility for variances

Assessing supervisory performance is usually based on efficiency aspects, meaning those portions of variances that supervisors may directly influence. Price aspects are subject to external influences outside supervisors' control, for example economic conditions and abrupt price changes.

Efficiency is normally measured as a ratio of inputs and outputs and understandably is a relative term. Therefore variances are simply indicators demanding attention and investigation; they do not provide answers.

Labour variances

Apart from obvious levels of productivity varying through degrees of motivation and disputes, labour costs may be accurately budgeted. Predictable changes can be seen generally well in advance since they often depend on trade union agreements and general wage rises. However there are some unpredictable features such as changing the hourly rate to suit emergencies, or placing an employee with a wage rate unrelated to the job.

Material variances

Acquisition and usage are treated separately. The purchasing manager's responsibility is to buy at economic prices and terms while the production manager aims to use materials efficiently. In practice the two are interrelated since a sudden unforeseeable change in usage may mean buying at uneconomic rates and increased carriage costs to hasten delivery.

Efficiency is usually measured by comparing the bill of materials (a specification of quantities allowed for a number of production units) with the quantities used. Variances may occur through pilfering, poor handling, imperfections, poor standard of work, methods changes and machine maintenance problems.

Variance analysis

Random variances tend to be ignored if they are within reasonable or set limits. Significant variances demand an investigation, but of course someone must decide what is significant. This decision is often based on judgment, hunches, or a feel of the situation.

The alternative is to set a percentage deviation from the budget based on its financial implications. With a machine maintenance budget of £500, 20 per cent is obviously insignificant compared with a 5 per cent deviation from a £500 000 material budget. Nevertheless analysis might show the latter deviation is due to the former.

Analysis usually conforms to cost-benefit examination by applying statistical techniques and problem-solving approaches. These isolate randomness from controllable events and indicate courses of action.

Marginal costing

Definition

The technique of marginal costing was briefly described in the previous chapter. Marginal cost has been defined as the direct costs of labour and material plus variable overhead expenses, or as the additional cost of producing one more unit or product. The procedure of marginal costing is best shown in tabular form as in Fig. 28.1.

Explanations of the terms used are given below before discussing the theory on which marginal costing is based.

1   *Variable costs*   Those costs that tend to vary in relation to output. They include direct labour, material and expenses (i.e. prime cost), variable overheads for the factory and, under some systems, the variable element of selling, distribution and administration cost.

2   *Fixed costs*   All costs that tend to remain constant for a period of time, and within a specified range of output. Typical examples are management and supervision costs, depreciation of fixed assets, rates, rent, heating, lighting, power, insurance and subscriptions.

3   *Sales revenue*   The actual amounts received from selling the products.

4   *Contribution*   The sales revenue less the total variable costs (the marginal costs) for a product.

5   *The fund*   The total sum of the contributions.

The total fixed costs are finally deducted from the fund to give the net profit.

A comparison between the conventional systems of costing and marginal costing is shown in Fig. 28.1.

Conventional Costing

| Sales revenue | *less* Prime cost and factory overheads | = Gross profit | *less* Administration overheads | = Net profit |

Marginal Costing

| Sales revenue | *less* Marginal costs | = Contribution (fund) | *less* Fixed costs | = Net profit |

Conventional Costing

Products		£000s			
	Sales	Prime cost and factory overheads	Gross profit	Administration overheads	Net profit
W	10	− 4	6	− 6	0
X	14	− 5	9	− 8	1
Y	12	− 4	8	− 7	1
Z	8	− 2	6	− 5	1
Totals	44	− 15	29	− 26	3

Marginal Costing

Products	Sales	Marginal costs	Contribution fund	Fixed costs	Net profit
W	10	− 7	3		
X	14	− 10	4		
Y	12	− 10	2 } 10	} − 7	} 3
Z	8	− 7	1		
Totals	44	− 34	10	− 7	3

Fig. 28.1 *Conventional costing and marginal costing compared*

This illustrates the distortion factor met in conventional costing when attempting to apportion fixed overheads to cost centres fairly. The marginal costing technique eliminates this factor

The theory of marginal costing

Provided fixed costs tend to remain static, an increase in production should normally result in a reduced cost per unit. If production is decreased, an increase in cost per unit should be expected.

This theory is based on the assumption that all fixed costs are segregated and not affected by fluctuations in output, therefore as output rises the spread of fixed costs is greater and a smaller amount will be attached to each unit. As output falls the load attached to each unit will be larger. (The term *attached* does *not* mean apportioned; it is used here to indicate the portion of fixed costs which will appear when calculating the average cost per unit).

The term *marginal cost* – in accordance with this theory – will represent the change in variable costs when one unit more, or one unit less, is produced. This amount of change will be the difference between the two total costs when output changes by one unit.

Main aspects

Variable and fixed costs

Supervisors may assume that variable costs will be constant per unit regardless of fluctuations in output. They should remember, however, that possible changes may occur through price alterations for raw materials and components and, if production is increased to a point where overtime is incurred, the rates of pay will be affected and variable costs will rise.

In practice, fixed costs also tend to vary over long periods of time as policy decisions involve additional capital expenditure on new factories or extensions of existing premises. Such costs are known as semi-fixed or semi-variable.

This aspect does not nullify marginal costing, as many decisions are based upon short-term runs of periods of up to a year.

The important factor connected with fixed costs is that irrespective of production level they remain the same. Even when production ceases completely the fact remains that fixed costs continue. This outlook, when the significance of this factor is appreciated, indicates the critical role played by those who control variable costs. The effectiveness of controlling these variable or marginal costs decides the amount of contribution which governs the profit margin.

Contribution and new products

The importance of the contribution may now be extended to consider its effect on decisions involving new products. The question of whether to introduce a new line or to decrease the range of products and increase production on particular lines becomes easier to solve.

The following calculations for a proposed new product B are based upon apportioning the load of fixed costs according to the sales value of each product. This calculation is misleading because it attempts to split fixed costs among the products and, therefore, distorts the situation. In reality the new product will contribute another £500 towards fixed costs and profit; thus in this case, as the contribution from existing product A already covers fixed costs, the contribution from the new product B directly increases the profit by £500, i.e. by 50 per cent.

A simple example should clarify the issue involved:

Proposed new line – Product B

Product A			Proposed Product B		
		£			£
Sales	=	27,000	Sales	=	3,000
Less Marginal cost	=	20,000	*Less* Marginal cost	=	2,500
Contribution	=	7,000	Contribution	=	500
Less Fixed costs	=	6,000	*Less* Fixed costs	=	600
			(apportioned on total sales)		
Profit	=	1,000	Loss	=	100

The calculation using the marginal costing technique is shown below:

Product	Contribution	Fund	Fixed costs	Profit
A	= £7,000			
B	= £ 500	£7,500	−£6,000	£1,500

A further example which may be of interest to the supervisor involves a concern which manufactures three products. Under certain marketing conditions the company may need to investigate the possibility of reducing its range of products and determine the effect on profitability. The current situation is given first, followed by the effect of the proposal to abandon product A and divide the surplus capacity equally among the remaining products, B and C.

Existing Lines

	A	B	C	(£000s)
Sales	10	10	10	
Less Marginal costs	7	6	5	
Contribution	3	4	5	
Fund				= 12
Less Fixed costs				= 11
Profit				= 1

Proposed Change	A	B	C	
Sales	Abandoned	15	15	(increased)
Less Marginal cost		9	7½	proportionately)
Contribution		6	7½	
Fund				= 13½
Less Fixed costs				= 11
Profit				= 2½

Provided market conditions prompted such a change, the proposal stated above would show a substantial increase in profitability.

Unfortunately the proposed change of product range indicated above is often not straightforward because of certain limiting factors. These factors, such as availability of trained labour, shortage of raw materials, production capacity available, limited cash resources and the state of the market, must be considered in order to identify those products which will make best use of available resources.

Break-even techniques

An essential part of marginal costing is the break-even technique which includes calculations to indicate the change in profitability when output is altered or the product range is revised.

Break-even analysis is a technique which locates the level of production where sales revenue equals all the costs. It also indicates the relationship between sales revenue, variable costs, fixed costs and profit or loss at various levels of output. The *break-even point* is self-explanatory – it simply means the level of output where neither a profit nor a loss is incurred. The importance of this calculation and break-even analysis generally lies in its ability to indicate such aspects as the amount of sales necessary to cover the degree of profit required for various purposes, the revision of selling prices to provide sufficient sales revenue to cover estimated profit and establish a particular break-even point, and the variable cost per unit.

The break-even point may be calculated by formula or plotted on a break-even chart. The formula is given below:

$$\text{Break-even point} = \frac{\text{Fixed costs}}{1 - (\text{Variable costs} \div \text{Sales revenue})}$$

Example:

Sales revenue £10,000; Variable costs £6,000; Fixed costs £2,000.

$$\therefore \text{Break-even point} = \frac{£2,000}{1 - \dfrac{6,000}{10,000}} = \frac{£2,000}{1 - \frac{3}{5}}$$

$$= \frac{£2,000}{\frac{2}{5}} = \frac{£2,000 \times 5}{2}$$

$$= \underline{£5,000}$$

The break-even chart

Construction of a break-even chart is based upon the choice of information required.

The x axis is used to show output or sales, whether it may be desired to indicate the volume of sales in units or as a percentage, the output in value or units, or the capacity of the plant. The y axis indicates the cost.
An example is shown in Fig. 28.2.

The main features to note are the fixed costs line which remains static at £30,000 and the variable costs line which is the total costs less the fixed costs, amounting to £20,000. The chart indicates the break-even point where the variable costs line cuts the sales line. The vertical line – from the break-even point to the x axis – intersects the point where output will provide sufficient funds to break-even at 50,000 units.

The fact that costs do not behave in such a simple manner as drawn on the break-even chart has already been stressed. Costs do not always fit conveniently into fixed or variable groups; they vary for other reasons besides fluctuations in output. The supervisor will know by experience that when attempts are made to increase production, invariably extra costs appear – such as overtime and bonus – which explain the concept that maximum production does not necessarily match with maximum profit. On the marketing side it is quite common to make price reductions when the concern decides to increase sales.

Whatever its disadvantages, the break-even chart clearly shows the relationships between fixed costs, variable costs and sales revenue. Within

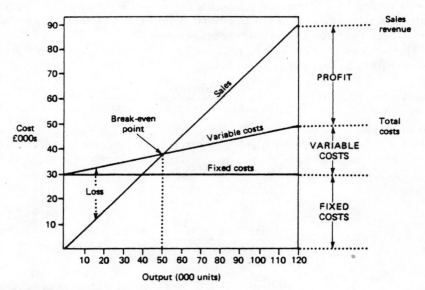

Fig. 28.2 Break-even chart

Here the x axis shows output and the y axis the cost. The x axis may be required to show the output in value, sales in units or as a percentage, or to show plant capacity. The dotted line indicates the point in output where sales exactly cover costs; neither profit nor loss is made

the relatively narrow limits of production fluctuations the errors inherent in straight line graphs are practically eliminated. Thus marginal costing and its techniques can help considerably in solving problems related to levels of production, range of products, pricing of products, and subcontracting.

There are many variations of the break-even chart which can be used for purposes other than analysing company output. For instance, in Fig. 28.3 the technique is used by the consumer to find the break-even point between two tariffs offered for gas. If the consumption in a house is below 53 therms, Scheme A will be cheaper; if consumption is over 53 therms the break-even point is exceeded, therefore Scheme B will be cheaper so long as the consumption does not fall below that point each quarter.

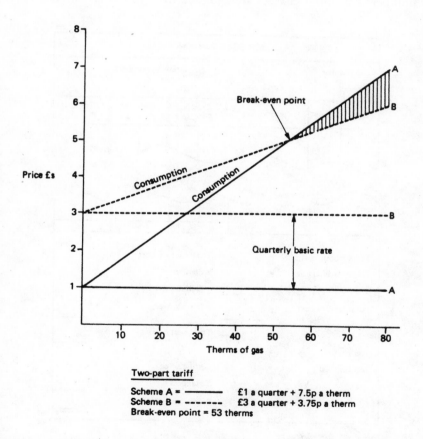

Fig. 28.3 *Form of break-even chart for domestic use (under the old scheme)*

In this illustration the break-even technique enables the consumer to determine which tariff of gas to adopt. If the consumption is below the break-even point of 53 therms, Scheme A will be the cheaper. If consumption is higher Scheme B should be adopted

Methods of costing

The two main methods are job costing and process costing. Various other methods are derived from these two. A description of each method is given below.

Job costing

This is the method of costing those jobs which have to be kept separate during production. These non-standard jobs include 'one-off' products such as a large transformer, a bridge, a ship or an office block. Each job is given a number and all costs connected with it are booked by allocating them to that number. All labour charges are allocated from job clock cards, materials

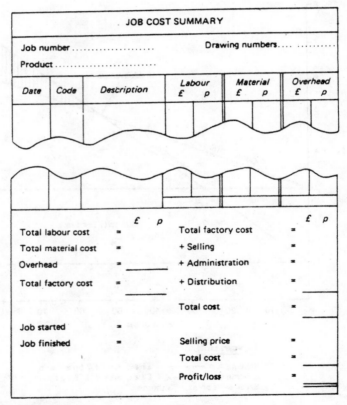

Fig. 28.4 *Job cost summary*

'One-off' products are costed separately. The card shows that the total job cost is made up of the production cost (labour, materials and overheads) *plus* an allocated proportion of selling, distribution and administration expenses. Research and development may be recorded separately or may be covered by 'administration'

from stores requisitions and a proportion of production overheads. A proportion of selling, distribution, administration and research and development expenses is allocated to give the total cost of the job *when* added to the production cost consisting of total labour, material and overhead costs. These details are shown in the job cost summary as in Fig. 28.4.

Process costing

This method is suitable where products are manufactured by set processes which are not isolated to individual jobs as in job costing, e.g. where materials for processes are derived from earlier processes where a number of products go through the same process but cannot be distinguished until

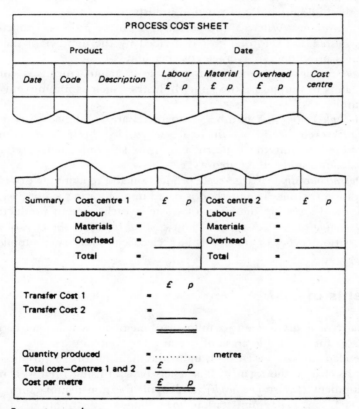

Fig. 28.5 *Process cost sheet*

Process costing is used when a product passes in sequence through several distinct processes. All charges associated with each process must be allocated correctly. Notice that the *transfer cost* (from the previous process) is separated, giving a clear indication of the present process cost. The cost per metre is in fact the *average* cost per metre for the period covered

further processes alter the standard form. Such industries as chemicals, foods, paints and textiles are, by nature, ideal for process costing.

Control of costs is achieved by ensuring that all charges associated with each process are allocated correctly. These charges include labour, materials and overheads, but the transfer cost (the cost from the previous process) is separated in the process cost sheet, thus giving a clear indication of the present process cost. Figure 28.5 shows a typical layout of a process cost sheet.

Other methods

These are generally based on job and process costing methods.

1   *Terminal and contract costing*   These methods are a form of job costing used in the building and construction industries.

2   *Batch costing*   Where a number of jobs can be processed together each batch is costed and the total cost is divided by the number of units in the batch, thus providing an average cost per unit.

3   *Unit costing*   This method is suitable if manufacturing is continuous and the units of output are the same. Industries such as mining and brewing are examples.

4   *Multiple costing*   A number of methods are combined to cost a range of manufactured products which are assembled both from components manufactured within the concern and from subcontracted parts. The car industry comes under this category.

5   *Operation costing*   Large-scale production and repetitive work is suitable for operation costing. The method is based upon locating a unit cost for each operation and assessing the effect of waste at each stage of production.

6   *Operating costing*   A form of unit costing to locate the cost of a service such as various types of transport, gas, electricity and water supplies.

Elements of cost

The total cost is divided into a number of elements which may be grouped together to form suitable areas of expense for control purposes.

These elements are based both upon the main factors of production, e.g. 1 *labour* to change the form of 2 *materials* by 3 utilising premises, machines and equipment (*factory overheads*), and upon the non-manufacturing factors (overheads), e.g. *(a)* administration, *(b)* selling, *(c)* distribution, *(d)* research and development.

The area of production consists of two groups of elements known as *prime cost* and *factory overheads* which together form the *factory cost*. The non-manufacturing overheads are added to the factory cost to form the total cost. The difference between total cost and selling price will provide the profit or

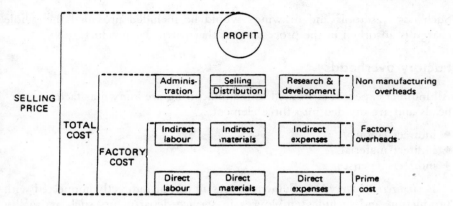

Fig. 28.6 *Elements of cost*

These elements are based on production factors (factory cost) and non-manufacturing overheads. The relationship between this total cost and the selling price determines the profit or loss

loss figure. The diagram in Fig. 28.6 illustrates the elements of cost and method grouping to arrive at the profit and selling price.

Each element of cost is now explained under its particular group.

Prime costs of production

Where expenditure can be directly allocated to a product or cost centre (a particular or isolated point of production), instead of being apportioned or shared, it is called a direct cost.

The three elements of direct costs are:

- direct labour
- direct materials
- direct expenses

1 *Direct labour* Those employees who directly work upon the manufacture of the product come under this element. The wages must be justified in allocating them direct to the product or unit and, in this connection, chargehands and foremen could be included as direct labour although generally they are classed as indirect labour.

2 *Direct materials* Those materials that are allocated to the product are called direct materials. They include raw materials, partly finished or finished components and sub-assemblies, i.e. all material that becomes part of the product.

3 *Direct expenses* All expenses, other than labour and materials, which are directly employed on a product or unit are charged as direct expenses.

Such costs as tools and drawings would be included provided the whole charge is absorbed in the processing of that particular product.

Factory overheads

All indirect expenses attributed to manufacturing are known as factory overheads and are divided into three elements:

- indirect labour
- indirect materials
- indirect expenses

1   *Indirect labour*   This element covers all labour indirectly connected with production and includes employees in service departments such as quality control and inspection, production control, tooling shops, internal transportation of materials, components and products, stores, the works dining room, maintenance and welfare.

2   *Indirect materials*   All consumables, such as oil, grease, cotton waste, sawdust, cleaning fluids, and small items such as nuts, bolts, and screws are included where they cannot be traced back directly to the product.

3   *Indirect expenses*   The remaining costs are running expenses such as electricity, gas, water, rent, rates and insurance.

Non-manufacturing overheads

All overheads other than factory overheads are included in this category and are divided into four elements:

- administration
- selling
- distribution
- research and development

1   *Administration*   This element absorbs all management expenses not covered under selling, distribution and production. The expenses of directing and controlling and of the administration of functions such as finance, accounting, auditing and secretarial and legal activities are included.

2   *Selling*   All expenses incurred to maintain and develop sales such as sales promotion, advertising, the sales general office and the sales force of representatives come under this element.

3   *Distribution*   This overhead includes all expenses connected with external transport, storage and warehousing.

4   *Research and development*   All costs associated with improving or developing the product are termed research costs. When the results of research are applied and create some practical benefit to the product these expenses are called development costs. If a new product is involved development costs apply until the prototype is completed.

Allocation and apportionment

Allocating and apportioning costs to products varies according to particular circumstances and the number of different products manufactured in the concern. The methods are discussed under the following headings.

1   *Direct costs* – allocated direct to the product by using the most suitable method.

2   *Factory overhead costs* – generally recovered in two stages: firstly, allocating (charging) them to departments (or cost centres), and secondly recovering (apportioning) to each product.

3   *Non-manufacturing overhead costs* – recovered in a variety of ways depending upon circumstances.

Each heading is now discussed.

Direct costs

The methods used to record and allocate direct costs vary considerably according to particular circumstances in an industry. The principal requirements, however, may be outlined as follows.

Labour control

Any method of allocating labour costs usually includes the following activities. Responsibility generally rests with the individual or department mentioned in brackets.

1   *Engagement of employees* Application form records details, wage rate and any revisions (personnel department).

2   *Record of attendance* Clock card or job card records hours attended daily (time office).

3   *Direct hours worked on each product or cost centre* Job card or time sheet records job numbers and hours (supervisor and employee).

4   *Calculation of direct labour cost for each product or cost centre* Total costs calculated and entered on job cost summaries (cost department).

5   *Weekly wages calculated* Total hours attended and bonus calculated from clock card, job cards or time sheets (wages department).

Material control

A typical procedure for controlling materials is outlined below.

Activity	Form	Responsibility
1 Establish stock levels	Authorisation sheet	Accountant, purchasing officer & production manager.

2	Cost pricing method	Authorisation sheet	Cost accountant.
3	Replenishing stocks	Purchase requisition	Storekeeper.
4	Ordering goods	Official order	Purchasing officer.
5	Receiving goods	Goods received note	Storekeeper.
6	Accepting goods	Inspection note	Inspector.
7	Payment for goods	Purchase invoice	Accountant.
8	Issuing materials	Materials requisition	Storekeeper.
9	Returning materials	Materials returned note	Supervisor.
10	Transfers	Materials transfer note	Storekeeper.
11	Recording stock	Bin cards Material control cards	Storekeeper and stores clerk.
12	Charging materials to product or cost centre	Materials requisition. Material returned notes Job cost summaries.	Cost clerk.
13	Checking stock	Stock check sheets	Stock checker or internal auditor.

Factory overhead costs

The first stage is to decide upon a fair allocation of factory overhead costs to each production department or cost centre. A cost centre is a point or area where cost control may be applied; it could be a section, a group of machines, an individual or a group of individuals. A supervisor or a manager is responsible for each cost centre.

Bases of apportioning factory overhead costs

The main bases are detailed below.

1 *Employees' wages* Such overheads as national insurance contributions and employers' liability insurance may be charged under this method.

2 *Number of employees* Some items which may be fairly apportioned under this method are dining-room costs, wages department expenses, welfare costs and costing expenses.

3 *Floor area or cubic capacity* Some examples which apply here are lighting, heating, rent, fire insurance and general upkeep.

4 *Technical measurement* Where actual measurement of the overhead is possible within the cost centre this method provides a fair means of apportioning the charge. Examples are: lighting by assessing the number of bulbs or kilowatts consumed, heating by the number of radiators, electric power and water consumed by metering.

5 *Value of buildings and plant* The values of plant and buildings may be used as a basis for such items as depreciation, insurance, rates and repairs.

6   *Direct charges*   In some cases a direct charge is possible when employees are engaged within a cost centre for such purposes as supervising and machinery maintenance.

Recovery and allocation

The second stage is to recover (or apportion) the factory overhead costs already allocated to each department or cost centre.

Recovery is straightforward when only one type of product is manufactured. The total factory overhead cost is divided by the number of products manufactured during the period, thus providing a uniform recovery rate for each product. When a range of products is manufactured, the allocation of a fair charge is more difficult. Job costing and many process costing systems have the same problems. Some of the methods used to allocate factory overheads in these circumstances are:

- prime cost percentage
- direct wages percentage
- direct material percentage
- labour hour rate
- machine hour rate

1   *Prime cost percentage*   The factory overhead for the period is divided by the prime cost and expressed as a percentage. In many cases expenses are omitted from the prime cost. The formula and an example follows.

$$Percentage \ of \ prime \ cost = \frac{Factory \ overhead}{Prime \ cost} \times \frac{100}{1}$$

Example

$$\begin{aligned}
&\text{Period: July 19-2}\\
&\text{Factory overhead} &&= \pounds2,000\\
&\text{Direct labour} &&= \pounds3,000\\
&\text{Direct material} &&= \pounds2,000\\
&\frac{2,000}{5,000} \times \frac{100}{1} &&= 40\%
\end{aligned}$$

Thus a job with a prime cost of £100 would be charged £40 for factory overhead cost.

2   *Direct wages percentage*   This simple method is generally inaccurate, but when such factors as wage rates, machines and work content are of a similar nature for all the products manufactured, a higher degree of accuracy is attained. The formula and an example are given below.

$$Percentage \ of \ direct \ wages = \frac{Factory \ overhead}{Direct \ wages} \times \frac{100}{1}$$

Example

$$\begin{array}{ll}
\text{Period: July 19-2} \\
\text{Factory overhead} & = \text{£2,000} \\
\text{Direct wages} & = \text{£3000} \\
\dfrac{2,000}{3,000} \times \dfrac{100}{1} & = 66.67\%
\end{array}$$

In this case a job with a direct wages cost of £100 would be charged with £66.67 for factory overhead cost.

3   *Direct material percentage*   Generally this method is unsuitable where various materials – within a wide price range – are employed in the manufacture of products.

$$\text{Direct material percentage} = \frac{\text{Factory overhead}}{\text{Direct material}} \times \frac{100}{1}$$

Example

$$\begin{array}{ll}
\text{Period: July 19-2} \\
\text{Factory overhead} & = \text{£2,000} \\
\text{Direct material} & = \text{£2,000} \\
\dfrac{2,000}{2,000} \times \dfrac{100}{1} & = 100\%
\end{array}$$

4   *Labour hour rate*   Where the operators' time is a very important aspect of the work, this method is useful because the calculation is based upon the number of direct labour hours for the job.

$$\text{Direct labour hour rate} = \frac{\text{Factory overhead}}{\text{Direct labour hours}}$$

Example

$$\begin{array}{ll}
\text{Period: July 19-2} \\
\text{Factory overhead} & = \text{£2,000} \\
\text{Direct labour hours} & = \text{8,000} \\
\dfrac{\text{£2,000}}{8,000} & = 25\text{p/hr.}
\end{array}$$

If a job takes twenty hours to complete the factory overhead cost would be £5.

5   *Machine hour rate*   Where the operating hours of machines are a dominant feature of production this method will be more accurate.

$$\text{Machine hour rate} = \frac{\text{Factory overhead}}{\text{Machine hours}}$$

Example

Period: July 19-2
Factory overhead = £2,000
Machine hours = 4,000

$$\frac{£2,000}{4,000} = 50p/hr.$$

If twenty machine hours were taken to complete a job the factory overhead would be £10.

Non-manufacturing overhead costs

The method of recovering these overheads again depends upon circumstances.

Administration costs may be written off as a general expense in the profit and loss account, or apportioned between work-in-progress and cost of sales, or averaged out among all products. Selling and distribution costs are generally written off to cost of sales account. Finally, research and development costs may be written off over a period of years (similar to fixed assets) and attached to factory overheads, or treated as a direct charge to the particular product, or written off as a general expense in the profit and loss account.

Estimating

In many respects estimating is similar to production planning and, of course, costing plays an essential part in both these activities. The need for estimates arises in job production as outlined in Chapter 25. A customer's inquiry which involves particular requirements cannot be met by a standard product, therefore an estimate or quotation must be calculated for the manufacture of the specific item required.

A reliable estimate must start at an earlier stage than production planning. The expense involved in research, design, drawings and specification preparation can be very costly. Reference to past records of cost in these overheads is essential, but the future always contains the unknown factors which demand an intelligent guess by the specialists concerned with forecasting.

The actual cost of estimating must also be taken into consideration. The responsibility for an estimate is a heavy burden as an error may involve the concern in a considerable loss which cannot be claimed from the customer in normal circumstances.

The estimator must have a clear idea of the customer's requirements and be able to couple these with cost records. Although it is possible to build up an estimate by calculating the direct labour, material and expenses involved this tedious lengthy process can be sidetracked by concentrating on the total cost of sub-assemblies or components which may be common to a number of jobs, thus building up a quotation in this form. Naturally some parts will require the full treatment of prime cost establishment and, where variable components are involved, it is possible for the estimator to build up a library of information by using statistical methods to cover a range of costs for a variable. The use of standard costs, if they are available, helps considerably in assessing the cost of components.

The problem of loading the total cost with a suitable profit margin rests with top management. The estimator may be given a percentage to work with, but on some occasions the loading varies with circumstances, e.g. the need to win a particular contract for prestige purposes or for lack of other work, or the desire to discourage the customer because of an over-full order book.

The importance of the delivery date is often overlooked by companies. Delay can be costly to the customer and it is not unusual for penalty clauses to be included in contracts to overcome this problem. Such clauses operate on a set sum to be paid by the supplier for every day or week that delivery is overdue.

Questions

1 Define costing and outline its main objectives.
2 Write an account of job costing and process costing.
3 Draw a diagram illustrating the main elements of cost and describe each element briefly.
4 Outline a typical procedure for controlling materials.
5 Describe the various ways of apportioning factory overheads.
6 Write an essay on standard costing.
7 What are the purpose and advantages of budgetary control?
8 Describe a simple system of marginal costing.
9 How can costing help the supervisor?
10 When would it be worth while to accept an order at less than total cost?
11 Explain the use of the principle of exceptions in connection with standard costing.
12 What is meant by break-even technique? Illustrate your answer with a diagram.

Case study

Mark Johnson established a small business thirty years ago. Previously he worked as an engineer for a large electronics firm, found a gap in the market for a complex component and decided to manufacture it himself. The business was successfully developed into a medium-sized company with 250 employees.

Approaching retiring age, Mark brought into the business his daughter Alison who had studied management with the object of eventually taking over. Alison, straight from university, chose to spend some time on the shop-floor to get the feel of the place. Within a short time it was obvious to her that control was poor although there was little discontent. The company still had no major competitors and employee benefits were high.

She overheard two supervisors: '. . . and I seem to spend most of my time filling in control reports but they don't seem to do any good. It would be much better if we could just get on with the job.'

'Why worry, Colin?' the other replied. 'You're well paid; you have an easy time really; everything goes like clockwork here.'

'And what happens when the "old man" packs up soon? That girl of his is going to be in dead trouble if she tries to use any management science or whatever they call it here.'

'The management information system is what they call it. Should be renamed the mis-information system!'

Alison withdrew quietly and decided to check up. When asked about the variances and what happened the chief accountant replied, 'We don't do anything but we've got the records if you'd like to see them.'

Her father replied to the same question: 'It's all there. We know exactly what is going on. I try to discover the sources and reasons, but it's a very complicated system. Hard to say who is really responsible when we have problems but we get by.'

By now Alison was very worried. 'But what happens if the rumours are true about Rodgers Industries developing a cheaper model?'

Consider the options open now to Alison. How could the supervisors help her?

29 Improving productivity

Measuring productivity

Productivity indicates the degree of effectiveness of resources. Often defined as the ratio of input of resources to output of goods or services, productivity is generally difficult to calculate and interpret accurately. Comparing productivity ratios also indicates organisational effectiveness, the efficiency of control systems, and the effect of applying various techniques.

Measuring productivity generally refers to labour as the resource factor, but understandably all other resources affect labour effectiveness. Labour productivity is defined generally as the ratio of employee to output, or man-hours to output; materials productivity as cost (or amount) or material consumed to output; and capital productivity as assets employed to output.

Cost reduction concepts

Inherent faults with costing systems are their historical nature and the tendency to treat standards as objectives. A healthier outlook is to incorporate cost reduction (through costing systems) as a continuing updating process of preventive measures, in keeping with quality assurance in Chapter 26. This philosophy avoids complacency through misinterpretations such as:

1 Low productivity may be hidden if related to high profit in a flourishing new market.
2 Low productivity in one section may be hidden by high productivity in another.

Four main approaches to reduce costs are distinguishable:

- cost reduction programmes
- use of specialists
- prognosis
- collaboration

These are now discussed, followed by an examination of waste and cost reduction checklists which are useful for the supervisor. Note that more than one approach is not uncommon in some concerns.

Cost reduction programmes

Historical in nature, costs and waste are investigated. Often sectional boundaries restrict improvements; local attempts are made to rectify faults without sufficient back-up. Programmes may be established on an ad hoc basis when senior management is suddenly confronted with poor profit results, or to a timetable coinciding with reports.

Such arrangements suffer from spasmodic efforts to improve; sometimes they are inherently wasteful themselves. Work study and work measurement techniques are often used to study existing activities. There is also a reliance on basic control procedures.

The specialisms approach

This approach relies on specialists to find the most appropriate resource and to ensure its most economic use. Typical examples are:

1   scientific and technological expertise provided by engineers who may make enormous savings through the introduction of new technologies
2   effective financial and non-financial incentive schemes recommended by a personnel manager.

Effectiveness often depends upon the conceptual capabilities and co-operativeness of specialists; and the expertise of the managing director in achieving co-ordination.

The prognostic approach

This scientific concept relies on sampling, diagnosing excessive costs and waste; attempting to anticipate, forecast, or predict trends or faults; and recommending courses of action to remove the problems and prevent recurrences. It differs from the above approaches but still relies on historical information for diagnosis.

Common applications are statistical quality control techniques and planned maintenance.

Productivity culture

This approach accepts the systems philosophy, creates a collaborative management style, and encourages full development of participative concepts. Rapid adaptation to change occurs in all parts of the system.

Scientific and technological updating is automatic, as is improving the organisation and developing creative approaches to jobs. A quality assurance culture and human resource management are fundamental.

Waste

On a national level, any form of waste drags a country down to a slightly lower standard of living. When all waste is coupled together the economic loss can be considerable. Waste is a complete loss of all the resources needed to produce that proportion which is discarded or misused.

Probably most people in the community are guilty of improper use of some service or product. Small incidents such as throwing away milk from a nearly empty bottle, discarding small quantities of food, leaving lights on and dripping taps are examples of useless consumption. The immediate retaliation from some individuals might be that they have the right to do as they please – they pay for the privilege of burning a light in an empty room; there is democratic freedom to buy an article and destroy it if they wish. Whether the same people would be prepared to hand out pound notes to strangers as they pass by would be doubtful as they may think it is ridiculous to throw money away after it has been earned.

A more subtle sense of responsibility and understanding of economic life is needed before the same reply is forthcoming when pointless destruction of goods or services is committed. Shallow thinking and dilatory attitudes are often fostered by mistaken beliefs about freedom and what it really means. Freedom does not mean that individuals should be free to destroy and misuse the creations and efforts of individuals although those individuals have been paid for their work.

Most people who pay income tax react sharply when they hear of waste connected with government expenditure as the connection is clear. Thinking out how people indirectly pay for waste is very involved and difficult to understand.

Within a company similar problems connected with the identification of individuals and waste exists. Attitudes are indicated by such remarks as 'It is not my business', 'The company can stand it', 'They will not miss these few nuts and bolts', 'Plenty more where those came from', 'Why worry? There's another one in the stores', and so on.

The supervisor's part

The supervisor must appreciate the problem of attitude towards waste. He or she is responsible for reducing waste to a minimum which involves continually probing all forms of expenditure – in its broadest sense – to see whether cost reduction is possible.

Cost reduction may be defined as being able to reduce – on a long-term basis – any item of expense without interfering with the effectiveness of the service rendered. The breadth of cost reduction – under this definition – includes some costs outside the direct control of the supervisor. The main areas generally associated with cost reduction are production, design, marketing and finance. Within the field of production the supervisor is concerned with labour, materials, plant and machinery, and other factors of expense. Possible improvements in design can often be seen from shop-floor level which may escape designers at a more remote point.

The supervisor ought to develop a searching attitude towards costs which means something more than inquiring into the possibility of reducing the cost by direct means. Some examples are the use of a time switch to control lighting and heating, buying a more expensive tool which is cheaper in the long run, applying one coat of expensive covering instead of three coats of cheaper covering, replacing an unsuitable machine by a new one which will produce savings eventually. Such changes require expenditure first, while the savings come later. More direct ways should not be ignored, such as cutting out shapes from a metal sheet in a more economical way by altering the position of the pattern, or using a cheaper grade of material which does not impair the efficiency of the product.

Control factors

Some of the factors the supervisor may consider when planning a method of operating cost reduction as a continuing process would be the following.

The time factor

Does the item vary in cost on a regularly occurring or an intermittent basis? Waste may occur through an employee regularly having half a day off each week, or there will be cases of epidemics such as influenza or enteritis. An intermittent example may be absences to attend a race meeting or a football match.

Classes of items

These may be divided into labour, materials, machines, equipment, tools and services.

Significance

The item may be measurable or estimated from the aspect of amount of waste. From this aspect it may be decided that the item is controllable, partly controllable, or uncontrollable.

Recording

The various factors mentioned above should be recorded together with a description of the item or type of waste. The question of responsibility is also involved and timeliness of information is important so that action may be taken early.

Cost reduction checklists

A guide to each class of item is now given in the form of a checklist which indicates the main points but is not intended to be a comprehensive summary. The supervisor should write out a list for use from his or her own knowledge and experience. The causes of waste vary with circumstances.

Labour checklist

1 Skilled workers must be on skilled work, semi-skilled workers on semi-skilled work, and on so.

2 The wage should be appropriate to the job. It is wasteful to pay a high wage to people and place them on low wage tasks. The importance of 'servicing' (providing assistance to) highly paid employees is obvious but often neglected.

3 Use the knowledge, skill and experience of employees. Unfortunately the problems of rising and declining industries make this task extremely difficult at times.

4 Avoid time wasted by employees through walking about; examine the possibilities of cutting down this factor. For example, it is cheaper for an unskilled employee to bring materials to the skilled operator.

5 Aim to cut out idle time completely. Aim high, question the schedules, check the work flow, and try to close the gaps.

6 Reduce frustration of the employee through poor product design. Ferret out the ideas and make a fuss about the proposed improvement. Get something done!

7 Poor training produces poor workers. Try to improve training schemes.

8 Unsound incentives speak for themselves. Ensure that financial and non-financial incentive schemes are suitable and are operating properly.

9 Inability to motivate employees. Learn more about motivation. Practise and experiment until better results are achieved. Motivating is an art which takes years to perfect unless you are one of the fortunate few.

10 Poor management attitude. You must make the best of a bad job; the managers cannot help – they do not know any better, but you do! Make excuses, point out to employees how busy managers are, the heavy burden they carry, the tremendous weight of responsibility, the shortage of time, which makes them easily misunderstood. Deep down they mean well and tolerance is essential. There is no logical alternative because unless you align yourself with managers and attempt to excuse their conduct, you will naturally side with your subordinates which is obviously unsound and widens the gulf between management and employees.

11 Using inexperienced labour. The danger of accidents, excessive scrap and the effect on other employees is apparent. Such causes as poor selection and lack of suitable labour are outside the supervisor's scope. He or she

should complain and try to train the unfortunate individual as soon as possible.

12 Carelessness, laziness, accidents and absenteeism are four examples where the supervisor must take positive action after adequate investigation by personnel counselling.

13 Quality being neglected for quantity. An appraisal of the financial incentive scheme and attitudes is essential.

14 Working conditions below standard.

15 Unsuitable tools, machines, equipment and materials.

16 Poor maintenance resulting in breakdowns and frustration.

17 Inadequate instructions.

18 Inadequate induction schemes.

19 Avoidable overtime. Often employees and supervisors get into the habit of working overtime unnecessarily.

20 Low morale and high labour turnover. Better supervision and selection procedures, training schemes and closer control should improve this situation.

Materials checklist

1 Cheapest for the purpose. The important factor is that the quality of the finished article is not impaired.

2 Not requisitioning sufficient supplies (orders too small).

3 Inadequate supplies available at the stores.

4 Damaged material through negligence.

5 Salvage. In some cases savings are possible by salvaging scrap and selling it already sorted to concerns.

6 Poor storage facilities – some materials are easily soiled and become shop worn if they are not properly stored at the work place.

7 Inadequate materials handling. Damaged materials and delays may be overcome by paying more attention to this factor.

8 Faulty materials. This problem should be investigated and reports sent to the purchasing officer or executive responsible for supplies.

9 Excessive consumption of consumable materials. Such items as sandpaper, solder, emery, paint, files and twist drills, also office supplies, tend to be treated carelessly and are subject to pilfering. Costs may rise considerably unless these items are strictly controlled.

10 Careless use of small parts or components. Small parts tend to be mixed together and waste can develop unless provision is made to separate them by placing in individual boxes.

Machines checklist

1 Replacement of obsolescent machines by more efficient models.

2   Maintenance programmes to minimise breakdowns and prompt attention when they occur.
3   Most effective layout of machinery and equipment.
4   Remove redundant machines.
5   Ensure economic operation of machinery by scheduling to reduce idle time.
6   Use the correct type of model for each operation.
7   Ensure that attachments which save time are fitted and used.

General checklist

1   Application of work study to simplify, standardise and generally improve methods, and to measure the work content.
2   Work planning and scheduling.
3   Correct use of jigs and tools.
4   Tolerances should be opened to limits which do not affect the quality of the product.
5   Check on housekeeping. Slackness leads to more accidents, increased cleaning costs and loss of materials.
6   Excessive use of services such as lighting, heating, compressed air, water and power.

Maintenance

Unless a programme of maintenance is conducted on sound principles of control the amount of waste can be considerable through breakdowns and the employment of an excessive number of maintenance staff. Although many executives recognise the problem of maintenance, there appears to be considerable reluctance to plan and control it. Some individuals insist that maintenance work cannot be measured, yet others have actually measured and successfully set standards by using the technique known as analytical estimating which is explained in Chapter 24.

There is no doubt that maintenance problems will increase as machines are driven faster and higher precision is required. Automated equipment still needs attention, and higher purchase prices will inevitably demand more output from machines which, in turn, place a heavier cost load when breakdowns occur.

To achieve the object of maintaining the efficiency of buildings, plant and equipment maintenance must be arranged so that production is not interrupted and the safety of employees is assured. A planned maintenance programme is a typical example where expenditure is essential to achieve savings in the long run.

Planned or scheduled maintenance

This form of maintenance is designed to reduce the number of sudden break-downs of machinery and equipment. The scheme aims to keep plant running continuously during production time by adopting a programme of continuous maintenance which reduces emergency maintenance to a minimum. Careful keeping of maintenance records and control procedures helps to reduce maintenance costs by making the best use of maintenance staff.

The two methods of planned maintenance are called preventive maintenance and long-term maintenance.

Preventive maintenance

This programme specifies periodic cleaning, servicing, inspection and replacement of parts prone to breakdown. The scheme includes duplication of vital parts which are built in to the machines (where practicable) such as two valves or two motors which can be quickly switched from one to the other in the event of a breakdown. Where this system is not possible, provision is made for spares to be immediately available for replacement. Schedules are set for servicing time so that maintenance may be conducted without interrupting production.

Within this scheme vital parts are replaced after a specified number of hours running time; they are then serviced and ready for replacement next time the change is due. The advantage is that the changeover time can be arranged in preference to a sudden breakdown which always seems to occur at the busiest period.

Preventive maintenance must be justified on a cost reduction basis. Records of previous waste through breakdowns compared with the new scheme will show the economies. Unfortunately plant still breaks down at inconvenient times in spite of preventive maintenance. A balance of savings must therefore be kept, otherwise the tendency for the programme to grow and grow in an attempt to stop breakdowns completely would be uneconomic and practically impossible to achieve.

Long-term maintenance

More sophisticated forms of maintenance come under the heading of long-term maintenance. Briefly they include 'built-in' maintenance devices which automatically compensate or provide facilities for switching to duplicated sections when breakdowns occur. Lubrication is a typical example where automatic or semi-automatic devices lubricate moving parts.

The use of protective covers and guards ensures that certain parts of the machine which are susceptible to dust and corrosion are safely sealed. Where practicable, permanently sealed units within a machine are built in. These units are stringently tested for endurance and are replaced at the end of their recommended life.

The supervisor's part

In circumstances where the supervisor can call upon a maintenance department, his or her assistance in helping the department to plan the work may be invaluable. Much depends upon the attitude of the maintenance or plant manager and the programme of maintenance, if any. The supervisor should press for planned programmes if they do not exist, as invariably the cost of maintenance is more than offset by increased output.

If maintenance is largely the responsibility of the supervisor, the time spent on planning will be rewarding in the long run. Each item should receive a periodic overhaul and records should be kept for control purposes. A procedure for reporting and dealing with emergency breakdowns should be in operation.

From the human aspect the supervisor must convince operators of the importance of treating machines and equipment with care. Any carelessness or deliberate negligence is a serious offence; the supervisor should investigate the circumstances and interview the employee to find out the basic cause of the act. The loss may be considerable through someone's lack of responsibility towards plant and the case must not be treated lightly.

Conclusion

Responsibility for developing a cost-conscious outlook among employees rests largely with the supervisor who can assess the general attitude towards equipment and materials and impress upon employees the important role they play in keeping costs down.

Eliminating waste is a vital part of the supervisory function. The supervisor must wholeheartedly support the use of various techniques which attempt to improve a generally poor situation. Value analysis is a typical example where the supervisor can play an important part. This technique is described in Chapter 26. The success of such a scheme relies upon contributions from *all* employees. Supervisors must appreciate the significance of this fact and stress its importance to subordinates.

Similarly, the use of committees to control costs is becoming more popular as a means of creating enthusiasm among employees to be cost-conscious. A carefully-run suggestion scheme is a further method which is described in Chapter 12. Some suggestion schemes have been very successful, and this technique is still undeveloped in many companies. Finally, the supervisor can make great improvements by attending to the many causes of waste which have already been described.

Questions

1   Discuss the problem of attitudes towards waste in the factory.
2   Outline the main sources of waste in a factory and state how you would attempt to reduce them.
3   There are two main ways of reducing costs which are termed direct methods and indirect methods. Explain how the supervisor can use both methods effectively.
4   As a supervisor, how would you conduct a cost reduction programme?
5   Discuss the ways in which labour costs could be reduced.
6   What methods would you employ for a survey of materials costs in your section?
7   In what ways could you develop a cost-conscious outlook among your subordinates?
8   What arguments would you use to convince an employee that cost reduction is very important?
9   How would you deal with this attitude from an employee who has carelessly broken a tool: 'I can't see that it matters; there are plenty more in the stores and the firm can afford it'?
10   What measures can a supervisor take to cut down waste?
11   Describe way of improving plant efficiency.
12   Outline a plan for an initial survey of the effectiveness of your department.

Case study

A feud had developed between Clifton, the works manager, and Howard, the maintenance engineer, in Robson Company. Howard was responsible to the managing director and seemed to be in favour. Clifton was similarly responsible but did not receive the support he expected. He was intent on introducing a planned maintenance programme to avoid the continuing breakdown problems, but Howard would not entertain the idea.

As a supervisor working for Clifton how could you assist him with this problem?

Part III: Suggested projects

1   Conduct a small work-study project in your establishment. Outline the procedure to be adopted, record your findings and any resistance by subordinates, give an account of the installation of the new method and follow-up. Keep a detailed record of your study and include your personal observations.

2 Revise the layout of your workshop. Draw up diagrams to show the existing layout and the proposed layout. Include a detailed account of the reasons for your proposals and the probable snags you would expect to encounter during the changeover period.

3 Choose two assembly operations and carry out a thorough study of the methods in use. Revise the operations using the principles of method study and motion economy.

Write a detailed report on the existing operations and the proposed changes.

4 Conduct a survey of the existing production control system in your establishment. Analyse the system and the requirements; redesign a new system utilising Gantt charts if they are not already employed.

5 Study labour and machine utilisation in your concern. Draw up the existing scheme and redesign, or design a scheme if one is not already in existence.

6 Study the production system in your concern and plan or revise a system of progressing. Illustrate your method with suitable diagrams and explanations.

7 Investigate the inspection activities in your establishment and devise a suitable system of quality control.

Make an account of the existing arrangements and justify your proposed scheme.

Bibliography

Adair, J., *Action Centred Leadership*, Gower Press, 1979

Allen, C. R., *The Instructor, the Man and the Job*, 1919

Atkinson, P., *Achieving Results through Time Management*, Pitman, 1988

Bain, G. S. (Ed), *Industrial Relations in Britain*, Blackwell, 1983

Batty, J., *Management Accountancy*, Macdonald & Evans, 1982

Beer, S., *Cybernetics and Management*, English Universities Press, 1968

British Standards Institution, 'Anthropometric Recommendations for Dimensions of Office Machines, Operators' Chairs, and Desks', No. B.S. 3404 *Glossary of Terms in Work Study*

Corke, D. K., *Production Control in Engineering*, Arnold, 1987

De Bono, E., *Lateral Thinking*, Penguin, 1980

Drucker, P. F., *The Practice of Management*, Heinemann, 1955

Drucker, P. F., *Managing for Results*, Pan Books, 1967

Feldman, D. C. & Arnold, H. J., *Managing Individual and Group Behaviour in Organisations*, McGraw-Hill, 1983

Fry, T. F., *Computers Appreciation*, Butterworth, 1981

Glautier, M. W. E., Underdown, B. C. & Clark, A. C., 3rd Edition, *Basic Accounting Practice*, Pitman, 1985

Goldsmith, W. & Clutterbuck, D., *The Winning Streak*, Penguin, 1985

Graham, H. T., *Human Resource Management*, Macdonald & Evans, 1980

Gray, I., *Henri Fayol's General and Industrial Management*, Pitman, 1988

Gregory, D. & Ward H., *Statistics for Business Studies*, McGraw-Hill, 1974

Guest, D. & Knight, K., *Putting Participation into Practice*, Gower, 1979

Handy, C., *Understanding Organisations*, Penguin, 1982

Hanson, J. L., *A Textbook of Economics*, Macdonald & Evans, 1983

Houldon, B. T., *Some Techniques of Operational Research*, English Universities Press, 1969

International Labour Office, *Accident Prevention*

Koontz, O'Donnell & Weihrich, *Management*, McGraw-Hill, 1980

Lawrence, P. R. and Lorsch, J. W., *Organisation and Environment*, Irwin, 1967

Likert, R. & Likert, J. G., *New Ways of Managing Conflict*, McGraw-Hill, 1976

Livy, B., *Corporate Personnel Management*, Pitman, 1988

Lockyer, K., et al, *Production and Operations Management*, Pitman, 1988

Luthans, F., *Organisational Behaviour*, McGraw-Hill, 1981

Mintzberg, H., *The Structuring of Organisation*, Prentice Hall, 1979

Murrell K. F. H., *Ergonomics*, Chapman & Hall, 1965

Peters, T. J. & Waterman, R. H., *In Search of Excellence*, Harper & Row, 1982

Pocock, M. A. & Taylor, A. H., *Handbook of Financial Planning and Control* Gower Press, 1980

Watson, T. J., *Sociology, Work and Industry*, Routledge & Kegan Paul, 1980

Urwick, L. F., *Elements of Administration*, Pitman, 1974

Index